Challenging Racism
in Higher Education

Challenging Racism in Higher Education

Promoting Justice

Mark Chesler, Amanda Lewis,
and James Crowfoot

ROWMAN & LITTLEFIELD PUBLISHERS, INC.
Lanham • Boulder • New York • Toronto • Oxford

ROWMAN & LITTLEFIELD PUBLISHERS, INC.

Published in the United States of America
by Rowman & Littlefield Publishers, Inc.
A wholly owned subsidiary of The Rowman & Littlefield Publishing Group, Inc.
4501 Forbes Boulevard, Suite 200, Lanham, Maryland 20706
www.rowmanlittlefield.com

PO Box 317
Oxford
OX2 9RU, UK

British Library Cataloguing in Publication Information Available

Library of Congress Cataloging-in-Publication Data

Chesler, Mark A.
  Challenging racism in higher education / Mark Chesler, Amanda Lewis, and James
Crowfoot.
    p. cm.
  Includes bibliographical references and index.
  ISBN 0-7425-2456-6 (cloth : alk. paper) — ISBN 0-7425-2457-4 (pbk. : alk. paper)
  1. Discrimination in higher education—United States—Prevention. 2. Multicultural
education—United States. 3. Prejudices—United States. 4. Stereotype
(Psychology)—United States. I. Lewis, Amanda E., 1970- II. Crowfoot, James E. III.
Title.

LC212.42.C54 2005   2005003656
378.1'9829—dc22

Printed in the United States of America

♾™ The paper used in this publication meets the minimum requirements of American
National Standard for Information Sciences—Permanence of Paper for Printed Library
Materials, ANSI/NISO Z39.48-1992.

CONTENTS

Tables and Figures

Acknowledgments

We acknowledge the assistance of many people in the preparation of this work. Undergraduate and graduate students who provided essential documentary and library research include Sarah Bowman, Shirley Greene, Judith Harris, Michelle Hughes, Lisa Landresman, Ellen Meader, Christine Navia, Luis Ponjuan, Rachel Ross, Inna Schulz, Erica Soloway, and Mary Wright. On numerous occasions these student-colleagues shared their own wisdom and thoughts in ways that extended our own thinking and writing.

Several colleagues in the academy read portions of this work and provided critical feedback and commentary that stretched our own thinking and undoubtedly improved the final product. Many have themselves been pioneering analysts and advocates of multicultural change in higher education organizations: Jessica Charbenneau, Patricia Gurin, Mark Kaplan, Jerome Rabow, David Schoem, Alford Young Jr., and Ximena Zuniga.

Assistance in editing and word processing has helped iron out much of the jargon and tortuous phrasing so common in works of this sort: Steven Gray, Barbara Lewis, and Patricia Preston. The editorial staff at Rowman & Littlefield has made the process of producing this work much easier, and we salute their foresight in making this investment. And Community Resources Ltd. has provided essential financial resources along the way.

Finally, we acknowledge several colleagues whose long-term comradeship and leadership on these issues have provided us with inspiration and support in this volume and in other aspects of our work: Bunyan Bryant, Harley Flack, Tyrone Forman, Bailey Jackson, and Maria Ramos.

Preface

Challenging Racism in Higher Education is both analytical and practical. We provide conceptual frames for understanding the current state of intergroup relations in higher education. We also present the voices and experiences of college students, faculty, and administrators, integrating this first-person material with research literature. We show concrete actions people and organizations have taken to alter institutional racism and other forms of discrimination on campus and what further action they can take to work toward social justice. We link people's experiences, institutional programs, and potential future steps with more generalized scholarship about diversity, multiculturalism, and organizational change.

OUR HOPE FOR THIS VOLUME

We are at a critical moment in the history of our nation and the world. The world scene is characterized by long-standing patterns of political and economic domination and subordination, along with technologies of cultural control. News of terrorism, civil strife, starvation and disease, reliance on militarism and violence, and environmental destruction is daily fare. Globalization brings these issues to the doorstep of our personal and national consciousness and penetrates domestic politics and social life. Increasing disparities in wealth and income cut across racial and class lines and impact every level of the U.S. educational system. Both overt and more subtle patterns of discrimination based on race, class, gender, sexual orientation, ability, and religion sustain privileges and advantages for some citizens and disadvantage and oppression for others—including access to and success in higher education.

At the same time, the opportunities for change are present in the racial demographics of population change, market demands for a racially/ethnically competent workforce, mobilized efforts of people to improve their life circumstances, and abiding visions of justice. Throughout the world—with the leadership of some national governments, the United Nations, and voluntary organizations—there is a growing understanding of the unsustainability of current inequitable ways of organizing national and global social and economic systems. Courage and imagination are needed to understand these trends and their impacts, to counter some and facilitate others. Challenging racism in every aspect of our national and international life, but especially in our systems of education, is a key element for the future of a democratic, just and sustainable society. Education is the key to exposing historic and contemporary forms of racism and its individual and institutional intersections with sexism, classism, heterosexism, and religious oppression. It also is the key to mobilizing individuals and societies to engage in behaviors that are more just and respectful to different groups.

The study of racism and other forms of discrimination in the United States is a complex undertaking. Even limiting our inquiry to institutions of higher education has proven to be a daunting task. Many chapters in this book have themselves been the focus of multiple research studies and entire books. We know that in analyzing these issues in one volume we foreshorten some inquiries that could be treated in more encompassing ways. Nevertheless, by examining a wide range of issues under one cover, we hope to give readers a view of the organizational dynamics supporting racism and discrimination in higher education. Concurrently, we hope to make clear some ways to alter these dynamics and to move on to more egalitarian, democratic, and multicultural forms of teaching and learning.

While we draw primary attention to issues of race and racism in the context of a multicultural perspective on higher education organizations, we do not think that racism is the only form of discrimination operating in our colleges and universities, nor that racism is the most potent and pervasive form of discrimination at all times and in all institutions. Subtle and overt discrimination on the bases of gender, socioeconomic class, sexual orientation, physical ability, ethnicity, and religion are also present on most campuses and in virulent and pervasive forms on some. Moreover, the ways in which individuals' multiple social identities overlap and intersect with one another make a focus on any one dimension of identity somewhat artificial. While we recognize this limitation, we hope that our focus on race and racism, about which there is the most available scientific information and the most heated public conversation, will provide a context for understanding other dynamics of identity and domination-subordination.

We hope that the conceptual frames we present in part I (chapters 1–3) help make sense of the often murky and covert workings of institutionalized racism and other forms of social discrimination and privilege in the general society and in colleges and universities. We hope that they stimulate discussion among members of the academy and that these discussions provoke rich dialogue about the state of affairs on particular campuses. We hope that the first-person reports from and related scholarly material about students, faculty members, and administrators in part II (chapters 4–7) remind readers of what's at stake—of the ignorance, pain, and confusion affecting many members of our institutions, and of their often innovative and courageous efforts to survive and thrive. We hope that readers can draw upon the principles of change making and the practical examples provided in part III (chapters 8–12) to plan for change in their own institutions, change that challenges racism and other forms of discrimination and that promotes multiculturalism and social justice.

WHO WE ARE

The three of us have been struggling with the central issues of this volume for all our adult lives. Over the past four decades we have done so as undergraduate and graduate students working from below; as faculty and senior administrators working from above; as internal advocates, negotiators, and cajolers within our own institutions; and as researchers, external critics, and consultants trying to educate and assist those in institutions where we are not centrally involved. Most of our professional experience has been in large, research-oriented universities, although we all have studied, taught, or led programs in smaller, liberal arts colleges.

As three white people trying to challenge racism and other forms of discrimination, we constantly work to be more aware of the privileges accorded to us by our racial and other memberships. As a result, we are continually engaged in conversations with white allies as well as opponents—or bystanders—and in coalitional work with members of underrepresented groups.

In many ways this book represents an act of "tempered radicalism." (See our discussion of this concept in chapter 8 and in Meyerson 2001.) Throughout the process we have regularly juggled the contradictions between our collective belief in the deeply embedded nature of racism and other forms of discrimination, and our faith (sometimes sorely tested) that change is possible and that it sometimes can be accomplished from within organizations. While we agree with Audre Lorde (1984: 112) that "the master's tools will never dismantle the master's house" and that institutions of higher education are resistant to change, we see no alternative to trying to transform them into more democratic and just organizations. And we have discovered that some of the tools we learned to use as academics are powerful and may provide important leverage in the change process.

Finally, we have learned much from one another and have explored and worked through complicated disagreements, have become comfortable with (or at least resigned to) contradictions and challenges, have negotiated new ways of working and writing collectively, and have realized the benefits of collaborative work. Each of us has participated in the conceptualization, drafting, editing, and reediting of each chapter. Thus, the finished product reflects not so much each or any of us as individuals but our best collective work. We hope that others who engage with the ideas and information in this volume, and who undertake to grapple with these issues as they challenge discrimination, reap similar benefits.

Part One

CONTEXT

On college campuses across the country students, staff, faculty, and administrators struggle with how to share space, build meaningful communities and survive in what sometimes feel like inhospitable institutions. The very nature and extent of their struggles vary considerably depending on individuals' social location (e.g., race, class, gender, sexual orientation) and status in the institution. What for some are places that affirm their worthiness, reward their contribution, support their worldviews, and value their participation are for others places of exclusion, denial of their perspectives, marginalization, and pain. Universities are operating within a much larger context in which not only high levels of racial inequity persists but also racial minorities continue to be denigrated, women continue to be underpaid, and gay, lesbian, bisexual, and transgender people continue to be harassed and locked out of many basic civil rights. Universities themselves differ in their willingness and capacity to address inequities, bridge the gulf in understanding between those who live and work there, and respect and learn from the different experiences and ideas of their members.

Members of campus communities have quite different experiences of the diverse and stratified world in which they live and the environment in which they teach and learn and work. These experiences differ by their racial/ethnic and gender background and by their role or function in the institution. We illustrate and discuss these issues throughout this volume, but perhaps a taste at the outset will alert readers. As some students report, for instance:

The community I came from—white, suburban, upper class—assumed that we were superior. I mean, after all, we had to be brighter, work harder, et cetera, to get to where we are. Right? You were good because you had money. Race wasn't even an issue. (*white student*)

One of my TAs [teaching assistants] was talking about students having to work, and he said, "None of us have to work to earn money because we can write home to our

1

parents." I was working thirty-five to forty hours a week. If I wasn't a strong-willed person, I would have really felt bad. (*African American student*)

I've always felt left out of study groups. It's almost like they [white students] have these cliques already. They're going to do much better because of the groups they have. They have their friends who took the class before, and they have all these resources that we don't have. (*Latina student*)

I never considered before how much of an advantage I have by being white. I'd heard of discriminatory hiring practices before and things like that, but I'd never really associated those things to me. Just because I don't often think of myself as white doesn't mean I won't be given special privileges at the expense of others. (*white student*)

And some members of the faculty reported their own experiences in these matters.

As the only tenured woman of color in my department, I feel responsible for mentoring the junior faculty who are women and minorities. I feel like I need to be in there to make sure that things get done and get done in the right way. So in many ways it's almost like because of my identity I actually have too much to do. (*Latina faculty member*)

I don't walk into a classroom expecting that my white students and particularly my white and male students will automatically accept that I'm a scholar in my area. My white colleagues can do that. I think a lot of students come in expecting that "Oh, a black professor—I'm not going to learn that much about anything that's real." (*African American female faculty member*)

The fear of being called a racist if you're a white liberal is very strong. (*white female faculty member*)

It's benign neglect. Even here in this school I was marginalized. I was not put on any committees or made chairman of any major committees. I was just marginalized. And that's how the school dealt with me as a black faculty member. When I first came here, these faculty members had never dealt with a black person as an equal. (*African American male faculty member*)

When women who were going through a Women's Studies Department started speaking in my [science] classroom, I began to hear new and exciting voices that had been very rare before. And they really transformed what was possible in my classroom. The same would be true when gay students came out in classrooms and began to speak. It was at those historical moments, I think, that I began to listen and to deal with what before I'd been unable to look for. (*white male faculty member*)

And administrators also addressed these experiences:

My experience from graduate school through the academic affairs vice presidency has been a legacy of having to demonstrate my credentials. It is a given that I have to work harder and produce more than my white make counterparts to be taken seriously. I often say to audiences that true equality will be reached in this country when mediocre men and women of color and white women are hired at the same rate as mediocre white males. (*African American female administrator*)

It is hardly surprising that many mistaken notions persist about Asian American academics since we are relative newcomers to higher education. . . . The pervasive stereotype of Asian Americans is that they are inscrutable and mysterious. (*Asian American administrator*)

The pain and struggle reflected in these voices, along with the positive experiences cited, are part of the on-the-ground reality of institutionalized discrimination in society generally and in higher education in particular. While we leave the elaborated discussion of these different experiences on campus to chapters 4–7, they highlight in personal terms the issues we undertake throughout this volume. These personal experiences are neither incidental nor occurring in a vacuum; they are embedded in the nature of institutional racism in the society and in the organization and operation of most colleges and universities.

As discussed in the preface, we recognize that there are many other forms of institutionalized discrimination operating in higher education (e.g., sexism, class inequality, and heteronormativity) and that socially just multicultural communities address all these forms. While we give some attention to these multiple forms we have decided, for reasons specified, to give the bulk of our analytic attention to issues of race and racism.

In this first part, we set the stage for the analytic, experiential, and pragmatic chapters that follow. In chapter 1, we lay the groundwork for the volume by discussing the nature of race, race relations and racism in the U.S. society and by reviewing alternative meanings of diversity and multiculturalism and their relevance for promoting justice in higher educational institutions. Chapter 2 reviews the history of racial, gender and other forms of discrimination in higher education—from exclusion to segregation to assimilation to the present. Chapter 3 presents an organizational framework for understanding the operations of race and racism in higher education organizations; it presents an analytic template that will be referred to throughout the volume.

Chapter One

Contemporary Struggles over Race and Racial Equality/Justice

We begin this work with the understanding that the United States of America is a nation divided by race. In the sixteenth, seventeenth, and eighteenth centuries, large numbers of people from northern Europe and Spain came to the land that would become the United States. One group entered from the Northeast, symbolized in our history by the establishment of the Plymouth Colony in 1620. The other entered from the Southwest, symbolized historically by the building of the Palace of Governors in Santa Fe in 1610. Both groups moved onto land inhabited by indigenous peoples—variously referred to as Indians, Red Men, Savages, and later Native Americans—and in the process subjugated them physically, economically, socially, and culturally. At the same time that the newcomers were displacing and conquering (and in many cases simply eliminating) Native Americans, they also were importing indentured white Europeans and enslaved Africans to the Americas and using them as forced labor. The subjugation of both Native Americans and Africans became formalized into the laws and legal practices of the new nation's organizations, communities, and families, as well as its religious and cultural beliefs and traditions. Initially, many indigenous people sought to be helpful to the settlers; but once their ill treatment began, they and enslaved Africans focused on surviving and, as much as possible, resisting their domination and exploitation. Still later, when people from Latin America and Asia (first from China and Japan and later from other Asian nations) were either forcibly incorporated (via the Treaty of Guadalupe Hidalgo) or immigrated to the United States, they, too, were subordinated and forced to adapt to physical, economic, social, and cultural constraints. During their early years in the United States, many indentured members of white ethnic groups were also treated harshly—were forced to work in dangerous and low-paying industries, were regularly discriminated against, and were often subjected to violence. But while early immigrants from Ireland and southern and eastern Europe, in particular, struggled for decades, they did eventually acquire the rights and protections of citizenship which were denied to both recent arrivals and long-standing residents who were racially categorized as nonwhite.

People of different racial and ethnic groups still typically live in different neighborhoods, create different family and friendship circles, think of themselves and their country in different ways, and have dramatically different access to privileged organizational or community roles and the riches and resources of our nation. People of color and white Americans have different average lifespans, unequal economic resources, different experiences with courts and police and public services, and differential access to safe working conditions, good health care, and even to clean air and water. Even among different groups of so-called people of color and distinct groups of so-called white people, inequalities based on economic class result in substantial differences in experience and in access to the means of satisfying basic human needs. The rights and privileges of being a citizen of the United States are not available to all of us in equal measure. Over and above the common threads of belief and commitment to "e pluribus unum"—to the things that unite us as a people and a nation—we are different, divided, and stratified.

At the same time that these inequalities persist, beginning during World War II and increasingly since the 1960s, we have seen widespread use of various policies and practices to combat discrimination and advance racial justice. These programs have arisen at national, state, and local levels, as part of voluntary as well as governmental efforts. Some have been effective in empowering previously oppressed groups, in awakening white Americans to the destructive nature of unearned privilege, and in changing the racialized structures of our society. Others have been ineffective. Overall, substantial racial injustice and inequality persist, despite the progress that has been made. Similarly, injustice and inequality are experienced along gender and socioeconomic lines, by gay/lesbian/bisexual/transgender (GLBT) people, by differently abled people, and by members of minority religious groups.

INEQUALITY IN EDUCATION AND HIGHER EDUCATION

Chapter 2 reviews how some of the realities of racial life in the United States were instituted and have been maintained. They are part of our history and are reenacted daily in the operations of our major institutions. They add up to socially constructed systems of domination and subordination, of greater and lesser access to life opportunities and often to life itself, and of resistance and struggle against oppression. It is important to understand how these realities are present in our systems of education, especially higher education. Designing and implementing a public K–12 educational system represented an important strategy for creating a fair and democratic society. But the process also served as a means of socializing a rapidly growing industrial workforce and "civilizing" and Americanizing people of color, poor people, and what were thought to be uncivilized hordes of immigrants from abroad. As economic advances have made a higher level of educational attainment necessary for economic success and positive life outcomes, institutions of higher education have come to play a greater role in our public political and economic life (Zumeta 2001). They now have greater impact, both on hopes for creating a truly just and democratic society and on efforts to maintain racial inequality and injustice.

Throughout our racial history, educational organizations have been a central arena for defining racial justice and the appropriate means to realize or frustrate it. For example, struggles over racial segregation and desegregation in elementary and secondary schools occupied federal courts, city governments, and communities throughout the latter half of the twentieth century. In recent decades, affirmative action programs in higher education and elsewhere have taken center stage. Many of these affirmative action efforts face political opposition from conservative leaders, who assert that they are unnecessary and unfair. College administrators, faculty, and students are challenged in new ways to address the question of who can or should be members (students, faculty, staff) of their organizations. On the one hand, many people value racial diversity and recognize the role of historical and present-day discrimination in limiting the educational opportunities and experiences of students and faculty of color. On the other hand, efforts to take race seriously as a factor in admissions, hiring, and promotion are being challenged in the courts, in other policy arenas, and by some groups on campus.

The content of the curriculum, what is to be learned or the "canon," is another focus of struggle in what some have called the "culture wars" (Carby 1992). Some progressive scholars have created new courses that investigate and teach about the plurality of cultures, experiences, and outlooks of people throughout our nation and the world. Others have concentrated on integrating such views into the core elements of the current curriculum. Part of both ventures involves not just "understanding and appreciating others," but understanding the tradition of western and white (and male) dominance, and resistance to such dominance, in the control of world affairs, in the maintenance of unequal societies, in scholarly literature, and in the nature of what traditionally has been taught in collegiate classrooms. Conservative and/or concerned scholars and administrators have resisted this movement to understand and resist domination and subordination, bemoaning the "degradation of our Western heritage," the "attack on dead white males," and indeed the "disuniting of America" (Bloom 1987; D'Souza 1991; Schlesinger 1992).

These collegiate and university struggles are often linked to parallel or related contests taking place within the larger community. Understanding the nature of race and racism in higher education is inseparable from understanding the nature of race and racism in our society in general. It seems essential then to spend some time defining our terms. What do we mean by race? By racism? Why—in the language of the title of this book—would we wish to challenge it?

RACE AS A SOCIAL CONSTRUCTION

Since the early part of the twentieth century, social scientists have recognized race to be a social rather than biological construct, an ideational category reflecting little if any distinct biological nature or essence (DuBois 1968; Gossett 1975; Omi and Winant 1994). While biological arguments about different racial groups' talents have not totally disappeared, they now are routinely condemned. For example, following the publication of Herrnstein and Murray's (1994) work, *The Bell Curve*, which argues that there are fixed and enduring racial differences in intelligence, a spate of books challenged this analysis (see, e.g., Fraser 1995; Jacoby and Glauberman 1995; Kincheloe and Steinberg 1996). Survey research has shown that few whites now support the idea of the biological inferiority of people of color (see Schuman et al. 1997; Sniderman and Piazza 1993).

The boundaries and meanings of racial categories, along with the rights and resources associated with them, have varied across time and space. For example, who counts as black, white, Latino/a, or Asian and what it means to belong to one or another of these groups, have varied in our national history and around the globe. Southern European, eastern European, Irish, and Jewish immigrants to the United States initially were categorized as racially "other" in relation to Anglo-Saxons. Italians' racial status was contested well into the twentieth century, when they clearly were accepted into the dominant white racial category (see Guglielmo 2003; Higham 1963; Omi and Winant 1994; Roediger 1991; Saxton 1990; Takaki 1993). Some groups have lobbied successfully for the option to select more than one racial category when filling out official government forms, and others such as Native Hawaiians, Arab Americans, and multiracial people, continue to engage in political struggles with the U.S. Census Bureau to change their official racial designation (Wright 1994).

Despite these shifts, an individual's placement into a racial category within a particular spatial and sociohistorical context has always had profound implications for that person's identity, life chances, access to social and material rights and resources, and physical safety. Thus, even though there is nothing biologically real or natural about racial categorizations, placement into a particular category has had and continues to have serious physical, psychological, social, economic, and political consequences. Each individual is socialized by their family, school, and local community about their own race and the race of others who appear different. They are taught, sometimes explicitly and often implicitly, which groups are (and should be) superior and which inferior, and consequently how they are expected to behave. Institutions of adulthood reinforce and maintain these early and deeply internalized lessons. People behave as if the categorizations are real and incorporate them into laws, policies, and social and individual practices. Consequently, they are socially real and have real consequences.

At the societal level, blacks, whites, Asians, and others "have race," and are accorded or blocked from certain statuses and privileges based, at least in part, on their racial group membership. In a system in which being white provides benefits, and being designated as a racial "other" carries severe physical, psychological, and material disadvantages, persons do not have to have a conscious racial identity to benefit from or be penalized because of their racial designation (Almaguer 1994; Farley 1995; Feagin and Feagin 1986; Feagin and Sikes 1994; Hacker 1992; Harris 1993; Oliver and Shapiro 1995; Roediger 1991). What matters is the social fact that race continues to organize social life for everyone. Class, gender, sexual orientation, religion, and ethnicity matter as well. There is not one way of being black or one way of being white, but in a racialized social system like ours, every person's life is shaped by race, class, gender, and so on.

At the personal level, racial knowledge helps shape individual identities and often leads to preferences about who to be close to as well as distant from. The development and enactment of a personal and social racial identity—consciously or not—is as much a part of the process of learning and growing into an adult as is the establishment of a sexual identity. More or less consciously, individuals know they "have race" and have membership in a racial group. But it has been particularly difficult for white Americans, especially, to feel a part of a racial group. On the one hand, their numerical and cultural dominance suggests to them that whites are not a group among other groups but, rather, represent the norm or the whole, from which other groups stand out or deviate. On the other hand, the plurality of national and ethnic divisions within the large European immigrant population, and loyalties to these divisions, seem to vitiate any tendency toward an overarching white group identity.

Even as race, gender, and class operate in ways that benefit some and subordinate others, dominant American discourses about individualism, opportunity, and freedom undermine the ability to attend to such divisions. Popular narratives suggest that every person has an equal chance to be successful and that we all succeed or fail based on our individual merits. This rhetoric leads to high levels of denial and rationalizations about the obstacles many people face and the privileges others enjoy. For example, in recent years many commentators have argued that race is no longer important, that we should all be color-blind, that even talking about race is racist in that it perpetuates racial classification (Berg 1993). But if we fail to recognize the existence of racial groups and collectives, and of their differential treatment, we obscure relations of domination and oppression of people of color (Young 1994). In this sense, it is not important to speak of racial groups as having specific and uniform cultures or immutable and natural essences, or even as having self-conscious group identities, but as possessing shared histories that result in similar present-day social locations and treatment within the social structure (Lewis 2004).

Thus, although we recognize that race is not genetically or biologically meaningful and that the categories are neither fixed nor even mutually exclusive and dichotomous, race is quite clearly real in psychological, social, and material terms. Our society and its institutions and their members use it to organize lives, guide social interaction, shape social institutions, and provide greater or lesser access to social opportunities and resources. Deeply embedded notions of racial superiority or inferiority are used to justify and legitimate patterns of domination and subordination. Only through careful analysis of institutional, organizational, and interactional processes can we come to a more conscious and complex understanding of why and how this socially constructed category continues to have such profound impact on our personal and national lives. An analysis focusing on these processes is essential for planning and implementing effective policies and programs to reduce and someday hopefully eliminate racism.

INDIVIDUAL PREJUDICE OR INSTITUTIONAL/ORGANIZATIONAL RACISM?

Changes in our society and its cultures, legal rules, and ways of understanding racial matters have altered scholarly and public understandings of race, racial prejudice, racial discrimination, and racism. The twentieth-century American traditions of scientific inquiry and public policy debate consistently emphasized various forms of prejudice, or individual racial attitudes, as marks of racism and as the cause of discrimination and inequality in private and public life. We argue for a more systemic and institutionalized definition and analysis of racism.

Racism as Individual Prejudice or Mental Quirk

We take seriously Frantz Fanon's (1967) admonition "The habit of considering racism as a mental quirk, as a psychological flaw, must be abandoned" (77). In many ways, this psychological understanding of racism still predominates in social analysis and in popular practice. Thus, in 2000 the commissioner of Major League Baseball reacted to a widely quoted and nationally circulated racist tirade by John Rocker, a highly paid and successful relief pitcher, by requiring Rocker to undergo psychological counseling. In 2002, Senator Trent Lott was deposed from his position as Senate majority leader on the basis of having said things that were construed as evidencing his individual racial insensitivity. The fact that both individuals' remarks also reflected a form of institutional racism, deeply traditional and broadly held views about people of color or about the struggle for civil rights, was quickly overlooked. Similarly, many universities have reacted to racist incidents on campus as if they were aberrations and the actions of lone individuals or small groups of disaffected students. Such psychological analyses have led to individual-level responses such as expelling certain students, sanctioning individuals, instituting classes in other cultures, or counseling and sensitivity training.

This perspective on prejudice as an individual-level phenomenon still drives much social science research, leading to numerous studies of racial attitudes that show apparently contradictory trends. While most measures of traditional or old-fashioned prejudice show decreases over the years, this has not been an uncomplicated harbinger of good things to come. For while scholars have found increasing support for principles of racial equality (such as the idea that people should be able to attend any school of their choosing or live in any neighborhood), most measures of public support for policies that would make such principles a reality have not shown a complimentary increase (Hughes 1997; Schuman et al. 1997). Moreover, studies which have explored racial attitudes in more depth through the use of interviews or participant–observer strategies have found higher levels of prejudice than surveys have captured (e.g., Bonilla-Silva and Forman 2000). These varying trends have been interpreted in several different ways (Blalock 1967; Blumer 1958; Bobo 1999; Bobo, Kluegel, and Smith 1997; Bonilla-Silva 2001; Dovidio and Gaertner 1986; Gould 1999; Kinder and Sanders 1996; Kinder and Sears 1981; McConaghy 1983):[1]

- The seeming diminution in racial prejudice may be largely illusory. Studies that rely more on personal interviews than paper and pencil questionnaires suggest that not much has changed in the public's view of people of color.
- The shift in racial attitudes is real but does not easily translate into behavioral change or into support for public policy initiatives.
- The shift in racial attitudes involves replacing old-fashioned racism with politer and more politically correct forms of culturally based "aversive" or "symbolic" racism that focuses on the ways in which people of color "fail to live up to" traditional American values—those rooted in the Protestant Ethic's notions of hard work, restrained or suppressed expressions of emotion, delayed gratification, and individualism.
- The shift from overtly antiblack attitudes to more covert forms helps maintain a defense of one's own (or one's parents') hard-earned status and privileges— one's material self-interest—in the face of increased competition and threat.
- The shift in racial attitudes has convinced people that their own and others' views have become sufficiently race-neutral that programs to counter discrimination are no longer necessary.

Many of these trends are likely to escalate. Indeed, changing population dynamics indicate that the proportion of people of color in the United States is growing rapidly relative to the white population, due to differential birthrates and to immigration from Latin America and Asia. This shift has major implications for school-age populations and the new workforce. Meanwhile, the global economy, overwhelmingly populated and staffed by people of color, continues to grow in economic and political importance. As the proportion of white people in the United States and worldwide dwindles, their economic, political, and cultural power may be threatened as well. Whites' defense of their "group interests" and historically privileged positions may become an even more important factor in future race relations and in future struggles for social justice.

Attitudes and Behavior

Racial attitudes, prejudiced or not, are complex. No single data set or single theory is likely ever to explain the full range of public and private attitudes about race and racism, or the behaviors that may flow from these attitudes. But perhaps most astonishing is the relative dearth of scholarship on individual *behavior*. Studies of the relationship between attitudes and behavior have long indicated that behavior is not necessarily consistent with expressed attitudes. In common parlance, this is a matter of whether people with seemingly tolerant or liberal attitudes really "walk the talk." More than fifty years ago, Robert Merton (1949) emphasized the difference between "prejudice" and "discrimination," suggesting that either can occur without the other. People can hold prejudiced attitudes yet not engage in behavior that discriminates against the targets of these attitudes, or they can hold nonprejudiced attitudes and still engage in discriminatory behavior. If a person who expresses minimal overt prejudice acts in ways that reflect negative attributions and assumptions about others, what shall we say? That the expression of minimal prejudice was inaccurate or dishonest? Or that there is evidence of attitudinal-behavioral inconsistency? Our preoccupation with the role of the conscious or deliberate element in discriminatory behavior often blinds us to the role of nonconscious or unconscious factors. This orientation similarly has influenced judicial decisions and has often led the courts to require evidence of specific intentional acts of discrimination in order to find a constitutional violation (Flagg 1993; Lawrence 1987).

Racism as a Structural and Institutional Phenomenon

Even less attention has been paid to the powerful actions of organizations and collectivities—to institutional forms of discrimination and racism. Fortunately, some authors recently have offered structural analyses of racism, suggesting that racism is only one part of a racialized social system—and that prejudice is merely the ideological component of societies in which race is a central feature of economic, political, and social patterns (Bonilla-Silva 2001).

The establishment and maintenance of racial difference—and the economic, political, and cultural dominance of white people and groups—are part of the history and traditions of our nation. Many citizens and students need be reminded, by a rereading of the federal Constitution and other founding documents of the Republic, that support for slavery and a noncitizen class of people of color (blacks and Native Americans) is part of our national birthright (just as are noncitizen classes of women and poor people). The continuing domination and oppression of people of color by generations of white people, and their cumulative impact, is important to remember and retell: it is reviewed with particular relevance to the history of higher education in chapter 2.

Feagin and Feagin (1986: 28) emphasize the potent roles of both direct and indirect institutionalized discrimination in this process. "Direct Institutionalized Discrimination refers to organizationally prescribed or community-prescribed actions which have an intentionally differential and negative impact on members of subordinate groups . . . carried out . . . routinely by a large number of individuals guided by the rules of a large-scale organization" (30). Examples relevant for higher education institutions include deliberate efforts to track or counsel minority students out of college preparatory courses and collegiate attendance, to guide them into certain low-status curricular and career paths, to direct them to technical schools or two-year colleges, or to exclude minority content from the curriculum or social life of educational institutions.

Of greater subtlety—and therefore of greater interest to people working in rhetorically liberal or progressive institutions—is Indirect Institutionalized Discrimination. This category "refers to practices having a negative and differential impact on minorities and women even though the organizationally prescribed or community-prescribed norms or regulations guiding these actions were established, and are carried out, with no conscious prejudice or deliberate intent to harm lying immediately behind them. On their face and in their intent, the norms and resulting practices appear fair or at least neutral" (Feagin and Feagin 1986: 31). Examples of indirect institutionalized discrimination in organizational operations include denying minority scholars access to faculty positions because they lack appropriate or traditional credentials, credentials that may have been foreclosed to them by prior discrimination, or because they lack cultural attributes that are assumed to be relevant for certain positions but that, upon examination, may not be essential. Examples also include acts of omission, such as failing to adopt admission standards that take students' different preparatory opportunities into account, not providing minority students information about collegiate opportunities, and not recruiting minority students vigorously. Further examples might include the use of collegiate rituals and symbols that reflect only Eurocentric traditions or that appropriate Native American ethnic traditions, lack of supportive services for students from disadvantaged backgrounds, governing organizational elites composed entirely of white men, and a lack of support for efforts to confront racist speech, behavior, or organizational policies/practices (see chapter 3). Such actions or nonactions reinforce the continuation of discrimination and differential advantage.

Personal prejudice and bigotry continue to exist, finding expression in both covert and overt behavior. Moreover, individual discriminatory acts continue to be manifested in hate crimes that threaten and damage members of subordinated racial groups (ironically, many hateful acts are protected by constitutional guarantees of free speech). The analytic problem, however, is that many people think of racism as only including personal and deliberate acts involving a consciously harmful purpose. It is important, therefore, to emphasize the minimal role that personal awareness or conscious intent plays in the expression of prejudice, and the limited role that personal prejudice plays in institutionalized discrimination. The analytic concept of institutional racism emphasizes that societal and organizational mechanisms and procedures can have discriminatory impact (either to deprive of or to confer benefits) even if individual actors are unaware of those impacts and are seemingly nondiscriminatory in their personal actions and not consciously prejudiced in their personal beliefs. As a result, individual racial attitudes or behaviors must be analyzed in the context of organizational and societal parameters and frames of reference (Alvarez and Lutterman 1979; Carmichael and Hamilton 1976; Feagin 2000; Gould 1999; Hall 1990; Jones 1970; Pincus 1996). Racism would not persist in individual attitudes and behaviors if organizational and societal norms and explicit practices did not teach, support, and reward such activity (and sometimes punish deviance from them).

This analytic perspective suggests that indirect or subtle/invisible institutional forms of racism are more important today than ever before. Following long struggles, overt styles of racism have largely been outlawed, as have forms of direct or intentional institutional discrimination that explicitly exclude certain groups. As Bobo and colleagues (1997: 16) have argued, however, the explicitly racist practices of the past have not been systematically replaced by their opposite: "a thoroughly antiracist popular ideology" in which a "democratic vision of the common humanity, worth, dignity, and place in the polity for" all is embraced in cultural or institutional terms. As a result, persisting racial inequalities "are now popularly accepted and condoned." Thus, the manner in which institutional structures and cultures continue on and reinforce historic patterns of disadvantage and dominance—what we call institutional racism—is largely ignored.

The widespread but distorted belief that we now live in a color-blind society, or should act as if we do, has emerged as a central way of thinking about race in the United States (Bobo et al. 1997; Bonilla-Silva 2001; Crenshaw 1997). In this vein, the dominant culture officially stigmatizes explicit, traditional, or old-fashioned racial prejudice and overt discrimination (though it often tolerates these in informal or private contexts). At the same time it condemns efforts to raise racial issues, label racist values and practices as unjust, or mobilize racial consciousness to challenge institutionalized racism. The dominant culture further challenges efforts to create social policies and programs that explicitly recognize race as a valid basis for redistributing societal resources (resources that are or have been maldistributed as a result of institutional racism), including efforts to increase opportunities for people of color to attend first-rate colleges. A belief in the irrelevance of race and advocacy of a color-blind ideology stands in the face of "substantial and widening racial economic inequalities, high levels of racial residential segregation, and persistent discrimination experienced across class lines in the black community (Bobo et al. 1997: 40). Thus, color blindness may suit a hoped-for future in which racial discrimination does not constrain life opportunities, but it is at odds with today's reality.

In parallel fashion, a long and continuing history of explicit white dominance tends to be officially ignored or minimized. Many whites lack awareness of what their "whiteness" means to them and the racial privileges they would not enjoy if they were not perceived as "white." Instead, these privileges are viewed as givens—as just the way things are. Many are unaware of why they predominantly socialize with and live near other white people, why they generally feel more comfortable with groups and individuals whose skin color is most like their own, or how they are members of a rapidly diminishing numerical minority globally. White people also regularly deny or substantially underestimate the degree of discrimination experienced by people of color. This deep denial with regard to racial matters characterizes most whites irrespective of differences in educational, economic, and geographic backgrounds (Brown et al. 2003; Kenny 2000; Krysan and Lewis 2004).

As a result of this lack of personal awareness of the role race, institutionalized racism, and organized white privilege play in their lives, many whites are unable to see how these forces operate in the lives of people of color. In fact, as Gould (1999), Bonilla-Silva and Lewis (1999), and others have outlined in their discussions of the new forms of racism, much discrimination takes place under the guise of "facing facts." Defenders of the status quo interpret persistent minority group failure in education and on the job market as evidence of minority cultural deficiencies or inferiority—an instance of blaming the victim (Ryan 1971). This conclusion follows from a belief in egalitarian values—the notion that equal opportunity is now available to all—and clear indications that blacks and Latinos/as have not attained the same level of success as whites have (Gould 1999). If prejudice and discrimination are essentially things of the past, then the dismal performance of minorities in the job market or in schools becomes objective evidence of their lack of ability. Similarly, the successful performance of whites serves as evidence of their superior ability or hard work, and not as the logical outcome of their accumulated privilege.

This ideological framework conveniently explains the racial and class status quo and provides a rationale for maintaining it and excluding people of color further. Failure to hire, admit, or promote blacks and Latinos/as can be rationalized on the grounds that everyone has an equal shot in the existing economic and educational systems. Similarly, admissions offices can treat standardized tests—which largely measure "accidents like birth, social position, access to libraries, and the opportunity to take vacations or to take SAT prep courses" (Fish 1993: 136)—as neutral, decontextualized measures of individual merit.

The national belief in a meritocracy has deeply penetrated higher education. As Bonacich (1989) describes it, this set of assumptions suggests that society operates as a sort of foot race in which everyone is assumed to have lined up at the same starting line (called the assumption of equal opportunity) and started at the same moment. "The meritocratic ideology of winners and losers is deeply embedded in our schools and universities. . . . Teachers and professors are the judges of performance. They define who will win and lose. And they are themselves caught up in a race to win at their own level" (Bonacich 1989: 7). Obviously, however, everyone does not begin at the same starting line and the race is not fair. By suggesting fairness while countenancing unequal starting positions, the meritocratic system legitimates and reproduces inequality and injustice.

SELECTED EXAMPLES OF INSTITUTIONAL
RACISM IN HIGHER EDUCATION

A critical examination of the history of U.S. higher education reveals numerous examples of how racial domination has been institutionalized in and maintained by higher educational organizations. These examples by no means provide a comprehensive description of the operation and effects of racism in U.S. higher education. But they illustrate a range of the ways in which racism historically has been institutionalized. For example, many early university scholars provided an intellectual rationale and justification for racism, thereby helping implement and reinforce racist social constructions and practices. The earliest manifestation of this dynamic in higher education involved selected religious classics that constituted the core curriculum in the seventeenth and eighteenth centuries. Scientific racism emerged later in the form of books that treated slavery as a "benign institution" and promoted beliefs in the inherent biological inferiority of people of color, supported by "intelligence tests" and the study of eugenics (Kailin 2002; Washington 1996). Scientific racism, as developed and rationalized in academic communities, served as a defense of white supremacy, and as Washington (1996) puts it, "the university curriculum became the training grounds" for indoctrinating students "with the belief that the universe was designed for the Afro-American to be the servant of whites" (81).

Public financing of colleges and universities provides another example. In its earliest forms, U.S. higher education was privately financed and governed; but after the passage of the 1862 Morrill Act, states began to play a much greater role in creating and maintaining public colleges and universities (Lucas 1994). Part of this movement toward public financing of universities—specifically, the second Morrill Act of 1890—resulted in creating segregated institutions for blacks. The legislatures and governors of the states heavily influenced the financing of these higher education organizations and often their educational policies as well. Thus, as Wilson (1994b) outlines, the second Morrill Act of 1890 "provided states particularly strong incentives to create public universities congruent with this legislation to serve black students and other racial minorities even though these new institutions would be part of 'separate but equal' and thus racially segregated" (198).

During the latter part of the nineteenth century and throughout the twentieth century, most persons of color who could attend institutions of higher education were enrolled in segregated institutions. White women had similar experiences during these years. These colleges were founded because persons of color and white women were excluded from the states' primary higher education institutions. Sometimes the basis of exclusion was legal; at other times it rested on traditions embodied in policies specific to individual colleges. Furthermore, many students of color and white women were counseled and steered toward these options even when other possibilities were available. Later, when mainline institutions became more open to persons of color and white women, the historically segregated institutions continued to attract students based on the negative experiences of many students of color and white women students in predominantly white male institutions (Allen 1992; Feagin, Vera, and Imani 1996; Fleming 1984). Often the strongest attraction of black-only (historically black college and universities, or HBCUs) or female-only colleges lay in the presence of faculty role models who shared the students' race and/or gender. Such faculty members were rarely found in colleges and universities intended to serve the white male population. Classroom and campus dynamics at these colleges were in many cases less racist and sexist as well. As these various patterns of steering aggregated, they formed systemic barriers (based on race and gender) to full access.

One current example of how racial domination has been institutionalized in educational organizations connects to our society's larger racialized economics (Calhoun 1999; Keller 2001; Paulsen and St. John 2002). Race and class separation or segregation in neighborhoods—and thus in elementary and secondary schools—often combines with the ways in which states and municipalities fund public schooling to produce inequalities. Students from different neighborhood schools have differential access to pivotal educational resources, from outstanding teachers to adequate books and laboratory supplies to physical safety. Thus, students of color and white students from working-class or poor backgrounds are systematically at a disadvantage in their preparation for college and for college entrance examinations, and in their access to the skills required to successfully negotiate the college selection process. With less access to adequate college counseling, advanced courses, and well-qualified teachers, these students find their ability to compete for access to highly selective colleges severely hampered.

Another mechanism that helps maintain the racial and class exclusivity of elite colleges and universities stems from the structure and cost of college admissions tests (such as the SATs and ACTs). These tests focus on students' general knowledge and knowledge of specific subjects such as world history, biology, environmental studies, and chemistry, and "Data for the class of 2000 in California show that while only 13 percent of African-Americans and 11 percent of Mexican-Americans took four or more SAT II tests, 24 percent of white and 32 percent of Asian-Americans did so" (Zhao 2002: 13). Not only do students from the most elite and competitive high schools get a better preparatory education, and thus score better on these tests in general, but they can afford to take them multiple times in order to obtain the highest possible scores as supporting evidence of their suitability for university admission.

The cost of attending college adds to current patterns of racial and economic inequality. Much of our higher education system is privately financed, so people with wealth can most easily afford access to the most selective colleges and universities. Particularly since World War II, the tremendous expansion of public, nonresidential, two-year junior/community colleges with open admissions and lower costs has increased access to higher education for people concentrated in the lower echelons of class and status. Consequently, many students of color and persons from less affluent backgrounds are steered or attracted to these postsecondary educational options. The wide geographic distribution and large number of these two-year colleges allow enrollees to live at home or in local communities where they maintain part-time work. Today a large proportion (estimated at 45 percent) of high school graduates who attend college in their first year after graduation enroll in community colleges, and a larger proportion of students of color than white students enroll in them. While these colleges provide students of color with greater access to postsecondary education, they also lead them toward vocational curricula and post-collegiate careers and jobs that offer lower earnings and lower social status than those available to holders of bachelor's degrees. Although more students of lower socioeconomic status (SES) are now attending college, the increases are almost entirely in two-year institutions. Meanwhile, high-SES students are attending four-year institutions in higher numbers than ever before (Calhoun 1999). As Calhoun (1999) argues, "U.S. higher education both reproduces and, at least to some extent, conceals a profound prestige and reward hierarchy" (13).

During the 1980s, the Reagan administration dramatically decreased the amount of financial aid available in the form of grants while increasing the availability of student loans (Wilson 1994b). The effect of the increased loans, Wilson (1994b) points out, was "a disincentive to poor minority students . . . who additionally faced . . . the doubling of tuition in the past 15 years [which] made the cost of higher education even more prohibitive" (204). A change from grants to loans discourages college students and potential college students from lower socioeconomic backgrounds from enrolling or completing their degrees (Becker and McSherry 2002). Obviously this student group includes a disproportionate number of college-age students of color. Loans may help such students enter college, but they also push economically marginal families even deeper into debt.

Notwithstanding all these examples of ways in which cultural, economic, and political forces have shaped the nature of race in the U.S. system of higher education, public discussion of race and colleges is commonly limited to admissions and the supposedly unfair advantage given to racial minorities. However, the legacy of racism in higher education organizations goes much deeper. It pervades the curriculum, pedagogy, structure of departments and disciplines, formal and informal relationships among participants, and decision making about hiring, promotion, and retention. The question is, What needs to be changed in order to increase racial equality in higher education? Though we address this question throughout the book, in part II we outline a definition of critical multiculturalism that guides our work and offers a foundation from which to challenge institutional racism and promote justice in higher education.

THE STRUGGLE OVER MULTICULTURALISM IN HIGHER EDUCATION

Historically, multiculturalism has meant a concern for the many ethnic and cultural traditions that make up the United States and for the people associated with them. Traditional strategies dedicated to achieving multicultural educational change have been oriented toward improving the school experiences of students of color. Their foci have been on curricular changes aimed at either teaching the culturally different in order to promote assimilation or increasing the sensitivity of majority group members so as to reduce prejudice and improve intergroup relations (Rezai-Rashti 1995; Sleeter and Grant 1988). For the most part, such efforts have promoted understanding of cultural differences and the traditions of different racial/ethnic groups, but have failed to challenge majority students' views about the priority of their own cultural traditions in the world or about the ways in which institutions and organizations perpetuate inequality. Privileged groups' "ways of learning" — as well as their ways of telling stories about the world that reaffirm their position in the dominant narrative—remain at the center or are advocated as the true "American way" (Crichlow et al. 1990).

Thus, where they are present at all, multicultural educational curricula and pedagogy generally do little to challenge the status quo racial reality and the wider reality of domination; instead, they serve primarily to help those in the institution get along or feel good about themselves. Unfortunately, this does little to confront the gaps in the educational experiences of different students and even less to challenge social inequality. Partly for this reason, Rezai-Rashti (1995) and others (Giroux 1998; McCarthy 1995) have turned to a type of educational reform variously called "critical multiculturalism," "insurgent multiculturalism," or "antiracist education."

By incorporating an understanding of the structural nature of inequality, antiracist education, social justice education, or critical multicultural education offer alternative frames of reference for viewing educational problems. For example, while traditional multicultural education argues that societal institutions are partly to blame for the origins of student failure, most of its focus remains on the individual, family, or culture. In contrast, although critical multicultural education acknowledges that cultural and familial factors cannot be ignored, it argues that institutionalized racism must bear much of the blame. Without directly discussing education, Gould (1999) provides an example of this kind of analysis: "If blacks sometimes do not succeed, even when they appear to be given a fair chance, this may be due to the fact that facially neutral organizations often have an adverse impact on blacks. Such organizations implicitly privilege white cultural attributes and devalue the cultural performances blacks bring to them" (173).

Individual prejudice or intention to discriminate is not the issue here: White people often are not aware of the ways in which they themselves, as well as major organizations and societal mechanisms, operate in ways that violate their personally egalitarian values (just as white people often are not aware of their racial identity and its impact on others).

In the U.S. context, many blacks and Latinos/as tend to be somewhat bicultural; in order to be successful, they must understand whites and white culture as well as their own. However, most whites are not bicultural and are not required to understand others' cultures. The kind of misunderstandings and judgments that result can have severe and profound consequences even for middle-class people of color. It's not enough, therefore, for people of color to have the same abilities as whites because abilities are perceived and assessed through evaluations of one's culturally based performance. Cultural differences as manifest in such performance become deficiencies in the context of structural discrimination. People in positions of authority often rank differences, label them better or worse and good or bad, and then use them to explain behavior. They then ascribe differences in performance or in basic conditions of living to supposed differences in ability or motivation, but not to the organization and conduct of societal institutions. Thus, decision makers seldom consider housing segregation and poverty, which correlate strongly with the quality of local schools and thus with students' opportunities for learning and learning, as structural determinants of individuals' educational performance and life chances—including their credentials for college admission. In short, they often overlook the presence and effects of contemporary and historic patterns of indirect institutionalized discrimination.

Challenging the operation of a monocultural framework and its attendant overt or covert institutional racism requires efforts that go far beyond traditional forms of multiculturalism. The more critical forms of multiculturalism include an inherent concern for issues of social justice and attend to the following (Adams, Bell, and Griffin 1997; Giroux 1998; McCarthy 1995; Olneck 1990; Rezai-Rashti 1995):

- A systematic critique of how knowledge is constructed and a recognition that knowledge is socially produced, imbued by human interests and implicated in unequal social relations
- A more nuanced discussion of racial identities, including the role of power relations and domination in structuring racial and ethnic identities and in allocating rights and resources
- A focus on organizational practices as well as pedagogy and the content of the curriculum
- A close study of the sites, institutions, and methods that foster and sustain racism in higher education institutions

This more critical educational examination focuses not only on students of color but also on white students. It emphasizes the relevance not only of race but of class, gender and sexual orientation, and religion. It suggests that curricular and pedagogical changes play an important part, but only one part, in challenging traditional exclusionary and unjust practices. It considers not only students but also faculty, staff, and alumni. It especially scrutinizes the institutions that serve them all, in hope of helping all members better understand their place in the world, the way their current educational organization operates, and what learning and working in a multicultural context mean.

Thus, multiculturalism is not merely a matter of adding key books to the curriculum or including a few traditional outsiders in the organization. It also is a matter of redistributing power and resources and reevaluating the rules and practices that govern such institutions and the lives of people within them in order to eliminate unearned privilege and accompanying dominance and subordination. And beyond that it is a matter of defining and encouraging the kinds of changes in expectations and behavior that may enable us to live collaboratively with one another in diverse organizations and communities.

NOTE

1. The research on racial attitudes overwhelmingly focuses on black–white relationships and comparisons and ignores the multiracial nature of intergroup attitudes in U.S. society. While many of the broad principles and themes discussed in this literature apply to whites' attitudes toward all groups of people of color, there are many complexities, nuances, and variations between and among the views of whites and groups of people of color that are missing.

Chapter Two

A History of Racism in U.S. Higher Education

Appreciating the extent and depth of racism in higher education requires paying explicit attention to ways in which higher educational institutions are inextricably intertwined with the larger history of racism in the United States. In describing the history and current status of racism in education, we outline predominant patterns in the history of people of color in K–12 and higher education—exclusion, segregation, forced assimilation, and limited inclusion. This historical context helps give meaning to contemporary racial patterns in education that show positive progress toward reducing racism as well as others that maintain, reproduce, and in some cases increase racial disadvantage and injustice.

A BRIEF HISTORY OF RACE IN THE UNITED STATES

In the fifteenth and sixteenth centuries the planet was circumnavigated and subjected to the rule of a core of nation-states (Holland, Spain, Portugal, and Britain) seeking new sources of land, wealth, and labor. One outcome of European travel across the globe was confrontations with people in Africa and the Americas and the emergence of some of the earliest notions of racial difference. These early racial ideas did not merely involve attempts to describe newly "discovered" peoples, but led to attempts to take over the resources of those being described (Said 1978; Winant 2001). Thus, from the beginning, the creation of racial categories was deeply connected to colonization and subjugation. Although racial hierarchies prevailed across the emerging world racial system, specific racial arrangements differed according to local circumstances. Some developing racial systems distinguished as precisely as possible between "whites" and "others," while other systems relied on a continuum of racial categorization that admitted more intermediate positions (*mestizo*, *mulatto*, *moreno*, and a large variety of other mixed identities).

The United States developed a racial system commensurate with evolving conditions within the newly developing nation. The origins of this system reach back to the period of early colonization and involved the confrontation of European settlers with those already living on the land. Most of what was to become the United States had been home to an array of indigenous tribes. Recent estimates of the size of this indigenous population at the time of European settlement range from five to eighteen million people north of what is now the U.S.–Mexican border (Lomawaima 1995). The earliest European explorers, conquerors, and settlers came bearing instructions from their monarchs to claim ownership of these lands that were previously unknown to them.

In the late 1700s, the new federal government of the United States temporarily dealt with the Native American tribes as equals and negotiated treaties with them. As the demand for land increased with the growth of European immigration, however, and as the military power of the U.S. government increased, settlers aided by the U.S. Army continued to press westward, abrogating treaties and forcing Native American groups farther and farther beyond the Mississippi. Following these initial removals, whites pursued further legal and extralegal actions to expropriate more land from Native American control. Against a backdrop of political and economic subjugation, tribes continue to this day to seek legal redress in court to have their early treaties honored (Cornell 1988; Feagin and Feagin 1999; Snipp 1995; Takaki 1993).

Despite the best efforts of these native tribes to maintain themselves, military actions interspersed with hostile legislative and judicial initiatives had the cumulative effect of a slow-moving campaign of genocide. Millions of individual Native Americans and many whole tribes were wiped out. The sources of this devastation included diseases brought by the Europeans, military attacks by U.S. forces, expropriation of tribal land and water by white settlers backed by the government, and physical banishment and incarceration. This was followed by a long-standing policy known as "cultural stripping" in which whites sought to convert the indigenous people to Christianity and otherwise acculturate or assimilate them.

As U.S. forces conquered the indigenous people, reduced their numbers and banished them to the most undesirable lands, whites established farms, small towns, and large plantations as their means of livelihood. All of these enterprises required laborers; the largest enterprises—agricultural plantations in the southern area of the United States—were presided over by landowners who eagerly sought inexpensive and controllable labor. Attempts to enslave indigenous groups largely failed, and the supply of white indentured servants from Europe could not keep up with demand. Instead, landowners increasingly turned to a new and growing source of labor: captured Africans. A highly profitable international trade involving northern ship owners and operators arose to enslave African captives who were imported in chains to the Caribbean Islands and then to North and South America. The European and American slavers and the slave owners to whom they were sold viewed them as uncivilized pagans who were inferior even to the extent of being subhuman. Once sold to the owners of plantations they endured life-long bondage as property and sources of cheap labor. Like subjugated Native Americans, newly imported Africans were often forced to give up their language, religion, and cultural traditions. Laws prohibited them from receiving an education, in hopes of rendering them more tractable.

A long period of enslavement was followed by systematic exclusion and segregation in most areas of public life. While formal Jim Crow laws in the South forced African Americans to use separate public facilities, attend segregated schools, ride in separate train cars, sit in the back of the bus, de facto segregation in the north had many similar effects with African Americans segregated into overcrowded neighborhoods, into the most dangerous and lowest-paying jobs and into the worst schools (DuBois 1996; Drake and Cayton 1993; Sugrue 1996; Takaki 1993). Not until passage of civil rights laws in the mid 1960s were African Americans most basic rights protected.

Throughout the nineteenth and twentieth centuries, a flood of European immigrants came to the United States from all over northern, southern, and eastern Europe. Groups received quite different receptions based largely on their ethnic origins, and many white ethnics (including Jews, Irish, and Italians) faced severe discrimination in housing, jobs, and social interaction (Roediger 1991; Takaki 1993). For example, as Guglielmo (2003) documents, Italians were seen as racially inferior whites and thus were often despised and excluded. However, despite such poor treatment, these white ethnics always had access to basic protections (particularly those of citizenship) and resources not available to racial minorities (Guglielmo 2003; Steinberg 1996). Recent European immigrants moving out into newly acquired western territory (e.g., Texas and California) had more rights and protections than those whose families had lived in the United States or on the land for generations.

Early interactions between white settlers from the United States and citizens of the former Spanish colony of Mexico occurred in the area of southwestern North America. In 1845, the United States formally annexed the territory of Texas, which had declared independence from Mexico ten years earlier. The annexation triggered a war between the United States and Mexico, in which the Mexican army was defeated. In 1848, by the Treaty of Guadalupe Hidalgo, the United States fixed the border between Texas and Mexico at the Rio Grande and for $15 million took from Mexico the land area that would eventually become Arizona, California, Nevada, and Utah, and parts of New Mexico, Colorado, and Wyoming (more than 525,000 square miles). Despite treaty provisions intended to protect the Mexican residents living on the ceded territory, this conquest set the stage for the eventual subjugation of Mexicans who owned land and lived in these areas (Montejano 1987; Takaki 1993). These wars and land appropriations began the long tradition of economic exploitation and social segregation of Mexican and Latino/a immigrants to and residents of the United States.

The first Asian immigrants arrived from China in the mid-1800s. Fleeing economic hardship in China and seeking the greater economic opportunities perceived to be present on the West Coast of the United States (Chan 1991; Le 2001a, 2001b; Takaki 1993), these mostly male sojourners intended to make their fortune and then return to China. Business owners on the west coast and in Hawaii turned to Chinese and other Asian immigrants to perform difficult and dangerous work on farms, in mines, and on railroad construction projects. Once in the United States, these immigrants and their successors from other areas of Asia and the Indian subcontinent experienced frequent violent oppression and continuous discrimination. In daily practice and by law these early Asian immigrants were deemed racial inferiors, similar to Africans or Native Americans (Almaguer 1994). From the latter part of the nineteenth century through World War II, laws and executive actions officially sanctioned exclusionary and racist practices against Asian immigrants and informally encouraged periodic racial violence. In addition, the national-origin immigration laws of the late 1800s and early 1900s virtually stopped Asian immigration to the United States for decades. Not until Congress passed the 1965 Immigration Act were these restrictive laws and policies overturned.

Thus, while the United States valorizes its historical record of racial and ethnic pluralism, it exaggerates its success and denies the continual exploration and oppression of racial and ethnic minorities (Steinberg 1996). This oppression pivots on territorial expansion and economic exploitation, but has also involved the social construction of race and the institutionalization of racist practices. American ideals and values about democracy and pluralism often have served to minimize, cover up, and rationalize historic and contemporary racism. However, oppressed groups—sometimes with the assistance of allies in the majority community—have energized struggles to bring social, political, and economic practices into closer congruence with these ideals.

A HISTORY OF EDUCATIONAL EXCLUSION, SEGREGATION, AND FORCED ASSIMILATION OF MINORITY GROUPS

Although commentators have often characterized our educational system as a force for ameliorating social inequality, evaluation of its history also reveals a long record of exclusion, subordination, and forced assimilation. Educational organizations at all levels, including higher education, have often helped to reproduce existing racial hierarchies.

Exclusion

All racial minority groups in the United States at one time or another experienced exclusion from formal schooling. The black experience in the South provides a clear example of what was at stake. Early in the history of the new country, many states passed laws known as *black codes* (Marable 2000; Takaki 1993). The black codes comprised a range of laws designed to control both free and enslaved blacks, including defining who was black, regulating their movement, and limiting their rights. These laws included many restrictions on the education of both free and enslaved blacks. As Litwack (1998) puts it, "Knowledge encouraged independence and free thought. Knowledge opened up new vistas, introduced people to a larger world than the local town and county. Knowledge permitted workers to calculate their earnings and expenditures" (54). Not only was it illegal to teach slaves to read or write but many state laws prohibited providing instruction to free blacks. Whites viewed educating blacks as a threat to the South's racial hierarchy and people (slaves or slave owners) who flouted the law faced severe retribution. The laws against educating blacks were part of a larger racial project to subjugate and control a large and potentially rebellious population, and the pattern of excluding subjugated peoples from formal or informal educational arrangements was repeated again and again in U.S. history.

    Another key example of the relationship between educational institutions and racial heirarchy comes from the early history of California. Although the state's first school laws, passed in 1851, did not mention race at all, the implicit understanding was that only whites were to participate. Later revisions to the state school law explicitly provided that districts should count only white children in disbursements of funds. "This 'White children' clause effectively denied Negro, Chinese and Indian children the right of attending public schools" (Cloud 1952: 44). In the late 1850s, the state superintendent of schools, Andrew Moulder, discovered that some districts were admitting blacks on an equal basis with whites and informed them that California's schools were for whites only. Moulder helped get a law passed in 1863 that specifically disqualified Negroes, Mongolians, and Indians from being admitted to public schools (schools risked losing all state funds if they failed to comply) (Savage 1976).

    California authorities occasionally made exceptions to this tendency toward complete exclusion from public schools. The structure of exception and its justification reflects another pattern in the educational history of racial minorities in the United States: the creation of segregated public schools for those understood to need assimilating and acculturating to white values and behaviors. Thus, some districts in the state eventually had the option of providing separate schools to "children of African descent and Indian children," if white citizens did not object, on grounds of the civilizing effect of education (Cloud 1952: 45).

Around this time, a black resident of San Francisco attempted to enroll his daughter in the local public school. When she was turned away, the family sued. The final decision in the case, *Ward v. Flood*, issued in 1874, confirmed the doctrine of separate but equal education, requiring districts to provide schooling to all children, but not in the same facilities.

Several years after the decision in *Ward v. Flood*, 1,300 Chinese residents tested the parameters of the school laws by petitioning the legislature for access to separate schools for Chinese children. Their petition was denied:

> The petitioners claimed that in San Francisco alone Chinese had been taxed $147,000 for educational purposes, yet the money had been used for schools benefiting "children of Negroes and White people, many of the latter being foreigners from European countries, while our youth have been excluded from participation in the benefit." (Wollenberg 1976: 37)

Unlike the very small African American and Indian populations, by the late 1870s, Chinese immigrants constituted 10 percent of the state's population and were seen as a threat to white laborers (Almaguer 1994). The movement to end Chinese immigration was at its peak as "'anti-Coolie clubs' and labor organizations merged into the Workingman's Party which campaigned on the slogan 'the Chinese must go'" (Wollenberg 1976: 37). In this context there was little support for providing any educational facilities for the Chinese.

Even though by 1880 all racial barriers were removed from San Francisco's school laws (though they still existed in other parts of the state), this new inclusiveness still did not cover Chinese children (Wollenberg 1976). Only in 1885, following the state supreme court's decision in *Tape v. Hurley*, did the Chinese win the right to separate public schools. Mamie Tape was a U.S. citizen of Chinese descent, and the court affirmed that there was no legal basis for excluding American citizens from the schools or for forcing Chinese parents to pay taxes for schools they had no right to send their children to. This was a decidedly unpopular decision; the state superintendent of schools was quoted as stating that the decision was a "terrible disaster" (Wollenberg 1976: 41) and the superintendent of schools in San Francisco rushed to get a state bill passed to establish separate facilities for "Mongolians" so that the court wouldn't order Mamie Tape admitted to the predominantly white school involved in the original suit. Even with the *Tape* decision only San Francisco and Sacramento opened Chinese schools. Not until 1929 did the state's school code expunge all provisions regarding racial segregation and specifically mandate that all children, regardless of race, should be admitted to all schools in the state (Heiser and Almquist 1971).

California's experience had many parallels across the nation. Typically, whichever racial minority group was seen as the largest threat to white authority and as the one most necessary to control was the one most completely excluded from schooling. As we will see in the following sections, California's educational history also paralleled nationwide dynamics in the movement from initial total exclusion of racial minorities from school, to slowly beginning to provide segregated and inferior schools, to eventually (after organized resistance) extending new school opportunities for racial minorities on the rationale that doing so created opportunities for civilizing ignorant or heathen peoples.

Segregation

In response to organized efforts by racial minorities to gain access to schools—and to good schools—authorities in many locales begrudgingly ended the total exclusion of various groups by creating separate, segregated schools. As in the California example, separate schools for racial minorities often arose in response to concerted struggles by people of color to gain access to educational opportunities for their children. In the South, blacks first gained access to education during Reconstruction. During and after the Civil War, the American Missionary Association and other northern philanthropic organizations played a key role in setting up and supporting segregated schools for freed former slaves throughout the South. In fact, following the Civil War, the pursuit of education became a main focus of southern blacks. As Franklin and Moss (1988) outline, it was "viewed by many as the greatest single opportunity to escape the increasing proscriptions and indignities that whites were heaping upon blacks" (239). Thus, black children attended school even when it caused their parents great hardship or inconvenience. By 1900, more than half of all black southern children age ten to fourteen were attending school (Anderson 1988b).

The commitment to have children attend "neighborhood schools" was based on apparent concerns about preserving local community integrity, avoiding children having to travel for lengthy times and distances, and encouraging parental participation. Given the residential segregation of most communities, community integrity usually meant racial/class integrity. Therefore, this commitment led to racially segregated and separated schools, another example of "indirect institutionalize discrimination" and at times of intentional and "direct institutional discrimination" (Feagan and Feagin 1986). When black and white families lived close to one another, even this commitment to neighborhood schools was overridden by the desire to maintain racially separate schools, and black children were often bused long distances to outlying and separate schools. Moreover, despite legal requirements that separate black facilities be equal to white institutions, the two diverged dramatically. Both de jure segregated black schools in the South and de facto segregated black schools in the North were unequal to white schools in their facilities, the salaries paid to teachers/administrators/staff, and their teaching/library/laboratory materials. As a result, they provided a seriously deficient education to African American students. Though the best-known system of segregated and unequal schooling involved blacks in the South during the Jim Crow era, the same circumstance confronted many groups in the North and West.

Early in the twentieth century, a separate Mexican school system was established in Texas. It began in central Texas in 1902, and by 1930 almost 90 percent of all schools in southern Texas were segregated. In the 1940s, segregated Mexican schools existed in 59 counties and 122 school districts across the state (Montejano 1987). Much like Jim Crow segregation of blacks in the South, the educational segregation of Mexicans in Texas formed part of a larger set of rules that limited interracial contact and attempted to control and exploit a vast laboring class (Takaki 1993). Educational segregation thus served two purposes: by limiting the education of Mexicans it kept them available as cheap labor; and it separated a supposedly racially inferior population. As Montejano (1987) describes:

> The [Anglo farm] settlers understood well the potentially corrosive force of "educating Mexicans" for the maintenance of their divided world. The divisions of the racial order made little sense if Mexicans were "better educated" than some Anglos or if both were "mixed" in school. Educating the Mexican also raised the danger that Mexicans might seek "social equality." . . . The key element in Mexican school policy was the concern of farmers in securing and controlling farm labor. If farmers were to keep this labor reservoir, Mexicans had to be kept ignorant. (191)

Some districts in Texas and throughout the Southwest refused to spend any money on Mexican schooling; others restricted Mexican children to an elementary education; and still others created separate, underfunded Mexican primary and secondary schools (Takaki 1993). Such schools had poor facilities and few supplies, and they were staffed by poorly paid white teachers who often shared widely held beliefs about Mexican racial inferiority (Montejano 1987). Despite the inadequate and limited education available, Mexican parents pushed to get their children educated. Like some of their employers, these workers recognized the key role that education could play in improving their children's chances of securing better jobs and wages.

A similar pattern existed for Japanese workers on plantations in Hawaii (Chan 1991). Between 1885 and 1924, two hundred thousand Japanese immigrated to Hawaii as government-sponsored contract laborers to work on large sugar plantations. Though the migrants were comparatively well educated (because of the compulsory educational system in Japan), planters in Hawaii resisted educating workers' children. First opposed to any education, planters later worked to limit education, trying to end it at sixth or eighth grade and to have it be entirely vocational. Employers also argued that a public school system was unnecessary and too expensive (Takaki 1993). One plantation manager explained that there was no need to fund a "ruinous system that keeps a boy and girl in school at the taxpayers' expense long after they have mastered more than sufficient learning for all ordinary purposes"; another remarked, when asked whether schools might create intelligent citizens, "they'll make intelligent citizens all right enough, but no plantation laborers—and that's what we want" (Takaki 1993: 265). In fact, as children of plantation laborers learned about the Declaration of Independence and other precepts of equality, freedom, and democracy, many recognized the limitations of plantation life and decided that they did not want to end up like their parents. The plantation owners and managers had rightly feared that education might undercut the availability of generations of poorly paid and subordinated laborers.

Forced Assimilation

Interest in assimilating supposedly uncivilized or heathen populations to white culture and norms has been a dynamic in the educational history of all U.S. groups. Until the late 1960s and early 1970s, as McCarthy (1995) argues, assimilationist ideology dominated all levels of the educational system. Public schooling was intended to open up some opportunities to immigrant and minority groups and at the same time create a single cohesive culture through the transmission of putatively American values, norms, and identities. Though many of these efforts targeted non-English and non–northern European immigrants, other vigorous assimilationist projects focused on people of color, including African Americans, Native Americans, Mexican Americans, Puerto Ricans, and Asian Americans. Many white ethnic groups may have benefited from the assimilationist model; but for racial minorities, assimilationist propaganda often took the form of withering attacks on their native cultures and "a special kind of cultural incorporation into a racial order in which they were accorded a secondary status" (McCarthy 1995: 24).

The earliest group aggressively targeted for assimilation was Native Americans. Their formal education began during the 1880s with the inception of white-controlled boarding schools designed to assimilate the allegedly uncivilized Indians and destroy tribal cultures. Private philanthropic agencies, including religious organizations, played a major role in establishing reservation and nonreservation boarding schools, such as the Carlisle Indian Industrial School in Pennsylvania. Off-reservation boarding schools often forcibly removed children from their families and other tribal surroundings, arranged to have their hair cut, replaced their traditional clothing with school uniforms, and often punished them for speaking their native languages (LaFlesche 1963: Standing Bear 1975). In many cases, boarding schools also physically and sexually abused their Native American students (Smith et al. 2003). "Such education . . . often resulted in loss of tribal identity" (Kidwell 1994: 242). By the late 1880s, 14,300 Indian children were enrolled in 227 boarding schools nationwide. Most were operated by the federal Bureau of Indian Affairs or by Christian religious groups that received government subsidies. The boarding schools were a key component of larger programs designed to force Native American groups to assimilate or be obliterated. Some scholars suggest that these schools constituted a final, unacknowledged "Indian War," specifically targeting Native American children (Adams 1995).

Assimilationist projects circumscribed the curriculum available to blacks who secured access to education in the North or eventually in the segregated South. While many segregated black schools were staffed by African Americans, their curricula and textbooks were controlled by whites (Banks 1995; Weinberg 1977; Woodson 1977). As with the Japanese in Hawaii and the Mexicans in the Southwest, the white elites controlling the schools tried to ensure that the education offered to minority children did not generate "inappropriate expectations." Their objective was not to create independent and thoughtful citizens who understood their rights and could demand greater opportunity. Instead, it was to teach respect for and acceptance of white authority, temperance, Christian morality, and a work ethic that incorporated racial subordination; the curriculum's sanitized version of history celebrated white superiority and denigrated blacks (Litwack 1998). Some of the disagreements around the content of Black education are reflected in the famous debates between Booker T. Washington and W. E. B. DuBois about the relative merits of industrial versus academic education.

By the 1960s, resistance to these assimilationist projects grew to the point that many urban blacks demanded local community control of schools (to reflect community traditions), greater representation of racial minorities in educational institutions, and increased attention in the curriculum to racial groups' history, literature, art, and music. By the mid-1980s, these challenges coalesced into a call for multicultural education at all levels—elementary, secondary, and tertiary (including graduate and professional schools).

Resistance

Underrepresented groups have always resisted educational subjugation. From their early days in North America, African Americans have struggled first for access to education generally and later for higher-quality education. Although African slaves received very limited education (Franklin and Moss 1988), they sought such opportunities and masters and overseers throughout the South sometimes taught select slaves to read and write, ignoring laws against teaching blacks. A small number of Negro schools were organized and funded by free blacks themselves in parts of the South and some Northern cities during the early and middle 1800s (Anderson 1988b; Franklin and Moss 1988). Driven by their strong desire to be educated, some blacks overcame the many barriers and found a way to educate themselves or attend school (Litwack 1998). During the period of abolition and reconstruction, some progressive whites actively advocated and supported these efforts.

Similarly, wherever they were located, Mexicans, Japanese, Chinese, and Native Americans organized to gain access to education for their children. In the post–World War II period, these struggles acquired renewed vigor with the flowering of the civil rights movement, the end of legal segregation in the *Brown v. Board of Education* decision, and the enactment of new civil rights laws.[1] During the 1960s and 1970s, many groups struggled for community control of schooling, most notably in black groups' efforts in major urban areas of the North. In addition, Native American groups fought for and eventually won passage of the Native American Self-Determination and Education Improvement Act (PL 93-638) in 1975. This law allowed tribes to assume management of various programs, including education, on a contract basis from the Bureau of Indian Affairs. Despite concerted attempts to deny them access to high-quality educations, various groups of color fought long and hard to overcome their exclusion. But despite individual and group struggles of resistance, the dominant racial ideology and the influence of the political and legal system continues to position most groups of people of color on the margins of the educational system.

RACE IN HIGHER EDUCATION

The available history of people of color in U.S. higher educational institutions is severely circumscribed, largely because few people of color aside from those who gained access to Black colleges were able to attend colleges and universities prior to World War II. Similarly, there is very little record of Latinos/as and Asians in U.S. higher educational institutions before then. Though stories exist of individual triumph in securing a college degree, the collective experience of people of color in colleges and universities prior to World War II was one of almost total exclusion.

Most book-length treatments of the history of U.S. higher education pay little attention to race or to the practice of racial exclusion. The scholarly coverage of the pre–Civil War colonial period makes almost no mention of the higher education of people of color except for an occasional note regarding one of the few Native Americans or free blacks who managed to gain access to college. Only for the years after World War II, and particularly after the civil rights movement of the 1960s, do the histories of higher education explicitly address the topics of race, racism, and multiculturalism. Even today, book-length histories of higher education fail to include critical and in-depth treatments of how racism was institutionalized in colleges and universities and how it was maintained by the white majorities in most educational institutions and the larger white power structure.

As discussed in chapter 1, racism was historically institutionalized in U.S. society and continues to be practiced on college campuses, though in altered forms. Higher education in the United States historically has promoted the material interests (wealth, power, and status) and symbolic interests (assumptions, cultural styles, and visions) of white elites. These elites have used their economic wealth, political power, and ideological legitimacy to ensure that education helps them maintain their positions of privilege while continuing to subordinate people of color.

Despite the overarching history of racial exclusion, specific people or institutions within higher education have played a contrasting role by challenging racist practices and ideologies; these counterexamples suggest why we might expect higher education to serve different ends. For example, Berea, Antioch, and Oberlin Colleges admitted African Americans to their ranks long before other predominantly white schools. Moreover, while the hard work of many people of color to gain access to higher education or to start their own institutions was built on recognition of the importance of education for advancement, it also involved a few key white allies who supported these efforts.

During the colonial period, the first colleges established in North America were modeled after English culture and practices. The education they provided was unavailable to blacks, indigenous groups, and women. Initially, only propertied white males were enrolled at the private universities, and not until the mid-1800s did women and people of color begin to be accepted into higher education at all—often in small numbers or through the founding of separate institutions. And even these separate institutions were commonly run by white males. Major demographic transformations in the composition of higher education organizations did not begin for another hundred years, following World War II. In fact, with the exception of students attending segregated black institutions that had been created after the Civil War, few people of color had access to higher education before the mid-1900s.

While Latinos/as and Asians accounted for a relatively small part of the U.S. population prior to the late 1800s,[2] blacks represented a substantial population, especially in the South. Nevertheless, few blacks had access to or graduated from American colleges prior to about 1860 (Brubacher and Rudy 1997; Franklin and Moss 1988; Weinberg 1977). Most colleges simply did not admit blacks; for example, in refusing to admit a black student in 1845, Brown University authorities "explained that if he were admitted 'southern patronage would be withdrawn'" (Weinberg 1977: 263). In other instances, colleges capitulated to the racist sentiments of their students. In 1850, Harvard Medical School admitted three black students. In response, 60 of 108 enrolled students signed a petition asking for the black students to be dismissed. Ultimately, even though many other students opposed this initiative, the faculty eventually persuaded Dean Oliver Wendell Holmes to notify the students that they must leave after completing the semester in which they were studying (Weinberg 1977).

After the Civil War, the history of African Americans in U.S. higher education shows a continuing pattern of exclusion and discrimination: "Southern colleges, virtually without exception, barred black students from attending, and the situation was only marginally better in elite northern colleges" (Weinberg 1977: 266). Much as they did with regard to K–12 education in the period after the Civil War, southern state governments seldom acknowledged any responsibility to provide blacks with higher education. Northern missionary societies founded private colleges that, though designed to teach both black and white poor, eventually became Negro colleges when southern governments passed laws prohibiting interracial attendance. Furthermore, by limiting primary and secondary education opportunities for blacks, southern states forced most of these colleges to teach at a precollegiate level. One of the main proponents of the movement to found black colleges across the South, Booker T. Washington, argued that the goal of higher education for blacks should be "industrial education." Northern philanthropic gifts flowed to colleges such as Tuskegee Institute and Hampton Institute which embraced this industrial education and thus were not seen to represent a threat to the racial and economic order.

Substantial inclusion of blacks in higher education began with federal government initiatives. The first major change resulted from the passage of the GI Bill after World War II. This legislation enabled thousands of African American and Latino/a veterans (as well as many white veterans from poor and working class backgrounds) to attend college without being disqualified by financial constraints or a limited record of previous educational achievement (Greenberg 2004). The second major change in African American college enrollment resulted from the Civil Rights Act of 1964. According to Wilson (1994b), from 1965 to 1980 African American college enrollment doubled from 600,000 to 1.2 million, with only 20 percent still attending historically black colleges. To be sure, both in educational circles and in the nation at large, a wide range of people and institutions vigorously debated and resisted these efforts.

Similarly, the educational experience for Native Americans changed substantially in the 1960s. As one standard reference work on the history of U.S. higher education written prior to this time states, "college training for . . . the American Indian, has been practically nonexistent in any special or distinct sense" (Brubacher and Rudy 1997: 79). Beginning in the late 1960s, however, a system of tribal community colleges began with the Navajo Community College in Tsaile, Arizona (Feagin and Feagin 1999). According to Thornton (2001), following the founding of the Navajo Community College, a total of twenty-nine tribal colleges were established solely or primarily to educate Native Americans. These two-year institutions offer a range of degrees in academic, vocational, and technical areas. They also provide access to curricula on Native American history, language, and culture. A major challenge for these colleges has been that, "to adequately serve the needs of the people a tribal college . . . [must draw on] . . . the history and culture of tribal people" (Badwound and Tierney 1996: 445). Such strategies reflecting central values of traditional Native American cultures may conflict with the pervasive meritocratic values and practices of U.S. higher education. Since the 1960s, American Indian studies programs also have been created on a number of traditionally white college campuses. With increasing mobility and urbanization, Native Americans are more likely to attend a wide range of colleges and universities.

Current Racial Patterns in Education

Racial patterns in K–12 education today show a complicated pattern of progress, stagnation, and retreat. By the end of the 1960s, the percentage of Native Americans with fewer than nine years of education had substantially decreased. Still, the percentage of Native American high school graduates continues to lag far behind the national average, and Native Americans have the highest dropout rate of any racial or ethnic group (Feagin and Feagin 1999).

With regard to the struggles of African Americans, while the 1960s and 1970s marked considerable progress in efforts to desegregate the nation's elementary and secondary schools, the last several decades have seen a major slowdown. In a number of recent reports, the Civil Rights Project of Harvard University notes that the last ten to fifteen years have seen a trend toward resegregation with "*virtually all* school districts analyzed . . . showing lower levels of inter-racial exposure since 1986" (Frankenberg and Lee 2002: 4; emphasis in the original). This is not only an issue of interracial contact, since predominantly black and Latino/a schools tend to have high levels of poverty. As a result, "These schools are also associated with low parental involvement, lack of resources, less experienced and credentialed teachers, and higher teacher turnover—all of which combine to exacerbate educational inequality for minority students" (Frankenberg and Lee 2002: 4–5). Data from various sources confirm that blacks in the United States still have less access than white students do to educational technology, attend schools with older and inadequate physical structures, have a higher proportion of teachers who are not trained for their subject area, attend schools with higher levels of poverty, have less access to college preparatory curriculum and programs, and so on. These persisting inequities have major consequences for blacks' college enrollment.

Though many Latino/a groups have shown improved educational achievement since the 1950s, Latinos/as are the most segregated racial minority group in our country's schools today (Orfield and Gordon 2001). Most continue to attend schools composed predominantly of children of color and to receive inferior educational resources (Frankenberg and Lee 2002; Orfield and Gordon 2001). Between 1950 and 1980, the median number of years of schooling for Mexican Americans improved from 5.4 to 9.6, yet it remained far behind the national median of 12.6 years. In 1980, under 38 percent of Mexican Americans older than twenty-four years had graduated from high school (compared to 67 percent of the total population), and in the mid-1990s, under half were high school graduates (compared to 80 percent of the total population) (Feagin and Feagin 1999).

Asian Americans, the fastest-growing group of color in the United States, represent an educational success story across a number of measures (Ong and Hee 1993; Pang 1995). Since the 1970s and 1980s, they "have been touted by the media as the model minority who have enjoyed extraordinary success in American society despite their long history as an oppressed racial minority" (Suzuki 1994: 275). However, use of the "model minority" stereotype minimizes or denies the racism that Asian Americans continue to face. It also contributes to blaming other people of color for their social and economic problems by implying that if the others would follow their example they would be successful, too. Thus, it pits Asian Americans against other racial minority groups. Within education, the model-minority stereotype minimizes the particular educational challenges that different Asian American subgroups face and ignores the bimodal distribution of Asian American educational success: Whereas many groups such as Indians, Japanese, and Koreans have achieved success because they immigrated to the United States with college degrees, other groups from Southeast Asia have come as political and economic refugees with little formal education and have struggled.

With particular regard to higher education, table 2.1 indicates that college and university enrollment rates of all racial groups have substantially increased since the 1960s, with black and Hispanic students making the largest gains (parallel timeline data on Asians or Pacific Islanders and Native Americans are not available). Nevertheless, these groups continue to have a lower percentage of college-age adults enrolled in higher education than do whites. Moreover, as table 2.2 shows, the percentage of degrees conferred on people of color (except for Asians/Pacific Islanders) drops considerably between lower and higher echelons of the educational hierarchy. For example, whereas African Americans acquired 10.9 percent of all associates' degrees in 1999–2000, they secured only 6.6 percent of all doctorates. Both of these percentages are below blacks' corresponding percentage in the national population of eighteen- to twenty-four-year-olds. The same is true for the Hispanic population.

The picture gets worse when we examine not merely those attending college today but overall educational attainment patterns among different groups. U.S. Census Bureau data reveal that blacks, Latinos/as, and Native Americans have much lower college graduation rates than either whites or Asian Americans, a result of the decades of exclusion from higher education (U.S. Census Bureau 2002). As of 2000, of the U.S. population twenty-five years or older, 44 percent of Asian Americans and 27 percent of non-Hispanic white Americans were college graduates, compared to between 10 and 15 percent of non-Hispanic Blacks,

Table 2.1. Enrollment Rates of 18- to 24-Year-Olds in Degree-Granting Institutions, by Race/Ethnicity, 1967 to 2000

| | | Race/Ethnicity | | |
| | | White | Black | |
Year	Total	(Non-Hispanic)	(Non-Hispanic)	Hispanic
1967	25.5%	26.9%	13.0%	———
1970	25.7%	27.1%	15.5%	———
1980	25.7%	27.3%	19.4%	16.1%
1990	32.0%	35.1%	25.4%	15.8%
2000	35.5%	38.7%	30.5%	21.7%

Note: Data are based on sample surveys of the civilian noninstitutional population.
Source: National Center for Educational Statistics (2002: 225, table 186).

Table 2.2. Percentage Distribution of Degrees Conferred by Colleges and Universities, by Race/Ethnicity and Degree Level, 2000

		White (Non-Hispanic)	Black (Non-Hispanic)	Hispanic	Asian/ Pacific Islander	American Indian/ Alaskan Native
Degree Level	Total[a]					
Associate	100.0	73.7	10.9	9.3	5.0	1.2
Bachelor's	100.0	77.5	9.0	6.3	6.5	0.7
Master's	100.0	79.9	9.0	4.8	5.8	0.6
Doctorate	100.0	82.0	6.6	3.8	7.1	0.5
First professional	100.0	76.3	7.1	4.9	11.0	0.7

[a] Total does not include data for nonresident aliens.
Source: U.S. Census Bureau (2002: 175).

Latinos, Native Hawaiian and other Pacific Islanders, or American Indian or Alaskan Natives. As these data and the following brief discussions of the current status of different groups of color in higher education suggest, there is still much room for progress in opening educational opportunities to all.

African Americans

While the total percentage of eighteen- to twenty-four-year-old African Americans attending institutions of higher education increased steadily between 1967 and 2000 (see table 2.1), the percentage of black males has actually been decreasing (Bennett 1995: 668). Overall, blacks are approximately half as likely as whites to have secured a college degree (U.S. Census Bureau 2002). Explanations for the persistently low rate of African American college enrollment include, in addition to overt political and economic discrimination, inadequate precollegiate education, increased enlistment in the armed forces and other sectors of the labor force, changes in the family structure of many blacks, increased serious teenage problems, inadequate financial aid, and high rates of attrition in the early years of college. Moreover, although the percentage of blacks enrolled as undergraduate students in higher education roughly equals their percentage in the population, they continue to constitute a higher proportion of the enrollment in two-year colleges than in four-year institutions (National Center for Educational Statistics 2002). Brint and Karabel (1989) clearly delineate the caste system that pervades the U.S. higher education apparatus. All institutions are not equal, and the hierarchy generally begins with Research I universities and elite liberal arts colleges, proceeds to other large state universities, through smaller state colleges, ending in junior colleges and community colleges. Despite notions of a linear pathway, it is very unlikely that a student entering junior or community college can access the elite institutions at the top of the ladder. The National Center for Educational Statistics reports that while about 75 percent of community college students enter with a goal of getting a degree, only about 33 percent of this group intend to go further to obtain a bachelor's degree; further, only slightly more than 50 percent of those students who initially intend to pursue a bachelor's degree actually transfer to a four-year institution (Hamilton 2003). The overall conditions of black Americans in higher education has best been summarized by Allen and Jewell (2002): "Education generally, and higher education in particular, has been and continues to be fiercely contested ground for African Americans. Black educational gains have been hard won. Because our victories tend to be partial and/or precarious, African Americans often find themselves revisiting the same battlefields" (256).

Latino/as

Today, Latinos/as are less likely than members of most other groups to earn a bachelor's degree (Falbo, Contreras, and Avalos 2003). They have one of the highest dropout rates from high school, are generally underprepared by their elementary and secondary educational experiences, and have little access to college preparatory courses or information. As of 2000, only 57 percent of the Latino/a population twenty-five years old and older had graduated from high school as compared to 88 percent of non-Hispanic whites. And Latinos/as were only about one-third as likely as non-Hispanic whites to have a college degree (10.6 percent vs. 26 percent) (U.S. Census Bureau 2002). Even within the overall average of 10.6 percent, Cuban Americans (at 23 percent) are far likelier to hold a bachelor's degree than the two other largest Latino/a groups, Mexican Americans (6.9 percent) and Puerto Ricans (13 percent). Many of these Cuban immigrants arrived with college degrees they had earned in their home country.

The low college graduation rates for Mexican Americans and Puerto Ricans restrict the upward economic mobility of members of these groups. Because they are such a rapidly growing percentage of the population of eighteen- to

twenty-four-year-olds in the nation, their numbers in higher education will increase even if the percentage of Latinos/as attending college does not (Carnevale
2003). But their current disproportionate enrollment in two-year colleges and
Hispanic Serving Institutions is likely to continue (Leon 2003; Carnevale 2003).

Asian Americans

According to the 2000 census, Asian Americans twenty-five years old and older
were more likely than any other racial/ethnic group to have graduated from college. However, their rate of college graduation varies extensively by ethnicity.
While people of southern and eastern Asian ancestry have high educational at-
tainments, those of Southeast Asian heritage have much lower rates. Moreover,
many Asian Americans with college degrees secured them before immigrating
to the United States. Thus, in sharp contrast to most Latino/a immigrants, many
Asian immigrants begin their experience in the United States with a high level
of education. Another issue raised recently by a number of Asian American
scholars is the potential backlash against high levels of Asian American educational achievement. As Suzuki (1994) summarizes:

> The second access issue . . . is whether some of the most selective and prestigious
> institutions of higher education have imposed unofficial "quotas" on the admission
> of Asian American students. During the past 10 years, Asian American enrollments
> have steadily increased in a number of such institutions and now comprise a sub-
> stantial proportion of the total enrollments in those institutions. . . . These high per-
> centages apparently created considerable concern in these institutions that Asian
> American students may be "overrepresented" and upsetting the "ethnic balance" of
> the student population. (265–66)

Thus, despite their seeming success, many Asian Americans often face discrimination in admissions and hostility on campus (Chan 1991).

Native Americans

Native American college attendance rates increased by 54 percent from 1988 to
1997. As of 1997, the total enrollment of this group was approximately 142,000,
or about 1 percent of all college students. Native Americans collectively still
have very low educational attainment rates, however, only approximately one in
ten Native Americans being college graduates. They also continue to be overrepresented at two-year colleges and underrepresented at four-year colleges. In
1996, they made up 1.3 percent of the enrollment at two-year colleges but only
0.8 percent in four-year institutions (National Center for Educational Statistics
1998). Moreover while it is important to recognize that Native American enroll-

ment in all colleges practically doubled in the two decades between 1976 and 1996, their number relative to the total number of all students enrolled increased by only 30 percent.

Progress Overall?

The increases in the numbers of students of color since World War II and of white women students since 1900 in higher education deserve notice, even while they evidence the need for much more improvement. Currently white women are still underrepresented in certain disciplinary arenas (such as science and engineering), even though they have achieved and surpassed the enrollment level of white males in undergraduate degree programs overall and in some graduate program areas. Persons of color continue to be underrepresented at all levels of higher education, and this pattern is even more extreme when enrollment analyses exclude community/junior colleges and technical institutes from consideration. Students from poor or working-class backgrounds are similarly underrepresented in general in higher education and, when present, are concentrated in nonelite institutions.

In concluding its analysis of education and race/ethnicity, the Clinton-era President's Council of Economic Advisers (1998) emphasized that "completing of a four-year college degree has become increasingly associated with economic status and success in the labor market" (22). In the United States, higher education is the primary path to elite status and select professions. The upward trend in numbers of people with baccalaureate or higher degrees is unmistakable. Students of color remain underrepresented at every level of higher education, with potentially devastating effects to their future life opportunities and earnings.

People of color are similarly underrepresented in other prestigious roles and statuses in higher education (including faculty and higher administration). In the twenty-two years from 1975–1976 to 1997–1998, the percentage of faculty of color in higher education increased from 8 percent to more than 13 percent; but most of the change is accounted for by the increased presence of Asian Americans, whose percentage representation increased from slightly over 2 percent to over 5 percent. Other groups of faculty of color increased much less over this twenty-two-year period—less than 1 percent in the case of blacks and Native Americans.

CONTINUING ACCESS TO HIGHER EDUCATION

A key policy change that aided in the positive (albeit limited) shift in college demographics was affirmative action, which has opened doors for thousands of

students, faculty, and administrators of color. After enactment of the Civil
Rights Act of 1964, universities' "stated goals now had to include strong
counter-balancing affirmations concerning social justice" (Marsden 1994: 420).
Chief among these newer goals was greater representation of people of color in
admissions and hiring and in determining curriculum content and social climate. Struggles over the nature and extent of affirmative action today are part
of the ongoing struggle over racial groups' access to higher education and to
the reproduction and/or transformation of racism in our society and educational
institutions.

The Johnson administration's advocacy of "affirmative action" was presaged
by the Civil Rights Act of 1964, which suggested that superficially equal treatment could not unravel the effects of prior (and current) discrimination and disadvantage. Title VI of the Civil Rights Act of 1964 prohibits public and private
institutions that receive federal funds from discriminating on the basis of race,
color, or national origin. It permits educational institutions to take such factors
into account in attempting to diversify their student population and to mitigate
the effects of past discrimination (although it prohibits using race as a sole factor in admission, hiring, or promotion). Moreover, President Johnson's 1965 Executive Order 11246 called on all federal contractors to "take affirmative action
to ensure that applicants are employed . . . without regard to their race, creed or
national origin." Title IX of the 1972 Education Amendments extends this antidiscrimination agenda in higher education to include gender, and Section 504
of the Rehabilitation Act of 1973 extends it to people with disabilities. The ambiguity of these statutes explains why the nation continues to debate the meaning of efforts to approach racial equality in education (and also indicates why
places like Bob Jones University do not accept any direct federal aid).

The *Bakke* case (*Bakke v. Board of Regents* 1978) was part of the effort to
challenge affirmative action and assert a new concept: reverse discrimination. In
Bakke, the U.S. Supreme Court affirmed (in a two-part decision by separate 5–4
votes) that on the one hand explicit racial quotas in admissions were impermis-
sible and that on the other hand some consideration of race was permissible in
order to achieve valid goals, especially in undergraduate education. Over time,
as part of the trend identified in chapter 1, the federal courts have continued to
be away from "proactive affirmative action policies that assume the existence
of institutionalized inequality" (Platt 2000: 324), in favor of narrowly tailored
remedies intended to address identified, intentional discriminatory acts.

In the *Hopwood* case (*Hopwood v. State of Texas* 1996), which involved four
white plaintiffs who had been denied admission to the University of Texas Law
School, the law school relied heavily on LSAT scores and grades, but it also used
a special committee to review African American and Mexican American applicants. The U.S. District Court found in favor of the plaintiffs on grounds that
their equal protection rights under the Fourteenth Amendment had been violated.

The Fifth Circuit Court of Appeals upheld, finding that there was not a clear case of a compelling state interest in diversity, per se, and that the University of Texas's affirmative action policy was not narrowly tailored. The court argued that the only compelling state interest is overcoming the effects of past discrimination and not educational benefits that might result from a diverse student body. Although the Circuit Court of Appeals agreed that the University of Texas Law School did have a history of discrimination, it concluded that this discrimination had ended by the late 1960s, and discrimination in secondary education in the state of Texas was neither proved nor deemed relevant.

After *Hopwood*, and in response to a rising tide of white opposition to explicit race-based affirmative action programs, several states (including Texas, California, and Florida) developed programs to maintain diversity in student bodies by guaranteeing admissions to public colleges and universities to a set percentage of high school students who graduate near the top of their class. These programs attempt to address some racial and social class biases built into the public schooling system by guaranteeing that at least the top students from the state's worst schools will gain access to college. They promote racial fairness in a backhanded way, however, since their success in continuing to bring a diverse group of students to college campuses depends on the existence and maintenance of segregated secondary schools. Though relatively recently implemented, they also have begun to come under attack. In some cases, wealthy white families are protesting the policies, claiming they make it harder for their children to gain admittance into states' flagship institutions (Glater 2004: 1). In contrast, several research groups have concluded that the plans are problematic because they are in fact having the opposite effect, and are "not adequate substitutes for affirmative action when it comes to diversifying the study body" (*Academe* 2003: 7) Because the plans also do not specify which public colleges the qualifying students will be admitted to, the most likely pattern is for white and affluent students, with the highest exam scores, to attend elite or flagship state institutions, while students of color and relatively impoverished students attend institutions of lesser status.

Alternatively, a number of scholars and policymakers have suggested moving to a policy of socioeconomic-based affirmative action rather than race-based affirmative action. A significant challenge in trying to implement such plans is that they are typically based on family income data which does not address major and persisting racial differentials in access to wealth. In general, African Americans earn about 60 percent as much as whites and even when controlling for differences in education and other characteristics Blacks still earn over 10 percent less (Bonilla-Silva and Lewis 1999). However, even more important for educational experiences and college admissions than these income gaps are the gaps in wealth between similarly situated Blacks and whites. As Oliver and Shapiro (1995) powerfully demonstrate, Blacks lag far behind whites in accumulation of wealth—even when they bring in the same income. Even low-income whites have more net wealth than middle income blacks. As Starr (1992) reports, white households with incomes between $7,500 and $15,000 have "higher mean net worth and net financial assets than Black households making $45,000 to $60,000" (12). These wealth gaps are largely a result of intergenerational transfers, the persisting legacy of historic discrimination. In fact, even if all direct, present-day racial discrimination against them was eliminated, "African Americans would [still continue to] be disadvantaged because of the cumulative and multidimensional nature of historic racial oppression in the United States" (Bobo et al. 1997: 17). Thus, socioeconomic-based affirmative action, drawing solely on family income data, will consistently underestimate black disadvantage.

The most recent major U.S. Supreme Court cases focused on affirmative action in higher education (both of which were decided in 2003) involved the undergraduate college and law school of the University of Michigan (*Gratz et al. v. Bollinger et al.* 2003; *Grutter v. Bollinger et al.* 2003). In these cases, white plaintiffs argued that they were unfairly denied admission due to special consideration given to potential students of color. In the undergraduate admissions case, which has drawn greater attention because of its implications for other higher education institutions, the plaintiffs focused their criticism on the point system used for ranking potential students. Plaintiffs' attorneys and amici curiae (including the U.S. attorney general) labeled this system a quota, while defendants' attorneys and amici argued that the system attempted to guarantee diversity. With a maximum possible score of 150 points, a maximum of 98 points could be awarded for a combination of the student's secondary school GPA (up to 80 points), the school's type and quality (up to 10 points), and the difficulty of courses taken (up to 8 points). Up to 12 additional points were given for students' scores on standardized tests, such as SAT or ACT. Another 40 points were available to be given for other factors, as follows: geography (up to 10 points for a Michigan resident or 2 for an underrepresented state), legacy status (4 points for children of University of Michigan alumni), personal essay (up to 3 points for an outstanding one), personal achievement (up to 5 points if outstanding), leadership and service (up to 5 points), and miscellaneous (up to 20 points). The miscellaneous category included such factors as membership in a socioeconomically disadvantaged or racially/ethnically disadvantaged group, being a scholarship athlete, being a man in the nursing field, and the provost's discretion. Although race was clearly not the only factor in admissions' decisions, it was obviously one of a number of factors the university wished to use to ensure a diverse student population.

In writing for the Supreme Court's 6–3 majority in the undergraduate admissions case, Chief Justice Rehnquist argued that the "University's policy, which automatically distributes 20 points . . . to every single 'underrepresented minority' applicant solely because of race, is not narrowly tailored to achieve the interest in educational diversity that respondents claim justifies their program" (*Gratz et al. v. Bollinger* 2003: 2427–28). In the Court's view, this admissions policy did not allow for individualized consideration, and as such was deemed a violation of the equal protection clause of the Fourteenth Amendment. In contrast, Justice O'Connor wrote the Supreme Court's 5–4 decision upholding of the admissions policy of the University of Michigan Law School based partly on the law school's use of a more individualized and flexible set of procedures (*Grutter et al. v. Bollinger et al.* 2003).

In a dissent from the Court's majority view in *Gratz v. Bollinger*, Justice Ginsburg used a markedly different argument than did the other Justices. In addition to focusing on the university's admissions policy, she emphasized the relevance of the social and historical context of these policies and of the nation's history of institutionalized discrimination. Justice Ginsburg observed that "we are not far distant from an overtly discriminatory past, and the effects of centuries of law-sanctioned inequality remain painfully evident in our schools and communities," and she argued therefore that "decision-makers may properly distinguish between policies and exclusion and inclusion" (*Gratz et al. v. Bollinger et al.* 2003: 2443–44). Justice Ginsburg's view is close to our own, emphasizing the history of racial and other forms of exclusion and discrimination in society at large and in higher education in particular. This history, together with the continuing state of racial inequality in society, requires remedies that avoid the illusion of color blindness in order to achieve a more just and egalitarian future. Taken together, the majority opinions in these two cases yield support for affirmative action policies that promote racial diversity in higher education while giving individual attention to each applicant's talents and motivation while creating a diverse educational community. That was the case in the Supreme Court's approval of the University of Michigan Law School's admissions policy. Even so, this support was tempered by Justice O'Connor's words, "We expect that twenty-five years from now, the use of racial preferences will no longer be necessary to further the interest approved today" (*Grutter v. Bollinger et al.* 2003: 2347).

However universities respond to these rulings, and whatever the course of future litigation, reasonable policies must acknowledge and cope with the reality of historic and contemporary forms of institutional racism and sexism. In trying to make decisions about college admissions that take into account a number of criteria, including academic potential, demonstration of hard work, and skill, it does not make sense to match decontextualized applications from elite and affluent suburbs against those from impoverished rural or urban areas, or those from elite boarding schools against those from underfunded and underperforming public schools. If students (of whatever race/ethnicity) fail to receive equal primary and secondary educations, how can they fairly be compared with others unless these race- and class-based factors are taken into consideration?

The critical question for all people involved in these discussions is how to achieve diversity (and/or remedy discrimination) as fairly as possible. Since more students apply to universities (especially elite ones) than can get in, some degree of unfairness will probably always exist. But the central policy choice involves deciding how to apportion the burden of unfairness. How much of the burden should be borne by members of traditionally disadvantaged groups, who generally have fewer life options to start with and have historically borne a disproportionate burden of unfairness, and how much should be borne by members of traditionally privileged groups, who generally have more life options to start with, at least in part because others were denied access to those same opportunities? Perhaps equally important, how will the postadmission policies adopted by higher education institutions reflect or implement these decisions? Such questions take us beyond discussion of affirmative action itself to the nature of change in organizations of higher education that are attempting to deal with racism and racial equality. In chapter 3, we describe and analyze higher education organizations, setting the stage for later chapters that discuss these issues in further detail.

NOTES

1. Although seen as a clear victory at the time and in the decades immediately following, more recently several authors have begun to question whether and how much the *Brown* decision actually improved educational experiences for African American children. Evidence of increasing resegregation in elementary and secondary schools, large racial/ethnic gaps in school performance data, and substantial differences in postsecondary school and work opportunities make it clear how tenuous progress is. See, for example, Bell (2004), Clotfelter (2004), and Orfield and Gordon (2001).

2. Although it is true that large numbers of Native Americans lived on land that was to become the United States, by the time that those who remained were incorporated as citizens, their numbers had been totally decimated. By the end of the nineteenth century, it was estimated that fewer than 250,000 remained. Asian immigration was severely curtailed prior to the 1965 and completely cut off during the first part of the twentieth century. Although many Mexicans lived on lands ceded to the United States in the Treaty of Guadalupe Hidalgo, their growth as a significant population was uneven due to periodic efforts to recruit them as cheap labor during periods of growth and then to deport them when economic tides turned. Significant numbers of other Latino/a groups did not begin to enter the United States until the mid-1950s.

Chapter Three

An Organizational Framework for Analyzing Racism in Educational Organizations

U.S. national history is fraught with contradictory values and information about equal rights and slavery, equality of opportunity, and the reproduction of poverty and wealth. As a result, many people, especially white people, who encounter obvious examples of racial inequality find it difficult to recognize or acknowledge the injustice embedded in these circumstances; instead, inequality is seen as the result of merit and fair play or of the natural workings of the society and economy. It often is difficult to recognize the institutional and organizational factors that create and maintain privileges and advantages to whites while penalizing and negatively impacting people of color. Both privileges and penalties occur in the present, but they often invoke and incorporate historical accumulations and lead to future expectations of entitlement or of deprivation. When people do not understand the historic or contemporary bases on which inequality exists, it is hard for them to act with fairness, much less to serve as effective advocates for racial justice.

Organizations are the key intermediaries between the larger society and the lives of individuals and groups. They typically mirror the larger society and are in the position of either passing on or sometimes challenging dominant patterns and their effects. In their internal culture and operations formal organizations of all kinds, including colleges and universities, are contested systems. While the people and groups in an organization work together for overarching goals and purposes, they also have different interests—based on their identity, role, functional unit—and these interest groups often compete for limited resources. For instance, different colleges within a university may compete for scarce funds; different departments within a college may compete for undergraduate concentrators; schools of social work (or public health or education) may have different notions of how the university should relate to the local community than do departments of English or history; and athletic departments and academic units may have different visions of how students should spend their time. Upper-level administrators often minimize or deny the presence of these contested realities, and represent specific decisions as the outcome not of political struggle but of rational and fair deliberation, hopefully reflecting what they see is best for the organization and all its members and clients.

As we argued in chapter 2, colleges and universities are embedded in the unending legacy and power of societal and institutional racism in the United States and its penetration into all aspects of organizational and community life. As a result, some observers have suggested that meaningful change in higher educational systems is impossible. At the very least, any serious attempt at challenging racism requires a coherent framework for understanding organizational life, and this task is the focus of this chapter.

FROM INDIVIDUAL INCIDENTS
TO INSTITUTIONAL RACISM

In chapter 2, we reviewed the work of several contemporary scholars and activists who have updated gaps in various groups' history in the United States and have drawn attention to the recent state of race relations and racial injustice in higher education (Allen et al. 1991; Altbach and Lomotey 1991; American Council on Education 1999; Bowser et al. 1993; Feagin, Vera, and Imani 1996; Hurtado et al. 1999; McClelland and Auster 1990; Oliver, Rodriguez, and Mikelson 1985; Osajima 1995; Smith et al. 1997; Smith, Altbach, and Lomotey 2003). Part of this work documents how commonplace are racial incidents in which students of color (as well as gay or lesbian students and Jewish or Moslem students) have been harassed, humiliated, and threatened on campus. For instance, during the 1980s, Bayh (1989) noted incidents targeting students of color at 174 different colleges, including the following:

- Citadel: A group of white students dressed in white sheets and hoods threatened a black cadet with racial obscenities and a burnt cross.
- Dartmouth: White students destroyed shanties that had been erected in protest of corporate investment in South Africa.
- Macalaster College: Five Asian women found their room vandalized, with the letters *KKK* written on the door.
- University of Massachusetts: A mob of white students physically attacked black students.
- University of Michigan: Black women in dormitories received harassing flyers announcing an intention to "get them" and suggesting that they go back to Africa.
- University of Mississippi: Arson destroyed a black fraternity house.
- University of Wisconsin: A group of fraternity men held a mock auction of black slaves with white pledges wearing blackface and Afro wigs.

- Yale University: A swastika and racist comments appeared scrawled on the Afro-American cultural center.

Incidents of this sort continued to occur on a variety of college campuses after 1990:

- A court case at a university in the Northeast involved a student who left an anonymous racist and threatening message on an African American student's answering machine.
- At a southern land grant university, a fraternity held a party with members wearing blackface and KKK costumes and simulated a lynching of a member in blackface.
- At a historically black college, a local white man who was charged with setting off pipe bombs on campus stated that he was trying to "get rid of some of them niggers."
- At a large public university in a central state, a black male–white female couple was attacked and beaten up on campus amid cries of "nigger lover."
- At a large public university on the West Coast, at the beginning of the fall semester Klan cards were left on several cars at a school football game and a black college student was allegedly beaten with a metal pipe by a man who is a member of a skinhead group.
- At a public university on the Eastern Seaboard, black student leaders received letters with racial epithets threatening their lives.
- At a mid-Atlantic state college, three white males attacked an Asian American student in a "racially motivated assault" that left him with a broken skull.
- A New England state court case involved a student who allegedly used anti-Semitic slurs and threatened to kill a fellow student.
- At a community college in the Northwest, a threatening racist flier was posted on bulletin boards across campus.
- At a public university in California, three white males allegedly attacked a student because they believed that the student was gay.

The Federal Bureau of Investigation (FBI) announced that 222 colleges and universities had reported 241 incidents of hate crimes in 1998: "The FBI data indicate that 57 percent of hate crimes were motivated by race, 18 percent were motivated by anti-semitism, and 16 percent were motivated by bias based on sexual orientation" (Wessler and Moss 2001: 5). Considering the difficulty of gathering such data systematically, and the reluctance of universities to report such events, this is likely to be an underestimation of actual incidents. Moreover, such statistics cover only the most overt and aggressive forms of racism and discrimination on campus, leaving out many subtle or less aggressive daily experiences—what Solórzano, Ceja, and Yosso (2000) call "microaggressions." Following September 2001, attacks on Muslim students and people of Middle Eastern appearance or dress increased as well: CNN reported that "across the country, universities have become a focal point of anger directed at Arab-American, Muslim, and Southeast Asian students" ("Racial Backlash Flares at Colleges," 2001).[1]

Aside from the demeaning and often brutal nature of these events and attacks, they appear constant over time and similar across geographic locations and types of campuses. The similarities suggest that the events themselves reflect underlying, regularized, and well-institutionalized patterns of racism in our society at large. And beyond the immediate damage to individual victims, the incidents affect and poison the entire campus climate.

These sorts of incidents are not the only realities of interracial life on campus. As we note in later chapters, many students report good relationships and lasting friendships with students of other races and ethnicities. Many white students report learning about their own racial selves and the nature of societal racism and racial relations as a result of intergroup encounters on campus. And many students of color report substantial growth from and satisfaction with their collegiate experience, despite both egregious incidents and the prevailing tone of awkward and distant racial relations. The core problem is that all too often college faculty and administrators fail to promote such positive intergroup encounters and learning, and they fail to respond to such incidents as those noted here in ways that might challenge racism and improve the campus climate.

When first noticed by or brought to the attention of collegiate administrators, many of these incidents are described as accidents—as departures from prevailing norms of civility, tolerance, and justice. Indeed, many administrators characterize them as being not racial incidents at all, but instances of drunkenness, playfulness, or political protest (e.g., Hunt et al. 1992). Or authorities may see them as reflecting problems that reside solely in the student community, reflecting ill on the state of mind of American college youth. Or they may analyze the incidents as the actions of an individual or a small group of deviants who are ignorant, prejudiced, hate filled, or partially deranged. These analytical approaches are consistent with the general process of denying racism by deracializing or otherwise minimizing obviously racially inspired phenomena (Essed 1991). It also shifts the focus from the operations of institutionalized racism to individual prejudice, as discussed in chapter 1. The fact that such incidents are experienced so often, in so many different settings, makes it clear that they are not individual incidents. Such individualistic interpretations not only fail to provide a basis for understanding racial processes and outcomes but also deny the culturally and structurally embedded nature of institutional racism and its accompanying patterns of domination and subordination.

Blauner (1972) provides a closely related perspective on the different analytical frames used to interpret the state of race relations and race conflict on college campuses. He draws attention to differences between the analytical frames typically deployed by even liberal white academics and those typically used by students of color that are still relevant today:

For the liberal professor . . . racism connotes conscious acts, where there is an intent to hurt or degrade or disadvantage others because of their color or ethnicity. . . . He does not consider the all-white or predominantly white character of an occupation or an institution in itself to be racism. He does not understand the notion of covert racism, that white people maintain a system of racial oppression by acts of omission, indifference, and failure to change the status quo. The Third World definition of racism focuses on the society as a whole and on structured relations between people rather than on individual personalities and actions. From this standpoint, the university is racist because people of color are and have been systematically excluded from full and equal participation and power—as students, professors, administrators, and, particularly, in the historic definition of the character of the institution and its curriculum. (276–78)

These different perspectives, mirroring the distinctions between individual actions and the operations of organizational or institutional structures discussed in chapter 1, still exist.

Individual incidents of racial unrest and individual acts of racial harassment both reflect and foster institutional racism; they both stem from and reinforce such dynamics. Racially motivated incidents that occur on campus illustrate not only the tension between students of color and white students but institutions' failure to create safe and secure environments for anyone's interracial interactions and learning. We focus on incidents of racial hostility here not because they are the central or even most important manifestation of racism on college campuses, but because they often trigger thinking about race on campus and constitute one of the few expressions of racism that are acknowledged as such. Thinking about the continual and repetitive nature of such incidents and the inadequacy of administrative responses to them, demonstrates clearly the shortcomings of either a microlevel focus on individual perpetrators and actions or an exclusively macrolevel focus on broad social phenomena and processes. The former captures only a small part of the problem while the latter fails to identify local organizational and community movements that provide the impetus for organizational change. Instead, in the next section, we introduce a mesolevel or organizational-level framework for analyzing college and university dynamics and for eventually challenging institutional racism and promoting multiculturalism and social justice in higher education.

ORGANIZATIONAL FACTORS PROMOTING/SUSTAINING INSTITUTIONAL RACISM

Understanding institutional racism in colleges and universities—especially the operation of "indirect institutionalized discrimination" (Feagin and Feagin 1986)—requires attention to the nature and operation of these organizations. Drawing on a framework first generated by Terry (1981) and later modified by

Chesler and Crowfoot (1990), we suggest that eight generic dimensions can describe the structures and operations of any organization and influence local policies and practices, including those affecting racial attitudes, racial relations, and racism as well as other patterns of oppression and discrimination (see figure 3.1). The dimensions are mission, culture, power, membership patterns, social climate and social relations, technology, resources, and boundaries. At the end of this chapter (in figure 3.2), we demonstrate how to use these dimensions to depict the status of an institution on a continuum from monocultural to multicultural. In chapter 8, we use the same framework to distinguish the relevance and utility of various change strategies and tactics.

Most organizational theorists and researchers would agree that all eight of these dimensions are present in all organizations, although scholars disagree about which dimension is most likely to dominate the others. As a theologian and ethicist, Terry (1981) emphasizes the primacy of mission and culture. The structural-functional school of social thought emphasizes the role of social relations and technology. Power-elite theorists emphasize the vital driving force of power in organizations. Educational theorists or faculty development specialists might stress the crucial nature of technology—the curriculum and pedagogy. Organizational development scholars and practitioners often emphasize the centrality of social relations and climate as well as culture. In addition, the university reflects the organization of wealth and power in the society at large, and some historians and economists would focus on the elite capitalist structure that lies at the root of historic and contemporary patterns of university life and how it influences the process of resource allocation via the boundary management system.

These organizational dimensions are interdependent and generally reinforce one another to create, for the most part, orderly and predictable patterns of organizational dynamics and behavior. Thus, for instance, the mission of a university influences its culture, and vice versa. Similarly, if the resource base changes dramatically, the mission might change, and the technology might follow suit. For example, if the organization's culture promotes inadequate respect for or unfair treatment of people of color, its power system is unlikely to deliver on the mission's commitment to racial justice. If the mission and culture do not express a concern for reducing racial injustice and ignorance, resources probably will not be allocated to support curricular or environmental innovations relevant to such issues. Without specifically allocated resources, the technology is not likely to serve the goal of actively pursuing antiracist results and practices.

At the same time that this set of interdependent dimensions operates to hold the organization together, it also reflects internal inconsistencies, contradictions, and conflicts. Multiple missions and cultures exist, and subordinate ones constantly struggle with the dominant one. As a result, incremental adjustments and changes always are being made. While formal power structures represent and

Figure 3.1. Institutional Racism in Higher Education Organizations

Mission
Explicit attention to justice and racial equity as a goal is lacking.
Recognition of plural goals is absent.
Commitment is to the status quo of the society and the institution.
Multicultural/antiracist rhetoric is not tied to action strategies.
Culture
Monocultural norms for success are promulgated.
Traditional rules of the game exist for appropriate expression/dress/behavior.
No explicit rewards allocated for antiracist innovations.
Diversity and excellence are seen as competitive/contradictory.
Stance toward racial incidents is reactive.
Rituals, technology, and standards of competence reflect white and Eurocentric
  dominance/exclusivity.
Power
Power holders in most senior positions are white.
Informal access to the power hierarchy is limited to members of the white male
  club.
Constituencies of people of color have no formal access to power holders.
Protests by students of color are seen as trivial and disruptive.
Innovations and challenges are dealt with via short-term solutions.
No unit accountability exists for challenging racism or promoting a multicul-
  tural agenda.
The Office of Minority Affairs, if it exists, is not a central or powerful function.
Membership
No procedures exist to solicit or guarantee diverse student, faculty, and staff
  composition.
Retention/advancement of diverse participants is not a priority.
Social Relations and Social Climate
Social networks of the faculty/staff generally exclude people of color.
Meetings are run via traditional rules of efficiency.
Interracial relations among students are not seen as a university-wide concern.
No proactive policy/program exists regarding racial incidents or harassment.
Climate is not socially or academically supportive of faculty, staff, or students
  of color.
Technology
Traditional pedagogies for classroom instruction are unaltered.
Curriculum does not explicitly address issues of racism, various groups' contri-
  butions to knowledge, or the need for multiracial study groups.
No/few opportunities available for (re)training the faculty to mentor
  students/faculty of color.
Information systems are not responsive to different ethnic/racial/gender styles.
Traditional modes of scientific inquiry are privileged.

(continued)

Resources
> Funds are generally not available to support new antiracist practices.
> Active recruitment of students and faculty of color does not exist.
> Postrecruitment financial and social support for students and faculty of color is minimal.
> Other agendas have priority for scarce resources.

Boundary Management
> Community and physical settings usually include pervasive racism.
> No special procedures exist to recruit/admit a diverse student body and hire a diverse faculty, staff, and administration.
> Racist community settings and incidents are not challenged.
> External stakeholders prioritize educational benefits to affluent white males.
> Alumni of color are not seen as vital contributors/resources.
> Public relations and public information are not explicitly antiracist and multicultural.
> Information about the local community is not interpreted from different racial perspectives.

Source: Chesler and Crowfoot, 1990, "Racism on Campus." In W. Mays (Ed.), *Ethics and higher education* (pp. 195–230). New York: Macmillan. Copyright © (1990) by American Council on Education and Macmillan Publishing Company, a Division of Macmillan, Inc. Reproduced with permission of Greenwood Publishing Group, Inc., Westport, CT.

extend the prevailing culture, informal power arrangements curry favor and wheedle special deals that depart from and may even sabotage formal decisions and policies (Rowley, Hurtado, and Ponjuan 2002). These contradictions and conflicts in the organization's dominant patterns open up essential paths of access and opportunity for people committed to innovation and reform.

The content of these organizational dimensions or domains also vary depending on the nature of the institution and its historical development. Though each dimension is found in all formal organizations, they find different operational expression in large research universities, small liberal arts colleges, religiously oriented colleges, and community or junior colleges. In later chapters we apply this schema to broaden our analytic understanding and frame our suggestions fo change.

The Evidence for Institutional Racism: Organizational Principles and Examples

Aspects of institutional racism potentially present within each organizational dimension of higher education institutions are listed in figure 3.1 and elaborated here.

Mission refers to the official and unofficial purposes of the organization, as reflected in written policy statements, informal understandings or priorities, and symbols or public images. Some colleges and universities merely refer to their mission and the means for attending to it in official documents like accreditation reports and the college catalog; others regularly include it in organizational rituals; and still others refer to and use it in organizational planning to develop goals, solve problems, or create and maintain context and focus.

Mission statements tend to be abstract and sometimes vague presentations of principles and goals. Most advocate transmitting Western cultural traditions, advancing knowledge, providing an education to the young, sustaining individual and social productivity, and performing public service. They speak more to the conservation of tradition than to the creation of change, although they often are influenced by current political struggles and the developing economic needs of the larger society. The emphasis on preserving and passing on the traditions of Western (Eurocentric and Anglo-Christian) civilization reflects higher education's origins in service by and for privileged white males. Concerns for alternative civic traditions or international problems and perspectives are rarely a priority but may be expressed in response to developing national needs.

The mission of a college or university is determined by the board of trustees or governors, in conjunction with the president and senior staff. Planning efforts, from market concerns to human resource management, generally flow from and clarify the organization's mission in response to logistical demands and future options. Since most organizations have several secondary missions as well as a primary one, their complementarity or balance is quite critical. Consider, for example, the way that modern universities try to satisfy their commitments to public service and to the advancement of scientific knowledge, or the way members of the faculty try to balance teaching, research, and service. Mission may become a focus of conflict when debate centers on competing standards of excellence or when different types of higher education institutions (public or private, secular or religious, liberal arts colleges or research universities, four-year institutions or community colleges) commit themselves to different research, teaching, or public service priorities. Even internally, professional schools/departments of social work, education, or nursing often emphasize service to the local or national community more than do the "core" academic disciplines of liberal arts departments.

Mission statements rarely are reviewed, debated, or discussed vigorously. Yet matters of what and how knowledge and wisdom are sought (for example, which cultural traditions and epistemologies are studied or used), who is to be educated (which regional, racial, gender, and socioeconomic groups), which public services are to be performed (to benefit which interest groups or stakeholders), and what leadership should be committed to doing (what characteristics and commitments they should reflect) are cornerstone issues underlying a university's mission. These considerations (whether overt or not) typically set the stage for maintaining established traditions, including discriminatory patterns promulgated in the larger society of which the university is a part.

Although many institutions of higher education have added support for diversity to their existing mission statements (Rowley et al. 2002), Turner (1997) suggests that colleges and universities must instead fundamentally transform their missions in order to accomplish multiculturalism and social justice. However, articulating a commitment to reduce institutional racism may appear to some organizational constituencies (internal or external) to announce a partisan mission — a departure from the supposedly neutral or nonpolitical stance of the university and from the continuation of "value-free" methods of research and learning.

A *culture* of core values and beliefs permeates organizational functioning and is evident in common understandings, assumptions, or preferences regarding how people should behave — from dress and deportment to language and speech cadence — and are often embodied in symbols, traditions, and public images. Organizational culture is deeply rooted in the history of each college or university and gives special meaning to the unique lifestyles that predominate at each (Clark 1970; Dill 1982; Masland 1985). Like other organizations, a university generally contains several different cultures that operate simultaneously and may come into conflict; where a dominant culture and alternative cultures exist, the latter often serve as "safe haven[s] for the development of innovative ideas" (Martin and Siehl 1983: 52). Alternative cultures may be rooted in racial, gender, religious, sexual orientation, or class traditions that differ from the dominant pattern, although they are generally marginalized or seen as less legitimate. Universities may also include several different faculty, staff, or student cultures, an academic culture, an administrative culture, an athletic culture, a scientific culture, a humanistic culture, an activist culture, and so on (Austin 1990; Hurtado et al. 1999; Kuh and Whitt 1988; Peterson and Spencer 1990).

The culture of contemporary colleges and universities usually reflects the core values of the dominant organizational coalition and its perception of the core values of the society within which it operates. Indeed, one basic mission of a university, at the apex of an extensive system of public and semipublic education, is to prepare the young for full acceptance of and participation in the dominant culture, exemplified by the rhetoric of individual freedom and democratic governance. The prevailing influence of ideologies of utilitarianism, and of individual merit and mobility through competition, effectively link the university culture to the dominant cultural assumptions of the broader society and the needs of the political and economic system — as perceived and promulgated by prevailing elites. All too often, critics view efforts to achieve racial and other forms of diversity as undermining the university's cultural commitment to universalistic norms of academic excellence as defined in individualized, meritocratic, and Eurocentric terms. These traditional norms are operationalized internally in debates about the centrality of different curricular programs, standards for student admissions and graduation, criteria for faculty tenure and retention, and the quality of administrative leadership.

Generally, the ruling modes of inquiry in universities are those of Western, Eurocentric civilization in which a narrow range of scientific methods predominate. Positivist and reductionist methods of inquiry break phenomena apart into their constituent elements and then reconstruct or reassemble them. Distance and detachment are maintained between the knower and the thing to be known and scientists often depreciate emotion or intuition and preference as sources of bias to be controlled except in the areas of the arts. Ethnic studies, women's studies, and postmodernist interpretations of the humanities and to a lesser extent the social sciences have begun to challenge some of these assumptions, values, and practices.

The dominant culture of the university is passed on by the faculty as they act upon and interact with students in the classroom. As Zorn (1986) states:

> Most of what students learn about the faculty's values comes from observing the examples set by individual faculty functioning in the teacher/scholar role. The structure of courses and curricula, the use of language, the priorities on use of time and the mode of student-faculty interaction all convey faculty values in an implicit and sustained way that can be understood by every student. (8)

The pervasive culture of the lone, specialized expert and the moral commitment to maintain adult control of the young transmutes into the authority of the teacher as the fount of wisdom in and out of class. Despite diverse intellectual specialties and their distinctive subcultures, the wisdom of the specialized adult expert is passed on to students, or "banked" into them, in the language of Freire (1970). Faculty members often interpret the organization's support for the cultural values of academic freedom and freedom of speech to mean that their classroom behavior should not be criticized, nor should their choices of content and their impacts on various groups of students.

Kochman (1981) points out that black people and members of white ethnic groups often are embedded in a culture different from that of non–ethnically identified whites/Anglos; and that women often constitute a distinct subculture in male-dominated organizations. These groups may have different ways of talking, relating, fighting, and learning—and potentially of teaching and administering as well. Since most contemporary universities are enmeshed in white/Anglo culture, the entrance of substantial numbers of people of color and women inevitably escalates cultural conflict and creates extraordinary pressures on the new populations. For instance, several scholars have indicated how difficult it is for African-American students to negotiate the alien and often hostile culture of predominantly white colleges and universities (Allen 1988). Fiske (1988) emphasizes the problems encountered by Hispanic students who have to find their "way in institutions built around an alien (Anglo) culture" (29); and Richardson, Simmons, and de los Santos (1987) note that successful programs for minority students "rely on the student culture to establish an environment conducive to involvement and achievement" (23). Most colleges' and universities' enmeshment in middle- and upper-middle-class and heterosexual cultures often presents similar problems or tensions for students, staff, and faculty from less wealthy backgrounds and for those with a different sexual orientation.

One very visible aspect of a university's culture is the symbols by which it presents itself to the public and by which it generates feelings of loyalty. Notably, the athletic mascots and nicknames of several colleges and universities have become the focus of protests and struggles. For instance, critics have accused the University of Illinois's mascot, Chief Illiniwek, of being a stereotypical and destructive representation of Native Americans. At Florida State University (Seminoles) football games, the crowd traditionally cheers its team on with chopping movements of the arms, representing Native American tomahawking. Thus, images of Native Americans as violent warriors have been incorporated into the sports culture. In quite a different vein, the University of Hawaii recently decided to change its teams' nickname of Rainbow Warriors to just Warriors. According to some reports, administrators did so to avoid any association of the university's athletic teams with gay people (the rainbow is a symbol of some gay pride/gay advocacy groups).

An organization's *power* dimension consists of its leadership composition and style and its decision-making structures and processes. These mechanisms center legitimate authority, and the right and power to influence or coerce the behavior of other organizational members, in a small group of leaders. In the modern university, the legal and practical foundation of power is established and the public trust protected by appointed or elected boards composed of individuals from outside the academic organization. In practice, however, these trustees primarily represent the white, male, and upper-class part of the public (see chapter 7). As the U.S. economy has come to rely more and more on science and technology produced by universities, the relationships between higher education and private business have multiplied and intensified, thereby increasing the representation of U.S. business leaders on governing boards. The dominant perspectives of these trustees generally reflect the cultural assumptions and practices of the wider society and thus they do not generally advocate placing a high priority on programs designed to increase racial and other forms of social justice on campus.

From the beginnings of U.S. higher education, boards of both public and private institutions have vested policy control and day-to-day management in collegiate presidents. As later faculty professionalized, and in a few cases unionized, they gained a degree of formal organizational influence. But most official power generally is still located in bureaucratically defined central offices where presidents, vice presidents, and provosts preside. These members of the dominant coalition often depend on collegiate deans, department heads, and key senior faculty for the implementation of policies and procedures. The administrative and staff sectors of higher education organizations mirror bureaucratic hierarchies. But the academic sectors of most universities seldom operate on these principles, nor do they reflect civic notions of democratic management or participation; instead, they generally are organized as decentralized, hierarchical fiefdoms with considerable autonomy and only loose connections (Weick 1976). Thus, formal power in academic organizations often is difficult to exercise, either via hierarchical or collaborative processes. And unless they are organized into unions (much less likely in Research I universities and small liberal arts colleges) faculty members have minimal opportunity for meaningful influence regarding university policies, exert formal power only at the departmental level, and even there sometimes minimally so. Their power to make decisions usually extends no further than the content of the curriculum and the conduct of research projects and classroom activities. In the classroom, however, faculty members have virtually exclusive power to decide what to teach and how to do so. Students, the nominal consumers or clients of the institution, have little official power to influence major organizational decisions. The same is true for midlevel and lower-level administrative, clerical, and staff employees. On occasion, external stakeholders such as boards of visitors, alumni organizations, state legislatures, boards of education, and federal courts exert influence on university decisions.

The power of the president and vice presidents is much greater in some colleges than in others, and the way these executive officers exercise power differs, too. In some colleges, official leaders dominate decisional proceedings and seldom listen to subordinates; in others leaders consult with and receive input from other groups; in still others, multilevel collaborative arrangements prevail. For instance, staff and finance departments commonly operate on a corporate or bureaucratic model. Departments of student affairs try to involve students to some degree as participants (although seldom as decision makers) in cocurricular matters. The academic sector of most colleges and universities consist of a large number of decentralized and autonomous units defined by particular specializations (such as schools of education, public health, and social work, and departments of biology, English, and psychology). Whatever the style, authority is implemented most practically via budgetary and financial policies, supplemented by centrally controlled personnel policies. Nevertheless, people at lower levels of the power structure can readily resist senior administrative efforts to alter the prevailing power structure of the university—such as those required to challenge racism—because of the decentralized academic control of specialized units. This is especially likely in elite institutions, where departments are likely to have the greatest reputations and strength. The delicate balance of power between centralized authority and decentralized autonomy complicates the process of instituting centrally mandated programs of change effectively or of implementing institution-wide changes.

One common change in university power structures over the past several decades has been the creation of a special office in charge of minority group affairs. Generally, this office is responsible for recruiting, counseling, and arranging financial aid for minority students; occasionally it has a broader organizational agenda of achieving affirmative action or of reducing institutional racism. Whether its charge is broad or narrow, its ability to carry it out successfully depends on several factors: (1) whether the mission or goal statement of the university reflects the existence and purpose the office represents; (2) whether it is a staff office/position with little authority or power rather than a line office/position; (3) whether it is located in the central administration but not also represented in each subunit of the system, and thus isolated from the places where most critical decisions are made; (4) whether it is staffed by people other than prestigious faculty members and thus has little significant impact on the majority of the faculty; (5) whether its charge is to deal with social relationships and not with pedagogical and curricular change, and thus strikes at the margin but not at the heart of the academic enterprise; (6) whether it can influence the institution's research program through incentives and thus carries significant intellectual power; and (7) whether students—especially students of color—are involved in its formation, staffing, and ongoing functioning, and thus is likely to reflect their unique experiences of racism, sexism, classism, or heterosexism in the university and their visions of how things might be different.

Most often efforts to alter the monocultural white and male makeup of organizational elites generally have sought diversity in staff rather than in line positions and in peripheral rather than in core units or offices—often in these specific "minority jobs" such as affirmative action officer or head of multicultural affairs (Collins 1997). Only when members of minority race, ethnic, or gender groups demonstrate their loyalty to the prevailing culture are they likely to be appointed to truly powerful positions or to have their views considered carefully on key decisions. Even then, they may meet resistance from middle-level managers and from established centers of white and male faculty power. Where people in authority are predominantly white and male, and where authority is silent or inactive on the unrepresented nature and impact of this pattern, the organization can easily maintain its racism and sexism.

In the aftermath of racial incidents on campus, the lowest power group—students of color—often have taken the lead in requesting institutional change and in creating the pressure to bring it about (see chapter 11). More than faculty members of color or white staff members or white administrators, many students of color have correctly assessed the deeply entrenched cultural and structural racism within our institutions of higher education. White faculty and administrators who ignore or dismiss their concerns and demands have been caught by surprise when these students generate the initial thrust for change. Since students are excluded from the formal and informal power structure of universities and colleges, their path to express their needs and desires for change often uses channels the administrative hierarchy deems illegitimate, such as public protest, disruption, and demonstration. Since the culture of the university promotes a view of itself as nonpartisan, objective, and nonpolitical, its administrators, faculty, and students in the dominant cultural group often are shocked and outraged by political protest of any sort, especially from students—the most marginal, temporary, and nonexpert members of the system.

The *membership patterns* of a modern university are the demographics of its population, together with the criteria and procedures for becoming a member and for participating, including admissions/hiring, retention/tenure, and advancement/promotion. The members include students, faculty, and a wide variety of administrators, clerical staff, support staff, and board members. Critical questions for any organization include "who are to be members of this organization?" and "what kind of people do we wish to include?" In addition to establishing individual criteria for membership, organizations must set collective criteria based on their functional needs for certain skills, styles, or resources. Public conversation about racism and race relations in these organizations has recently centered on student membership criteria and processes, although faculty and administrator hiring and retention often is a focus as well. Personnel offices typically handle staff issues, which seldom reach a high level of visibility or public discussion. In many colleges and universities, the issues of student recruitment, enrollment, retention, and graduation have become so complex and important that administrators have created a new staff function called enrollment management.

The individual standards for student membership generally involve high school grade-point averages, standard admissions test scores, letters of recommendation, and personal statements about life experiences and goals. Other factors include special backgrounds, such as coming from an underrepresented geographical area, belonging to an underrepresented race, being the son or daughter of an alumnus or alumna, and being a talented athlete, musician, or artist. Current debates about affirmative action in collegiate admissions focus on the appropriate balance among these individual attributes. Beyond admissions, affirmative action concerns highlight issues of student retention, development, and graduation.

Debate over the criteria for hiring or retaining faculty often involves the definition and size of the appropriate pool from which new faculty members may be drawn. As noted in chapter 2, in the first century of U.S. higher education, white women and men and women of color were almost totally excluded from faculty roles. Initially, white women's faculty positions were overwhelmingly in colleges where the students were all female, and people of color were predominantly faculty members in historically black higher education institutions. In both cases, senior administrators were white men. Even now, white men are significantly overrepresented in the ranks of faculty, administrators, and board members (see chapters 2, 6, and 7). When community/junior colleges and post-secondary technical schools are removed from consideration, the underrepresentation of women and people of color relative to their proportion in the U.S. population becomes even greater. The implications of this demographic skew are enormous for all students, as Smith (1989) and Trueba (1998) point out.

> An institution that is primarily created and maintained by white faculty will present perspectives and values that exclude, penalize, or ignore students of color. The consistent reluctance of higher education institutions to diversify its faculty is clearly impinging on the quality of education offered for all students. Even white students need to understand ethnically and racially diverse populations in this country. Their insulation from minorities perpetuates their prejudices and inabilities to deal with populations of color. (Trueba 1998: 76)

The presence of substantial numbers of students, faculty, and staff from different backgrounds and identities can help overcome such insulation and misunderstanding. In the absence of a diverse membership, or the presence of only a few token members from different backgrounds, stereotypes and ignorance abound, and it is impossible to see variation within racial/ethnic groups. Then only differences between racial/ethic groups are obvious and they become highlighted and overemphasized. But while a diverse membership is a necessary condition for multiculturalism, it is not a sufficient condition without change in other organizational dimensions.

An organization's *social climate and social relations* involve the degree and quality of associations and interactions among its members. Beyond the question of membership, this dimension draws attention to whether and how faculty and staff, as well as students and student groups, relate with one another. It also addresses the relationships between these groups and any of their subgroupings, such as faculty and staff and students of different ages, genders, races, sexual orientations, and disciplinary interests. The organization's overall climate or morale depends not just on the level of intergroup interaction, but on the degree of mutual trust, respect, and satisfaction its members have regarding their life in the organization. This organizational dimension probably receives the greatest attention in most colleges' attempts to understand and respond to racism and racial relations.

In universities, as in other organizations, racialized patterns of interaction and communication determine the campus climate, and climates that include informal barriers to open and easy relationships among individuals and groups from different racial backgrounds are ubiquitous. Many social events are monoracial gatherings or include only a few token members of minority racial/ethnic groups; even when social or semiofficial events are desegregated, people generally sit or talk in racially separate areas or groupings. The absence of social activities that overcome prior exclusionary patterns and that stimulate positive interracial interactions in formal and informal settings precludes multicultural collaboration.

Especially in research-oriented universities, faculty members often are torn between loyalty to their discipline and to their local department, between commitments to research and to teaching or service to the local community. The character of relationships among department members varies considerably, with some departments marked by strong and close friendships and others by distant and cautious interactions. Given the historical numerical domination of most faculties by white and male members, efforts to fully integrate new faculty members of color and women faculty are deeply affected by these peer and departmental patterns of relationships. One common situation faced by faculty and graduate students of color and women is the relative absence of mentoring and sponsored access to important informal information about opportunities for funding, contacts with influential people in a particular field of specialization, and local opportunities for participation in formal organizational activities.

The patterns of social relations that dominate the faculty and the classroom inevitably permeate the student culture. Since the administration and faculty typically pay little attention to the intricacies of the student peer culture, most students ignore these issues as well. Many students socialize in racially separated domains; this inhibits them from having contact that might enrich them, demolish their narrow preconceptions, and help create a multicultural community. Among the possible outcomes of such racially separated patterns of learning and living are exclusion and overt and covert acts of discrimination against students of color that diminish everyone's quality of life. These patterns are an outgrowth of a culture, power structure, and set of social and intellectual relations that fail to teach people who are different from one another how to work with one another or how to live in multicultural communities.

An organization's core *technology* is the means by which it converts raw materials into finished products. In higher education, the curriculum and pedagogy, including courses, teaching techniques, graduation requirements, grading and other forms of evaluation, are the means for helping entering first-year students develop into university graduates. The faculty generates the curriculum, and the dominant instructional pedagogy generally involves considerable faculty autonomy and the one-way transmission of knowledge to students in isolated classrooms. In parallel fashion, technologies of scholarship are embedded in a dominant form of scientific inquiry. In both arenas, those in authority treat some technologies as privileged and may hesitantly tolerate others that are defined as less legitimate.

To the extent that the technology of instruction (pedagogy) relies on teacher dominance and student obedience, lone teacher and massed students, teacher expertise and student ignorance, it establishes a pernicious structure of social relations between the faculty and students that erodes mutual respect and curtails learning opportunities (Freire 1970; Giroux 1998; Palmer 1987). While this limited sort of pedagogy reveals systematic and universal insensitivity to students' needs, it falls especially hard on students of color. As minorities in a predominantly white institution, they are vulnerable to any form of oppression or callousness. The same is likely to be true for white women and economically disadvantaged white male students. Suzuki (1994) emphasizes the negative impact of sole reliance on traditional pedagogies such as the standard lecture:

> The standard lecture approach to teaching may have worked with the more selective group of students enrolled in higher education thirty years ago (and even that conjecture is open to question), but it is unlikely to be effective for the increasingly diverse student population entering our institutions now and in the future. For example, many Asian American students are reticent to respond to questions (if indeed, any are asked) or engage in class discussions without special encouragement. Alternatives to the lecture approach, such as small group discussions, are more likely to be effective with these, as well as with other, culturally different students. (271–72)

College and university faculty, rooted in their disciplinary interests, rarely receive preparatory training in teaching and almost never learn antiracist or equitable classroom approaches to instruction. Most faculty members were socialized in predominantly or exclusively white environs, were educated in predominantly or exclusively white undergraduate and graduate schools, teach in predominantly white universities, and live in predominantly white communities. Such segregated and privileged backgrounds and experiences do not equip them with the skills and commitment required to live and teach in a multicultural environment (see chapters 6 and 10). Much of the faculty, especially the white faculty, report a lack of knowledge and skill in dealing with issues of racial and gender diversity in the classroom (Weinstein and O'Bear 1992; Stassen 1995). If the university's culture and norms presume the faculty to be fully competent and experienced in their particular disciplines—and by extension, in all aspects of teaching pertinent to their subject—it is hard to invest in developing the skills or competencies helpful to working with a diverse student body.

Most institutions do not make the formal topic of racism a required part of the curriculum, the topic of reducing institutional and individual racism has not been popular with many faculty and some students, and the curricular priority on studying other cultures has not often been accompanied by serious analyses of white power and privilege (Takaki 1989). On the other hand, faculties in many colleges and universities have extensively debated whether to have a curriculum requirement focused on racism and ethnic studies. In the late 1980s, faculty at the University of Michigan, the University of Wisconsin, and the University of California voted for such a requirement. Similarly, "Stanford University expanded its required Western Culture Program to include the study of minorities, women, other cultures and class issues" (Maclay 1988: 15). Others have followed suit.

Given the priorities of many colleges and universities in favor of research and knowledge generation, the practice of science itself is an important dimension of institutional technology. Historically, science in higher education has fostered strong beliefs in objectivity, detachment, and distance by the scientist in relation to the objects of study and the information yielded. Based on semipositivist principles, most science has come to be perceived and practiced as value-free, though few scholars would claim that their work qualifies as completely value-free. Substantial criticism of traditional science, by white women scholars and scholars of color, has focused on the ways in which the semipositivist epistemology, research topics, methods, and uses of science are culturally embedded and thus have been misused to mischaracterize nonwhite and nonmale cultures and experiences or to overlook their concerns. They argue that other, more ethnographic, inferential, or participatory methods may be better able to uncover the understanding of people of different cultural backgrounds. Indeed, knowledge created in monocultural ways or contexts is only partial knowledge. Since the traditions and power of science and university leaders continue to legitimate traditional epistemologies and methods, however, efforts to depart from this orientation often meet with marginalization and scorn.

In addition to these aspects of the social technology of instruction and research, technologies of people management that affect staff, faculty, and student relationships are reflected in choices among bureaucratic and human relations principles of management. As information technology continues to burgeon, colleges also struggle to manage how people contact, communicate, and instruct one another via e-mail, course and program websites, and distance learning programs. University administrations are increasingly using information technology for purposes of human management and resource control (e.g., monitoring grade and salary distributions).

Resources are monies, goods, materials, and people that constitute the raw materials an organization transforms into finished products or services and the people and materials needed to accomplish this transformation. As people-processing organizations (Katz and Kahn 1978), colleges and universities have the ability to create diverse patterns of membership that help define the available level of human resources that can address or achieve a multicultural agenda. Money is an especially critical resource, since its allocation generally reflects organizational leaders' sense of what is central to its mission and culture and what is not. Colleges and universities also utilize the physical plant and equipment as other tangible resources. Information is another critical resource for academic organizations, and books, libraries, and now electronic databases are both the repositories of this resource and the means of supporting research investigations that produce new generations of scientific knowledge. Finally, a university's reputation, as a center of learning, as an athletic powerhouse, as a stepping stone to economic and political power, is a symbolic resource that also helps to define the organization.

In the process of garnering and allocating these resources, higher education organizations encounter a range of constraints and dilemmas. Appealing to wealthy and powerful individuals, private corporations, or public agencies may require deemphasizing a commitment to racial change and to altering structures of social privilege and oppression. Members of such elites may see the university's efforts to create a plural culture or an antiracist program as caving in to special interests, selling out Western civilization, bending core values under pressure, abandoning tradition, or sacrificing excellence. In addition, powerful social and economic institutions such as governmental agencies, public foundations, and corporations allocate the vast majority of research funds. Most of these sponsors are enmeshed in the same systems of institutional discrimination as the universities themselves, and most of them and their elite members also benefit from the socioeconomic status quo. Despite the prevalence of these patterns, some foundations have vigorously supported colleges' efforts to promote diversity and multiculturalism, and their provision of financial resources have made possible a number of important innovations.

Student tuition is another important source of financial resources. To a major extent, the ability to pay a student's tuition depends on the wealth of the student's family. Since the family wealth of African American and Latino/a students is generally lower than that of whites, many students of color must depend on the university's student financial aid packages to supplement student loans. As an example from the California State University system illustrates (Fields 1988: 25), financial aid often determines whether students of color can stay in school: "Expanded financial aid, better information about it and simplified financial aid processing were among the more important things that students [of color at California State-Long Beach] said the campus might do to help them remain in college." St. John (1991) observes that in view of low- and moderate-income families' economic status, direct grants are far more effective than loans as forms of assistance. Most recently, in the face of public and political pressure, many colleges and universities have begun to redesign their financial aid programs so they are "race-neutral": "colleges throughout the nation are quietly opening a wide range of minority programs to students of any race, mainly to avoid being accused of discrimination" (Schmidt 2004: A17).

Public universities receive appropriations from state legislatures, and the appropriation levels to some extent depend on the university's ability to satisfy the interests of concerned state officials. Public policies generally favor the interests of white and upper-middle-class people and their families, so states generally do not make support for university efforts to combat racism and create a multicultural environment a priority. When some activist legislators do pressure the university to challenge discrimination, some administrators tend to see such involvement as an unwarranted intrusion on the institution's academic freedom or as examples of special-interest-group publicity seeking. University responses often include denying that problems exist or, if they do acknowledge problems, asserting that significant efforts to remediate these situations are already underway.

The *boundaries* of the university environment are both physical and symbolic. They include the geographic connections between the university's physical plant and the surrounding local and national environment; the university's relationships with external suppliers of key resources (secondary schools from which new student members are drawn; purveyors of goods and materials used in classrooms, dormitories, and cafeterias; state or federal oversight and funding agencies); and university alumni. The broader and diverse cultures of the local and national society also affect internal operations, as the university screens and filters societal norms and values with shifting generational and political/economic pressures. Authorities officially maintain and manage these boundaries through a variety of boundary-spanning activities, although certain individuals may also play unofficial roles connecting or crossing these boundaries with particular external constituencies.

How the organization's external boundaries are maintained or managed has a major impact on internal university commitments and operations (Brown 1983). In general, racialized social and economic environments have a pervasive influence on college and universities and their interactions with other institutions. Most public colleges and universities have external elected or appointed governing boards, and these boards are bound to reflect the state's political and cultural climate as well as the relationship between the institution and its regional environment. In turn, these boards exert considerable influence on campus and "are extremely important in the evolution of a college's mission statement . . . [and] . . . affect policies about tenure, new degree programs, budgets, and the institutional president" (Harris and Nettles 1996: 341). Beyond the role of board members, declining state financial support for public colleges and universities threatens the very notion of higher education as a public good, and potentially reifies it as a privately available opportunity.

Most people expect higher education organizations to be nonpartisan and to ignore racist practices in other community or societal institutions. The struggle to convince universities to reallocate their investment portfolios in response to antiapartheid organizing efforts in the 1980s is one counterexample; more recent efforts to boycott products made in foreign or domestic sweatshops is another. Still another involves the action of several law schools in the late 1990s to prevent certain government agencies or corporations from recruiting on campus because of court findings or media reports of discrimination in these organizations.

The physical plants of many colleges and universities lie in or near white neighborhoods and predominantly white communities. These settings carry a history of racial exclusion, and people of color often find them uncomfortable environs to enter and live in (Carby 1992). On the other hand, some universities located in the hearts or on the margins of communities of color rely heavily on land ownership patterns that further the economic exploitation of poor and minority communities (Jacobs 1963).

A number of Research I universities have extended traditional boundaries by engaging in joint economic arrangements with the government or with private corporations. Well beyond the practice of government or corporate funding of university research projects, we now see joint funding of new product development, and exclusive patenting of research-produced drugs and technology that return profits to university researchers and research centers.

ORGANIZATION-WIDE PATTERNS: OVERVIEWS

Each of the eight major institutional dimensions operates in ways that can transmit societal racism, maintain patterns of white and male domination and privilege (and the corollary subordination of people of color and women), and constrain the potential for multicultural change. They also can alter these historic patterns, challenge racism and sexism, and promote multicultural options. As a result, conflicts often exist within each of these dimensions, as day-to-day realities contradict institutional ideals, as people of color seek improved opportunities, as white allies do or do not support them, and as external pressures (e.g., globalism, domestic demographics, improved human resource development systems, and renewed pursuit of social justice) influence institutions of higher education in either direction. In the context of these conflicting forces, universities often act in ways that knowingly or unknowingly encourage and promote oppression and domination within their own operations. Identifying, diagnosing, and assessing such patterns are necessary steps in planning changes to reduce institutional racism. By altering their mission, culture, power dynamics, membership patterns, or resources, universities can alter the basis of their own institutional racism. In turn, as institutional racism in colleges and universities changes, the organizations must alter aspects of their organizational missions, cultures, power, and resources.

Figure 3.2 represents each of these eight dimensions in models of organizations at three different stages of dealing with institutional racism and moving toward a multicultural, antiracist environment. These generic models are ideal types: they exist in our conceptual frame but not in pure form in reality. One stage or type of organization is *monocultural* (called "monolithic" by Cox 1991; "white male club" by Jackson and Holvino 1988; and "resistant" by Katz 1988). A second stage or type of organization is *transitional* (called "plural" by Cox, "affirmative action" by Jackson and Holvino, "transitional" by Katz, and "diverse" by others). Many of these first two stages' attributes have been discussed in this chapter and also are illustrated in figure 3.1. The third stage or type of organization is *multicultural* (called "multicultural" by Cox and by Jackson and Holvino, and "proactive" by Katz). Along any particular organizational dimension, institutions exist on a continuum from monocultural to multicultural. The boundaries between them and movement from one stage to another is neither linear nor necessarily unidirectional.

The monocultural stage generally is characterized by self-conscious (and often announced) commitment to maintaining traditional forms of white male domination and privilege and by resistance to multicultural change. To succeed in these organizations the few women and people of color (students, faculty, and staff) who are not simply excluded must assimilate into the dominant cultural mode. Social events are segregated (although not necessarily officially so) and little contact and communication occurs across racial/ethnic lines. The antiracist and multicultural agenda, if it exists at all, focuses on token diversity and the representation of small numbers of people of color in lower levels of the organization.

Organizations in the transitional stage of multicultural development have announced concern with issues of race and gender equity, and their diversity efforts go beyond tokenism in recruitment to a focus on retention and fair play in organizational operations. Intergroup contact and collaboration are encouraged, as are efforts to broaden the curriculum and approaches to students' academic needs and concerns. As a result, the transitional stage is likely to describe a wide variety of organizations, some of which have only recently or partially emerged from the monocultural stage and others that have made considerable progress toward a more multicultural structure and operations. Because traditional white male power holders, their constituencies, and their dominant cultural assumptions have been challenged, typically by vigorous protests or litigation, or by their own values, we can expect organizations in the early phases of this stage to be characterized by significant upheavals and overt conflicts. The backlash to challenge can be vigorous or subtle and can target the change process or specific advocates. As progress is made these conflicts are likely to be accompanied by some successful efforts to create cordial and collaborative relations among different groups. At the same time, little attention may be devoted to the racism and sexism that are deeply embedded in the organization's core mission, culture, and technology. Thus, all the confusion and contradictions about race and gender relations that beset our society are likely to be highlighted in the transitional stage. Most colleges and universities are in this transitional stage or somewhere on the margin between the monocultural and transitional stages.

The multicultural higher education organization has made considerable progress toward removing racial and sex-based barriers to success, although much work remains to be done. This stage represents an ideal type or a vision of

Figure 3.2. Organizational Stages on the Path to Multiculturalism and Justice

Organizational Dimension	Stage		
	Monocultural	Transitional	Multicultural
Mission	Deliberate exclusion of diverse issues and people. Exclusive focus on Western tradition.	Diverse student and faculty membership sought. Diversity and educational quality are linked.	Diverse student and faculty body and service to underrepresented groups valued. Diversity and academic are excellence linked. Global and social justice perspective advocated. Need expressed for change in societal arrangements.
Culture	White, male, and Eurocentric norms prevail. Prejudice and discrimination unquestioned and prevail. Assimilation into dominant traditions encouraged. Individual merit and responsibility for performance emphasized.	White and male norms questioned but prevail. Prejudice and discrimination lessened but continue. Comfort/tolerance for minorities sought. Group identities reified in separate student groupings/programs.	Campus incidents of discrimination constantly confronted publicly and negatively sanctioned. Alternative norms embraced. White, male, and Eurocentric symbols changed. Group identities synthesized with a transcendent community.
Power	White and male throughout. Others excluded or at the bottom of faculty/staff ranks. Access to "the club" limited. Strong hierarchy.	A few minority members reach middle staff and faculty levels. White and male leaders sponsor minority and women faculty/staff. Narrow access to positions of power.	Multicultural teams of faculty and staff leaders. Relatively flat and multilevel decision making, with wide access—including students.

	No designated responsibility for diversity agenda in admissions, hiring, retention, advancement.	Conflict occurs between change advocates and power holders. Special staff/office for diversity programs. Bureaucratic innovations undertaken.	Different decisional styles valued. Multiple centers of power engaged. Multicultural initiative in all units/levels seen as line function. Departments/colleges accountable for progress on minority hiring, success.
Membership	Exclusionary. Token minority presence.	Minority recruitment office exists. Culturally assimilated minority women included.	Plural representation guaranteed. Plural sense of community.
Climate	Social Relations/Social Segregated social events. Communication occurs within racial/gender groups. No external intergroup contact. Lack of trust across group boundaries. Emphasis on order and low level of conflict. Traditional management and meeting style.	Distant but cordial intergroup relations. Informal circles open to assimilated minorities. Communication on deeply held issues mostly within social identity groups. Some external intergroup social contact. Cooperation and conflict occur among identity groups. Attention to intergroup processes.[1]	Proactive inclusiveness in class, dorms, and external relations. Homogeneous and heterogeneous student and faculty groupings coexist. Much communication across race/gender lines. Conflict resolution mechanisms widespread.
Technology	Curriculum rooted in Western and classic traditions. People required to adapt to the existing technology, which is seen as culture-neutral.	Discussion occurs about ways traditional pedagogy may not fit/serve/reflect diverse groups' needs/styles/histories. Desegregated work teams occur.	New pedagogies adapt to diverse groups' needs/styles and contributions. Integrated work teams cherished. Curricula responsible to different

(continued)

Stage

Organizational Dimension	Monocultural	Transitional	Multicultural
	Segregated work and study teams common. Traditional definitions of research excellence prevail.	Cultural critiques surface of established research and teaching methods. Innovative curricular designs supported.	groups' traditions/histories. Active pursuit of plural forms of research responsive to minority communities and their epistemologies.
Resources	No special funds for diversity programs. Traditional recruitment paths and admissions criteria.	Special funds for diversity events. Recruitment focused on promising people of color and women. Retention efforts focused on minorities. Alternative admissions criteria.	Diverse membership a priority. Multicultural programs built into unit budgets. Multicultural retention and mentoring programs common. Multiculturalism a priority for resource development/use. Funds available for students in need.
Boundary Management	Traditional separations of work and home. No external socializing with diverse peoples. Fit in external market and cultures is a priority.	Changing demographics of markets/clients/suppliers/members recognized. Support for external socializing. Contradictions and conflicts in local community life acknowledged.	Work and home conflicts resolved creatively. Minority suppliers and markets sought. New external cultures and municipal policies advocated. Global focus. Multicultural vision and mission exported to peer institutions.

possible futures; no contemporary organization fully fits this model. Only as colleges and organizations approach this stage of development will the vision of this type of organization become clearer and better defined. Given the ways in which demographic and other societal changes continue to occur, it is likely that efforts to create multicultural organizations will entail considerable adaptation or struggle, with periods of resistance and retrenchment.

Although we have suggested that entire organizations can be identified with one of these stages, they are also applicable to various units and subunits. But different units or subsystems of the larger organization may be located in different stages and progress toward multiculturalism at different rates (if at all). For instance, as a function of its core mission, a college of social work may move much more quickly to the transitional stage than a college of pharmacy. And student groups, staff associations or units, and faculty departments or enclaves each may assess the importance of multicultural change differently and commit to different types or rates of change. Moreover, the process of transition from monocultural to multicultural is not a linear as organizations may make progress at some points only to experience retrenchment at some later date. An organization's dimensions are also not necessarily in balance at any moment, and colleges and universities may have achieved different stages on different dimensions. Internally, an organization may make swift progress toward changing some of its racially offensive cultural symbols, but may not yet have altered white male dominance in the power structure. Successful minority recruitment programs may increase the number of people of color, but they may not immediately improve interracial relations or achieve a multicultural climate on campus. Nor are successful efforts at multicultural curriculum reform always matched by parallel changes in traditional forms of pedagogy.

Thus, the multicultural ideal type of higher education organizations, as a stage beyond monocultural or transitional, involves a complex process of development that requires a deeper consciousness and multifaceted programs of change that integrate people, policies, and programs without promoting homogeneity in thought or action. This stage requires a college or university to deeply transform all the dimensions through which racism are institutionalized and to attend simultaneously to institutionalized sexism, heterosexism, classism, ableism, and discrimination against groups on the basis of nationality, religion, and other factors. These key aspects of the multicultural stage require identification of the similarities and differences among these different forms of discrimination as well as their interaction or intersectionality. Subsequent efforts at transformation no doubt will discover that efforts to address a specific form of discrimination can help catalyze efforts to alleviate other forms—but they also may promote competition for attention among variously disadvantaged groups.

Figure 3.2 and the monocultural-transitional-multicultural framework, like most of the discussion in chapters 1 through 3, focus on race-based and to a lesser extent gender-based discrimination. But the discussion of these organization dimensions, the discrimination that typically occurs within them, and the ways colleges and universities might look at different stages of coming to grips with and changing these patterns is also relevant to the experience of other groups which encounter discrimination and oppression. This discussion and figures 3.1 and 3.2 could be extended, or parallel figures created, to record and analyze the experiences of gay, lesbian, bisexual, and queer people, people with different abilities, and people experiencing discrimination on the basis of gender, religion, ethnicity, or economic status.

In fact, Sears (2002) does something quite similar in distinguishing between institutions characterized as "gay hostile" or "gay intolerant" (monocultural in our terms), "gay neutral" or "gay tolerant" (transitional in our terms), and "gay affirmative" (multicultural). In his terms, a gay hostile or intolerant institution "promoted an antigay agenda, including the restriction of homosexuals from its student or faculty bodies and the inclusion of antigay content in its curriculum" or "did not support pro-gay initiatives in its policies, procedures, curriculum, personnel or student body" (17–18). A gay-neutral or tolerant institution "took actions neither to encourage nor to curtail the presence of sexual minorities" or was "supportive of initiatives undertaken by its student body and faculty, such as the offering of courses with homosexual content, the adoption of a nondiscrimination statement" (17). A gay-affirmative institution, on the other hand, was one where "campus leaders worked in a proactive manner to reduce homophobia and heterosexism through actions such as modifying affirmative action and non-discrimination statements to include sexual orientation, and establishing gay/lesbian studies in its curriculum, providing domestic partner benefits . . . hiring/admitting other lesbian, gay and bisexual faculty and students into the university community" (17).

Fitting some of these items into our framework, a cultural focus on moving beyond a monocultural orientation on issues related to sexual orientation would emphasize the need to introduce language prohibiting discrimination against students, faculty, and staff on this basis to the college's mission statement. It would note the need for cultural centers, clubs, support groups, and services directed at the unique experiences and needs of this population as part of climate concerns. It would include full domestic partner benefits as part of resource allocation decisions. And it would commit the institution, as a boundary issue, to advocating for equal access and treatment for gay, lesbian, bisexual, and queer people in local community stores, restaurants, bars, and sports facilities. Likewise, a focus on the organization's movement to a transitional or multicultural stage with regard to ability issues would ensure that the culture cease use of offensive terms such as "handicapped people" or "cripples," that the climate fully support tutoring and note-taking services for students, faculty, and staff who hear or see differently, that faculty members learn how to teach effectively to students with different abilities, and that the physical structure of the institution be fully accessible to all members.

While our description and conceptualization of the organizational dimensions and dynamics of institutionalized discrimination and its transformations has emphasized their multiple and discrete dimensions and stages, it also is important to understand the concrete realities of these issues in the lived experience of different groups on campus. Part II of this volume is devoted to providing such a concrete understanding of how students, faculty and administrative staff members experience race and racism in higher education organizations. Still later, in part III, we consider various assumptions and strategies of change making, explicitly returning to figures 3.1 and 3.2 as guides to creating a campus audit or assessment. Several of these later chapters examine innovative programs that universities have developed in their efforts to challenge racism and approach multiculturalism and social justice.

NOTE

1. A regularly updated documentary source on hate crimes by state is compiled by the Southern Poverty Law Center and published in its periodical, *The Intelligence Report.* Sometimes such incidents in higher education are included. We learned through conversation with relevant staff people at this center that often colleges and universities don't officially report these incidents to the appropriate federal agencies. The *Journal of Blacks in Higher Education*, in a regular column titled "Race Relations on Campus," lists racial incidents that occur at colleges and universities across the country.

Part Two

CAMPUS MEMBERS' EXPERIENCES

In the last part, we reviewed the current and past context of racial hierarchy in U.S. society and education systems and provided an organizational framework for understanding the operations of discrimination in higher education organizations. These dynamics provide the context for understanding not only the demographics of who runs, works in, and attends colleges and universities across the country but also people's experiences of daily life on these campuses.

In the following four chapters, we examine how various members of university communities experience diversity in their organizational contexts. Much of the recent literature on higher education has agreed there are problems with regard to race relations on college campuses. Some articulate it as "a racial crisis," whereas others imply that the problems, though present and important, are not quite at a critical level (Allen, Epps, and Haniff 1991; Feagin 2002; Smith, Altbach and Lomotey, 2003). At the very least, researchers have pointed to a significant gap between white students' and students of color's assessments of their schools' racial climate. Once students of color are present on campus, what occurs in their relationships with their peers has important implications for both their academic and social success and for deciding whether and how institutions can overcome the societal legacy of racism and racial isolation.

What happens when white students and students of color meet and try to work and learn with one another? How do faculty members deal with their own internalized concerns, with the challenges posed by a diverse student body, and by an increasingly diverse peer community? And what are the experiences and outlooks of collegiate administrators as they try to provide leadership under these circumstances? These issues are crucial for the ability of all members of higher education institutions to succeed and thrive. They exemplify the organizational parameters of membership, climate, power, and technologies of instruction discussed in chapter 3.

Each of these chapters examines scholarly literature and firsthand reports from key constituencies. Chapters 4, 5, and 6 all examine data from research conducted at the University of Michigan. As a leading institution in efforts to challenge racism and promote multiculturalism, Michigan illustrates both the pain and struggle of U.S. race relations as well as some of the important innovations and gains associated with diversity. We recognize other aspects of the specificity of this institution (e.g., Research I, public, four-year, Midwest region) and thus in each chapter augment and test our findings by drawing on research done at other institutions and nationally. In chapters 4 and 5, we report results from student survey questionnaires (Matlock, Gurin, and Wade-Golden 2002) and our own individual and small group interviews with students (Chesler, Peet, and Sevig 2003; Chesler, Wilson, and Malani 1993; Lewis, Chesler, and Forman 2000). In chapter 6, we report results from an interview study with University of Michigan faculty. The interview data from chapters 4, 5, and 6 come from several distinct studies done at different times and not part of a single design. Chapter 4 explores the experiences of white students in their approaches to and interactions with students of color. Chapter 5 describes the corresponding experiences of students of color in the classroom and social interactions with white peers and faculty in higher education institutions. Chapter 6 reports the experiences of faculty members as they discuss encounters with students and with their faculty colleagues in diverse circumstances. And chapter 7 examines the situations of administrators working in diverse collegiate environments.

Because the primary focus of this volume is on race as a central component of diversity and multiculturalism, the data chapters that follow focus primarily on race. We provide examples of parallel trends and patterns for some other axes of difference/inequality (such as gender, class, sexual orientation, ability, and religion) but recognize these efforts to be incomplete. Moreover, a broader multicultural approach would require not merely the inclusion of gender, sexuality, class, and so on, but the recognition that one's experience on campus is shaped by the intersections of particular identities (such as white, upper-class, Christian, lesbian student vs. white, working-class, Jewish, heterosexual student, etc.). Thus, there is a great deal of diversity within the larger categories that we deal with in only superficial ways.

Chapter Four

White Students in the University

The context for the racial interactions that occur among college and university students includes not only the campus culture and structure but also students' own life histories and experiences. The racially separated and segregated neighborhoods and schools that most students come from predispose many to think in abstract and stereotypical terms about people of other races and ethnicities. Given the nature of class and race relations in most communities, these relatively few white students who have interacted with students of color are more likely to have met and learned with Latinos/as and Asian Americans than with African Americans. At the same time, media attention and private conversations focus most attention on white–black relations. Thus, even when incoming white students hold liberal racial attitudes, their views typically are embedded in a vague rhetoric that is untested in real encounters with people whose attitudes differ from or conflict with their assumptions of privilege.

Once students arrive on campus, important aspects of the internal organization of contemporary U.S. colleges and universities pose barriers to racial change and to the development of antiracist or multicultural student orientations and interactions. For instance, the student (and faculty) membership patterns on most campuses underrepresent the proportions of people of color in the nation as a whole. Even if white students encounter peers of color in these settings, those racial and ethnic groups' representation is still minimal (Hurtado, Dey, and Trevino 1994). If higher education is the first place where white students have sustained classroom or social contact with students of another race, it also may be the first time they encounter the need to think about their own racial identity.

The organizational technology of higher education (the curriculum and instructional approaches) often fails to address this legacy of racial separation and racism directly, and thus does not take systematic advantage of possibilities to facilitate positive racial interactions among students. Traditional notions of liberal education

79

have not addressed the knowledge and skills that students of all races and ethnicities need in order to act and interact successfully across their differences. Indeed, "liberal education has predisposed educated people toward a preference for identifying the common or universal themes in human experience, which means, in practice, discomfort with approaches that reveal basic, perhaps unassimilable, differences" (Association of American Colleges and Universities 1995: 11). Too many interracial encounters in classroom settings are sporadic and hesitant, and reproduce prior hierarchies of racial advantage and disadvantage. Too few curricular efforts thoughtfully address, or urge students to address, racism and the rationales for combating racism and approaching multiculturalism; such education in citizenship is rarely considered part of the purpose of a liberal education.

At the same time, the very fact that a diverse collegiate community exists provides the opportunity for racial interactions that are not possible in a monocultural or racially homogeneous setting. Indeed, Gurin and her colleagues (Gurin 1999; Gurin et al. 2002) argue that some of the most powerful positive interactions that students engage in across racial/ethnic lines occur outside the classroom, in the context of what they call "informal interactional diversity." These extra-academic settings permit challenges to prior messages and opportunities for learning new forms of racial exchange, new racial attitudes and behaviors, and (for white students) new meanings of whiteness.

In this chapter we explore the racial outlooks and experiences of white college and university students. In so doing, we draw upon scholarly literature and on surveys and direct conversations with white students at the University of Michigan between 1990 and 2001 regarding their racial attitudes, experiences and interactions with students of color and with other white students, and on their views of racial issues such as affirmative action on campus.[1] Wherever possible, we compare the patterns discovered at the University of Michigan with those found in other studies of campuses nationwide.

THE SOCIAL GEOGRAPHY OF RACE AND
STUDENTS' PRECOLLEGE EXPERIENCE

In her book *White Woman, Race Matters*, Frankenberg (1994) defines the "social geography of race" as the ways in which both social and physical spaces are racialized and how race influences patterns of life experiences, social interaction, and access to resources. Like most white young people in the United States today, white students on college campuses across the nation grew up in predominantly white neighborhoods and attended predominantly white elementary and secondary schools (Orfield and Gordon 2001; Orfield et al. 1997). Students we interviewed talked about the effect these segregated experiences had on their conceptions of themselves and others in two major frames of reference: a lack of meaningful contact with racial minorities, and subtle or overt racism. Understanding white students' precollege years can illuminate how these students behave in the university context and how their thinking about and understanding of race develops and is expressed during their college years.

Many white students indicated that the segregated nature of their neighborhoods and schools involved minimal contact with people of color and thus left them without direct experience and information. Whites who had been exposed to a liberal racial rhetoric assumed the view that all people were the same, or at least equal. This egalitarian viewpoint often coexisted with negative stereotypes generated and reinforced in their families and via the media. Others, unsympathetic to this liberal rhetoric, saw racial issues and race relations in starker terms. White college students of both types spoke clearly about their prior lack of contact with people of color.

[My city] is close to [a largely black city]. It's so close that when you cross the street you're in [the black city] and you can tell. You cross the other side of that street and you can tell the difference between the wealth and stuff like that. People in my city are afraid; they don't want their city turning into this other city. You cross that border, you see a bunch of slums, a bunch of poor people. I mean, I was going down there 'cause I heard cruising was cool down there. Like we drove past this point to turn around, and we were in slumville. We were afraid to turn around in these streets.

My parents are pretty open-minded, but a lot of their language is definitely prejudiced. They'll just talk about people who commit all the crimes and say, "Oh, well, it was in *this* kind of neighborhood" or *"These people* were doing that."

The community I came from—white, suburban, upper-class—assumed that we were superior. I mean, after all, we had to be brighter, work harder, et cetera, to get to where we are. Right? You were good because you had money. Race wasn't even an issue.

Some students who grew up in racially mixed neighborhoods and elementary or secondary schools had had more contact with students of color. But this did not necessarily translate into substantial or accurate racial knowledge of themselves and others. Even in relatively diverse neighborhoods and educational settings, white students commonly experienced racial separation; only about 30 percent of white students reported having any close nonwhite friends prior to attending the University of Michigan (Matlock et al. 2002). As one said:

At the moment when I went to high school, my high school was 55/45 [percent] white/black. But you weren't really in classes with other people, except for there were like five black kids who were on the college track, and they were in the social group with the white kids.

Issues of race and race relations were not totally absent from the precollege academic experiences of these students. Many secondary schools, especially those populated by college-bound young people, included instruction on our national racial history and struggles. However, students suggested that many of these efforts amounted to minimal and token attention.

> I think the only thing I learned in school was that Washington Carver was a black man, and he discovered peanuts or something like that. I think that was about it. I think we might have peripherally dealt with Martin Luther King. But four years, two years of history, two years of government, we really didn't touch on African Americans or any other issues at all . . . that just didn't even exist, as far as anybody was concerned. In elementary school we dealt with the Indians; you know, we did all the things that everybody did—you know, you put your hand on a piece of paper and you draw around it and you cut it out and you make a turkey, or you make little Indian hats and things like that with feathers.

Much existing U.S. history curriculum, as Wills (1996) states, "undermines students' ability to use history as a resource for thinking about contemporary race relations" (365). Lacking a formal education or classroom discussions about race and racism, many white students learned not to talk about race at all.

Hurtado and her colleagues (2002) argue, on the basis of a multiuniversity study involving several thousand students, that the key predictor of first-year college students' openness to diversity is the degree of their prior engagement with diverse peers. Students without sustained prior interracial experiences are hampered in their present day efforts to understand or interact in racialized situations. A great deal of scholarly work has shown that childhood and adolescent experiences deeply affect white students' sense of themselves in relation to others and their ability to interact successfully with others (Forman 2001; Frankenberg 1993; Kenny 2000; Lewis 2001; Perry 2002). For the most part, white students' precollege experiences teach them not to see themselves as having a race and do not give them a lens for seeing or understanding their own exclusionary attitudes and behaviors.

CAMPUS ENCOUNTERS WITH RACE

The social and cultural context of U.S. race relations that precedes white students' entry into college does not disappear when they matriculate. At the same time, a diverse campus environment provides opportunities for new encounters and learnings. In this section we describe several major ways in which white students understand and experience race and racial matters on campus. Specifically, we describe white students' reports of occasional racial ignorance and blindness, efforts to understand and overcome separation and distance, and the persistence of stereotyping—themes that reflect dominant themes in U.S. racial relations. We also review white students' reports of positive changes in their views of students of color, due primarily to positive interactions with a racially/ethnically diverse group of peers or to innovative classroom or collegiate practices.

It is important to remember that not all white students have the same college experiences. White students of different ethnicities, sexual orientations and economic class backgrounds often have precollege and in-college experiences that mark them as different from and somewhat disadvantaged in comparison to the majority of their middle- and upper-middle-class collegiate peers. Coming from families without an academic or professional orientation, having fewer economic resources, attending poorly staffed and financed secondary schools, needing to work while in school, and not knowing the "rules of the game" of the collegiate peer culture, students from working-class backgrounds often experience peer disdain and rejection. As one academic from a working-class background notes, she didn't know what to do when her dormmates talked about their travels abroad and when her "roommate was crying because she couldn't fit all her Pendleton wools in her closet and drawers and had taken over some of mine" (Black 1995: 20). In addition, some white students from working-class backgrounds encounter faculty members who make stereotypical assumptions about their talents. Peckham (1995) notes that "working class students are identified by their habits of language, thought and social behavior, and these working class habits are precisely the habits that professional/managerial-class teachers have learned to interpret as evidence of intellectual inadequacy" (268).

Color Blindness

Many white college students remained blind to the meaning—to themselves and to others—of whiteness and to their roles in interracial encounters. As members of the racial majority on campus, they experienced themselves as white reflectively or reactively, rather than proactively. As two white students stated:

I don't ever think about my race . . . or being white.

I consider myself white but I don't think about it. The only time I think about it is when we have to do these dumb forms and think about what race we are. But I just normally don't like to think about it.

The experience of being in the majority often makes their own race "invisible" to white students (Doane 2003; Flagg 1993; Tatum 1997). Moreover, their inability or unwillingness to see or understand their own racial identity and status in systems of social relations leads many white students to downplay the importance of race in general. Furthermore, some understand themselves to be "color-blind," to "not see race," and therefore to be without prejudice or racism.

There are a lot of bad people out there being racist. But it's not like I am one of them. I don't hurt people.

When I was asked in a class to describe my beliefs about race, it was easy. I said that I think that the whole idea of race has gone too far, that we need to stop thinking about race and start remembering that everyone is an individual.

White students who do not understand their own racial membership cannot understand the reality and status of students of color. Indeed, the position of being in the dominant racial group often prevents white students from seeing, knowing, or understanding the experiences or perceptions of others. As some contemporary scholars have suggested, especially among apparently liberal whites, these views exemplify the growing tendency of a color-blind ideology that obscures the experiences of students of color and further reinforces barriers to whites' ability to acknowledge their own distinctive racial identity and experience, particularly as members of a dominant or privileged group (Bonilla-Silva and Forman 2000; Crenshaw 1997; Lewis 2001). Group differences in access to resources, lived experiences, and worldly orientation do exist. When not acknowledged or dealt with they are not reduced but are reinforced. In this way a color-blind ideology supports subtle exclusion by both denying and reinforcing racial boundaries (Bonilla-Silva 2001; Doane 2003).

Separation and Distance

In their responses to surveys conducted during their senior year, white students at the University of Michigan provide a complicated and somewhat contradictory picture of the social geography of their relationships with students of color (Matlock et al. 2002). Only about 35 percent of white students reported significant exposure to diversity in informal interactions and friendships (in contrast, 50 percent of Asian American and Latino/a students, and 44 percent of African American students reported "quite a bit" or "a great deal" of interracial exposure). On the other hand, about 90 percent said that their relationships with students of other groups had been positive; few white students reported that the interactions they had with students of color were hostile. Of those whites who interacted with students of color, the largest percentage reported interacting most often with Asian American students followed by African American students and then Latino/a students. The proportion of white students who reported having at least one close friend of color increased during their time at Michigan, and about 60 percent acknowledged that since coming to the university they had learned a lot about other groups and their contributions to society. Nevertheless, many white students seemed ambivalent about the university's focus on diversity, with almost two-thirds reporting that they felt that the university put too much emphasis on differences between groups and about 40 percent believing that it inhibited students' ability to talk honestly about race and gender issues.

How is it that while more than a third of University of Michigan white students report substantial exposure to or interaction with students of color, many others perceive extensive segregation? Antonio (2001) argues that this discrepancy reflects the difference between students' perceptions of their campus' general environment, influenced perhaps by signal events, rumors, or media coverage, and their personal experiences of life on campus. It may also reflect the difference between the perceptions or experiences of many who have not tried or had the opportunity to connect meaningfully with students of color, and the quite different perceptions or experiences of a substantial minority of white students who successfully made the effort to cross racial borders.[2]

White students' complex feelings about diversity on campus also were evident in individual and focus group interviews.

> You do make friends of other cultures, but I think there's still so much segregation. I mean, black African American fraternities and sororities and Hispanic sororities and things like that are very, very segregated. We think of ourselves as such a diverse group of people that we kind of ignore what's going on, like, even if you go to a party here it tends to be the same kind of people.

Some white students are distressed by these divisions, while others see and understand them as parallels to the racial separation they experienced in their pre-college years and that are present in society at large.

In the excerpt just cited, the student refers to "black African American fraternities and sororities and Hispanic sororities" but not to white organizations, such as traditional campus fraternities and sororities. Thus, white students' failure to understand their own racial position leads to an inability to see or understand the racial position of others, and to recognize how they themselves may contribute to students of color's experiences of exclusion, stereotyping, and the like. As a further example, some white students at the University of Michigan expressed annoyance at patterns of racial separation that they saw as a voluntary choice by students of color.

> Isn't it [the Afro-American lounge] the same thing as black and white water fountains from what seems like the dark ages ago? The black and white bathrooms? The black person sitting in the back of the bus, separate areas, separate schools, and separate classrooms? This just seems ridiculous—that when blacks are trying to equate everyone and they're trying to racially integrate the university, the society, everything, they go and put up a sign and make a separate room for the minorities. I mean, they want equality and desegregation, and now they want to be all by themselves in an Afro-American lounge. And it doesn't make any sense . . . it infuriates me, as a matter of fact.

I don't understand why the black students all sit together in the dining hall. They complain about white people being racist, but isn't that being racist?

These white students' criticism of apparently black-only seating patterns, fraternities, lounges, and clubs ignores the fact that white-only associations and seating patterns also exist in practice, even if they are not officially labeled as such.

This common form of white racial myopia involves the notion that minority students are "self-segregating" (Elfin and Burke 1993; Tatum 1997). Meanwhile, whites' exclusionary or demeaning behaviors and various organizational pressures or norms promoting separatism that encourage students of color to seek support from one another remain unseen. Longitudinal research in higher education that included more than two hundred thousand students from 172 institutions concluded that it was white students who had the most separatist behaviors, particularly when it came to dating (Hurtado et al. 1994). In the same study, "more than one-half of the African American students (53 percent) felt excluded from school activities because of their race/ethnicity, as did nearly one-quarter of the Asian students (24 percent) and 16 percent of the Chicanos. By contrast, only one out of every 20 white students felt excluded from school activities because of their racial/ethnic background (6 percent)" (16). Similarly, in the Michigan Student Study, white students were the least likely of all groups to report that at least one of their close friends was of a different race (Matlock et al. 2002). Thus, the view that minority students voluntarily segregate themselves for no understandable reason ignores the ways in which white students—and the organizational processes of the white-dominated university culture, climate, and technology—often separate themselves and stereotype or exclude others.

Consider, in this regard, the experience of a white student who inquired publicly into the supposed phenomenon of black student self-segregation:

> One of the things I see the most on campus is that all the different races tend to stick with people just like themselves. Once, in a class, I asked why all the black students sit together in the dormitory cafeteria. A black student then asked me, "Well, why do you think all the white kids sit together?" I was speechless. At first I thought that was a dumb question, until I realized that I see white people sitting together as normal and black people sitting together as a problem.

Because she expressed her perception in class, and because a black peer responded in a thought-provoking way, the white student was able to recognize the reciprocal racial dynamics involved. Without this encounter, her new insight might not have developed. This kind of opportunity to interact openly with others, and to pose and learn from even naïve or seemingly "dumb" questions, is one of the obvious benefits of social diversity on campus.

Despite this example of a positive encounter, on-campus racial assumptions too often go unchallenged in classroom curricula and in informal classroom, dormitory, and social exchanges. Under these circumstances, old explanations for diverse phenomena and old stereotypes prevail.

> I took an American history course last semester that covered 1865 to the present. Slavery was discussed, but as a monolithic, unified movement. Women in World War II was discussed, but only the experiences of white women. No wonder I didn't know anything other than stereotypes about people of color. I never had to learn it.

Although many white students report learning about other groups while on campus, there is much more work to do in helping students learn how to interact across difference. White students often respond to their own growing awareness of the racial divides on campus with awkwardness and discomfort. For example, even many of those who were interested in crossing racial boundaries did not know how to do so, given the prevailing norms of campus life.

> Last year in the dorms there were two girls who were black; and on the hall, they lived together. I could go in there and hang out with them, and then I felt fine. I mean, I like them a lot, but when a lot of their friends would come over who were all black and I'd be in there, I definitely felt like I didn't fit in. And it bothered me a lot, so that made me feel that my whiteness was the reason.

If they are unable or unwilling to explore interaction across these boundaries, and to move beyond these feelings of discomfort, white students cannot take advantage of the many opportunities for informal interactional diversity that do exist and have been shown to have positive impact.

White students' distance from students of color, and their awkwardness, caution, or fear in their presence, stem in part from patterns of stereotyping that they learned before going to college. But if the campus social climate, culture, and formal learning opportunities do not promote open and honest conversation and sustained interactions about race, racism, and multiculturalism, students of all races and ethnicities may retreat into polite and distant conversations. According to Bourassa (1991), "Many white students are often unsure of how to interpret or respond to the attitudes or behavior of students of color" (13–14). She also draws attention to "feelings of awkwardness and fear experienced by white students who have never socially interacted with people from other racial or ethnic groups." The common nature of these reactions is expressed by two white students at the University of Michigan.

> I remember the time when I wanted to understand them a little better, but as I questioned things, I felt I had to watch what I questioned and watched how I said things because I was constantly being labeled. It seems like because I'm white it's easy to get labeled as something. I had to be very careful and I was afraid to ask certain questions, and I was afraid to express certain views.

We are always talking about a lot of multicultural things. But what that often boils down to is people start calling this a predominantly white institution and that there is all this white privilege that goes along with it. I'm just not aware of this privilege. You are always reading about black concerns and this idea of affirmative action rallies and stuff. It's like well, you know, what did I do? What am I supposed to do?

In the absence of an understanding of their own racial socialization, and without a supportive climate for inquiry, the mode of white racial interaction too often becomes withdrawal, sometimes accompanied by defense and attack. Some observers have drawn attention to the phenomenon of caution, tying it to the muting of whites' views and to whites' growing feelings of victimization (Feagin and Vera 1995; Fine and Weiss 1998; Gallagher 1995). But white students are not alone in their hesitancy about racial encounters; these feelings occur among students of color as well.

Stereotyping

Racial stereotypes and perceptions are confirmed and reproduced when the formal or informal curriculum and patterns of social relations on campus fail to challenge prior patterns of non- or negative interaction, and the negative or naïve individual viewpoints that underlie them.

I'd be walking around, and these stereotypes will pop up into my head, and I don't voice them, and I don't feel like I act on them, but still every day they will pop up into my head, and I get frustrated with myself.

In a finding similar to that identified by Hurtado et al. (2002) and Pascarella et al. (1996) with regard to the precollege and college experiences of students, Astin (1993) reports, "The frequency with which the student socialized with persons from different racial/ethnic groups [had the] strongest positive effect on cultural awareness and commitment to promoting racial understanding" (47). Under the right conditions, both formal educational activities and informal interracial encounters can lead to sustained engagement. Thus, one of the core arguments for diversity is that it provides the opportunity for white students to unlearn and relearn their understanding of contemporary race relations and their own racialized identity and role. Sometimes students and the collegiate environment interact in ways that take advantage of that opportunity and transformation occurs, and sometimes not.

Positive Change and Growth

It is clear that a diverse college experience does provide opportunities for white students to alter their prior racial views and behaviors. Matlock et al. (2002) report that the proportion of white students at the University of Michigan who had at least one friend of color increased from about one-third (32 percent) at the time they entered the university to about half (46 percent) four years later. In interviews, many white students voiced new understandings of racial/ethnic relations. Some reported having recognized their own prejudices and stereotypes, faced their own fears and awkwardness, and had more positive racial experiences and effective interracial encounters.

> It took me a long time to be able to get to a point where I can say that I have prejudices—I mean, just because everyone does.

> I think one of the big issues that I confronted a lot last year was the issue of racism that I have within myself that I don't recognize. And I recall specifically one friend who just harped on the idea that "I have black friends. I'm not racist." And that's all she would ever talk about. You know, I had friends of other races and colors in high school, but I never had the in-depth . . . I never had somebody who I was so close to that I was able to discuss difficult issues with. Here is the first time that I ever had that kind of intense interaction with someone of another race, of another ethnicity.

New educational input and experiences also helped some white students to understand the privileges normally accorded them as a function of their white skin color, socioeconomic status, and educational advantages.

> I'd never really considered before how much of an advantage I have by being white. I'd heard of discriminatory hiring practices before and things like that, but I'd never really associated those things to me. Just because I don't often think of myself as white doesn't mean I won't be given special privileges at the expense of others.

And for some white students, these explorations of privilege helped them to create a clearer sense of their identity as white persons.

> I was always fighting to say, "I'm not these white people over there. I'm unique; I'm me; I'm an individual." Now I'm able to say, "You know what? I'm very much white."

> It kind of hit me one year that really my identity isn't about how I'm Jewish or I'm disabled, but that most of it is being white. I came into the university pretty defensive about that, I think, wanting everyone to know that I wasn't a racist or that I wasn't a prejudiced person, and that I was really open. And then I've realized over time that just by being white I'm given things.

Of course, as Bonilla-Silva and Forman (2000) argue, even when whites provide generally progressive responses to attitude surveys, these may not accurately reflect their internal contradictions or their actual behavior in racialized situations. The test of their enlightenment rests in how they respond to instances of racism in themselves and in other whites.

> If I am not doing anything to help change occur, if I am just quietly sitting around and not disturbing anyone, nothing will change. So I have to do something.

> Now that I've made the decision to try to deal with that oppression, it is something I feel I have to be constantly working at it. Whereas if I were just ignorant about racism and didn't really think about it, it would be less of a responsibility.

These latter comments stand in contrast to what Forman (2001) calls "racial apathy" and what Tatum (1992) calls "passive racist behavior." Rather than viewing racism as none of their business or as something they are not responsible for addressing, some white students are prepared to proactively challenge institutional racism in society. They have gone beyond seeing these issues as ones faced exclusively by students of color.

The potential positive outcomes of a more diverse environment, and especially ones that provide deliberate opportunities for students to relate with one another in new and more positive ways, go beyond helping white students gain insight into their own and others' racial relations and identities; they also are intellectual and academic in nature. For instance, Gurin's research at the University of Michigan (1999) shows that "students who had experienced the most diversity in classroom settings and in informal interactions with peers showed the greatest engagement in active thinking processes, growth in intellectual engagement and motivation, and growth in intellectual and academic skills. The results are especially impressive for White students" (45).

EXPERIENCES WITH AFFIRMATIVE ACTION ON CAMPUS

Many white students express tolerant or progressive views about racial relations, but act or behave in contradictory and hesitant ways. These contradictions are most evident when racial issues directly confront white students' understandings of themselves, their world, and their own real or imagined material interests. The case of affirmative action is one such example, since it challenges structures and processes of historic white privilege and appears to threaten whites' traditional advantages in school and in occupational access and mobility. The heightened degree of attention to and public policy debate about affirmative action on campus, and the passionately heated and sometimes vitriolic nature of these debates itself can sour campus race relations and make open and searching student discussions even more difficult. Nevertheless, the fact that on most campuses reasoned and sometimes unreasoned discussion and debate do occur means that the opportunity for racial (re)learning exists and can be taken up.

Recent federal court decisions and politicians' pronouncements have affected universities' admissions policies, social climates, and sometimes even curricula. Reaction to the U.S. Supreme Court's decisions in two cases involving the University of Michigan (*Grutter v. Bollinger et al.* 2003; *Gratz et al. v. Bollinger et al.* 2003) indicate that affirmative action, diversity, and the status of students of color on predominantly white campuses will continue to be contentious issues. The national debate over affirmative action also has played a role in shaping how white students see themselves (and their apparent self-interest) and how they see and behave toward their peers of color. The dominant contemporary and oppositional description of affirmative action not only reflects white racial ideologies, but also reproduces and reinvigorates whatever patterns of racial stratification, separation, and distrust may already exist on campus. Alternative rhetorics that are more supportive of affirmative action could help advance racial inquiry, engagement, and patterns of intergroup collaboration that could improve the campus climate.

Sax and Arredondo (1999) report results of a study of 277,000 freshman attending 709 U.S. colleges and universities. Over 57 percent of white students surveyed said that they "agreed" or "strongly agreed" that "affirmative action in college admissions should be abolished." African American (21 percent) and Mexican American (30 percent) students were much less likely to agree with this statement. An even more recent national study (CIRP: Cooperative Institutional Research Program 2000) indicates that 52.4 percent of public university students feel that "Affirmative action in college admissions should be abolished" and that 21.8 percent feel that "Racial discrimination is no longer a problem in America."

The Michigan Student Study reports somewhat similar patterns to the national data, with some interesting caveats. As table 4.1 shows, most University of Michigan seniors agreed in principle that racial inequalities exist in higher education (similar numbers agreed that colleges have a responsibility to address such inequalities). White students were somewhat less likely than students of color to agree, but they still did so by a large majority (Matlock et al. 2002: 60). But the picture changes dramatically when the students were asked about specific policies that address such inequalities. This table shows that 64 percent of white students did not agree with the use of different admission criteria for some students of color. The biggest racial/ethnic differences occur between blacks and whites, with Latino/a support substantial but not as high as blacks, and with Asian American students evenly split (Matlock et al. 2002: 61). These trends are consistent with what some analysts have referred to as "symbolic racism," wherein negative feelings about race are expressed primarily at the policy level, in opposition to what are seen as special privileges for people of color (Kinder and Sanders 1996).

Table 4.1.   Percentage of Seniors Agreeing with Varied Statements

"Continued racial and ethnic discrimination within higher education requires that universities aggressively remove institutional barriers that promote inequality."

Race/Ethnicity	Percentage
White	80
Asian American	89
Latino/a	88
African American	96

"Different admission criteria with respect to the ACT and SAT may be justified for some students of color."

Race/Ethnicity	Percentage
White	36
Asian American	49
Latino/a	63
African American	76

"The hiring of faculty of color should be a top priority for this university."

Race/Ethnicity	Percentage
White	29
Asian American	51
Latino/a	58
African American	94

Source: Used with permission of Matlock, Gurin, and Wade-Golden (2002: 60–61).

Although a majority of white students opposed affirmative action both in student admissions and in faculty hiring, white opposition decreased between their first year and fourth year on campus. Thus much of the opposition seems to have originated from students' precollegiate years rather than arising from their experiences on campus; in fact, collegiate experiences appear to lead to greater support for diversity initiatives.

Despite white students' general opposition to affirmative action as assessed by survey items, extended interviews reveal important nuances in their views (Bonilla-Silva and Forman 2000; Bowman and Smith 2002; Chesler and Peet 2002). One view is that racial discrimination is no longer a problem and need not be directly addressed as part of an undergraduate education. The underlying assumption is that the playing field is now level. As several white University of Michigan students stated:

Equal opportunity exists now, and all people have the same potential for learning, so blacks can succeed as long as they work hard.

> I think it is ridiculous to have affirmative action now that everything is equal—no one is being discriminated [against] anymore.

Sax and Arredondo (1999) observe that the belief that racial discrimination is not a problem in the United States is a strong predictor of white students' opposition to affirmative action in collegiate admissions. Holding this belief also affects how white students think about and behave toward students of color and their claims of exclusionary or discriminatory treatment.

As attitudes regarding race have changed, most public discussion of affirmative action has become ahistorical. Framed by its opponents as a policy that unfairly punishes innocent whites, most objections to affirmative action fail to acknowledge the persistence and consequences of centuries of institutional discrimination. The dominant argument is that affirmative action gives minorities something they have not earned, and that these unearned advantages come at the expense of white middle-class Americans who deserve the benefits themselves.

> I had white friends who worked really hard in high school to get in here, and they were angry when they got rejected because affirmative action changed the standards. I think we should get rid of affirmative action and start letting people know that if they don't work hard to get into college, they won't be successful.

Like other popular racial myths, this is an exaggerated reading of the demographic realities of racial tensions. Given the small number of students of color applying to most elite colleges and universities, white students' primary competitors are other white students, not students of color. Nevertheless, this interpretation does reflect much of the public's view of affirmative action as a challenge to white male prerogatives.

> I think it's a real disadvantage to let people into this school because of their ethnicity. And, it's a terrible disadvantage to me and everybody else who goes to this school. It also drags the class down.

In addition to expressing their views of a basically fair and meritocratic system, these sentiments demonstrate that some white students see themselves as systematically being placed at a disadvantage because of the presence of students of color. Further evidence of the group position or self-interest perspective discussed by Bobo (1999) is present in the following student comment:

> People are punishing white people now because of our past, our actions. I don't agree with that. To equal out the past they're going to turn tables here and make it difficult for white people.

Here is another example of the connection between opposition to affirmative action and defense of perceived self-interest in some whites' thinking.

> If you're going to try and make your university or country the best, you should
> have the smartest, the most motivated people. If you take the less qualified student
> to meet your quota, I think that's terrible. It's almost like making someone feel like
> "Don't work as hard—your skin's the right color." . . . I think it's going to come
> back and it's going to affect us if we keep trying to level things out by not going
> with merit as such.

Predicated on assumptions of an idealized meritocracy and on stereotypical
beliefs about the inferiority of people of color, these student quotes reflect the
attitudinal system that supports and maintains "subtle modern racism" (Dovidio,
Mann, and Gaertner 1989). They carry a sense of superiority that, when coupled
with many white students' prior educational advantages, often leads to the exercise of unequal power relations in diverse classrooms. White students who see
students of color as academically inferior also are less likely to study or work
with them, leading to exclusion and marginalization. Views about the unfairness
of affirmative action go hand in hand with the emerging notion of white victimization and "reverse discrimination" (Doane 1997; Gallagher 1995; Pincus
2000). White students' resentment at their imagined victimization may be expressed in the form of racial hostility toward students of color.

Some white students argue that when unqualified or underqualified students
are admitted to a university, they cannot succeed anyway. Whether a function of
their poor prior educational experience, lack of talent, or unwillingness to work
hard, the argument goes, affirmative action does not really help students of color.

> I have seen black friends of mine get into schools on the basis of affirmative action,
> rather than on the basis of grades or scores, and thereby feel as if they are being
> given a leg up somehow, [but] they don't belong there. I have other black friends
> who have gone on to become lawyers and simply haven't got the training and the
> backgrounds. It's not that they aren't bright enough; it's just that they have been
> jumped along, and they find themselves in a law firm, and they are unqualified and
> are aware of that and are fired, and this reinforces the stereotype.

The view that affirmative action does not work and does not increase the educational success or life chances of its supposed beneficiaries is an element of contemporary white ideology that is widely asserted but unsupported by the facts.
Bowen and Bok (1998) present strong evidence that students of color generally
do quite well in college and afterward (see also Lempert, Chambers, and Adams
2000 for a report on the outcomes of affirmative action programs for law school
students).

All these forms of white student confusion or opposition to affirmative action
reflect broader ideologies about race in the society at large. They are deeply embedded in long-standing attitudes and public rhetoric or ideologies about white
entitlement, the existence of a meritocracy, and assumptions about people of

color. While current debates about affirmative action may provide the opportunity or stimulus for such views to surface, there is no evidence that they are caused by white students' actual experiences and encounters with students of color on campus.

Many white students who do support affirmative action do so either as part of a larger commitment to racial equality and justice or because they feel it promotes student diversity and a more positive learning environment on campus. Gurin (1999) reports that many white students at the University of Michigan saw benefits to their own education from attending a campus marked by racial (and other) diversity. Here is the comment of a student with similarly positive views:

> Without it [affirmative action] we wouldn't be able to have diverse classes. Like, I wouldn't be able to sit in a class on race and have students who are not white talk about their experience so I can learn from them. . . . You know, most of your education in college comes from living with people and interacting with people, and hearing people's experiences and learning how to deal with people you don't get along with, who you can't understand and can't see eye-to-eye with, and how to function in those situations. And I think that, as a white student, that's where affirmative action benefits us the most.

As the Michigan survey data show, a significant number (35 to 40 percent) of white students do support affirmative action as well as other pro-diversity policies on campus. For example, two-thirds of white students at the University of Michigan agreed that writers of different racial and ethnic groups should be part of the core curriculum and a little more than half agreed with the university's policy requiring students to take at least one course on the role of race/ethnicity in society to graduate (Matlock et al. 2002).

Moreover, some white students have developed sophisticated and complex understandings of racial issues on campus and in society at large, as confirmed by Gurin and her colleagues (1999; Gurin et al. 2002). They see evidence of past or present discrimination, understand some of its effects, wish to connect and work with students of color, and seem prepared to push for antiracist and multicultural objectives.

> I think that I thought it was crap, because you're letting a less qualified person in just because of the color of their skin. But I started learning about the discrimination throughout history, and I think that it's necessary right now. If you didn't make a culturally diverse place, then the people who had been forced down by the discrimination of society wouldn't ever have a chance to have the opportunity.

These last comments indicate that some white students have transcended the dominant white position on the affirmative action debate. Evidently, collegiate experiences can alter the ahistorical claim that discrimination is a thing of the past and that remedial efforts are unnecessary. This is supported by Michigan Student Study data showing that white opposition to affirmative action actually declines over students' years at Michigan. It also is confirmed in comments from student interviews.

> If people come into school and everyone assumes that they're there because of affirmative action, is that an argument against affirmative action? No! We should take the people who have those views and teach them and show them how to change their views.

Some white students appear to recognize the ways they benefit from current social arrangements and the role that white privilege plays in their life experiences, their perceptions of racial issues in the United States, their understanding of affirmative action, and their experiences with students of color on campus. They understand that our educational system does not function as a race-neutral meritocracy, see affirmative action as part of a broader program of social change, and are prepared to play an active role in that effort. In particular, white students who are more likely because of some other aspect of their identity to have experienced some discrimination in their lives (e.g., white women) tend to be more supportive of affirmative action and other policies for racial justice.

TAKING ADVANTAGE OF THE OPPORTUNITY DIVERSITY PROVIDES

Multiracial campus environments such as classrooms, clubs, social events, and dormitories give students the chance to learn how to work together with people who are different from themselves and to decide how to think and behave in future racially integrated settings. As white students struggle with these issues on the verge of adulthood, their identities as racialized beings are at stake. At this age and in these settings, they may be more willing and able to take risks, to unlearn old patterns of social interaction, and to discover new intellectual and social evidence about their own and others' race/ethnicity than at any other time in their lives. Too often, colleges design diversity programs that stop at the admissions process, at the educational doorway, missing the opportunity to teach positive forms of interracial interaction and to lay the groundwork for real changes in the nature of race relations. Examples of programs that do seek to attain these goals are discussed in chapters 11 and 12 (see also Cheatham and Associates 1991; Hurtado et al. 1999).

The evidence makes it clear that substantial numbers of students of color must be present to avoid the continuing costs of white isolation and minority tokenism. Representational or structural diversity is a necessary condition for student growth but not a sufficient condition. Just as important are curricular, pedagogical, and campus life innovations which may reduce some of the negative experiences reported by students of color as well as the racial ignorance, awkwardness, and isolation of many white students. Gurin (1999) has reported the educational benefits of diversity in college life for white students (e.g., growth in active and complex thinking skills, motivation to achieve, and racial and cultural engagement). However, taking full advantage of these positive effects and extending them into other realms (e.g., interpersonal interactions, racial attitudes) requires new programming and organizational innovation. Dispelling white myths of color blindness, uncovering disturbing intergroup patterns, and creating more just patterns in campus peer race relations are not merely matters of fairness or of enriching everyone's educational experiences. They are essential to constructing a more realistic, just, and livable future for our society. Moreover, as racial demographics in the United States continue to change, and as the world itself becomes smaller through increasing global movement of people and products, the ability to interact competently and comfortably across difference will be a necessary ingredient in personal success.

NOTES

1. The original data presented in this chapter come from white students at the University of Michigan. The quantitative data reported here come from the Michigan Student Study (Matlock et al. 2002: 6), which involved a "longitudinal series of surveys of the undergraduate class of 1994." All incoming students were surveyed in the fall of their freshman year and resurveyed at the end of their first, second, and fourth years at the university. The primary focus of these data, as presented in the Michigan Student Study report, is students' expectations and experiences with race and ethnicity at the university. The sample of seniors consisted of 1,129 white students, 187 African Americans, 266 Asian Americans, 88 Latinos/as, and 8 Native Americans. These data have been analyzed in a variety of univariate and multivariate formats, and they have been reported in several different academic and public venues.

The qualitative data were gathered from white students of varied backgrounds, genders, and collegiate interests between 1996 and 2001. A total of two hundred white students participated in individual and small group interviews and others wrote journals expressing their racial views and experiences. General questions sought to determine white students' views of and experiences with racial matters. Specific questions included the following:

- What were some of your early learnings about race—at home, in school, in your community?
- How do you think of your racial group membership? What brings it up?
- How would you define racism? How serious an issue is it?
- Do you think there are any disadvantages to being white in the United States? Any advantages?

- How does your being white affect your relationships with people of color here at the university?
- Have you seen any evidence of racism here at the university?
- What do you think about affirmative action—in university admissions or in employment situations?

These data were analyzed via inductive procedures, leading to the themes presented in this chapter. We do not claim that these particular quotes are geographically, temporally, or cohortwise representative of other white students' views and encounters, or of white students' attitudes and behaviors at other institutions. When joined with the Michigan Student Study's survey data and scholarly literature and studies conducted elsewhere, however, they provide a window into this generation of white students' racial consciousness and experience. Some of these data have been reported previously (Chesler and Peet 2002; Chesler, Peet, and Sevig 2003).

2. It also is possible that these differences are an artifact of different inquiry modes—surveys versus individual or small-group interviews. For instance, Bonilla-Silva and Forman (2000) argue that students they surveyed and students they interviewed responded differently. In surveys, students may seek to provide politically correct answers, although in the current context of U.S. racial relations it often is difficult to decide just what that means. While some authorities argue that students' responses in homogeneous focus groups are likely to be more thoughtful and forthcoming than their responses in surveys, others criticize homogeneous focus groups for fomenting orthodoxies and politicized expressions.

Chapter Five

Students of Color in the University

What do students of color experience on predominantly white college campuses? How do various groups of students of color interpret their relationships with their peers and their faculty in classrooms and in informal campus interactions? Several large studies and various smaller research projects, as well as numerous essays, have addressed these topics. Drawing on the general scholarly literature and on local research, we report the experiences of African American, Latino/a, Asian American, and Native American students on one college campus, the University of Michigan. We explore in depth the relations among students and between students and faculty on this large public university campus.[1]

Overall, seniors at the University of Michigan report having had a positive experience and having gained a "broad, intellectually exciting education" on campus (Matlock et al. 2002). We believe, and the survey data support, that students' overall experiences are good and that campus race relations tend to be positive. Nevertheless, different groups of students tend to experience the campus quite differently. Students of color often experience the campus differently from white students, and the views and experiences of college life of Latino/a and Asian American students differ from each other and from those of African American students. Students of color highlight their struggles with sometimes having racially coded characteristics ascribed to them, of sometimes feeling excluded, and of having self-perceptions that do not match others' expectations or treatment of them. What students of color report about their personal racial struggles reveals a great deal about the general campus climate and about the behaviors of white students and faculty. They also provide us with critical information about how to improve the campus climate. We scrutinize these campus peer and faculty relations within their societal and organizational contexts. Our national struggle with racism and racial issues and the university's culture, rules, and norms about membership have major impact on students' experiences and set the stage for microlevel interactions.

In chapter 2, we argued that most students of color—especially African American, Latino/a, and Native American students—have encountered (knowingly or not) educational racism and discrimination long before they get to college. Issues of class and race often leave them with less adequate elementary and secondary school curricula and facilities (including old and failing buildings, fewer academic resources, and minimally qualified teachers). In addition, neighborhood and community poverty deprives many of these young people of support systems essential for academic success.[2] Many are first-generation college attendees who lack (and whose parents lack) familiarity with higher education norms and procedures. Moreover, since much of public education continues to be racially segregated (Massey and Denton 1993; Orfield and Gordon 2001; Orfield et al. 1997), many students of color—particularly black students—experience interaction with large numbers of white peers and instructors for the first time following their entry into college. There are, of course, real exceptions to these trends. Many Asian American students and some Latino/a, African American, and Native American students come from middle-class or quite affluent backgrounds and have attended excellent elementary and secondary schools. Moreover a number of white students come from working-class backgrounds and face many of the same challenges as working-class students of color (e.g., poor schooling, having to work many hours, not having access to important cultural capital) (Dews and Law 1995). Some students from all racial groups have attended diverse high schools in which they had multiracial friendship networks. But for many students—particularly African American and white students—a diverse collegiate environment is a new and different experience.

RELATIONSHIPS WITH CAMPUS PEERS

Interracial relations at the University of Michigan, as at campuses across the country, are quite complicated and vary considerably by group. Many of the interactions are positive but others are problematic. The negative encounters seldom take the form of major racist incidents of the kind identified in chapter 1 and often reported in newspapers across the country. Instead they involve everyday, subtle expressions of stereotypes, moments of exclusion, and pressures to be different that are hard to capture but that continue to shape campus experiences for students of color.

In the University of Michigan survey of seniors, about one-quarter of most groups (and half of black students) felt that the campus had quite a bit of racial conflict; many fewer reported a great deal of hostility in their own personal interracial interactions (Matlock et al. 2002). On all of these survey measures, students of color, particularly African American students, reported more hostility than did white students, but even they characterized the majority of their interracial interactions on campus as positive. However, not all students of color have the same intergroup experiences in college, and not all groups of students of color experience the collegiate environment in the same way. Asian American and Latino/a students, in particular, reported that many of their interactions with white students involved cooperative and personal interactions (Matlock et al. 2002: 19): About two-thirds (67 to 70 percent) of the Asian American, Latino/a and white seniors, and about half (52 percent) of African American students felt that "quite a bit" or "a great deal" of "friendships between students of color and white students" marked the campus environment.

When asked in focus group discussions whether white students ever do things that offend them, several students of color simply replied "no." Moreover, some students of color talked about whites they knew who behaved in particularly positive and engaging ways. Here are just two examples:

> Since I've been here, one of my closest friends — she's white, and she's very aware of what it means for her to be a white woman, what it means to me, how she fits into the broad framework. You know, she's not necessarily knowledgeable about everything about Asian American culture, but I tell her. (*Asian American*)

> When it comes to white people, you can really tell who grew up in an all-white neighborhood and who didn't. I know this friend of mine, he lived in an all-black neighborhood, and he was just totally comfortable around any color of people, at any time. He could speak to anyone. He was totally natural about it, not tip-toeing making sure he didn't step on anybody's toes. (*African American*)

Students of color perceived these white students to be somewhat exceptional in their comfort with diversity and in their understanding of "what it means to be a white," and they believed that this made a huge difference in these individuals' ability to engage in relationships with others.

Despite these positive reports, many students of color reported difficulties in their relationships with white peers. Only a few interviewees mentioned direct insults aimed at them, but others cited more "benign" requests, expectations, or pressures (for conformity, assimilation, or ethnic-specific information). The impact of such tension and pressure should not be minimized. All such experiences trigger a response, at least internally (emotional stress, anger, or questions surrounding one's own identity and place) and sometimes also externally (defense, withdrawal, debate, or explanation). They raise questions about students' organizational membership (fully accepted, partially accepted, or barely tolerated), and highlight issues of social climate and culture.

The central interracial difficulties or challenges students of color reported in focus group interviews include racial stereotyping (on both academic and behavioral dimensions), exclusion or marginalization from interaction with white peers, pressure to assimilate and to deny one's group identity, white resentment about the supposedly unmerited gains of affirmative action, and the predominantly black–white focus of campus concerns about race. Although some of these issues arise overtly, many are quite subtle, and the latter forms of intergroup dynamics tend to be most confusing to students of color, threatening their comfort and interfering with their academic and behavioral adjustment to college. These experiences are best understood as the everyday micropolitics of race, what Solórzano et al. (2000) call "microaggressions," in which race shapes interpersonal interactions in ways that subtly yet potently subordinate people of color. Unless collegiate faculty and administrators implement programs that encourage new classroom processes and more structured and sustained opportunities for informal and equal-status or collaborative interaction, we can expect them to continue to occur.

Racial Stereotyping

Students of color reported that other students sometimes academically stereotype them, seeing them as less competent. As one student expressed it:

> They know that I'm there and in a sense expect lower scores for me because I am black. We had taken an exam and people were looking at the scores, and a white student was shocked that I did extremely well on the exam. (*African American*)

Other students talked about how specific racial or ethnic stereotypes led to assumptions about their preference for or proclivity in certain academic arenas.

> I've noticed that in my science classes people just assume that since I'm Asian American, I'm supposed to be good at this. I struggle through classes just as they do, but there's still that stereotype that if you're Asian American and in the sciences, you know your stuff—you don't have to study all the time. (*Asian American*)

> [In a Spanish class] because I was Mexican, people assumed I would know Spanish, and I didn't. When they found out I didn't really know it, they said, "You're just Latina on the outside, not on the inside." (*Latina*)

The (mostly white) peers of students of color may assume that they know something about them, their academic abilities, and their personal or academic preferences, based on their apparent or signaled race. Though stereotypes of Asian Americans as the model minority may seem relatively benign, they mask the discrimination Asian Americans experience in social and economic realms, place extraordinary pressures on Asian American students, and ignore the wide range of experiences of different Asian ethnicities (Chan 1991; Chan and Hune 1995; Chang and Kiang 2002; U.S. Commission on Civil Rights 1994). Similarly, as Feagin et al. (1996) note in their study of the experiences of African

American students at a predominantly white university, "A white gesture that might be seen as complimentary if it were solely based on achievement criteria is taken as offensive because of the racial stereotype implied in the white action" (66). The application of group stereotypes to individuals creates distress for students of color, generates personal struggles about identity and competence, and poses a challenge about whether to conform or not. Research suggests that treating students as though they have lesser ability can interfere with their academic achievement (Hummel and Steele 1996; Steele 1997). Furthermore, as Essed (1997) points out, for the targets of racist stereotypes these situations are related to a wider range of experiences where the dominant group treats them as other, excludes them, and behaves toward them as if they were inferior.

Some students of color also reported stereotyped expectations of their interpersonal behavior and cultural styles. These included assumptions about their life experiences, about their assumed knowledge of urban, street, or minority culture, and about their competence in performing culture. Here are two examples provided by students:

> The other class members would look to the Latinos for good stories about life in the barrio. (*Latino*)

> Every day little things happen; like one time when I was living on my hall, someone was playing loud music—like M. C. Hammer was rapping. So they said to me, "Show us the M. C. Hammer, how you do the M. C. Hammer." Like I'm supposed to know. I was the only black person on my floor, and it was like I was supposed to know how to do it. I said, "I don't even dance that well." I mean, I can dance, but I can't do the M. C. Hammer and the Running Man and this other stuff. (*African American*)

Behavioral stereotypes are similar to academic stereotypes: both express vestiges of older racial understandings about particular groups' innate talents and proclivities. The prevalence of some of these stereotypes is not surprising, given that most white students attending the University of Michigan grew up in white neighborhoods and had little prior contact with students of color. Among other things, some of them expect that all members of some racial groups (such as blacks and Latinos/as) know about poverty and urban life and expect them to behave in certain ways (such as angrily, meekly, rhythmically, or spiritually). Faced with these stereotypes, students of color must struggle with conforming and gaining immediate acceptance or rejecting interaction on these bases and risking exclusion or resentment. These phenomena do not necessarily reflect white hostility toward students of color; rather, they involve daily negotiations about the meaning of race in which students of color must deal with widespread group stereotypes.

Exclusion/Marginality

Some students of color reported experiences in and out of the classroom in which they felt white students excluded them from peer interactions. For example, one student stated:

> I've always felt left out of study groups. It's almost like they have these cliques already. They're going to do much better because of the groups they have. They have their friends who took the class before and have all these resources that we don't have. (*Latina*)

Thus, some students of color feel that dominant student networks are closed off, that a set of informal boundaries to acceptance is difficult to cross, or even that they are not wanted. Over half of the black seniors surveyed at the University of Michigan reported difficulty feeling comfortable on campus or feeling as though they belonged. Overall, students of color reported higher levels of alienation and lower levels of feeling accepted than did white students, although levels of alienation were much higher for black students than for Latinos/as and Asian Americans (Matlock et al. 2002). As Osajima (1993) reports, however, even for Asian American students, "being one of the few Asians on a predominantly white campus [can raise] doubts and questions about whether and where they belong" (84). Researchers found a similar phenomenon at the Massachusetts Institute of Technology (McBay 1986), where over 40 percent of black alumni said that they experienced "a sense of racial isolation"—of not fitting in or belonging to the larger community—during their student days. Similarly, at Wellesley College, more black students than whites reported a sense of loneliness and isolation (67 percent vs. 43 percent) (Task Force on Racism 1989). As one student in Michigan's focus group sample stated, "It's good for me to converse with people of my own race. But some days I can go the whole day and not see another black person on this campus."

In the face of such feelings of discomfort and alienation many students of color seek out members of their own racial/ethnic group and develop their own associations. Such in-group bonding is an important arena for support and socialization, peer counseling, learning how to negotiate one's identity with the larger white culture, cultural celebrations, links to home communities, and resistance to discrimination and marginalization. Indeed, hooks (1990) argues that there are important functions performed in such affinity groupings, that people of color "must create spaces within that culture of domination if we are to survive whole, our souls intact" (148–49).

The experiences of stereotyping and marginality students of color reported are also experienced by other groups on campus. Earlier we reported some of the negative experiences white working-class students reported in encounters with white middle- and upper-middle-class students and faculty. In another example,

McCune (2001) reports that many students with physical or learning disabilities or mental illness also had to deal with stereotyping: "Like students of color, those who can be identified at a glance as physically different experience assumptions about inferior intellectual capacity" (9). Such students sometimes are seen as using their disability status to gain extra accommodations in class or unearned advantages. Lesbian, gay, bisexual, or transgender (LGBT) students also document experiences of stereotyping, discrimination, and verbal and physical harassment by peers in dormitories, classrooms, and other informal spaces (O'Bear 1991; Rhoads 1997). Anticipating and dealing with such pressures makes the dilemmas of whether, when and how to "come out"—to announce one's sexual orientation to oneself and others—much more difficult. Like members of other marginalized groups these students also often form their own associations to seek out advice, support, fellowship, and opportunities to socialize without fear of harassment. In turn, these adaptations may be seen by members of the majority as another form of self-segregation.

White Ignorance

Racial separation and stereotyping create and reinforce cultural ignorance. Whereas students of color must learn about whites and their culture to survive and advance, white students are under little pressure to learn about minority cultures or traditions. Many students of color at the University of Michigan reported that white students often knew nothing about their group's history or culture, and often were uncomfortable in their presence or awkward and fearful about how to relate with them.

> They ask stupid things, like "Why is your hair straight?" "Why do you fling your hair around all day?" We have to know about their culture, and they don't have to take the time to find out about what we're about, what our culture is about, why we react to things, how we feel about certain things. (*African American*)

> When I was in an English class, one of the white men in the class said, "Well, I don't know what everyone's all worked up about; I've never seen any act of racism on campus." (*Latina*)

These students' experiences are not unique. Feagin et al. (1996) report similar results in their interviews with African American students, noting that white students sometimes act out of overt bigotry, but "at other times whites act inappropriately out of ignorance or a lack of experience with African Americans" (65). On some occasions students of color experience their white peers' ignorance as arrogance that springs from not having to know about others. Unfortunately, rather than opening discourse, these expressions of socially structured ignorance often reinforce a sense of difference and distance. Many students of color feel they are placed in the position of having to teach white students about minority cultures, or suffer misconceptions and implicit accusations of aloofness or resistance.

White Awkwardness and Caution

Students of color also often perceived white students as being very careful not to say the wrong thing. Concerned about being challenged or confronted (often experienced as expressions of hostility), many white students are seen to behave cautiously around students of color, as if seeking the illusion of peace and harmony, often withdrawing from or even denying uncomfortable racial realities. Several students of color elaborated on this phenomenon as follows:

> I find a lot of times, when talking about issues of race, white students want to feel good and hold your hand and don't want to see color and want to be unified. They want us to be white and not have to deal with us being black. (*African American*)

> I remember this one white woman saying, "I'm really a nice person, and I get along with Latinos." Like, "I want you to approve of me." I didn't say anything. I just let it go by. (*Latina*)

White students' caution or awkwardness can come across to students of color as unwillingness to engage in a meaningful discussion or relationship. When white students personalize all racial phenomena, attempt to reduce intergroup relations to the individual level, or profess color blindness, students of color may interpret this as a denial of structural racism or of group-level discrimination and a lack of recognition of differences. Some students of color at the University of Michigan also indicated that they interpreted such silence or withdrawal as a lack of caring about the issues or about their potential offensiveness or painfulness.

The combination of white caution or withdrawal, and stereotypical messages and behavioral exclusion, reinforces patterns of racial/ethnic separation in daily campus life. One response by students of color to perceived disrespect and exclusion is to search for community with people like themselves, among whom their racial and ethnic characteristics are not a bar to acceptance and intimacy. But when students of color do retreat to the company of others like themselves, unlike whites they face inquiry and often are chastised by whites for separating themselves.

While acknowledging these patterns of nonengagement and separation, we do not wish to overemphasize this tendency. Media reports—and some students' perceptions of campus life—lead some observers to believe that our campuses are highly segregated by race. But Antonio (2001) cautions against automatic acceptance of this view. He reports data from the University of California at Los Angeles indicating that only "one in six students report having racially and ethnically homogenous friendship groups . . . [, and] . . . the most common campus friendship group is racially and ethnically mixed" (74–75). Moreover, the greatest homogeneity occurs among white students (Hurtado et al. 1994; Matlock et al. 2002). How can we reconcile the discrepancy between reports of patterns of separation and the relatively high degree of reported interracial contact, friendships, and mixed friendship groups? (See the discussion in chapter 4.) The discrepancy may reflect a difference between abstract and generalized views of the overall environment (separation) and people's actual personal experience mixed friendships, or at least interactions.[3] Given students' prior experiences, some forms of social grouping are likely to be more visible to them (and more confirming of their expectations) than others. In actual practice, there may be no discrepancy in these interpretations, since students of all races and ethnicities (and genders and sexual orientations and religions) probably engage in and benefit from both intimate and supportive interactions with peers of their same social identity groups and the opportunity to interact successfully with people who are different from them. In noting the positive effects on African American students' learning outcomes of both interaction with diverse peers and having close friends of the same race, Gurin (1999) concludes, "These findings suggest the supportive function of group identity for African American students, and the potentially positive effects of having sufficient numbers of same-race peers, as well as opportunities for interracial interaction on diverse campuses" (46).

Pressures to Assimilate

At the same time that many students of color experience treatment marking their difference, they experience pressure to assimilate into the dominant white culture. Two students in the University of Michigan focus groups commented as follows:

> People tell me, "You're American—speak English, damn it." I have no patience for that whatsoever. When I'm in my dorm room and my next-door neighbors are Puerto Rican—they're from New York, and we're speaking Spanish—others come in and they're like, "What are you doing that for? We don't understand you when you speak Spanish. That's rude." (*Latina*)

> To be an Afro-American student here means you have to learn how to adapt and deal with the pressures, not only school but from the white majority. You have to build a tolerance to certain things, like the white majority structure. You really have to be within yourself and know who you are. If not, you could be caught in the system and lose your identity as an Afro-American person. (*African American*)

The pressure to assimilate is a salient theme throughout the literature on students of color in predominantly white colleges and universities (Feagin et al. 1996;

Thomas 1991). It is verified in detail by Bourassa (1991), who argues that "students of color are often expected to absorb, accept and adapt to the dominant white culture" (16). Furthermore, Osajima (1993) notes that such pressure often requires Asian Americans to make choices regarding becoming more Americanized—that is, choosing to jettison certain aspects of their ethnic identity or to retreat and bond solely with other Asian Americans. As Duster (1991) notes in his study at the University of California at Berkeley, "Those more integrated into the mainstream white culture noted that white acquaintances would frequently make a distinction between them and other Asian Americans, usually through remarks intended as compliments, such as, 'You're not like other Asians'" (23). Some of this could be the result of what emerging literature has suggested is whites' perception of themselves as the norm, without race or cultural specificity (the neutral, nonracial person), and thus of their own sociocultural norms of interaction as universal rather than particular (Doane 1997; Fine et al. 1997; Frankenberg 1994; Kenny 2000). As a result, white students and other players in the broader culture of the institution may be unaware that their assumptions about what constitute normal or appropriate styles of communication and interaction are culturally specific; as a result others' different styles may be understood and treated as deviance or divergence from objective norms of appropriate behavior.

In the University of Michigan focus groups, a number of students of color reported behaviors by whites that they felt attempted to treat students' race or culture as trivial, meaningless, or invisible (as in color blindness). Here are some examples:

> It really bothers me when a white person says, "Well, why can't we see each other as individuals instead of race being always an issue?" I always come out and say, "I can't understand why you would think we can separate race and see each other as individuals when my ethnicity is part of who I am and something I can't ignore." (*Latino*)

> When I met my roommate, who's white, she said, "Well, I'm not going to think of you as black, I'll just think of you as my friend who has a natural suntan." (*African American*)

> People are constantly saying, "Oh, I thought you were white." And I say, "No, I'm Native American." And they say, "Well, you look white." I tell them my mom is white. People expect this Indian with a feather in her hair. I think people make a lot of assumptions about your ethnicity. I don't mind if people ask, but it really upsets me when people make assumptions about who you are. (*Native American*)

Some students of color report that others want them to blend in and thereby become invisible (Tierney 1993). On the other hand, they often find that white students stereotype them academically and behaviorally, emphasizing their group characteristics and thus their difference, as in, "You're black—show me the M. C. Hammer." The dilemma for these students of color is captured in one student's statement, "either I was totally marginalized or I was 'the Asian American woman.'" These are two sides of the same coin—a push and pull that generates daily quandaries about who one is or wants to be. On a larger scale, it presents again questions of organizational membership: who are members of this collegiate community, who are full and appropriate members and who are special members.

Students of color also wrestle with these stereotypes in their own cultural groups. It is not only white students who press students of color to conform to a particular racial/ethnic image. Students of color often press one another to "stay black," join pan-Asian coalitions, or celebrate their Latino/a identity publicly and privately. One result is that these students may be engaged in a constant process of negotiating their multiple identities and memberships in both their unique and common cultures.

The Focus on Black–White Interaction

In 1994, Hurtado reported, "Most of the studies that document feelings of discrimination and campus race relations have been based on African American students" (25). The situation is hardly different a decade later. Not surprisingly, for groups of Latino/a, Asian American, and Native American students, the dominant campus (and societal) focus on black–white relations can create its own problems.

> If you're in class and they start talking about people of color issues, many of us are offended when it's always just the black issues that are discussed. (*Latina*)

> I remember a lot of times in class discussion when we talked, they would say something about an issue and I would bring up the Asian American perspective or what I felt about it and they would be like, "Yeah, that's nice, but here's the real issue." (*Asian American*)

Duster (1991) quotes from a Chicano student in *The Diversity Project*: "they [African American students] talk about racism and then a Chicano/Latino will go, 'Oh, yeah, I know what you mean,' and they'll just look at you or if you're not dark enough they don't think you've experienced it, and I've come out and say, 'Well, Chicano/Latinos face racism, too'" (35). In these kinds of exchanges Latino/a, Asian American, and Native American students are left feeling additionally excluded and marginalized. Moreover, as the Michigan Student Study data show, Latino/a, Asian American, and black students have very different experiences on campus that are not addressed adequately when the focus remains on black–white issues alone (Matlock et al. 2002).

Affirmative action programs and consequent debates that focus only on the admission of black students inevitably promote competition among groups of students of color for the scarce resource of college attendance and the even scarcer resources of respectful attention and engagement. And they contribute to white students' tunnel vision about the reality of diverse racial groups as well as the reality of diversity within racial groups.

Racial Resentments and Affirmative Action

While the specific legal and administrative issues surrounding affirmative action have changed shape through the years, the popular association of minority admissions and advancement with the notion of unearned preferences—and minimally or not at all with a history of educational exclusion and disadvantage—persists. The result is a common expectation by whites that students of color lack talent. In the University of Michigan focus group study, two students of color summed up the sentiments directed at them:

> Students directly asked me about affirmative action and was I a token student. It's like, "Yeah, you must of gotten here because you're a token student anyway. You must be stupid." (*African American*)

> I came from out of state, and I was . . . appalled when a white man got up and pointed his finger at me and said, "I don't think it's right that you go to school here when my best friend doesn't." I thought that was kind of outrageous. So I said, "You know nothing about me; you're just making generalizations." But then I felt bad because I started to try to justify myself for being here, and in my opinion I don't have anything to prove to him. I only have to prove things to myself. (*African American*)

These reports from students of color reflect reactions to statements about affirmative action such as those made by some white students in chapter 4, particularly the view that students of color are not qualified or do not "deserve" admission.

The reports by students of color that they often feel excluded, marginalized, and pressured to assimilate reflect and lead to broader power relationships between students of different races, and the generally privileged status of white students in white-dominated classrooms and systems of higher education. These unequal power relationships are often manifest in students of color having less air time in classes, less academic confidence and comfort, not being invited to join student work groups and teams, less access to the faculty, and in general a lesser sense that they are welcome as full members of these institutions. Duster (1991: 19) has documented similar feelings among by students at the University of California at Berkeley. "Black, Chicano, and Native American students routinely expressed the feeling of 'not belonging' at UC Berkeley." Students told Duster (1991), "I feel like I have Affirmative Action stamped on my forehead," "We're guilty until proven innocent," and "There's no way to convince whites we belong here" (13). Hurtado (1994) further documents the extent of the stereotypical message to Hispanic students at many college campuses that they are "special admits." Of course, people of color, young and old, were the recipients of such stereotypical and demeaning assumptions long before affirmative action on college campuses became a hot topic.

Feagin and Sikes (1994) and Cose (1993) have documented similar experiences among middle- and upper-middle-class African Americans in many public and private arenas. Thus, challenges to the legitimate status of African Americans in particular, and people of color more generally, are deeply rooted in the history and character of race relations in the United States; it is a broad societal phenomenon that is played out on campuses around affirmative action issues. It did not start on campus nor does it end there; it did not start with affirmative action programs nor will it end there either! In a society where higher education is a central element of cultural capital, attendance and graduation from a prestigious college is an important resource. Group-level struggles for access to good colleges are captured and illuminated in arguments about the numerical and symbolic representation of races on campus and are played out in interpersonal interactions such as those documented here (Blumer 1958).

RELATIONSHIPS WITH FACULTY

Among the most important factors in the collegiate organizational context are the academic curriculum and pedagogy (technology) and the role and behavior of the faculty. The faculty's presence and role in the organizational apparatus of college life touches students most strongly via their encounters in the classroom. The faculty's design of the curriculum, their choice of pedagogical strategies, and their ways of relating to students in and out of class (see chapters 6 and 10) all help shape students' experiences.

The majority of students at the University of Michigan, including all groups of students of color, reported positive relations with the (predominantly white) faculty. Overall, 71 percent of African American students, 72 percent of Latinos/as, and 57 percent of Asian Americans reported finding "at least one teacher" with a strong impact on their development (71 percent of white students reported similarly) (Matlock et al. 2002). And a clear majority of students of all races/ethnicities also reported that it was "very easy" or "fairly easy" to be taken seriously academically by their faculty.

Some students of color identified faculty behaviors that had a positive effect on them personally, on white students' behavior, and on their peer relations in class. Here are two examples:

> I know I did poorly on one exam, and I went to talk with the professor. After talking with the professor, he realized I knew the material but for some reason I just didn't do well on the test. After that he held regular sessions with me, and we kept the lines of communication open, and I began to do well. But if he had just blown me off, I probably would have continued to do poorly in the class. (*Latina*)

> In an English class, some students said that one of the authors was sexist as well as racist. It was put on the computer conference, and people actually wrote back. The professor got on and said that this was a very good thing to put on the system. He said people need to not just read the material but actually discuss the differences in perspective. (*African American*)

Despite these positive experiences, contradictory trends mark students' relations with faculty. Although some studies have reported that minority students generally feel satisfied with their relations with faculty (McLelland and Auster 1990), other work identifies racially problematic behavior by faculty (Trujillo 1986). Some problematic themes that emerged from focus group interviews with students of color at Michigan follow.

Absence from the Expressed or Hidden Curriculum

In some cases, students' relationships with the material presented in the classroom prompted their concern about exclusion from full academic membership. An Asian American student explained it this way:

> It's like something that gets added on to the syllabus if there's extra time in the semester. There were things that were on the syllabus that were about women and that were about Asian Americans too, and then we ran out of time, and so the professor had to cut some of the things out—the things about women and the things about Asian Americans. (*Asian American*)

A large majority of Michigan undergraduates surveyed (ranging from 67 percent of whites to 98 percent of blacks) agreed that the contributions of writers from different racial/ethnic groups should be essential elements in a college's core curriculum, but less than half of the students reported having had significant exposure to understanding other groups in their courses (Matlock et al. 2002).

Concern about the content of the curriculum is a theme echoed in colleges throughout the nation. At the graduate level, Margolis and Romero (1998) argue that the absence of regular courses on race and gender in the sociology curriculum maintain "an implicit hierarchy of knowledge" and a "deafening silence" for women of color. For many undergraduates this absence functions as another form of exclusion that minimizes their intellectual opportunities and frustrates their desire to find themselves in studies of U.S. society and to gain an understanding and appreciation of others. For instance, a Stanford University study indicates that, "students believe the current curricula and courses lack content that will promote an understanding of racial and cultural diversity" (University Committee on Minority Issues 1989: 7). Most of the respondents of color in that study (from 84 percent to 93 percent in each of the minority groups) reported that the Stanford curriculum "does not teach students about the contributions of diverse racial and cultural groups" (17). For students of all races, not learning about the intellectual contributions of diverse racial groups, and not learning the nation's or the world's histories of racial domination and subordination, diminish their ability to understand contemporary social dynamics and their own embeddedness in these patterns.

Margolis and Romero discuss not only the manifest content of the curriculum, but the operation of a "hidden curriculum" represented in the behaviors and norms modeled or expressed by the faculty (whether consciously or unconsciously). Several of the following themes in University of Michigan students' focus group responses illustrate such hidden or subtle influence.

Low Expectations for Minority Students' Performance

Even though most African American undergraduates and about two-thirds of Latino/a and Asian American students reported being taken seriously academically by their professors, some students of color said that the faculty seemed not to expect them to perform well in class, and thus did not encourage them or affirm their abilities (Matlock et al. 2002). Black students, in particular, registered dissatisfaction with the level of intellectual respect they received from faculty. For some, this affected their own expectations for themselves; for others, it created feelings of withdrawal and frustration.

> I wasn't doing well in the course and the professor said, "Oh, well, drop the course. There's nothing I can do for you, and there's nothing you can do." (*African American*)

> In class you can just tell that some teachers think that just because a student is black they don't know as much, and it makes you really mad. I can't really explain what goes on, but because I'm not black I see certain things from the outside. I see how they treat black students differently. Like if a professor or TA is trying to explain something to a black student, they talk to the student like the student is dumb. I don't even think they are aware of how they treat the students. (*Asian American*)

These experiences certainly are not unique. In the Massachusetts Institute of Technology's survey of one thousand undergraduates, followed by discussion forums, students of color reported feeling that "they were perceived as high risks by professors, teaching assistants, and students," and that this perception translated into "additional pressure to try to 'overachieve' in order to 'prove oneself.' Others described having feelings of alienation that increased their anxiety" (McBay 1986: 4). Indeed, McBay reports that in a survey of black MIT alumni, "31 percent voluntarily said that faculty members expected failure or a lack of ability in Blacks" (11–12). Several researchers have reported similar observations about the behavior or assumed attitudes of university faculty (Astin et al. 1972; Blauner 1972; Katz 1991; Rabow 2002; Trujillo 1986). This is such a pervasive and well-known phenomenon that many African American students at Michigan indicated on an entrance survey (before they got to a college classroom) that they did not expect to receive respect from the white faculty (Gurin et al. 2004).

Students of Color Are the Same as Everyone Else

Some students of color said that they felt estranged or excluded by assumptions that instructors made about students in general but that just did not apply to them.

> One of my TAs was talking about students having to work and he said, "None of us have to work to earn money because we can write home to our parents." I was working thirty-five to forty hours a week. If I wasn't a really strong-willed person, I would have felt really bad. (*African American*)

Such assumptions often are inaccurate when applied to the current generation of white students, and they certainly do not fit the realities of life of many students of color. Allen (1986) has reported that faculty members commonly make class- and race-based assumptions about students' past and current lives.

Failure to Recognize Differences among Students of Color

In contrast to the prior category, in which an instructor assumed that all students share his white and middle-class identity and experience, faculty sometimes seemed to separate, stereotype, or lump together students of color on the basis of invalid assumptions.

> When I went to pick up my exam in math class, the professor didn't look as if he knew exactly who I was, but he automatically found the paper with the lowest grade and handed it to me. I told him that that was not my name and not my paper. When I told him my name and he found my paper, my actual score on the exam was perfect. (*African American*)

In this example, the faculty member evidently did not know the name of this young African American woman—not in and of itself an uncommon or tragic situation in a large class. But to avoid the minor embarrassment of admitting this fact he made the situation far worse by resorting to a form of stereotypical racial profiling. Such overtly insensitive faculty behavior obviously creates pain and distress. Similar experiences also have been reported from other campuses. At the University of California at Berkeley, for example, Asian American students reported "being indiscriminately lumped together as a group, being subjected to a common stereotype or common racism for this reason, and being pitted against other minorities in the struggle for scarce resources" (Duster 1991: 42).

Singling Out Students of Color as Racial Experts and Spokespersons

Some students reported that they felt uncomfortable when they were identified and asked publicly to speak as an authority on issues assumed to be relevant to their own racial group, or on issues of racism and racial relations generally. They felt that to be made the expert in class escalated a single aspect of their identity, put undue pressure on them for expertise they may not have had, and led to stares from white students.

> When you take classes at the University, and you're African American, and you talk about black issues, they look at you assuming that you know all about the topic. For example, living in the ghetto—they look at you like you're the person who should know about it. . . . These are professors and students. (*African American*)

> An Asian article came up in class and the teacher looked at me and said, "I'm sure XXX will have much to say about this next article." (*Asian American*)

Graduate students of color at the University of Michigan's School of Public Health cited this sort of experience as a problem, too: "The expectation that all African American students are experientially expert in 'the black experience,' which is equated with poverty, and the expectation that they teach whites about racism" (Task Force on Racial and Cultural Concerns 1990: 3). Crenshaw (1989) also identifies the phenomenon of using students of color as "show and tell" experts or as "testifiers" as common in the experience of black students in law schools.

Faulty Discomfort or Caution

Some students, especially males, noted faculty who appeared overly cautious or intimidated—by them, by other students, or by their own concerns.

> She was very racist; she told us once that she was afraid of black people. (*Asian American*)

The professors never joke in class with black students. Their jokes are directed toward white students. You would think they know the white students personally. When professors and TAs favor the white students, that makes you feel uncomfortable; it affects you. (*African American*)

Some white faculty may indeed be scared of some students of color (Katz 1991). And some may be more comfortable and relaxed in their interactions with white students because of their similar culture, approaches to the classroom, and behavioral styles. Class issues also may be involved, since many university faculties have higher-status origins than do many of their students, often particularly students of color (Lipset and Ladd 1985). In any case, this situation can lead to perceptions of favoritism and to resultant alienation. The discomfort of white faculty members in interracial classrooms has been discussed by several observers (Blauner 1972; Mingle 1978; Peterson et al. 1978) and may help account for the common finding that African American students have fewer interactions and fewer informal contacts with faculty than do white students (Allen 1988; Fleming 1984; Stikes 1984).

As a consequence of some of these faculty stances, a number of students of color indicated that the faculty did not seem to care whether or not they learned the material. Willie and McCord's earlier studies (1972) indicate that students of color often felt that white faculty were uninterested in them, and Wolfman (1990) suggests that an institutional emphasis on research productivity often leads faculty in research-oriented universities to spend little time talking with undergraduates, particularly with students of color.

One undergraduate student described his assertive action in the face of this situation and noted why many students of color have difficulty adopting assertive behavior.

When I feel as though I don't get enough feedback, I will go to the professor's office and be very assertive. I think a lot of black students are hesitant to go to the professor's office, because they feel as though professors don't want to help them. They become intimidated because professors generally have a "don't give a damn" attitude. (*African American*)

In general, many students of color have positive interactions and experiences with their university faculties. But some white collegiate faculty have stereotypically low expectations for students of color, direct different types of questions to them than to white students, may not seem to care about or reach out to them, single them out as experts or spokespersons on racial/ethnic issues, and/or seem uncomfortable relating to them. In some instances, collegiate faculty evidently do not feel that their social relationships and interactions with students of color constitute a significant issue. Instead, they focus on delivering academic material in as efficient a way as possible and on testing students' learning of this material. Other faculty simply do not know how to address such issues. Most faculty have not been trained or educated to consider the classroom as a social group or social system in miniature, with interpersonal and intergroup dynamics that affect students' abilities to learn as well as their social comfort and identity. In most colleges and universities, faculty members receive little institutional support for challenging traditional patterns of racial understanding and interaction. Yet their actions and nonactions often cause or permit stereotypic, assimilative, exclusionary, awkward, and resentment-inducing experiences for students of color.

Students of color are not the only groups reporting that problematic situations occur with university faculty members. LGBT students also sometimes encounter stereotyping, exclusionary, or inappropriate behavior in the classroom. For example, students in one study reported being offended when a professor asked "what students looked for in the opposite sex," whereas another objected to a faculty member discussing "behavior modification as a way to treat homosexuals" without being open to the question of whether any treatment was necessary or appropriate (Rhoads 1997: 195). Students with physical and mental disabilities also occasionally reported facing discrimination, discouragement, or a lack of attention in the classroom. And McCune (2001) notes that "[some] instructors, perhaps out of ignorance, anxiety, or a misguided sense of fairness, refused to provide accommodations and often humiliated the students by publicly discussing their special needs" (10).

THE IMPACT OF RACIAL INTERACTIONS ON CAMPUS

Students of color on contemporary college campuses have benefited from recent advances in secondary education, the rising economic status of portions of the black and Latino/a communities, and affirmative action policies. They are the "best and brightest" of their ranks. Whether they come from racially segregated or desegregated secondary schools, once they enter predominantly white college environs many of them must renegotiate their identities, expectations, and relations with others. These young people of color confront a complicated set of pressures and/or demands. Too often asked to be representatives of their race and to embody racial stereotypes, they at the same time face criticism for emphasizing race and not just assimilating. Moreover, some students of color feel their cultural as well as academic qualifications are challenged by both whites and members of their own identity group. Contradictory expectations and assumptions from different directions often place students of color in awkward, objectionable, or painful circumstances.

One result of these experiences is that students of color at predominantly white colleges and universities carry an extra burden of mental and emotional stress and must struggle to determine what is real about themselves and their climate and what is imaginary. External events of the sort described earlier may prompt internal psychic struggles that amount to an extra cost of a college education. The resources of these students of color are taxed by the need to be on guard against, to deal with, and to counter the many direct or indirect negative messages they receive. As two students explain:

> In this environment the white students watch everything you do. Watch what you say around them, you might not want to offend them. (*Latina*)

> So much of our mental energy is used talking about these issues, about our anger and frustration in being asked ignorant questions and so on. White students don't use mental energy to do that. (*African American*)

Some African Americans who experience or anticipate such treatment matriculate at or transfer to historically black colleges and universities, where they hope to experience a feeling of family-like acceptance and support (Allen 1992; Fleming 1984; Fries-Britt and Turner 2002).

The MIT study succinctly describes the long-run costs of the extra burdens indicated above: while the black alumni surveyed clearly valued their MIT education, many indicated that "racism in the living and learning environments was not incidental but a fundamental factor in the high costs" of attending MIT (McBay 1986: 6). Negotiating these racial hurdles also leads to a great deal of "personal and psychological stress" and potential "damage to the students' self-esteem and self-identity" (Feagin et al. 1996: 44, 133). Students of color also incur tangible costs as a result of poor advising, counseling, and channeling. Nevertheless, most students of color cope with these demands successfully. That they do testifies to their strength, their ability to maintain an intellectual focus, and their emotional resilience in the face of far greater stress than their white peers experience.

The new literature on the changing nature of racial attitudes and institutional racism challenges thoughtful people to reevaluate these trends on college campuses in light of the broader social conversation about race and racism. While few of the students quoted in this chapter reported high levels of traditional racial prejudice, explicit exclusion, or hostility, they did point to numerous examples of subtle but potent negative interactions. The experiences of these students of color provide clear examples of current struggles with subtle forms of racism, both in individual interactions and in institutional encounters.

Clearly, a university's faculty members are little more immune from the segregated nature of our society and the prevailing patterns of racism and racial interaction in our communities and on campus than are students. Moreover, patterns of racial relations between students of color and the faculty and between these students and white students often mirror or reinforce one another.

Many of the views characteristic of university students reflect their precollege socialization, and the dominant ways in which race relations (including campus race relations) are dealt with in the media, and are not principally created by experiences on campus. Even so, in the absence of formal or informal experiences that effectively challenge and provide the opportunity for students to alter these views, we can expect them to play out on campus. Then negative cycles repeat themselves, and the contemporary collegiate environment sets the stage for many white students to see, to expect to see, and to behave toward students of color in stereotypical terms, and for many students of color to struggle with the intellectual and emotional burdens of living and learning in a difficult environment.

In many ways, the situation at the University of Michigan represents progress on many racially sensitive issues. Students of color, particularly Asian American and Latino/a students, reported high levels of satisfaction with their campus experience and only a small minority of students (10 percent of Asian American, Latino/a, and white students, and 20 percent of black students) reported that on balance their relationships with students of other racial/ethnic groups had been negative. A majority of students said that they had learned a great deal about other racial/ethnic groups and their contributions to American society while at the university (Matlock et al. 2002). Moreover, Gurin (1999) reports that African Americans who had greater experience with diversity on campus also achieved positive educational benefits, such as gains in active thinking, intellectual skills and abilities, and motivation for educational progress. Nevertheless, race relations on campus continue to be complicated by a multitude of subtle, everyday racial interactions that require students of color to come to grips with racial presumptions and less-than-open interactions. These patterns also require everyone else on campus to attend to these issues and to develop new classroom, residence hall, and informal interaction opportunities that can reduce the level of subtle as well as overt institutional racism.

NOTES

1. This chapter draws on findings from a number of national and campus-specific studies that have charted the experiences of students of color in colleges across the country. We also draw on examples from samples of students from a single campus in order to flesh out the nature and quality of peer interactions in more detail. The University of Michigan is a useful site within which to examine these issues, since its history closely mirrors larger patterns of racial struggle on universities nationwide. The quantitative data reported here come from the Michigan Student Study (Matlock et al. 2002). See note 1 in chapter 4 for details.

The qualitative data come from analyses of transcripts from fifteen group interviews, or small structured discussions, involving a total of seventy-five undergraduate students of color, lasting from one to two hours each. All of these group interviews were homogenous by race and/or social identity of the students being interviewed (several groups each of African American students, Latino/a students, Asian American students, and Native American students) and mixed in gender. The discussion leaders were specially trained in focus group interviewing techniques and in every case matched the group being interviewed in social identity (race/ethnicity). General questions sought explicitly to discover problems and problematic issues, such as these:

- How do you and students of other races relate to one another in class?
- Have you ever felt uncomfortable about assumptions or comments made in class related to race and/or ethnicity?
- How do your peers expect you to do in class?
- Have you ever worked with other students on a team project? How was that?
- What do white students do that offends or hurts students of color outside of class?
- Has an instructor ever done something constructive about race relations in or out of class? What do they do about in-class incidents? What could they do?

Various specific probes asked informants to identity, specify, and elaborate on these issues. Some of these data also have been reported in academic and public venues (Chesler et al. 1993; Lewis, Chesler and Forman 2000).

2. For example, the Michigan Student Study showed that almost five times as many black students as whites reported that financial aid support was a key factor in their decision to attend the University of Michigan. Black and Latino/a students were far less likely than white or Asian Americans to receive significant financial support from their parents. To be sure, many poor and working-class white college students also struggle financially and culturally to persist and graduate (Dews and Law 1995). As is the case for poor and working-class students of color, major transformation in federal student financial aid over the last three decades make their efforts to achieve a degree harder than ever. Moreover, because of large racial differentials in wealth many working-class white families still have equal or greater access to resources for college than do middle-class black families (Oliver and Shapiro 1995).

3. In addition, it also is possible that some of these different reports reflect differing questions, different ways of asking questions, and different interpretations of the meaning of friendships. As noted, different portions of the data come from the sharply divergent contexts of an individual paper-and-pencil survey and racially homogenous and problem-focused focus groups.

Chapter Six

The Experiences of Diverse Faculty Teaching in Diverse Classrooms

In this chapter we examine faculty members' experiences negotiating their identities and practices in teaching diverse groups of students in classes. In addition to drawing on a wide range of research from national studies we use original data from faculty at the University of Michigan to flesh out key issues.[1] The literature on faculty backgrounds and outlooks is quite useful, but there is a paucity of in-depth data on daily experiences with teaching in diverse classrooms. Conversations with faculty committed to working on these issues provide a window into what it means to take multiculturalism seriously in a large, predominantly white research university. The material in this chapter highlights several of the organizational domains portrayed in figure 3.2. Issues related to representing and retaining faculty of color reflect concerns about organizational membership; the discussion of classroom substance and procedure—curriculum and pedagogy—involves issues of technology in an educationally focused human service organization; and the examination of relationships among faculty and between faculty and students raises issues of organizational climate and power structures.

The picture captured by Sax et al. (1999) of the racial attitudes and views of this national professoriate suggests a pattern of generally tolerant and progressive educational outlooks. For instance, 58.7 percent of all faculty surveyed (at both public and private four- and two-year colleges) indicated that "promoting racial understanding" was a very important personal goal, and 57.8 percent indicated that enhancing students' "appreciation of racial/ethnic groups" was a very important goal they held for undergraduates. Nevertheless, faculty of color and women faculty often view things and do things differently from their white and male counterparts, and this highlights the importance of having women and people of color represented in university faculties. For instance, Sax et al. (1999) report that female faculty respondents were more likely than male faculty to have goals of "promoting racial understanding," to include in their courses "readings on racial/ethnic issues" and "readings on women/gender issues," and to attempt to "enhance appreciation of racial/ethnic groups." Female faculty also were more likely than male faculty to feel that it was important to "create a multicultural environment" and that "a diverse student body enhances education." For their part, faculty of color were far more likely than white faculty to state that "promoting racial understanding" was a very important or essential goal (Astin et al. 1997). Indeed, Astin et al. (1997) and Hurtado et al. (1999) report that faculty of color were more likely to act on these goals by utilizing a wide range of participative classroom techniques than were white faculty: they were more likely to engage students in discussion, peer evaluation, classroom dialogue, and readings focused on issues of race and ethnicity. The diverse backgrounds of faculty members obviously influence their approaches to classroom matters.

CREATING AND SUSTAINING A DIVERSE FACULTY

One key measure of efforts to create a multicultural educational organization is the diversity of its members—in this chapter the faculty. Of course, representation marks only the beginning of the process of diversification, but substantial numbers of faculty of color and female faculty is necessary to transform a monocultural organization into a more multicultural one. Without such numbers, "Women and minorities . . . are both under-represented in leadership roles and lack a critical mass—circumstances that afford them little leverage to reduce or eliminate cultural barriers to change" (Trower and Chait 2002: 9).

The history of efforts to increase the representation of female faculty and faculty of color is replete with arguments about the negative effects of an inadequate pipeline (such as a lack of qualified female and minority Ph.D.s in a given field), discrimination in hiring itself (overt discrimination or subtle preferences that impact differentially on women and scholars of color), and accumulated disadvantages (combining early disadvantage or discrimination in home and school with pipeline effects and potential hiring deficiencies) (CAWMSET 2000; Clark and Corcoran 1986). Whatever the comparative validity of these arguments, progress in representation has been slow (Allen et al. 2002; Turner Sotello-Viernes, Myers, and Creswell 1999). Trower and Chait (2002) report that, as of 1997, 64 percent of full-time faculty members were male and 87 percent were white, and only 5 percent of full professors were of African American, Latino/a, or Native American origin. As noted in chapter 2, in the mid-1970s, 79 percent of full-time faculty were male, and 92 percent were white. Some progress is being made, but the pace of change is quite slow.

Black faculty, in particular, tend to be overrepresented, relative to their numbers overall, at public two-year and four-year institutions and underrepresented at more prestigious public or private doctorate-granting universities (see table 6.1). A similar pattern applies to female faculty. Women and members of racial or ethnic minority groups also hold lesser ranks than do white male faculty, are less likely to be tenured and tend to teach at less prestigious institutions (Kulis, Chong, and Shaw 1999; Trower and Chait 2002). The same holds for working-class faculty, "The thousands of working-class academics who were assimilated into U.S. higher education in the years after 1945 tended to be concentrated in lower-status colleges and universities" (Mazurek 1995: 251). Since 1976, throughout the academy great changes have occurred in the reduction of the percentage of faculty of all races, ethnicities, and genders in the junior tenure-track ranks and the increase in the percentage of all faculty in the nontenured category (lecturers, instructors). Faculty not on the tenure track have less voice in departmental decisions and in determining their teaching assignments; they also face continual financial and employment uncertainty. Faculty of color and women are overrepresented in these categories.

The path to increased representation and advancement of female faculty and faculty of color is not easy. Local organizational characteristics, such as the college's mission and its prior experience with and hiring of faculty and administrators of color, along with local demographic and political factors, affect approaches to faculty hiring, retention, and tenure/promotion. Moreover, internal organizational factors may permit a legacy of racial discrimination to show up in "white control over faculty search processes, criteria, screening and interviewing; white-dominated nomination and insider information networks; and heightened scrutiny of minority candidates under the guise of maintaining standards and resisting special-interest politics" (Kulis, Chong, and Shaw 1999: 117). As one example, Tierney and Bensimon (1996) report that a number of faculty of color and female faculty found themselves insulted and sabotaged during the recruitment and hiring process or shortly thereafter. As Moses (1989) notes, "Verbal support [by universities] for affirmative action does not necessarily transform itself into support of a program or of new minority employees once they are hired. . . . Black women may be stereotyped, resented or even treated with disrespect because they are perceived as less qualified" (13).

Even when faculty of color and female faculty are represented on university faculties, they often experience life in the classroom and in departments quite differently from their white male colleagues. For instance, Niemann and Dovidio (1998) report survey results showing that "minority faculty members had lower levels of job satisfaction than did white faculty members and that this differences was mediated by feelings of racial and ethnic stigmatization" (793). The gender and racial/ethnic composition of a given department or unit may substantially affect faculty members' comfort level and job satisfaction. Tolbert et al. (1995) demonstrate that when women are in a distinct numerical minority in a department, they are likely to have higher turnover rates. In a large-scale research project examining thirty-three thousand faculty, Astin et al. (1997) indicate that faculty of color

Table 6.1. Percentage Distribution of Full-Time Instructional Faculty and Staff According to Institution Type, by Gender and Race/Ethnicity, Fall 1998

	Public Doctoral	Private, Not-for-Profit Doctoral[a]	Public Compre-hensive	Private, Not-for-Profit Compre-hensive	Private, Not-for-Profit Liberal Arts	Public Two-Year	Other[b]
				Total			
Total	34.9	10.6	14.8	6.7	8.5	18.3	6.2
Race/Ethnicity							
White, Non-Hispanic	34.8	10.5	14.4	6.9	8.8	18.3	6.3
Black, Non-Hispanic	23.2	8.2	21.8	6.0	10.7	21.5	8.7
Asian or Pacific Islander	46.8	14.2	15.0	4.3	4.2	10.6	4.9
Hispanic	34.8	11.7	16.0	5.5	4.1	25.5	2.4
American Indian/Alaskan Native	34.2	5.7	10.9	11.4	12.7	19.9	5.2
				Male			
Total	38.0	11.7	14.4	6.7	8.3	14.4	6.6
Race/Ethnicity							
White, Non-Hispanic	38.1	11.7	13.9	6.7	8.5	14.4	6.7
Black, Non-Hispanic	20.3	8.9	22.1	7.2	13.0	16.8	11.7

Asian or Pacific Islander	51.1	14.8	14.9	5.1	4.5	6.1	3.7
Hispanic	33.9	13.2	16.6	6.2	3.3	24.2	2.7
American Indian/Alaskan Native	34.0	5.3	11.2	13.1	10.1	24.7	1.6
				Female			
Total	29.4	8.7	15.6	6.8	8.9	25.1	5.5
Race/Ethnicity							
White, Non-Hispanic	28.9	8.5	15.3	7.3	9.3	25.3	5.4
Black, Non-Hispanic	26.3	7.5	21.4	4.7	8.3	26.5	5.5
Asian or Pacific Islander	37.2	13.1	15.3	2.5	3.5	20.7	7.7
Hispanic	36.2	9.3	15.1	4.4	5.5	27.7	1.8
American Indian/Alaskan Native	34.5	6.6	10.3	7.8	18.6	9.1	13.3

[a] Includes research, doctoral, and medical institutions.

[b] Other institutions include private not-for-profit two-year institutions, public liberal arts colleges, and other specialized institutions.

Note: Includes full-time instructional faculty and staff at Title IV degree-granting institutions with at least some instructional duties for credit. Percentages may not sum to 100 due to rounding.

Source: National Center for Educational Statistics (1999; www.nces.ed.gov).

were generally less satisfied with multiple aspects of their jobs and roles. Other research has found that such faculty members were more likely to report feeling isolated, unsupported, stressed, and subject to discrimination (Dey 1994; Garza 1993; Gmelch 1995; Smith and Witt 1993). They also more often report a burden of "cultural taxation"—the effect of being called upon to perform various services to multiple constituencies (students, faculty committees, and community groups) seeking access to the few female faculty or faculty of color available (Aguirre 1995). All these studies emphasize the role of organizational variables such as departmental composition, norms, support structures, socialization processes, tenure review processes, and overall social climate in creating or buffering stress and extra workloads for faculty of color.

THE CHALLENGES OF TEACHING
IN A DIVERSE CLASSROOM

Faculty members and classrooms function in the context of the larger university organization, and figure 6.1 presents an image of some of the forces that influence faculty approaches to teaching in diverse classrooms. The faculty member's conceptualization of and behavior in the classroom results from personal characteristics (race, gender, class origin, age, and organizational status) and substantive as well as pedagogical knowledge and skills. Also relevant are the instructor's attitudes and beliefs regarding racial matters; in this regard Stassen (1995) emphasizes that, despite the generally progressive picture of faculty members' racial attitudes, much of their behavior may be affected by their own and the society's racial ambivalence and complexity. The characteristics of the students who attend a particular educational organization, classroom, or course (class composition, class size, and subject matter, for example) set the stage for the actual teaching that occurs. Other organizational forces, detailed in figure 3.2, include the nature of peer/collegial and departmental norms, support for innovative teaching, the institution's mission or stance on diversity and multiculturalism, and the prevailing campus climate (including contemporary local struggles and incidents). Extraorganizational forces in the local or national community may also affect the pedagogical environment and incidents of racism/sexism/classism often intrude into the classroom and alter individual faculty members' approaches and students' responses.

The ways faculty face these challenges and approach the diverse classroom have great impact on how students learn to deal with one another, over and above their academic progress. For instance, reports from students in chapters 4 and 5 make it clear that faculty need to develop ways of engaging diverse groups of students in sustained forms of intergroup interaction in class in order to help them form successful working/learning relationships with one another. Such experiences not only

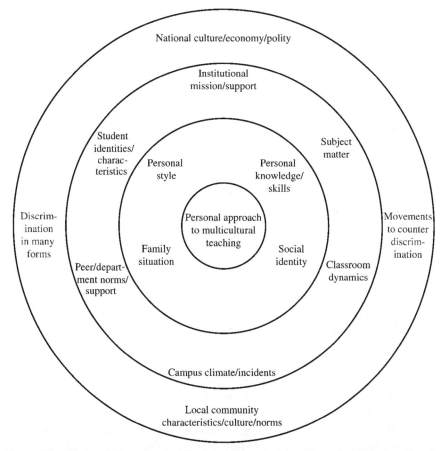

Figure 6.1.   Forces Influencing Faculty Approaches to Diversity and Multiculturalism in Classroom Teaching

can improve the classroom and collegiate environment, it also can lead to the gains in active thinking and intellectual engagement referred to by Gurin (1999). These considerations are relevant for the teaching–learning process in all classes, both those where the manifest subject matter touches on such issues and those where it does not. In all these situations faculty need to be alert to, and prepared to take advantage of, those challenging classroom times and events that highlight intergroup concerns and capture students' emotional and intellectual attention—those "teachable moments."

The combination of these factors makes teaching in diverse settings, and especially teaching in a proactively multicultural manner, quite challenging. Indeed, four major challenges typically are faced by faculty working in diverse educational settings: personal, pedagogical, curricular, and structural. These challenges are always present in the teaching situation; however, the nature of diverse and heterogeneous instructional settings highlights them.

Personal Challenges

Bell et al. (1997) have argued that clarity about one's own social identity is crucial to successful teaching in diverse environments. They suggest that as instructors we "need to be willing to examine and deal honestly with our values, assumptions and emotional reactions. . . . The self-knowledge and self-awareness that we believe are desirable qualities in any teacher" (299) become even more important in work with diverse student populations. All faculty work in ways that reflect their social identities, their personal and group-oriented understandings of themselves, and their roles as scholars. Thus, faculty members' social identities strongly influence students, predisposing some students to be more or less willing to relate with and learn from them—and obviously the reverse is often true as well. Furthermore, some faculty members' internalized biases (conscious or not) may make them more or less open to and respectful of students of particular races or ethnicities, genders, socioeconomic classes, and sexual orientations.

The role that social identity plays in the classroom and on campus varies for faculty of different origin. In many institutions, faculty of color stand out amidst a faculty membership that is largely white. Although their identities play different roles in their lives, the faculty of color whom we interviewed fairly consistently reported clear racial identities, both with respect to those they carried self-consciously and with respect to those that others ascribed to them.

> My identity began with the strength I had gotten from my mother in terms of the history of black folk . . . with the images of oppression. That was the basis for my identity. The acts of oppression plus the learnings and teachings I got from my mother are how I can survive here at the university. (*African American male*)

On the other hand, since white faculty members' racial identity is often taken for granted, it sometimes goes unrecognized or undiscussed (by them or others) as an important factor in their lives. Some claimed not to identify themselves racially to any great extent.

I don't feel like I have a very strong racial identity. My identities are much more wrapped up with me as a faculty member and things like that. (*white male*)

It is unclear whether this individual simply does not understand the personal and social meaning of his whiteness or whether he considers it minimally relevant for his role as an instructor. Other white faculty recognized the salience of their racial identity and its role in their lives inside and outside the classroom:

I know myself as a person of a certain skin color and with a certain location in the social structure of the society in which I live and all its organizations. . . . It means I am a person of privilege—mostly increasingly known privilege, but sometimes unknown privilege. And that's shorthand for having greater social resources and opportunities and access. I need to be very careful about how I act on that privilege, . . . and I have a responsibility to continue to think about ways of eroding or transforming the system of privilege that maintains things the way they are. (*white male*)

Social identities are relevant not only for individual faculty members' self-concepts but also for their racialized interactions with others. Faculty of color often confront a set of racial assumptions and dynamics (e.g., challenges to their authority) that complicate the instructional process. This may help explain why many faculty of color tend to be quite alert to the ways their racial identities and assumptions might play out in the classroom.

In many of our classes, you can't grade objectively. Some of our grading is based on, for example, oral presentations or oral qualifying exams for graduate students or a group presentation. Everybody's idea of race comes into play in that kind of an assessment. And I don't think that a lot of people are consciously racist, but I think a lot of people are racist. I think that how you view somebody when they get up to the board, and what you assume about what they know and their qualifications, impacts your assessment a lot. (*Asian American female*)

Similarly, some white faculty spoke explicitly about their social status as members of the dominant group working with a diverse student body that included people from subordinate groups. While they saw the dynamics of intergroup relationships as potentially limiting their effectiveness, they also sometimes saw them as providing an opportunity to talk about race openly or to point out experiences of privilege that students might learn from.

I'm a white teacher, and I'm teaching this class. I mean it's obvious that I need to be thinking and talking about that. . . . I'm wanting to encourage students to talk from their own experience because everybody has experiences with race and racism in this country, whether they think they do or not. As a white teacher I can model this by talking very frankly from my own experience about realizations I've had, ways I've been socialized, things that have happened. . . . I meet with all students individually and we talk about everything, but there are times that I know I'm connecting better obviously with some students than with others. (*white female*)

For the most part I feel like my race is read. And I'm very conscious that students of color are judging, evaluating, interpreting how safe they are with me, what I'm going to do if white students say, as they do, painful and hurtful things. (*white female*)

Many of these faculty members feel that having a clear sense of their own racial identity and social location with regard to race is essential to successful teaching in a diverse classroom.

Pedagogical Challenges

As the student reports from chapters 4 and 5 make clear, when teaching in a diverse setting faculty need to consider how the dominant institutional framework impacts students from different cultural backgrounds. A history of white and male dominance, and the primarily individualistic and competitive cultures of most institutions, suggest that monocultural pedagogical approaches may not be effective for groups of students who have quite different learning styles and preferences. As Anderson and Adams (1992) point out, "One of the most significant challenges that university instructors face is to be tolerant and perceptive enough to recognize learning differences among their students . . . in the way that they process and understand information" (19). These authors summarize differences in communication patterns, motivational styles, and psychosocial characteristics that often occur along gender, racial/ethnic, and economic class lines and that affect how students approach, interact in, and process classroom materials and events (see also Kolb 1981). Culturally responsive forms of instruction—ones that emphasize relational as well as analytical learning styles, oral as well as written performance, active as well as passive instruction, time as well as power tests, and so on—may be more effective with different groups of students.

While recognizing that one style of teaching does not necessarily work well for all students, faculty disagreed regarding the extent to which specific social groups displayed differences in learning styles.

I think that white students tend still to be very individualistic about their work; they're very competitive about their grades. I don't see that as much among Latino/a students. . . . My sense is that Latino/a students all want to get good grades, they are ambitious, and they feel good when they get good grades, but I don't think they have that sense of entitlement that I find sometimes in white students. If white students don't get a good grade, they're knocking on your door and calling your office, sending you e-mails and finding out what went wrong, and why and why and why. . . . Latino/a students tend to accept their grades and I don't find them being so aggressive about that. I think that Latino/a students work better in small-group conversations and when there's discussion. Rather than having to write their own papers, I think that they do a lot more learning—they're more comfortable, it seems to me—when they're doing learning like problem solving and discussing in a small group. (*Latina*)

A lot is made of differences in learning styles. . . . You can say things about groups but then you get individuals from those groups in a small classroom so that you're really focusing on the individual personalities, histories, et cetera. I'll have very affluent African American students who have lived only in white neighborhoods, and I'll have white working-class students who have lived only in black neighborhoods. (*white female*)

One of the critical challenges in this regard, as with all responses to gender and racial/ethnic/cultural differences, is how to address diverse styles without overstating, essentializing, or overgeneralizing them (and without denying or trivializing them). Without presuming that any particular tendency infallibly characterizes members of various cultural and class groupings, faculty should recognize that their potential validity calls for flexible and responsive forms of instruction.

The modern university often equates faculty subject matter mastery with instructional competence; but knowing "how people learn" (Bransford, Brown, and Cocking 2000) is also important. Such pedagogical knowledge includes "information about typical difficulties that students encounter as they attempt to learn about a set of topics; the paths typical students must traverse in order to achieve understanding; and sets of potential strategies for helping students overcome the difficulties that they encounter" (Bransford et al. 2000: 45). This is a difficult enough task when the student population is culturally and stylistically homogenous; when the student population is heterogeneous a wide base of cultural knowledge and a multiplicity of pedagogical options are necessary.

In addition to considering student attributes and styles, faculty must treat the diverse classroom as a social group composed of students who enter carrying various racial/ethnic assumptions and expectations about themselves and others. In acknowledging this issue, Canon (1990) writes that "over time, I gave more and more attention to classroom interaction, which, like all group interactions, is structured by inequalities of power among the participants" (126). Students of the dominant U.S. race (white), gender (male), economic class (upper middle), and intellectual cadre (superior high school and excellent standardized test scores) are likely to have experienced a great deal of time and attention in their elementary and secondary school settings. As suggested in chapter 4, they may

also assume they have superior skills and a greater right to be in college than do'
students of color. Thus, they may quite naturally expect and act out a greater
share of classroom power, ordinarily reflected in comfort, discussion time, grade
expectations, and informal exchanges and attention from with the instructor.
These expectations, or sense of entitlement, are addressed in the preceding excerpt from a Latino faculty member. Unless faculty members can generate educational environments that are safe or open enough to overcome or prevent such
intergroup patterns, that equalize classroom access, participation, and power,
many students (especially students of color, female students, and students from
working- and lower-class backgrounds) will be discouraged from fully engaging
in and benefiting from the learning process.

Faculty members vary considerably regarding whether, when, and how they
feel diversity is relevant to the instructional process. Some feel its relevance
mostly with regard to course content, while others feel its relevance in every aspect of the teaching enterprise. In conversations about what classrooms skills,
strategies, or tactics are important for successfully teaching in a diverse environment, a few faculty stated that no special skills were necessary.

I close my eyes and teach my science. (*white male*)

Even those who did not see any need to modify their teaching strategies, however, generally recognized that racial dynamics were part of the classroom.

Science is science. I don't teach any differently [in a diverse classroom], but I
strongly encourage students to sit in the front, and the black students usually take
me up on that. There is like a higher density of black students in the front than in
the back, and one consequence is that I think they [black students] are more comfortable in class or more comfortable asking questions. . . . If you were going into
a new environment and nobody looked like you or nobody of authority came from
your area, you'd feel a little intimidated. (*African American male*)

Obviously some subject matters lend themselves more directly to concern about
and attention to diversity (one's own and students') than do others. But all classrooms are composed of students and faculty members, and we know that the dynamics that occur overtly or covertly among students, and between students and
faculty, affect the climate of the classroom, students' learning, and faculty satisfaction and esteem. Thus, a concern for and skill in dealing with diverse classroom identities and interactions is always relevant. Moreover, all faculty can
help all students, particularly by recognizing and acting on the reality that the
classroom space (physical and social) may be far more hospitable for some students than for others.

For many faculty, awareness of the relevance of race and gender for the teaching and learning experience emerged over time. Sometimes faculty learned to be

more aware of the possibilities that diversity provided by watching or listening to their students.

> When women who were going through a women's studies department started speaking in my classroom, I began to hear new and exciting voices that had been very rare before. And they really transformed what was possible in my classrooms. The same would be true when gay students came out in classrooms and began to speak. It was at those historical moments, I think, that I began to listen and to deal with what I hadn't been dealing with before, what I'd been unable to look for. (*white male*)

Indeed, having a diverse class can bring dimensions to the academic enterprise not possible otherwise.

> We were talking about a study of men in a low-income, urban community in an undergraduate class, and one of the more outspoken students said, "You all are talking about these people like foreign beings; you never come in contact with them. [But] that's me, and I used to be on the corner," and he went on. Everyone just sort of froze at that moment. We got a real live person from this book, and they had been talking about these people like they were from another planet. That typified to me all the stuff I like—someone that made other people realize that there's some greater significance to what's going on here, it's not just an academic exercise. About eight students stayed after class and talked for another thirty. . . . I was getting ready to leave, and I realized they were still going on, so I sat with them. I felt particularly proud of the fact that people who weren't necessarily great performers felt compelled to spend thirty more minutes on this after class was over. (*African American male*)

For this faculty member, a "teachable moment" had arisen by accident.

Classroom interactions often involve students coming into contact with people who are different from them along a number of dimensions. Many faculty talked about the classroom as a social group with various dynamics that demanded understanding, monitoring, and occasional intervention. Some, when using student groups or teams in class, identified the necessity of deliberately creating mixed groups (thus overcoming the tendency of student segregation):

> The thing we do in science and engineering is emphasizing team building and working in teams. . . . One school of thought goes you should let students form their own teams so they can work together comfortably with people of their own election. . . . There's another school of thought which is basically do it randomly and that's what I do, except that in the middle of the semester I always change groups to allow people to get out of a bad situation. (*Asian American female*)

In addition, however one creates student workgroups or teams, students need preparation in the orientation and skills required to work collaboratively in these situations. They generally do not enter higher education with such skills, and this is especially the case if the teams are diverse. Complicated issues are at play in shaping students' classroom interactions, ranging from racial stereotypes about competence to issues of comfort with both peers and faculty members. Faculty must regularly make strategic decisions about whether, when, and how to pre-structure or intervene to ensure positive intergroup collaboration in work teams. Given the importance of such collaboration, or informal interactional diversity, for student learning, this matter is a critical arena for pedagogical attention.

When race itself becomes a topic of classroom discussion, whether by deliberate instructional plan or by accidental emergence, faculty must draw all students away from defensive and/or attacking postures and into discussion and dialogue. Making courses more multicultural sometimes means addressing difficult or controversial issues. At a minimum, it can bring to the surface topics of race, class, gender, or sexuality that are not normally part of polite conversation. Engaging students in such conversations involves a delicate mix of skills and instructional strategies. The key to doing this successfully, and to taking full advantage of dramatic teachable moments, is to monitor students' emotional and intellectual states, as well as one's own. In addition to content area knowledge, skill with communication and comfort with conflict are key to managing the multicultural classroom.

> A high tolerance for conflict [is important]. Because you never can anticipate exactly what's going to happen when you start pushing people's buttons. And you do push people's buttons, whether you intend to or not. You have to be relatively quick on your feet because things come up that you don't plan for. . . . If people can't challenge you, they won't feel comfortable challenging each other either. (*white female*)

Faculty fear or defensiveness about racial issues can shut down a provocative and enlightening conversation before it has a chance to begin.

> [It's important] simply not to be defensive. To be genuinely interested and unafraid, interested in what people have to say and to be unafraid to hear it. So that whatever happens, you can say, "Yes, I'm sorry I didn't understand that. Thank you for telling me." It's a skill or an attitude of being positive and unafraid and willing to negotiate something, and therefore not stuck on one's authority, privilege, power, that kind of thing. I suppose along with that come particular listening skills, really being able to read an atmosphere and hear what's beneath what's being said. (*white male*)

Some white faculty, especially white men, have been called racist or sexist in class, and have experienced considerable pain as a result. Indeed, it is increasingly common to hear white male faculty talk about feeling embattled or victimized by outspoken students of color in class. White faculty caught by surprise by such challenges, not knowing where they come from or what they might have done (or not done) to provoke such challenges, naturally become more cautious in diverse classroom settings. Irrespective of the merits of any particular case or incident, it is not hard to see how attempts to deal with complex issues of identity and diversity may backfire and cause distress for students and faculty alike.

It is unrealistic to expect students to engage in intergroup behavior that faculty themselves have not mastered. Although faculty in our interview group varied somewhat in their views of proper classroom deportment and the most effective pedagogical strategies, they stressed the importance of setting an example of openness and respect. Faculty often talked about mistakes that they had made in dealing with conflict and the lessons they had learned. Very few thought they had all the answers. Instead, they outlined an evolving set of understandings and skills that grew over time.

> What I learned to do was to not intervene while it's happening. One is where someone has simply spoken up and said, very strongly, "What you just said is racist." And that person is outspoken, has great command of language, and is very angry. . . . Your opposite case, of course, is the one where you're in a discussion and you know that the language you're hearing from other students is itself racist—innocently maybe. . . . You can feel other students getting ready to move in on them. Or they're just feeling very uncomfortable, feeling silenced. And again you can feel very high tension in the room. . . . Those I wait to see what happens [before jumping in]. And I really try to work with the person who made those comments, if they're keeping a journal or if I catch them after class. . . . So when I get tension in class, I didn't used to be able to do this, but now I don't intervene real quick, I let people play out what they need to do. Then we have something real in front of us because these are real expressions of what's in people's minds, [and we can learn from it]. (*white male*)

The principal multicultural pedagogical challenges reported by faculty involve techniques of delivering material so as to address diverse student styles and skills, managing the dynamics of heterogeneous classrooms that are embedded in institutional and societal cultures of racism and sexism, and dealing with emergent incidents or tensions among different groups of students.

Curricular Challenges

Curricular and pedagogical issues are intertwined. In chapter 10, we focus attention on the challenge of multicultural curricular reform, which Gurin (1999) refers to as "classroom diversity" and which refers to how fully course content attempts to include information about diverse groups. The content of the curriculum lies at the very core of the academic and teaching/learning enterprise. But trying to create multicultural curricular materials may lead some faculty to enter areas in which they doubt their competence. Many faculty have trouble deciding what new material to include, how to include it, and what changes in the standard disciplinary content are necessary to accommodate it. Moreover, initiating curricular change can raise issues with fellow faculty who feel that such reforms challenge disciplinary priorities and boundaries. Curricular and pedagogical innovations thus can have major organizational implications.

Structural Challenges

Departmental and organizational norms establish the institutional ground rules for the support (or lack of support) and rewards (or sanctions) that faculty members experience. In departments and colleges that do not place a priority on teaching excellence, faculty are unlikely to invest much effort in innovative teaching. And even in environments where teaching is genuinely valued, faculty at research-oriented universities must balance their teaching efforts with the demands of a research-oriented career. The reward structure for the professoriate strongly influences how faculty members allocate their time and energy. If teaching in a diverse classroom takes additional time and energy, and evidences the need to do some things quite differently, the level of risk that a particular faculty member will undertake depends to some extent on the degree of support offered at the departmental level.

Aside from the question of institutional support for teaching, challenges rooted in the organizational structure of faculty life often arise. For example, women faculty and faculty of color often discuss concerns about the quality of mentoring and peer collegiality (Chesler and Chesler 2002; Padilla and Chavez 1995; Rowe 1993; Tierney and Bensimon 1996; Turner and Myers 2000). Other challenges are generated by various organizational factors, such as those noted in figure 6.1, that influence the attitudes and expectations that faculty bring with them into their classrooms and their interactions with colleagues.

Given how difficult some of this work is, it is important to find support for multicultural teaching. Certain white faculty members, especially, reported that they had received substantial support from the institution for their teaching in general and for their multicultural teaching in particular. Some of this support came directly from their home departments.

> I think that most of my colleagues view how I teach [pursue issues in ways that may benefit racial or ethnic minorities] pretty positively. . . . I think generally that my commitment to teaching and the fact that I do a good job of it has been appreciated by the department. I think the way I've gone the extra mile . . . making sure that the students who come in less prepared have an equal opportunity to succeed has been appreciated more by some people than by others. (*white male*)

White faculty also endorsed teaching workshops or departmental retreats focused on diversity issues, on the special needs or styles of particular populations, or on their own identities and roles, as helpful to them.

Several faculty of different racial and ethnic backgrounds also talked about being regarded by their peers as instructional leaders, receiving respect and admiration from their peers for good teaching or for diversity-related work.

> My colleagues think that I am a fine teacher. I do have a bit of a reputation on that [diversity issues], so I think it's very positive. I'm not an expert on that [racial diversity], but people do seek my counsel sometimes. (*African American male*)

On the other hand, some faculty of color felt that their colleagues avoided dealing with these issues by using them as resources for anything related to diversity or race.

> When I was hired . . . my dissertation had to do with black people, and that was enough. They started calling me the multicultural person. But I don't do multiculturalism. So they'll send students to me and I'm like, "That's not my area—I can't help you." But anything dealing with black people or people of color, they just send all those students to me. (*African American female*)

Moreover, just because other faculty recognized a colleague as knowing something important about multiculturalism did not mean they valued that knowledge highly—at least not at tenure and promotion time. A reputation as a multicultural resource may not always pay off as well as other kinds of disciplinary mastery.

> I think most of my colleagues see me as somebody who knows a lot about this stuff [multiculturalism]. Now whether or not they value it is a whole other question. Some people think this is really important, it's really great, and we should be doing more of it. I have colleagues who, when they're working on an article that has to do with multicultural teaching or multicultural work, will ask me to read drafts of their articles. So I'm seen in some ways as a resource. There are other colleagues who think either this is a fad or it's not central, or who simply don't care about teaching at all. So it doesn't matter to them if it's multicultural teaching or any kind of teaching. (*Latina*)

Some of these issues arise because of assumptions and presumptions about race and gender that shape social interactions, including ones on campus. In particular, faculty of color often must deal with white colleagues who have limited experience interacting with racial minorities as peers.

> I mean, it's benign neglect. Even here in this school I was marginalized. I was not put on any committees or made chairman of any major committees. I was just marginalized. And that's how the school dealt with me as a black faculty member.

When I first came here, these faculty members had never dealt with a black person as an equal. (*African American male*)

The chair of the department said, "Can you write a memo explaining what a Hispanic is?" No one at the university seems to understand this, including herself. So that was interesting—like explaining basic Hispanic history and whatever in a memo for people with Ph.D.'s. (*Latina*)

Several other researchers have noted the degree to which faculty members of varied racial/ethnic groups experience feelings of ostracism and marginalization (Turner and Myers 2000).

Because of their small numbers, faculty of color on campus are often faced with the burden of multiple kinds of extra work. As one of a small number of faculty of color they often are asked to serve as minority representatives on multiple committees, to act as liaisons to racial/ethnic community groups, to participate in many minority-related programs, to advise or mentor large numbers of students of color, and to "handle" racial conflicts (Aguirre 1995; Fogg 2003; Garcia 2000; Harris and Nettles 1996). Several faculty talked about the different specific tasks that cost them time and energy.

In my current life, I think I've been a beneficiary of affirmative action and all that stuff, so in many respects my race has been a benefit to me. But I also think it creates an enormous amount of work for the same reasons. People want some woman of color or some person of color to be sitting on every committee, being everywhere, and that includes the students. . . . I feel like I get pressured, I get these e-mails from other Latino groups, and it's always like, "How come more of the faculty aren't at the various events we organize?" (*Latina*)

This includes feeling responsible for mentoring and nurturing junior colleagues and students.

As the only tenured woman of color in my department, I feel responsible for mentoring the junior faculty who are women and minorities. I feel like I need to be in there to make sure that those things get done and get done in the right way. So in many ways it's almost like because of my identity I actually have too much to do. (*Latina*)

Many faculty also detected institutional ambivalence about the multicultural work they undertook, whether in the form of innovative curriculum development or mentoring and advising students and colleagues of color. This ambivalence may arise from mixed feelings about multiculturalism or from the delicate task of prioritizing teaching within a research university. Beyond ambivalence and competing messages, some faculty noted that their expressed and demonstrated commitments to teaching and to multicultural teaching had real costs.

[I have been accused of being soft on minority students,] and I say, "That's fine, because that's what I'm here for." Well, not necessarily being soft but paying attention to them in class, validating what they have to say, recognizing their presence and the perspectives that they bring to class. . . . And when that has come up I say, "Good." Because the nonminority students get that validation every place else, and many of the [minority] students don't get it in the other classes. . . . At the same time, I think I'm not being soft on them because I have very high expectations of the work they can do, and I push them toward that. (*Latina*)

To transcend the institution's mixed messages and ambivalent support for multicultural teaching, faculty we spoke to focused various efforts on creating community on campus. Some faculty organized formal groups to share ideas and renew each others' energy; others sought opportunities to team-teach with colleagues who had similar teaching philosophies and commitments.

EXPERIENCES OF DIFFERENTIALLY SITUATED FACULTY

The challenges discussed above take different shape in diverse classes and faculty with different social identities do not experience and respond to these challenges in the same ways.

White Faculty

Although the literature on diversity-related views of elementary and secondary school teachers is quite broad, the available scholarship on white collegiate faculty is surprisingly small. Some white educators, however, have provided in-depth looks into their own and their peers' experiences and concerns. For example, Messner (2000) believes that white male faculty are likely to be evaluated more positively by students than are women professors or faculty of color. He attributes this tendency, in part, to the fact that white males more closely fit students' preconceptions of what a professor looks like. Goodman (2001) reflects on the "bond of unstated but understood affirmation between white male students and a white male instructor" (75, quoting Allsup). Under such circumstances, when a white male instructor "reveals and challenges the system of white male privilege, white male students may feel betrayed. They may become angry when the educator acts in ways that violate the implicit norms that maintain oppression and the assumption that 'he is one of us.'" Katz (1991) reports that white faculty he interviewed were very cautious about discussing racial issues in class for fear of raising either white guilt and anger or anger from black students. As one of our white female faculty respondents put it, "The fear of being called a racist if you're a white liberal is very strong." Weinstein and O'Bear (1992) have categorized some concerns of white faculty in response to a question regarding what things make them nervous about raising or attending to issues of racism in class. The concerns include confronting social identity conflicts, confronting or being confronted with biases, responding to bias and discrimination when it occurs, handling doubts about competency, needing approval from students, and handling intense emotions. All these issues may be universal for instructors in the teaching–learning situation, but in diverse and multicultural situations they generally are more potent and problematic. For here, the faculty (like the students) are more vulnerable, both in their clarity about their identities and attitudes, and in their location in the cauldron of contemporary intergroup differences, conflict, and struggle.

White Women Faculty

White female faculty obviously face many of the same dilemmas and challenges as do white male faculty. In addition, however, the press of workplace sexism poses additional challenges. Theodore's study (1986) of several hundred academic women who protested sex discrimination provides ample anecdotal evidence of their struggle against gender stereotypes, marginalization, and sexual harassment. In addition, campus personnel policies and departmental norms often operate in ways that make women's academic advancement more difficult. Of the 470 women reporting employment-related complaints in Theodore's study, 34 percent discussed concerns about salary equity, 19 percent discussed concerns about promotion procedures, and 40 percent discussed incidents of harassment.

Female faculty in the natural sciences, math, and engineering (SME) report some of the particular difficulties incumbent upon their entry, retention, and advancement in predominantly male academic fields. In 2001, for instance, only 8.9 percent of the nation's tenured or tenure-track faculty in SME were female, and only 4.4 percent were at the full professor level (American Society of Engineering Education 2001). While gender-based patterns of socialization and education may affect women's early career choices, once in the scientific academy female scientists report lower levels of social support and fewer collegial interactions than their male counterparts (Etkowitz, Kemelgor, and Uzzi 2000).

Women faculty in all academic fields constantly struggle with establishing balance between their professional and personal lives in ways different than do men. The nature of gender-based expectations and divisions of labor continue to place on women most of the demands of managing family life and the many decisions involved in having and caring for children. According to Wilson (2003; see also Mason and Goulden 2002), having children early in their academic careers can threaten women's job and advancement potential. The physical and emotional time and energy demands of motherhood often place women at a disadvantage compared to their male colleagues. These special responsibilities, and some of their costs, continue even in the face of enlightened policies of parental leave, tenure clock extension, and child care provision.

Faculty of Color

The literature discussing the experiences of faculty of color, which concentrates on African Americans and Latino/as, emphasizes that these faculty are numerically rare and feel considerable stress and pressure. For example, Padilla and Chavez (1995) note how Latino/a professors are "stigmatized and excluded from many of the social networks in academia" (7–8). And Johnsrud (1993) points out that faculty of color "cite everyday interactions, both social and professional, as sources of their feeling unwelcomed, unappreciated and unwanted" (7). The result is a loss of formal and informal collegiality.

Perhaps the most obvious evidence of such marginalization involves the reported difficulty junior faculty of color experience in finding mentors within the academy. Involvement in mentoring is important for all junior faculty, but it is especially so for colleagues who are culturally underrepresented in the institution. As Blackshire-Belay notes (1998), "If senior professors fail to reach out to junior colleagues from different racial or ethnic backgrounds, problems can arise. . . . White senior professors often seek out white junior faculty members whom they feel they can help. These senior white professors may be less willing to do the same with their black (or Latino/a or Asian American or Native American) junior colleagues" (33–34). Without such guidance, support, and advocacy, faculty of color often are unconnected to sources of funding and opportunities for professional presentations of their work, and may be uninformed about what it takes to be seen as a good departmental citizen or an appropriate candidate for tenure and promotion. Indeed, such isolation and lack of information amount to a form of institutional racism, inviting the perception that denial of tenure or promotion is due to racial/ethnic discrimination (Turner and Myers 2000). Similar difficulties in finding and using senior mentors are often encountered by junior female scholars as well (Chesler and Chesler 2002; Clark and Corcoran 1986; Johnsrud 1993).

Another example of marginalization is reflected in the ghettoization of black faculty or the barrioization of Latino/a faculty (Garza 1993). Faculty of color often are expected to advise minority students in their departments and are assigned to faculty committees dealing with cultural matters and student recruitment. Frequently they are asked to teach courses that focus on disciplinary issues related to race and ethnicity and to introduce their own identity group expertise into the curriculum—perhaps to be "the ethnic resource for the entire institution" (Turner and Myers 2000: 33). Since many departments and colleges generally see such roles as peripheral rather than central to their academic mission, they seldom reward faculty of color who play these roles; thus it is a form of "cultural taxation" (Aguirre 1995).

Faculty of color often reported that they faced other challenges, burdens, and obligations not ordinarily encountered by white faculty. For example, many reported that they faced a series of challenges to their authority inside and outside the classroom, necessitating a slightly different stance in the teaching process.

I can't do things that a white person can do and vice versa. I think white people can challenge white people in certain ways that may cause white people to listen [better] than if I challenge them because then—particularly if they're not open—they will just say that I have an agenda, or I become the racist in the classroom, or it becomes some kind of perversion like that. (*African American male*)

Women of color in particular felt that they did not have the same flexibility as their white and male peers when thinking about innovative or nontraditional pedagogical strategies.

I don't walk into a classroom expecting that my white students and particularly my white and male students will automatically accept that I'm a scholar in my area. My white colleagues can do that. I think a lot of students come in expecting that, "Oh, a black professor—I'm not going to learn that much and I'm not going to learn that much about anything that's real." I think my white colleagues can teach about lettuce heads for a whole semester, and that doesn't have anything to do with what they're supposed to be teaching, and it's automatically assumed that the knowledge is there but this may be sort of an eccentric person. I could not get away with that. Not at all. No. (*African American female*)

Regular challenges to their status meant that these faculty of color would find it difficult to, as a white colleague suggested earlier in this chapter, "close my eyes and teach my science." Indeed, regular challenges to their status as faculty (from students and from colleagues) meant that they often had to juggle the additional burden of repeatedly proving or demonstrating their expertise and maintaining their authority as faculty members while trying to be accessible to students. As Messner (2000) suggests, "Women and/or faculty of color faced a set of paradoxical options . . . either solidify your professional status at the expense of appearing rigid and distant or break down the social distance and risk undercutting your legitimacy as the professor" (413).

Peers and colleagues also sometimes questioned and challenged the status and authority of faculty of color as professors, and even their rightful place on campus. In some cases the questioning was subtle, paternalistic, and perhaps not consciously designed.

I wasn't getting across to the rest of my colleagues. And so I was commenting on this to this one colleague, and he said, "Well, you have a problem. Just tell me what you want to say, and I'll say it for you." I think he had a good intention; he was trying to be helpful. But he didn't understand the gender politics of that. That has been something I have seen a lot in committees, where you say something and then another person comes who has more authority, as deemed by others, as given by other people, and somehow they say the same idea and then they get recognized for that idea. (*Latina*)

The literature reporting and discussing the experiences of faculty of color has progressed beyond the black–white syndrome to include numerous analyses of Latino/a faculty. But there is as yet little discussion of the experiences of Native American or Asian American faculty. The recent work of Turner and Myers (2000) presents the voices of these faculty of color as well, and indicates some unique situations they face. As these authors indicate, American Indian or Native American faculty especially face the dilemma of maintaining "ties to their own community while at the same time being part of a culturally incompatible academic community" (98)—a situation exacerbated by there being very few colleagues of their own cultures on campus. Asian American faculty report concerns about language: not their own difficulty, but the ways in which "others often perceived them as not being able to adequately speak or fully comprehend English" (99). This reaction is part of a larger perception of the Asian American scholar as not American, an image embedded in patterns of a priori marginalization (see, e.g., Takaki 1993). For these scholars as well, the notion that they are part of a "model minority" often leads to overlooking the ways in which they also are subject to both blatant and subtle forms of racial/ethnic discrimination and exclusion from collegial activities.

Women Faculty of Color:
The Special Case of Double Jeopardy

The situation of women of color in the academy is so perilous that it deserves special attention. On a variety of dimensions, Allen-Brown (1998) argues, "African American women are even further away than Euro American women in achieving equality within the academy" (170). Moses (1989) discusses examples of the double jeopardy (on the basis of race and gender) in her interviews with black female academics: "barriers to growth and success . . . such as support, retention, research, teaching, and tenure are affected by the climate for black women at both predominantly white institutions and historically black institutions" (13). Similarly, the interviews conducted and excerpted in detail in Turner and Myers (2000) eloquently delineate some of the professional and personal dilemmas that women of color in the academy experience: feeling isolated and underrespected ("tokenism" and "lack of collegiality" in Moses's terms), being underemployed and overused (or "ghettoized/barrioized"), and being challenged by students with regard to their credibility, expertise, and authority.

Gay, Lesbian, Bisexual, and Transgender Faculty

Our interviews with University of Michigan faculty did not explore issues of sexual orientation; nor is there a large literature on faculty members who are openly gay, lesbian, bisexual, or transgender. No doubt these gaps represent both the limited number of out individuals on campus as well as the continuing existence of homophobia and heterosexism and its effects. They often combine to deprive gay/lesbian faculty of a sense of community as well as full participation in the larger academic enterprise.

The literature that is available points to a number of relatively unique challenges faced by these faculty. The central dilemma of coming out in a potentially hostile environment occupies many first-person stories, such as those presented in the collection by Mintz and Rothblum (1997). As Stuck (1997) notes, "Far and away, the major theme emerging from this collection of narratives is 'outness', with this issue reflecting both differences and similarities among the lesbian academics" (211). Rhoads (1997) also notes the ways in which fears of rejection, marginalization, and outright discrimination or harassment affect the personal and professional lives of lesbian, gay, and bisexual faculty. Decisions regarding openness or announcement of sexual orientation affected informants' approaches to job interviews and discussions (e.g., regarding acceptance or rejection and negotiating partner benefits and course focus), choice of research focus (e.g., whether to study and write about lesbian/gay topics), and expectations of interactions with students in and out of the classroom. Experiences with discrimination on both overt and covert bases were common, with many reporting a lack of institutional concern for their particular life circumstances.

Working-Class Faculty

Available literature also points to a number of challenges faced by faculty from working-class or poor origins. These range from having to contend with small everyday affronts such as affluent colleagues' stereotypical views of working-class families and casual and unthinking statements about vacation homes or social networks to lacking access to very basic information about the rules of the game, internal workings of the profession, and other resources which provide important competitive advantages (Dews and Law 1995). At every stage of the academic pipeline, poor and working-class students (and future faculty) are generally underrepresented and they are underrepresented to a higher degree at more elite and higher-prestige institutions. Aside from just being underrepresented, their daily experiences make persisting and thriving in the academy challenging. The few studies of working-class faculty generally report persistent feelings of never quite fitting in, of not being equipped for the norms of "genteel" interaction: "I still think of them as 'them,' although I have graduate degrees and have been on a college faculty for decades. I am not comfortable with middle-class gentility" (LaPaglia 1995: 177). Moreover, with the persistent invisibility of class in this country and our almost total silence about its effects, working-class faculty receive little unique support or recognition.

TAKING ADVANTAGE OF THE OPPORTUNITY DIVERSITY PROVIDES

Given the current state of race, gender, and class discrimination on campuses, as well as the ways in which many students from underrepresented or subordinated groups find themselves excluded and alienated from the academic environment, the natural social process is one of continuing separation, distrust, and nonengagement in mutual learning activities. In the face of these tendencies, faculty members must be proactive in dealing with the diverse classroom and must carefully plan and design ways to create a positive intergroup learning environment. Attention to the impact of one's own social identity on students—and vice versa, the creation of safe classroom spaces for exploration of these issues, the development of searching and compassionate dialogues among students and between students and instructors, and the construction of equal status relationships—can lead to transformed classrooms.

In addition to faculty action in classrooms, it also is clear that similar phenomena of monoculturalism and intergroup alienation pervade many departments and negatively affect faculty members' quality of life. Individual faculty, faculty leaders, departmental chairs, and administrative staffs must apply the same principles to faculty departmental relationships as faculty can apply to the classroom. Here, too, the creation of safe spaces for difference and for dialogue, conversations about social identity and its links to mutual engagement, attention to the impacts of social identity on divisions of faculty labor, design of activities that assume and realize equal status peer relations, and attention to the creation and operation of intergroup collaboration, can lead to transformed collegial and organizational relationships.

NOTE

1. The original material reported here comes from in-depth interviews with forty tenured and tenure-track faculty at the University of Michigan. We selected faculty for these interviews on the basis of their reputations as outstanding instructors and, especially, as thoughtful practitioners of teaching in diverse classrooms. Thus, we made no attempt to gather a representative sample (for survey data of a more representative character on similar issues, see Astin et al. 1997) but rather tried to solicit the most advanced thinking

and experience on these issues. The faculty interviewed had diverse racial/ethnic and gender backgrounds, taught in diverse disciplines, and held various ranks. We analyzed the interviews by a variety of techniques, most prominently ones using grounded theory procedures of inductive analysis to determine and organize central themes. The portions of the interviews presented in this chapter focused on what it meant for these faculty to try to teach a diverse student body and how they understood themselves, their students, and their roles in this endeavor. We identify the author of each excerpt by race/ethnicity and gender.

We appreciate the collegial efforts of Alford Young, Sherri-Ann Butterfield, Patrice Dickerson, Julica Hermann, Chavella Pittman, and Luis Ponjuan in generating and analyzing these materials.

Chapter Seven

Collegiate/University Boards, Presidents, and Senior Officials

Governing and Administering with Diversity

A third major membership group (in addition to students and faculty) in the operation of colleges and universities consists of administrative and support staff. In this chapter we focus on administrative leadership groups—the governing board and senior officers (president and vice presidents)—with lesser attention to other administrators (e.g., deans and department chairs) and staff members (comptroller and physical plant and student services staffs). Other administrators and staff members are important actors within higher education organizations, but the board and president set the tone and norms for the college, interpret and rank various priorities, distribute resources to and impose sanctions on middle management personnel, and provide leadership. They are among the most important players in the challenge to overcome racism and move toward multiculturalism.

We begin by identifying some characteristics of these complicated, multi-structured higher education organizations and their implications for leadership roles regarding diversity and multiculturalism. We then provide data on the racial and gender diversity of senior leaders and administrators and some of their views about diversity and multiculturalism in colleges and universities, paying special attention to the views of leaders of elite institutions because they so often define the framework for debates and struggles in higher education nationally. Finally, we look at future challenges faced by board members and administrators as they seek to maintain and increase diversity and to develop more fully multicultural higher education organizations.

ORGANIZATIONAL CONDITIONS AND CHALLENGES

Colleges and universities are substantially different formal organizations from corporations, governmental agencies, or community groups. As Sporn (1999) notes, "Colleges and universities . . . exhibit some critical distinguishing characteristics that affect their decision processes: goal ambiguity, client service, task complexity, professionalism and administrative values, and environmental vulnerability" (25; see also Baldridge et al. 1977; Bensimon, Neumann, and Birnbaum 1989; Gmelch 1995).

In dealing with institutionalized racism, diversity, and multiculturalism, administrative leadership is shaped and challenged by these organizational characteristics. The complexity of teaching, research, and service presents a challenge to all membership groups in colleges and universities, but it imposes particular dilemmas for officials who must mediate the allocation of rewards for these different and potentially conflicting tasks. The existence of multifaceted or contested goals and multiple tasks often makes establishing clear or measurable outcomes difficult, reducing the possibility of maintaining accountability for performance. Furthermore, whereas professional academics typically emphasize knowledge and autonomy, administrators generally emphasize operational efficiency and control, and students typically emphasize learning and social development. These disparate value clusters form the bases for multiple subcultures and conflicts among constituency groups within higher education. Greater diversity in academic organizations accelerates the tendency toward multiple goals, competing power centers, and increased vulnerability to external environmental forces.

Organizational theorists and researchers have applied various lenses or models to depict the different structures of academic organizations and to determine how presidents and other academic leaders use them to understand and act on their roles and options. Baldridge (1971) and Baldridge et al. (1977) originally suggested three models of the university: a bureaucracy, a collegium, and a political system. Bolman and Deal (1984) and later Bensimon (1989) and Bensimon et al. (1989) modified this typology by renaming two of the original lenses and adding a fourth: structural (corresponding roughly to Baldridge's bureaucratic model), human relations (corresponding roughly to Baldridge's collegium model), political (corresponding to Baldridge's political model), and symbolic.

The *bureaucratic or structural model* envisions an administrative organization that relies heavily on hierarchical authority and role specialization. The president and the vice presidents who report to her or him hold positions at the apex of this structure. Administrators make decisions authoritatively, each level being subject to the authority of the next higher level, with the president occupying the center of power. The key leadership group is composed of nonfaculty staff members, although a small number of the top officials are simultaneously members of the faculty, and others may be ex-members.

The *human relations* or *collegium model* interprets the university as a collegially structured academic organization in which academic professionals hold leadership roles. Decision making is characterized by consensus-based and democratic agreements among faculty peers operating with a high degree of interpersonal contact and with individual and subgroup autonomy. Subgroups comprise multiple and separate disciplines or professions whose members pursue teaching and research subject to the legal and fiscal authority of the board and administration. The president, typically a former senior faculty member, is seen as a member of this collective enterprise and as the first among equals.

The *political model* views the organization as being composed of multiple interest groups—some internal (staff, faculty, students), some boundary spanners (boards), and some external (state legislators, business leaders, and involved publics). Here, the varied groups or constituencies contend for power, each with competing needs and resources and with different disciplinary, professional, economic, and political visions for higher education. Decision making depends on processes of competition and conflict that lead to negotiated (and on rare occasions consensus-based) agreements. The president and sometimes the board mediate among competing interests and interest groups.

The *symbolic organizational model* emphasizes the relevance of common cultural beliefs and values among students, faculty, staff, administration, and board. Systems of meaning that validate the life, work, and study of organizational members are most apparent in the organization's distinctive identity, traditions and rituals. Individuals' tasks and roles are grounded in the deep culture of the organization, which often provides unstated or subconscious guidance in how to behave. The president is responsible for articulating the symbolic meaning of the organization, often leading important rituals and nurturing and facilitating others' growth. This model of collegiate and university organization is the least documented and most poorly analyzed of the four identified here.

While each of these models describes some aspects of all colleges and universities, one or another of them may be best for describing operational arrangements within particular organizations or organizational subunits. For instance, small liberal arts colleges and academic departments are likely to reflect major elements of the collegium model, although many departments may operate more like the political model. Major staff units, such as administration and finance, generally operate on the bureaucratic model, as do many community colleges; major research universities are less inclined to adopt this model. Religious colleges and some others with a clearly focused mission may appear to fit the symbolic model most closely. But the symbolic model also operates in secular institutions, where the core values and rituals of science, pluralism, and other aspects of modernity hold sway.

These four models also correlate with the dimensions of formal and academic organizations presented in figure 3.2. The bureaucratic model emphasizes the power and decisional system of the college or university and processes of re-source allocation. The collegium model emphasizes the importance of organiza-tional climate, while focusing attention as well on the culture of professionalism and expertise expressed through technologies of curriculum formation and ped-agogy. The political model clearly gives special weight to the power dimension of organizational functioning, including the negotiation of boundary relation-ships. And the symbolic model focuses on the importance of mission, culture, and membership.

MEMBERSHIP CHARACTERISTICS
ASSOCIATED WITH DIFFERENT MODELS

From the founding of the first colleges in colonial times through the emer-gence of universities in the latter part of the nineteenth century and continu-ing to the present, U.S. higher education has relied primarily on the bureau-cratic, political, and symbolic models. As a result, administrators have emphasized elite management of the organization, authoritarian control of subordinates, and a consensus or orthodoxy of basic values. Although the ar-chitectures of the bureaucratic and political models remain intact, the content of the orthodoxy upheld in the third model has changed substantially, as Christian religion has been replaced by secular humanism, rationalism, and the norms of science and empiricism. Moreover, as the size and status of the faculty grew, they gained the power to set standards for tenure and to be re-sponsible for setting and monitoring the content and standards of teaching, research, and students' education and degree requirements. Thus, the faculty gained substantial influence and autonomy vis-à-vis senior administrators, eventually leading to a more pluralistic notion of the bureaucratic model and widespread acceptance of norms of academic freedom in teaching and re-search. In the last decade, a consumer-oriented culture has encouraged stu-dent and parents (and in many instances community members) to try to play a more potent political role in organizational decisions.

Over time the core values, membership requirements, and sense of who be-longs in higher education have changed to include some people who stand out-side the dominant white male culture: people of color, women, and openly gay and lesbian people. These membership changes have forced greater complexity in all the organizational models that historically were developed and maintained by white males, primarily in their own interest and that of their core constituen-cies. For example, some women have challenged the degree of top-down au-thority and influence (characteristic of the bureaucratic and political models and practices) with more collaborative and consultative forms of authority. As the numbers of people of color have increased in colleges and universities their cultural values and practices have gained expression and legitimacy within the symbolic model and its applications. The general impacts of these basic changes in membership have included questioning any "one best way" to administer organizations, contests over the introduction of more diverse leadership policies and practices, occasional suppression of the expression of diverse values and practices, and the development of pockets of innovation potentially leading to redefinitions of these basic models.

U.S. higher education organizations became increasingly politicized in the mid–twentieth century (primarily after World War II), when universities expanded their number of academic specializations and their service relationships to the state and to external constituencies. The most influential of these new specializations developed around issues of national security and national or local economic development. As these changes occurred, the relationships between universities and local communities or regions became stronger and more complex. The effort to educate students for specialized professions added to the tension between disciplinarily defined basic research and applied research, and between the liberal arts and the professions and professional schools. These differentiations led to the formation of multiple internal interest groups, each with competing needs for financial resources and with differing understandings about the organization of knowledge, the primacy of basic or applied research, and the relationship and accountability of the organization to society outside the university. Today, as faculty specialization continues to increase, it poses serious challenges to collegial relationships and patterns of collective and collaborative decision making. In addition, faculty sometimes find their traditional autonomy in teaching and research roles increasingly challenged as outsiders pressure colleges and universities to achieve greater efficiency and accountability based on externally controlled evaluations, rankings, and accreditations. Throughout the course of these changes, and the entry of women and small numbers of people of color, a dominant coalition of white male administrators and faculty members continued to create and maintain the core structures and norms of higher education until the 1970s.

The daily impact of these structural, demographic, and political changes in membership patterns in higher education organizations resonate at all levels of the administrative system. Given the tendency for racial diversity to occur sooner and to be greater at the lower and middle levels of these organizations, the challenges of daily administrative leadership are especially severe for middle management. Whether as chairs of academic departments, supervisors of physical plant or service operations, or directors of residential life programs, middle managers face constant pressure to transform entrenched patterns of exclusion, discrimination, and domination. They often try to do this with insufficient training, resources, leadership, or models from above.

DIVERSITY IN BOARDS, PRESIDENCIES,
AND SENIOR ADMINISTRATIVE ROLES

Board Diversity

Boards of trustees, regents, or governors of higher education institutions have ultimate legal authority over the policies and practices of U.S. colleges and universities. They are the public's representatives in maintaining oversight and holding colleges and universities accountable to external constituencies; at the same time they act as protectors of these organizations and as buffers between them and external forces (e.g., alumni, state and federal legislators and agencies, and the public at large). As Zumeta (2001) points out, nonacademic governing boards of public colleges and universities interpose some distance between local and state political officials and the operations of these organizations. But how much influence boards have or should have, and how deeply they should get involved in internal organizational matters, are matters of ongoing debate and discussion.

The most recent comprehensive data on racial/ethnic representation comes from surveys conducted by the Association of Governing Boards of Universities and Colleges (Madsen 1997a, 1997b). Surveys sent to nearly 1,100 governing boards resulted in data from 67 percent (364 out of 543) of the independent colleges and university boards and 55 percent (293 out of 535) of the public college and university boards. As of 1997, 89.6 percent of the board members of the independent colleges and universities were white; 6.5 percent were African American, 2.1 percent were Latino/a, and 1.8 percent were members of other racial/ethnic minorities (Madsen 1997a). With regard to public institutions in 1997, 82.7 percent of board members were white, 10.8 percent were African American, 3.1 percent were Latino/a, and 2.6 percent were members of other racial/ethnic minorities (Madsen 1997b). Although these data show some progress in racial/ethnic representation over the past three decades, they document the continuing domination of whites on the governing bodies of higher education institutions. Moreover, these data evidently include members of the boards of HBCUs (historically black colleges and universities) and HSIs (Hispanic-serving institutions); if these institutions were excluded, the extent of white dominance would be even greater. The disproportionately low level of representation of people of color on these higher education boards is consistent with the low representation of people of color at the highest levels of most institutions in the U.S. economy and polity.

As current board members and presidents seek new board members, they typically call on people in their own social and academic networks. Thus, Floyd (1995) suggests, "Typically, the low representation of women and minorities on boards of trustees has been accounted for by the fact that few female or minority individuals have had the opportunity or connections which would prepare them for appointment to a board" (104). In addition, even when women and people of color are represented on boards, they may be marginalized and excluded from the most important board committees, and their views may be discounted by the white and male majority.

Presidential Diversity

While boards of regents or trustees play vital roles in legitimating organizational governance, college and university presidents are the most powerful figures within local higher education organizations. Gross and Grambsch's (1977) early studies of how participants are perceived on their local campuses demonstrate that others see presidents as the most powerful players. Their roles in setting goals, deciding policies, leading decision-making groups, and representing the organization to the external environment solidify their formal status. And despite the role played by individually powerful faculty members, visible or invisible coalitions of senior administrators and faculty, or interested state legislators, the preeminent status of the president on campus has remained largely unchanged.

Given the social importance of their role, and the racial/ethnic and gender characteristics of the governing boards who select or appoint them, it is not surprising that as of the late 1990s most college and university presidents (and provosts or vice presidents—particularly academic provosts or vice presidents) continue to be white males. The most recently available data on the gender and race of presidents of colleges and universities is available in an American Council on Education (ACE; 2002a) study indicating that as of 2001, 21.1 percent of college presidencies were held by women and 12.8 percent by members of racial minorities. These figures represent substantial increases from 1986 data, when women held 9.5 percent of these positions and members of racial minorities held 8.1 percent. However, the ACE study also indicates that the rate of growth in numbers of women and minority college presidents has slowed in the past decade. Even the ACE's figures must be interpreted cautiously, since a number of the minority presidents were leaders of HBCUs or HSIs. Further, women and minority presidents are more common at two-year colleges and at public institutions. As of 2001, in public two-year institutions, minorities held 14.9 percent of the presidencies and women 27 percent. At the other end of the status spectrum, in private doctoral-granting universities, minorities held 3.4 percent of the presidencies and women 8.7 percent (ACE 2002b).

Judith McLaughlin, head of the Harvard Seminar for New Presidents, has closely observed the results of searches for presidents of colleges and universities. Commenting on the differential rates of appointments of women to different types of higher education organizations, she says, "Higher education, like it or not, has always been a sort of status or class organization. . . . The sense is that the highest class or highest prestige are research universities. With any glass ceiling, it's easier to break into lower-prestige entities first. Institutions tend to look for their own for the presidential position" (Lively 2000: A31). McLaughlin further observes that even accounting for candidates' level of experience, race often acts as a filter for the lower evaluation of the credentials of minority candidates. And even while acknowledging that people of color are more likely to lead community colleges and two-year institutions than four-year institutions, Vaughan (1996) remarks on the low level of minority leadership in those institutions that enroll the largest number of minority students. In his studies of community college presidents and boards, he concludes, "Clearly minority membership at the presidential level does not reflect the diversity that we might expect to exist in an institution committed to embracing equal opportunity for all, at least in the student realm" (5).

Several college presidents also have commented on the continuing racial homogeneity and stratification of senior leadership positions in higher education. For instance, Barbara Gitenstein (2002), president of the College of New Jersey, notes:

> In the culture of academe, whether we like it or not, there is a hierarchy of institutions. At the very top, by most people's standards, are the Ivy League institutions. In summer 2001, there were three women who serve as presidents of Ivy League universities—two of whom began their tenure in summer 2001. And when Ruth Simmons was named president of Brown University, she became the first African American to assume a presidency in the Ivy League. (44)

Consistent with representational patterns in organizations throughout society, as well as in university faculty, fewer people of color and women occupy these leadership roles at the higher-status educational organizations.

Overall Administrative Diversity

Complementary 1999 data pertaining to the 159,000 executive, administrative, and managerial staff positions in U.S. higher education are also informative. Men held 52 percent of these leadership positions and white people (men and women) held 85 percent of them (National Center for Educational Statistics 2001). In sharp contrast, of the 932,000 nonprofessional job roles in higher education, men filled only 36 percent and whites filled only 32 percent. This is another example of the limited access of women, people of color, and people of working-class status to higher-status positions and reflects the general trend whereby white male managers and administrators, especially board members and presidents, continue the white and male domination of U.S. higher education that has existed since its beginnings.

Theodore (1986) documents some of the barriers to access to administrative positions reported by female academics: unadvertised positions and missing job descriptions, selection committees dominated by male administrators, assumptions about women's lack of "toughness," patronizing concern about neglect of the candidate's family, and a variety of related sexist attitudes. The lack of women educators and educators of color in senior managerial and administrative leadership positions sends a message to all concerned and deprives all institutional members, especially minority and women faculty and students, of an important resource. In terms that apply particularly to people of color (but relevant to women as well), Harris and Nettles (1996) argue that "a significant representation of minority administrators who identify with and relate to the culture of minority faculty enhances the climate in direct and indirect ways," including displaying role models of success, providing guidance and advice to minority colleagues and students regarding ways to navigate the institution, and promoting optimism and faith in the institution's commitment to diversity and justice (344).

ADMINISTRATORS' EXPERIENCES OF RACE

Relatively little research or firsthand information is available about the racial experiences of senior college and university administrators. Most of the available material comes from administrators of color publicly communicating their experiences in the leadership of U.S. higher education organizations. A few white administrators also have chronicled their racialized experiences.

White Administrators

James Tshechtelin (1999) has drawn four conclusions from his experience as the white president of a predominantly black community college.

> First, racism and white supremacy are immense problems in the United States. They are deeply rooted, and broadly dispersed throughout business, government, education, religion, sports and the media. Second, the problems of racism and white supremacy are not getting better. Although there are some areas of progress, there are other much larger areas that have made little progress or are regressing. Third, racism and white supremacy are taboo topics for discussion in our society, and an open dialogue on race is urgently needed. . . . A problem that we cannot talk about is a "double problem"—the problem itself compounded by the inability to deal with it. Fourth, the consequences of not dealing with racism and white supremacy threaten the social, economic and political stability of our nation. (7–8)

These comments mirror much of the analysis presented in this volume. Tshechtelin sees the United States as being dangerously divided by race, with negative consequences for our politics and economy. Moreover, despite evidence of some progress, he worries that our inability to talk forthrightly about racism and white dominance compounds the problems of race and bars further progress.

In somewhat less critical terms, but still directly, other white college presidents also support this line of analysis. According to David Carter (1991), president of Eastern Connecticut State University, educational reform is essential.

> More than ever before, our country needs the talents of the educationally disenfranchised. . . . For the first time in history, America's future depends on all of her citizens achieving their potential. Our changing demographics suggest that unless the disenfranchised gain the education and acquire the marketable skills that allow them to participate fully in society, we will face social instability. (1)

James Freedman (1991), president of Dartmouth University, also sees progress toward diversity as a crucial goal.

> The fundamental reason that diversity is important is that we are a diverse country, and our leadership is necessarily going to have to be drawn from a spectrum of ethnic, religious and racial groups. If we are to be successful as a democracy . . . this country is going to have very substantial numbers of minorities. . . . It is essential that American higher education commit itself to educating men and women—majority and minority—who will be the leaders of . . . communities. (25)

Carter and Freedman are among a growing number of educational leaders who emphasize the importance of higher education in providing diverse leadership for society. In so doing, they express a position consistent with that of the many corporate, military, and university leaders who signed an amicus curiae brief in support of the University of Michigan's position in its recent affirmative action case before the U.S. Supreme Court (see *Brief for Amicus Curiae 63 Leading American Businesses* 2003; *Brief of the American Educational Research Association* 2003; *Brief of the Amicus Curiae of the American Psychological Association* 2003; *Consolidated Brief of Lt. Gen. Julius Becton et al.* 2003).

Despite a willingness (in some cases) to analyze the nature of racism in higher education and the importance of countering it, however, white administrators rarely speak out professionally and publicly about their own racism and their struggles with themselves and other whites to approach greater diversity and multiculturalism in colleges and universities. One early exception to this pervasive pattern came from an interview study of a small sample (five European Americans and one African American) of presidents of technical colleges in a midwestern state (Hassamani 1973). Hassamani found that all of the presidents reported the positive influence of their families and religious commitments in creating a personal set of values supporting diversity. The European American presidents, however, reported a lack of prior interaction with people of color, due primarily to racial neighborhood and educational separation. On the other hand, the lone African American president reported experiencing during his childhood "legalized discrimination, and personal and institutionalized racism" (226). Hassamani concludes that most of the European American presidents, whatever their own ethnic backgrounds and experiences, viewed cultural diversity from an assimilationist perspective in contrast to the African American president's perspective of cultural pluralism. More telling is Hassamani's conclusion:

> The reluctance of the college presidents to make diversity a high priority was, in part, a reflection of their own values, attitudes, and beliefs. However, most of the college presidents also felt that they could have done more on the diversity issue if their constituents were more supportive of them on the issues related to diversity. . . . Most of the presidents did not hesitate to inform me that their communities held negative views of minorities and other marginalized groups . . . [and] that they were not in a position to affect changes in the values of their respective communities or society at large. (227–28, 232–33)

Thus, the administrative difficulties of providing leadership for a multicultural agenda are compounded by the threat of political resistance, whether such resistance is highly mobilized or quiescent.

Over the course of the past several years various college and university presidents and spokespersons have expressed worry that the need for excellence would likely be undermined by diversity, that they might be able to "achieve diversity without compromising excellence," that they could "balance excellence with diversity," that "diversity is part of excellence," and finally that "diversity is a necessary part of excellence." At each step of the way, of course, reformers encountered conflict and pressure to maintain the status quo, in language and in practice. While many administrative and faculty leaders are changing their understanding of the relationship between academic excellence and diversity of race, gender, and class, other members of the higher education organizations often lag behind.

Most of the presidents interviewed by Hassamani seem to have been prepared to act but were unwilling to undertake the personal and organizational risks that might accompany a more pressure-oriented strategy of organizational change. Unfortunately, waiting for support from below fails to supply necessary transformational leadership. It is instructive that Neil Rudenstine (1996), former president of Harvard University, advocated moving vigorously toward greater diversity despite realizing that such moves might cause turbulence and that "close association among people from different backgrounds can lead to episodes of tension" (B1). Rudenstine recognized that "common understandings often emerge only slowly and with considerable effort" (B2). A large part of this effort undoubtedly must come from university presidents and other administrative and faculty leaders.

Women Administrators and Administrators of Color

To understand why so few women administrators and administrators of color work in U.S. higher education, it is helpful to examine the search and selection processes leading to their employment. Reflecting on Woodbrooks's (1991) analyses of the selection processes at predominantly white universities as experienced by black women candidates for administrative positions, Sagaria (2002) states, "These candidates' narratives and the interpretation of them present the university selection process as a contradictory set of expectations created by a microcosm of white racist society reproducing tensions and conflicts for black women in a setting that is hostile to them" (681). Furthermore, according to Sagaria, the work of Reyes and Halcon (1988) illustrates the following discriminatory practices in the academic selection of Chicano administrative candidates: "type casting, practices of tokenism, limited minority hiring, devaluing of minority research and hairsplitting (a decision made on an arbitrary, hairline difference favoring a white candidate)" (681). Haro (1995) investigated the experiences of candidates for the presidencies or academic vice presidencies of twenty-five target campuses—two- and four-year coeducational institutions in regions with at least 9 percent Latino/a populations. He reports that compared to white men, Latino/a and white female candidates were required to have attained a higher level of accomplishment (both in academic/administrative credentials and in experience). Academic interviewers more often saw and labeled them as products of affirmative action and worried that they would favor the particular interests of Latinos/as or women.

Numerous writings by administrators of color—typically persons who served as president, provost, dean, associate dean, or department chair in different types of colleges and universities—describe the problems and challenges they encountered once they held positions as leaders in predominantly white institutions (PWIs). Some of these educational leaders provide complex visions of the goals and the barriers involved in going beyond representing people of color to attaining and sustaining multiculturalism and equity in higher education. John Slaughter (1998), president of Occidental College, addresses the purpose of diversity:

> Achieving diversity in those cases where it does not exist can be an important pursuit. But, in my opinion, it should not be seen as an end in itself. Diversity should be seen, I contend, as a necessary prelude to the creation of an environment of equity—the real goal to which we should commit ourselves. (8.2)

Gerald Monette (1998), president of Turtle Mountain Community College, speaks of the pressure exerted against diversity by people's "comfort zones":

> I believe that all people ought to have an equal opportunity to be diverse. This should be the goal for America. The challenge is to reach diversity while sustaining a comfort zone for each American. Diversity in America is acceptable only to the point where it does not remove us from our comfort zone. Proof of this is everywhere. Isn't it? (1.3)

As they attempted to provide institutional leadership, many administrators of color found themselves the targets of racial stereotypes and experienced prejudice, bias, and negative assumptions about their competencies. Three such administrators are Reginald Wilson, former president of Wayne County Community College; Enrique Trueba, former dean of the School of Education at the University of Wisconsin and senior vice president for academic affairs at the University of Houston; and Chang-Lin Tien, former chancellor of the University of California at Berkeley.

In addition to the usual issues—student conflict, declining state budgets—minority administrators face constant questioning of their competence and ability to be a leader. (Wilson 1994a: xi)

While advancing my career in academia as an administrator, I witnessed at close hand the political contortions white faculty used to rationalize their biases and the invocation of the sacred academic values, educational philosophy (read "cultural values"), academic freedom (read "white faculty control of academic processes") and "harmony" (read "fear of brown, black and other ethnics"). (Trueba 1998: 77)

It is hardly surprising that many mistaken notions persist about Asian American academics since we are relative newcomers to higher education . . . the pervasive stereotype of Asian Americans is that they are inscrutable and mysterious. More recently as the "model minority" myth has taken hold, we are regarded as "nerds"—serious, hard-working scholars who excel in computers and sciences, but shy away from playing fields. . . . These stereotypes confronted me as well. (Tien 1998: 45–46)

John W. Garland (2002), president of Ohio's Central State University, an HBCU, offers an extensive and thoughtful discussion of how these racial failings of U.S. higher education affected him personally:

I contend that higher education has focused on the formal aspects of diversity while permitting all of the substantive evils associated with chauvinistic attitudes to continue to thrive on our campuses. The academy has focused on form, not on substance. Form means bring more faces of color onto our campuses. Substance means the quality of their experiences, which includes stereotyping and other behaviors that have negative effects on people of color on our campuses. It also means that our campuses do little to raise the consciousness or change behaviors of white faculty, students and administrators. (38–39)

Oliver and Davis (1994) comment further on the racism experienced by African American administrators. They note that many of these men and women had attended special programs and workshops on higher education administration, but that their actual situations were unimaginably difficult.

No leadership development seminar, workshop on administration, nor management school prepares deans of color for demands such as: dealing with psychological warfare and feelings of alienation, dispelling myths among faculty of the leader's incompetence and inferiority, and assisting majority faculty in overcoming basic fears of professional interactions with people of color, particularly African Americans. (59–60)

The Special Situation of Women of Color as Administrators

Like women of color on the faculty of predominantly white institutions, female administrators of color face the twin oppressions of racism and sexism. In the words of Yolanda Moses (1994), former president of the American Association of Colleges and Universities and the American Association of Higher Education:

My experience from graduate school through the academic affairs vice presidency has been a legacy of having to demonstrate my credentials. It is a given that I have to work harder and produce more than my white male counterparts to be taken seriously. I often say to audiences that true equality will be reached in this country when mediocre men and women of color and white women are hired at the same rates as mediocre white males. (55)

And Rhetaugh Dumas, an experienced African American senior administrator who served both in the federal scientific establishment and as Dean of the School of Nursing and Associate Provost for Health Affairs at the University of Michigan, has studied the dilemma of African American women in leadership roles. She observes:

Whether she likes it or not, the black woman has come to represent a kind of person, a style of life, a set of attitudes, and behaviors through which individuals and groups seek to fulfill their own socio-emotional needs in organizations. It is not surprising, therefore, that there is a great deal more interest in the *personal* qualities of black women administrators than in their skill and competence for formal leadership roles. (Richards 1994: 40–41)

One result of the resistance that black women face in formal, high-status positions is the tendency of whites to ascribe to them functions that reinforce the view of the antebellum black mammy. As Richards (1994) notes, this attribution renders the black woman administrator's power illusory, and she is constantly asked to put herself at the disposal of those around her and take care of them.

Lesbian, Gay, and Bisexual Administrators

There is little available research or first-person testimony on the experiences of senior lesbian, gay, or bisexual administrators. The dilemmas of "coming out" as different in the midst of a heterosexist and often homophobic culture continue to render this population invisible and marginalized. However, some insights into these administrators' and staff members' concerns can be drawn from Croteau and his colleagues' studies (Croteau and von Destinon 1994; Croteau and Lark 1995) of lesbian, gay, and bisexual professionals in student affairs offices. Twenty-six percent of their 249 respondents reported experiencing discrimination in the hiring process, and 60 percent reported experiencing discrimination once they were on the job. Incidents ranged from paternalistic tolerance to verbal expressions of anti-lesbian and -gay sentiments to outright harassment.

ADMINISTRATORS AT ELITE
COLLEGES AND UNIVERSITIES

Colleges and universities are stratified in ways that reflect their prestige or reputation, exclusiveness (by cost or by the GPAs or standardized test scores of students), size of endowment, and postgraduate opportunities open to alumni. Thus, elite private and public research universities serve as models of high educational quality and legitimated organizational practices, both educationally and administratively. Recently, some leaders of these institutions have been publicly prominent as advocates and defenders of diversity, including racial diversity. For example, John DiBiaggio, president of Tufts University, offers the following analysis:

> I heartily concur that diversity is important to Tufts, and indeed to the nation, for three fundamental reasons: First, encouraging and fostering, within our community, a blending of ethnicities, cultures, races, religions and genders is educationally sound. It is our obligation to prepare our students to live and work in a highly diverse society . . . Second, diversity should be realized at Tufts and elsewhere for moral reasons . . . [to] address the vestiges of past racial injustices and to confront those that persist today. . . . Finally, the practical implications [of diversity] speak for themselves . . . to deny quality educational opportunities to the fastest-growing segment of our population simply does not make good business sense. . . . We simply will not be able to compete as a nation if the majority of our population has not been properly prepared. (ACE 1999: 22)

Many other presidents of leading colleges and universities publicly support diversity efforts that reach out to historically underrepresented groups, although they may or may not vigorously pursue this agenda in practice. For example, the *Journal of Blacks in Higher Education* conducted a survey of the presidents of the twenty-five highest-ranked universities and the presidents of the twenty-five highest-ranked liberal arts colleges. The presidents were asked to indicate which of the following statements they most agreed with (ACE 1999: 21):

1. All credentials being equal, I am in favor of giving the admissions nod to an applicant from a disadvantaged racial group.

2. Because there is a very large gap between the mean academic credentials of blacks and whites, I am in favor of admitting significant numbers of less academically qualified blacks provided they can meet our academic standards.
3. I am opposed to any form of preferential admissions based on race.

The presidents' responses demonstrated general but cautious support for affirmative action: 44 percent of these presidents most agreed with the first statement, 13 percent chose the second statement, and no one selected the third statement (ACE 1999).[1] However, since the racialized structure of social opportunities seldom results in situations where "all credentials are equal," one may wonder how likely support for item 1 is to translate into significant organizational change. Within the leadership of higher education—and even within the supportive statements presented here—are differing views and emphases with regard to diversity issues. For example, some statements are more specific than others about the issues involved; some leaders emphasize an educational rationale for diversity, while others champion an equity rationale; some address historic discrimination and racism, whereas others do not; and even the ways in which they speak about race varies considerably.

These college and university leaders are expressing their views in the face of a series of legal challenges to their institutions' affirmative action practices. With regard to affirmative action, Chang (2002) contrasts what he terms a contemporary "discourse of preservation" with a broader "discourse of transformation," the latter encompassing "a wide range of issues related to democratizing nearly every aspect of higher education" (129). Chang's two discourses resemble our distinctions between colleges' efforts to achieve diversity versus efforts to attain multiculturalism and social justice. The preservation discourse (or diversity argument) focuses on defending and maintaining current affirmative action practices, but seldom addresses broader goals and activities necessary to overcome racism and sexism on campus. The transformation discourse (or antiracist or multicultural argument) goes beyond most of these presidents' statements and challenges long-standing structures and processes of white and male privilege and power in higher education and in the society at large.

Consideration of these competing views raises the question of how university presidents' stated support for diversity relates to the actual state of affairs in their institutions. In one instance, the Ford Foundation, after years of financially supporting fellowships for students of color enrolled in Ph.D. programs, decided to investigate why elite research universities had so little faculty diversity. In 1994, the foundation invited the presidents of eleven elite research institutions to participate in a study of the situation: Columbia, Duke, Harvard, Princeton, Stanford, the University of California at Los Angeles, Chicago, Michigan, Pennsylvania, Texas, and Yale. Site visits to each campus included meetings with minority faculty members, minority graduate students, and administrators interested in and responsible for faculty diversity—the president, the provost, deans, department chairs, and related associates and assistants. The study also accessed institutional data on minority faculty recruitment and retention and on minority graduate student recruitment and retention.

Using the institutional data available to them and information about the 1,013 Ford Fellows (minority Ph.D. students) selected since 1986, Knowles and Harleston (1997) determined that only 70 fellows were on the arts and science faculties of these elite eleven universities. Furthermore, forty-four of them were on the faculties of the three state universities in the sample—the University of California at Los Angeles, the University of Michigan at Ann Arbor, and the University of Texas at Austin (distributed as fifteen, fifteen, and fourteen), while the other twenty-six fellows were distributed widely among the eight private institutions. Commenting on this pattern, Knowles and Harleston (1997) report:

> The "pool problem" was identified overwhelmingly as the number one issue in the recruitment of minority faculty members. . . . Even in those fields in which there were relatively more minority Ph.D. candidates, their still small number was offered repeatedly as the reason for the scarcity of minority group members on arts and sciences faculties. However, administrators and faculty members alike agreed that they recruit from only a few Ph.D.-granting institutions, institutions that do not award the greatest number of minority Ph.D.s. (1)

Senior administrators at these universities also identified the decentralized nature of faculty recruitment and graduate student admission as a key barrier to increased diversity. Several presidents and provosts indicated that they normally exerted very limited influence on faculty hiring decisions, and most senior officials indicated that faculty recruitment was usually undertaken at the department level and that faculty job descriptions and searches usually proceeded in traditional ways. According to Knowles and Harleston (1997), "The exceptions were at those few institutions where the president had made increasing the number of faculty and graduate students of color a top priority and had taken steps to make change happen" (3).

Knowles and Harleston (1997) also report that most administrators defined diversity as adding people of color, "but they do not consider the possibility that the institution itself might have to, or should change" (6). Clearly, a focus needs to be placed on creating in predominantly white institutions an environment that supports and develops graduate students of color and faculty of color. This perspective on where change must start also emerges in the comments of Barbara Gitenstein, president of the College of New Jersey.

> Without the will and the commitment of a critical mass of individuals, particularly the strong commitment of the senior administration, there will be no transformation change in an institution of higher education. . . . That person has to

know that understanding both the subtle and the not so subtle instances of racial, gender and religious discrimination is just the beginning—that person must help teach the majority community the power and importance of "interruption." (ACE 1999: 42)

In summarizing their findings with regard to the presidents and provosts of their sample of eleven elite private and public research universities, Knowles and Harleston (1997) write:

At each of the eleven universities, the president and often the provost spoke of the importance of diversifying the faculty and graduate student body. However, on only a few campuses had the president reinforced his or her commitment with action, and the numbers reflected that action. On those campuses, everyone with whom we met—administrators, faculty, and graduate students—spoke of presidential commitment and of action taken. Faculty and administrators knew who was in charge of and responsible for institutional efforts to increase diversity. They knew what programs had been implemented and what was and was not working. They had creative ideas and solicited input regarding other strategies they could pursue. Not everyone was satisfied with the action taken, but they knew of the president's commitment and volunteered their own impressions of it.

    On the other campuses, faculty members, administrators, or minority graduate students never mentioned the presidents' commitment to diversity. The difference was striking. One provost told us that the president had not made time to focus on increasing faculty diversity or recruiting minority graduate students. (17)

This evidence underscores the need for visible, proactive leadership by presidents and senior administrators. Faculty leaders and middle management officers take their cues from the actions as well as the rhetoric of such administrators. Presidents who do not take active leadership, or who take leadership without good information about the forces operating to resist or frustrate their desires, will achieve little in the way of minority recruitment. Beyond recruitment, administrative leaders who do not look deeper than representational diversity, who do not examine and challenge the discriminatory patterns in their institutions' structures and cultures, will not be able to sustain progress toward a multicultural organization.

NOTE

1. That means that 43 percent of presidents surveyed did not select any of the three alternatives offered. It is unclear from the ACE report whether their nonresponse reflects a desire not to participate in the survey, a dissatisfaction with the range of options available to answer the question, or something else.

Part Three

CHALLENGING DISCRIMINATION AND PROMOTING MULTICULTURALISM

The preceding chapters identified the persistent nature of institutionalized racism and other forms of discrimination throughout the history and current organization of the U.S. society and systems of education. The majority of members in colleges and universities, regardless of their status as administrators, faculty, staff, or students, have been socialized in segregated environs and carry with them the experience of being privileged and/or being subordinated and discriminated against by virtue of their race, gender, and economic class. Moreover, these patterns of domination and subordination are sustained by the policies, programs, and practices (staffing and admissions policies, curriculum, social relations, power structures) of most higher education organizations. Academic units are generally resistant to antiracist and multicultural concerns that are not seen as central to their academic foci or that might interfere with a priority on traditional (and often monocultural) definitions of intellectual quality. Resultant tensions, as well as growth, in the racial consciousness and intergroup interactions of these parties are thus to be expected.

It also is clear that our national system of higher education is itself stratified by race and class. The higher the status of a college or university (e.g., a Research I university or elite liberal arts college versus a state college or community college) the fewer the number of students or faculty of color or from working-class backgrounds. Colleges and universities typically have more people of color and people from working-class backgrounds in lower level staff positions than among senior administrative or faculty roles. Boards of trustees, elected or appointed, are likely to be filled by wealthy white people who reflect primarily the perspectives and interests of their social strata.

Under these circumstances, only a numerical minority of administrators or faculty members in these organizations are likely to actively seek to change patterns of discrimination and work toward multiculturalism and racial and social justice.

165

Students are most often the initiators of actions questioning or challenging discriminatory practices and seeking fundamental changes to reduce racism and increase multiculturalism. In addition, the most substantial changes in policies and programs related to social justice concerns have been the result of social movements and pressures rooted outside of colleges and universities, often involving formal or informal coalitions involving student and adult constituencies.

In these contexts, how does organizational change come about and what kinds of programs or initiatives make the most sense? In this part, several chapters discuss strategies to challenge organizational racism and promote multiculturalism. Our particular concern is the possibility of intentional and (more or less) planned change. Such intentionality requires specification of goals to be attained (or problems to be ameliorated), involvement of multiple constituencies, development of information systems to guide change planning, allocation of needed resources, implementation and supportive follow through of specific changes, and monitoring and evaluation of progress. It also requires both formal and informal organizational leaders, structures, and processes. Within these broad processes, the choice of particular change strategies depends on the specific nature of the local organization, its definition of its multicultural goals, ideological preferences regarding the use of persuasion and pressure, the specific nature and size of the unit(s) targeted for change and available resources.

Chapter 8 provides an overview of alternative strategies for change, all of which are located within an understanding of organizations as contested environments composed of differentiated subsystems and competing interest groups. Chapter 9 illustrates some of the principles involved in conducting cultural audits or assessments and examines their utility in planning, directing, and evaluating multicultural change efforts. It provides examples of varied instruments recently used by different colleges and universities. Chapter 10 further examines the important role of administrative leaders and faculty members in change making. The chapter emphasizes the role of administrators/managers in exerting wise and forceful leadership and in using systemwide strategic planning. It also analyzes the issues involved in efforts to improve faculty functioning, specifically with regard to (re)learning pedagogical techniques suited for multicultural learning environments and to reforming the curriculum in a more inclusive and antiracist, antisexist direction. Chapter 11 examines several multicultural initiatives that are focused on or initiated by the student community, including student service programs, intergroup dialogue programs, community service learning, and some of the ways students have mobilized independently (or in concert with faculty and community allies) to press their concerns for multicultural campus change. And chapter 12 presents and analyzes a number of specific multicultural innovations currently underway in colleges and universities. These examples further illustrate the principles and examples discussed in chapters 8 through 11 and are responsive in varying degrees to the issues raised in chapters 1 through 3 generally and chapters 4 through 7 more particularly.

Chapter Eight

Strategies of Organizational Change

The persistence of institutional racism and other forms of advantage/disadvantage and privilege/oppression discussed throughout this volume are currently the focus of change in many higher education institutions. The central problem for those committed to change these patterns is how best to bring it about. Changes in people and organizations are rooted in their individual and collective self-interests to survive and thrive, and new conceptions of self-interest must be developed that include understanding and advocacy of the benefits to whites and other people of privilege in a multicultural organization. Major innovations in organizations, moreover, are made and sustained when substantial internal leadership—from the top or the middle or the bottom of the organization—presses for such change and when social movements in the society or community external to the organization mobilize in support and advocacy. Innovative leadership by committed people of all social identity groups—men and women, white people and people of color, gay people and straight people, administrators and faculty and students—are required for multicultural changes to be made. The topic of this chapter is planned (sometimes termed *intentional*) organizational and programmatic change to achieve antiracism and multiculturalism and greater justice in colleges and universities.

The generic elements of planned change initiatives are not created nor implemented without substantial commitment, expertise, and time and energy of the organization's leadership group or some other team designated to lead the change effort. Whatever the goals, scale of operation, and strategies and tactics of the change effort (or efforts), it requires a team to be responsible for planning and implementation, including gathering relevant information and resources. Sometimes this group is an already existing unit—for example, the President's Cabinet, the Dean's Council or College Executive Committee, a departmental curriculum committee, the Program Committee of the Office of Student Services, or the Student Government Council. At other times it is a new group constituted expressly for this purpose, such as Faculty to Advance Multicultural Teaching, Student Affairs Committee for Enrolling More People of Color, Students against Racism, President's Advisory Committee on Race Relations, Community Group to Improve Town–Gown Relations. In either approach, the group responsible for leading the change effort should include people of different races and ethnicities and function as a multicultural team (see chapter 10 for information about such teams and the conditions for teamwork).

THE CHALLENGES OF PLANNING AND MAKING CHANGE

Our analysis finds a deeply entrenched state of racism, sexism, classism, heterosexism, and religious discrimination in higher education, one that carries forward a far-reaching historic legacy. Changes that alter these discriminatory patterns and promote multiculturalism require comprehensive efforts affecting the organizational domains of mission, culture, power, membership, social relations and climate, technology, resources, and boundary systems (see figures 3.1 and 3.2). Smith (1989) mirrors a portion of this agenda, emphasizing the need for "diversity efforts" to include an organizational mission that can support more cooperative campus cultures, a diverse faculty and staff, revisions in the curriculum and pedagogy, improved interaction, and an ability to deal with conflict in the midst of continuing inequality. Without such a broad and multidimensional view of needed change, we will continue to see pockets of innovation and special programs unconnected to core organizational operations.

Figure 8.1 graphically depicts a variety of activities related to the overall change-planning process: diagnosis, goal selection, choice of strategy, planning a specific project, acquiring resources, and implementing changes. The arrows on this diagram are reminders that this is not a linear and mechanistic process but an iterative one in which several activities influence one another. For example, the effort to acquire resources to implement change may lead to revisions in the goals, strategy, and plan itself. Although such adjustments will occur in several directions, these six activities must fit together and be mutually supportive. They eventually can lead to evaluations and corrective efforts that continue the cycle.

As the change leadership team prepares to determine organizational or programmatic goals and select change strategies and tactics, it should gather information on the current organizational conditions necessitating change and different interest groups' perceptions of these conditions. A broadly based audit or diagnosis is vital because administrators, faculty, and students are in different social locations, play different roles, and see the organization and any change goals and process differently; the same is true for people of color and white people, men and women, and so forth. The information in chapter 9 on multicultural audits is directly relevant to the information gathering, analysis, and interpretation

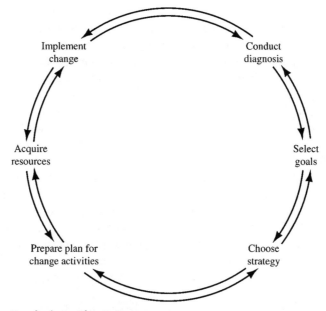

Figure 8.1. Developing a Change Program

that is required. Such diagnostic information and the conclusions they lead to is the change group's basis for finalizing its goals and undertaking its selection of strategies and tactics to accomplish them. It can also help plan the activities and timeline that will be implemented to accomplish these goals.

Incremental and Radical Change Goals

Institutional inequality in higher education is nested within the societal inequality and injustice that undergirds the entire society. Such a diagnosis might suggest that any change short of revolution—destruction and reconstruction of these institutions—is doomed. But as indicated in chapter 2, progress has been made in recent years by progressive educational leaders working internally, by mobilized student groups, and by important social movements pressing colleges and universities externally. Further incremental progress, and resistance to backsliding toward more racist and monocultural practices, can be achieved via incremental yet significant organization-wide changes that reduce discrimination and lead to a more just and effective educational environment. In this regard, the concepts of "tempered radicalism" (Meyerson 2001; Meyerson and Scully 1995) and "small wins" (Weick 1984) are helpful in responding concretely and pragmatically to the challenges of making multicultural change, preventing backsliding to former patterns of monoculturalism, resisting retrenchment, and sustaining progress. Meyerson proposes an approach to change that permits the advocacy of radical changes in a tempered way—*tempered* by moderation, fueled by the *temper* of passion, and sustained by the *tempering* of hardening. The combination of moderate and radical goals, passionate advocacy, effective tactics, and the annealing strength of struggle may permit change advocates to endure and work for change within unjust and oppressive institutions. The result may not produce dramatic and sudden large-scale change, but rather a series of small wins.

Of course, there are risks in settling for a strategy of tempered radicalism and for pursuing small wins or reforms rather than major victories. Retrenchment, co-optation, and achieving small victories that represent little or no meaningful change are among these risks, and there are many examples of negotiated agreements for reform that are never implemented fully in practice. Moreover, dangers lie in settling for incremental changes that reallocate minor resources but maintain traditional authority and practices and consequently maintain affluent white and male advantage.

Change strategies that seek to disrupt business-as-usual and target immediate and far-reaching transformation also have their risks. Rarely is far-reaching transformation sought, and even when it is, it is seldom gained. Moreover, to the degree that the status quo is disrupted by changes that seek to redistribute power and privilege, unbridled radicalism may stimulate resistance or backlash that results in no wins or retaliatory damage. In numerous instances, coercive tactics have resulted only in temporary rhetorical or surface level change. Indeed, in the history of U.S. race relations, periods of rapid progress (e.g., nineteenth-century reconstruction efforts and twentieth-century civil rights movements) often have been followed by long periods of retrenchment.

The dilemma posed by the alternatives of tempered or incremental strategies and radical or fully transformative ones is unresolvable in theory and each antiracist and antisexist change initiative must make strategic and practical choices based on local organizational conditions. Some readers will pursue strategies from the margins of established units that are more transformative relative to their organization's goals and traditions. Other readers will pursue incremental changes from within the mainstream of traditional higher education organizations. Still other readers working within visionary units or social movement organizations will pursue radical goals by mobilizing and deploying external pressures. Given the ongoing societal and global changes in racial demography and racial inequities, with resulting contest and conflict, colleges and universities will be subject to highly varied and constantly changing pressures from both their external and their internal stakeholder groups. These pressures will influence internal strategic decision making about the what, how, and when of change making. In the long run, most concrete efforts to challenge racism and sexism will require a mix of strategies to prevent retrenchment and achieve more diverse and socially just higher education organizations.

Choices among goals and strategies are not simply matters of leaders' and followers' ideologies and analytic frames; they also depend upon wider social conditions, the history and current state of the college or university, and the available resources. Figure 8.2 extends the view presented in figure 3.2, analyzing several different change foci and tactics that are more or less likely in higher education systems at three stages along the continuum between monocultural and multicultural. None of the stages are pure or static, and neither are the change strategies. Most organizations contain some internal elements in continual flux and others that are constantly attempting to stabilize or resist change, all at the same time. Both the internal and external pressures and the opportunities for change are always in flux. But if we people can identify the current stage of the organization or unit/subunit with regard to its movement toward multiculturalism along varied dimensions, change makers and change teams can adopt goals and design strategies most likely to be effective in their specific situations.

Monocultural higher education organizations are not all alike: some may be committed to a religious, political, or cultural agenda that excludes certain groups (including, particularly, people of color), while others may be less exclusive. Organizations in the transitional stage also vary considerably: most contain internal groups and leadership cadres that have already expressed some interest in making change although their multicultural vision and related programs

Figure 8.2. The Road to Multiculturalism and Justice (in Primarily White Colleges and Universities)

Factor	Stages		
	Monocultural	Transitional	Multicultural
Interest in multicultural change	Little interest unless pressed on survivability Low overt conflict	Social acceptability Fuller utilization of resources Taking advantage of special markets Adapting to external or internal pressure and resolving overt conflict	Equity and justice Belief in bottom-line rhetoric and growth potential Empowerment and organizational improvement
Major multicultural goals	Diverse racial composition of student body Assimilate students of color	Establish diversity training for faculty and administrators Recruit and retain students of color Modify curriculum in a pluralistic direction Hire faculty and staff of color Integrate student life	Change organizational mission Recruit and retain administrators of color Change curriculum to achieve multiculturalism Use broad range of pedagogies Promote student self-direction
Constituencies for change	Few External voices and pressures Some internal minorities	Some internal cadres A few leaders from the dominant coalition Cautious and informal faculty and administrative voices Legal claimants Students of color	The dominant coalition Strong and fully represented internal cadres People of color and whites together Internal and external forces joined

Major change strategies by high-power groups	Countersuit Some managerial listening and adjustment	Management diversity-training and awareness programs Organization development Affirmative action programs Administrative mandates Assessments and audits	Continuous (re)education of individuals and the organization Rewards for change advocates Multicultural norms and leadership Problem-solving groups Coalition formation Revision of policies and structures Combating external social oppression Multicultural organization development
by low-power groups	Litigation External demand or protest Coercion from below	Litigation Negotiations among interest groups Protest and pressure Student–community alliances Innovations on the margins Work stoppages	

are likely to be limited. Organizations at the multicultural stage of development (we acknowledge that we have seen few total organizations but have seen some units/subunits at this stage) will integrate values of social justice into their mission and operations, and many of their members and leaders will champion this agenda. At both the monocultural and transitional stages of organizational development, people who are located differently in the organization are likely to adopt different change strategies: members of higher-power groups (administrators and senior faculty, senior white men) are likely to perceive the organization differently, and have different goals and access to different types of resources than do members of lower-power groups (junior faculty and staff and students, people of color, and women).

Organizations at any stage vary in the degree to which they have made progress toward multiculturalism on the different organizational dimensions described in figures 3.1 and 3.2. For instance, some organizations may have very progressive mission statements but only moderately successful recruitment and retention efforts, and thus a minimally diverse membership. Some may have been successful at recruiting and maintaining a diverse student body but lack parallel change in a monocultural faculty; or perhaps both student and faculty composition has become diverse while the organization remains monocultural, assimilative, and oppressive in its culture and general orientation. Likewise, both mission and membership, and even climate, may be at a transitional stage but the power structure still monocultural. And so on. All such contradictions are likely to be sources of tension and highlight both the organization's interest in change and the existence of resistance.

In addition, these variations may distinguish different units or subunits from one another, even within a single larger unit or department. For instance, within a single university, Colleges of Liberal Arts/Sciences and Engineering may differ in their missions, admissions' and hiring histories, orientations to instruction, and relations to external constituencies, all of which reflect and affect their approach to challenging discrimination and approaching multiculturalism. Even within an academic department or staff unit faculty, students and administrators are likely to have different priorities and to evaluate their unit's progress on the dimensions of monoculturalism-multiculturalism differently.

Moreover, organizations undertaking multicultural change efforts vary in the breadth and depth of their agenda and programming. Some organizations may focus their change efforts on a single unit—a particular department, college, student dormitory or staff unit, while others may plan a broad institution-wide effort. Given the variations noted here, change efforts at the subunit level will be greatly affected by the degree of support and integration provided at the higher unit level, and change efforts at the unit level will be affected by the degree of institution-wide leadership and support available. They also may vary in the depth of the change goals, whether to undertake innovative or melioristic programming within existing structures or to attempt fundamental change in one or several of the dimensions.

The Value of Strategic Planning

Whatever the choice of change goals and foci, a coherent planning process can be helpful for either organization-wide or specific-unit efforts to make change. Such a process typically requires commitment and leadership from the relevant administration and involves "a formal process designed to help an organization identify and maintain an optimal alignment with the most important elements of its environment" (Rowley, Lujan, and Dolence 1997: 15). In this type of planning the focus is on an organization's or unit's changing external circumstances in relation to its internal capabilities. Analyses of these factors can help the organization determine how it can become more effective by identifying and exploiting its strategic market niche(s), where it has a comparative advantage relative to other organizations (Kotler and Murphy 1991). New understandings of planning are continuing to emerge in higher education organizations: as one example, contextual planning includes both long-range planning and strategic planning (Peterson 1997). Other refinements include tailoring such processes to specific higher education issues, such as enrollment management, diversity, and resource planning (Rowley et al. 1997).

Across the nation, there is a great variety of innovative teaching, programming, and conversation around issues of diversity and multiculturalism. However, many colleges and collegiate units have adopted simplistic and "weak" definitions of the problem and solutions (e.g., countering prejudice, celebrating differences, adding a few courses). Other efforts to achieve greater diversity or move in the direction of becoming more multicultural may be sporadic in nature and engaged in only at the margins of higher education institutions. Prior to the 1990s, most colleges' and universities' strategic plans did not include achieving racial diversity nor designs for the systemic changes necessary to become a multicultural educational organization. In the 1990s, however, some pioneering organizations (e.g., the University of Maryland at College Park [UMCP]) demonstrated that strategic planning can greatly aid the effort not only to increase diversity but also to create multicultural organizational change (UMCP and AACU 1998).

CHOOSING CHANGE STRATEGIES

In classic typologies of organizational and social change, Chin and Benne (1969) and Crowfoot and Chesler (1974) draw on the models of organizations discussed in chapter 7 (see also Burke 2002: 168–72). They distinguish among approaches emphasizing top-down strategic planning (the bureaucratic model), the exertion of political power from the organization's top (administrators and other formal power holders) or bottom (grass roots), and efforts to remake an organization's culture and norms (symbolic and collegium models). A new generation of scholarly discussion also has emphasized the relevance of political models of change that meld organizational theory and social movement theory (e.g., Zald and Berger 1978; McAdam and Scott 2002). In this view, one consistent with our own, political struggles and processes constantly take place in all organizations, including colleges and universities. Contending interest groups are ever-present, and their use of conflict and coercive or "transgressive interventions" (McAdam, McCarthy, and Zald 1996) that involve conscious mobilization of marginalized or aggrieved groups is endemic.

The overall means of influence used in change initiatives are what we mean by "change strategy." Influence in social relations between groups, as well as between individuals, is achieved through a continuum of behaviors that range from raw physical coercion through persuasion to discovery of grounds for collaboration through education and mutual inquiry. For purposes of illustration, in figure 8.3 we contrast a variety of strategies that differ along this continuum of the means of influence; they are also illustrated more specifically in chapters 9–12.

A fundamental distinction between these strategies involves the nature of authority relations, which in most of the U.S. society, including in colleges and universities, rests on a history of institutionalized domination and subordination and internalized attitudes and behaviors reflecting feelings and perceptions of superiority and inferiority based on race and gender and wealth. A shorthand expression to refer to these patterns is "power-over." On the other hand, in a few alternative settings authority rests on a history of mutuality of respect among people from different backgrounds and identities, along with shared power and patterns of mutual decision-making. A shorthand expression for these patterns is "power-with." Surely life is more complicated than this, and mixed strategies often exist, but for clarity in the short run we describe these alternatives as a dichotomy existing within a continuum of organizational relations.

The first of these two contrasting strategies can be distinguished by its reliance on coercion and threats of coercion, however communicated and exercised, whether using physical, psychological, or ideological force. Such coercion can be of the kind embodied in organizational and societal authority, and thus legitimated by military/police or cultural hegemony, or it can be based on the mobilized protests of organizational members who are challenging organizational authorities. The use of coercive force and pressure is aligned with the bureaucratic and political models of organizations and organizational change, which incorporate relations of domination and subordination. When low-power groups use coercion-based strategies, they often bring long-standing and suppressed issues to the fore, especially when the gulfs between groups of different organizational status or race, gender, and socioeconomic class are great. These strategies

Violent coercion

Nonviolent coercion

Strikes/boycotts/protests

Lockouts/firings

Litigation

Harassment

Unilateral decisions

Rewards and sanctions

Psychological intimidations

Pressure strategies
Power-over

Presentation of proposed solution

Press releases

Presentation of grievances

Debates

Mixed strategies

Skill development workshop

Information sharing

Education

Cooperative problem-solving

Mutual inquiry

Collaboration

Persuasion strategies
Power-with

Figure 8.3.   Alternative Change Strategies and Their Means of Influence

also can command attention, speed up action to redress inequities, and provide the means for ongoing monitoring of any changes. They may not work well if backed by insufficient power; then dominant groups who experience such coercive pressure and threat may counterorganize and overwhelm the change effort.

The second of these two basic strategies generally relies on persuasive communication that is aligned with the collegium model of organizations and organizing. The strategy of persuasive communication can also be found in modified bureaucracies that emphasize a reduced number of hierarchical levels and diverse leadership centers that operate as semi-autonomous subunits. This model is characterized by trust among the members based on minimal differences in power and commonly shared values and goals. Persuasion-based strategies anticipate cooperation and expect that any resistance is the result of insufficient explanation that can be overcome via clarification, conversation, and education. These strategies may work well in establishing a cooperative context for change. They may not work well in situations of great power difference and substantial resistance; they may then easily lead to delay, co-optation, tokenism, and agreements to make changes that ultimately are not implemented.

Given organizations' efforts to maintain the status quo, and the shifting nature of the status quo over time, senior leaders, other administrators, and the faculty usually rely on parts of both approaches. However, administrators typically operate within the established bureaucratic authority and secondarily within the collegial structure, while the faculty typically operates conversely. Mobilized student groups, especially students of color, may use a political model and the power of protest, especially if they feel they are not being listened to by institutional authorities. As in all change efforts undertaken by lower-power groups, a critical mass of active constituents is necessary as an alternative source of power.

Although these contrasts may help to clarify options, the concepts do not fully reflect the reality of organizational life and organizational change efforts. In practice, matters are much more complex. For instance, it may take sustained pressure and threats of disruption by students and faculty of color and women (coercion strategy) to convince white male colleagues and administrators to reeducate themselves (persuasion strategy) regarding racism and sexism and to engage in cooperative problem solving (persuasion strategy). Or, it may take several failed attempts at educating leaders about the need for change (persuasion strategy) to generate enough frustration to enable change advocates to mobilize support for the application of rewards and sanctions and sustained pressure (coercion strategy) to try new approaches in the classroom or in student life programs. One can start with either approach and moving back and forth is common.

Underlying these two strategies or families of strategies are different assumptions about the interests of different organizational members and functional units. Where members of the organization believe that leaders and power holders are operating in the interest of all organizational members persuasion is the more likely and appropriate means of exercising influence. Where organizational members perceive leaders and power holders—or vice versa—not operating in the best interest of all members, particularly not operating in their own specific interest, coercion is the more likely means of influence. Certainly the presence or perception of institutionalized racism and other forms of discrimination leads to greater willingness to use coercive strategies.

DESIGNING SPECIFIC TACTICS AND ACTIVITIES

Once a set of change goals has been selected, and an overall strategy decided upon, a number of tactical decisions still need to be made. These decisions involve identification of the specific activities by which influence of varied types (as noted previously) is exercised through particular people, structures, and elements of the organizational or unit and its environment.

The Force Field

A diagnostic and planning tool that can be used to aid such planning is the force field. Based generally on the work of Kurt Lewin, and his attention to the field of forces active in any situation, this technique can help identify and assess the situational elements that currently encourage or inhibit progress toward a change goal and the potential resources for an against such change.

The force field diagram illustrated in figure 8.4 assumes that at any single point in time an organization (or organizational unit) is relatively stable and thus the forces for and against change are in balance—a status quo is maintained. The change team's tactical decisions must upset this balance and overweight the system in the direction of change. The planning process utilizing this diagram proceeds as follows: (1) a multicultural concern or goal for change and its relevant organizational dimension or program (e.g., target) is listed at the top of the diagram; (2) forces (individuals, groups of people, organizational units or resources, external societal pressures or actors) that are or that might drive the change process are listed in the left hand column; (3) forces (individuals, groups of people, organizational units or resources, external societal pressures or actors) that are or that might restrain or resist the change process are listed in the right hand column. For instance, common drivers of multicultural change might include the college's senior leadership groups, particular figures in the state government, student organizations; common resistors might include particular administrators or faculty members, anti–affirmative action groups in the student or civic community, departmental curricula that are seen as sacrosanct. The next steps are to (4) assess the relative strength of each of the forces on either side;

(5) identify particular approaches that might strengthen forces driving the change and that might weaken the forces restraining the change; and (6) identify, perhaps through a brainstorming process, new forces that might be added to the driving side of the diagram. Specific forces can be listed both on the driving and restraining side, especially in the case of personal ambivalence or competing views within a particular unit or group. The result is a plan for action.

Multicultural Concern: _____
(goal for change)

Change Program or Target: _____

	Forces pushing for change (driving) +	Forces pushing against change (restraining) −
Individual	_____	_____
	_____	_____
	_____	_____
	_____	_____
Group	_____	_____
	_____	_____
	_____	_____
	_____	_____
Organizational	_____	_____
	_____	_____
	_____	_____
	_____	_____
Community	_____	_____
	_____	_____
	_____	_____
	_____	_____

Figure 8.4. Force Field Analysis for Planning Change

To take an example, consider the case of a department attempting to alter its curriculum to provide greater representation of the contributions and concerns of people of color, as well as the relevance of a subject for racial issues in the society (of course, the very approach to this agenda differs according to whether the department is in the social sciences, natural sciences or humanities, graduate or undergraduate, etc.). Driving forces might include the associate chair in charge of undergraduate studies, several faculty members, interested students, supportive statements from the dean's office, and a booklet of examples of such innovation available from the relevant disciplinary society. Resisting forces might include several other faculty members who lack the time and energy to participate in the effort, colleagues from various departments who are concerned about "revisionism," and recent articles in disciplinary journals warning against just such efforts. Attempts to strengthen the driving forces might include inviting the supportive dean to address the faculty, creating joint student-faculty committees to undertake curriculum revision, inviting leaders of the disciplinary society who support the innovation to visit campus to address people's concerns, and writing an article for a local newspaper connecting the curricular challenge to practical community concerns. Attempts to weaken the resisting forces might include gaining access to the dean's funds to grant released time to faculty to join the effort.

The diagnostic and prescriptive portions of a force field can be completed by individuals and then shared to create a common diagram, or people can work together in its joint construction from the outset. To the extent that the team creating such a force field is itself multicultural the resulting plan of action is likely to represent the wisdom of multiple perspectives. Regardless of how diverse such a team is, the development of an effective force field diagram may require a search for information beyond that possessed by team members. Once a plan is completed, specific assignments of responsibility, a time line for accomplishing specific actions, and a procedure for establishing accountability can be set.

Mobilizing Resources Needed for Multicultural Change Efforts

Once a plan of action is in place, the effort to alter an organization requires the development, mobilization, and deployment of resources that can support implementation. Acquiring such resources sometimes involves reorganizing currently available resources (e.g., reallocating merit increases to reward change makers, providing innovative faculty with released time to develop new courses, providing innovative units with additional funds and personnel); at other times it calls for developing new kinds of resources (e.g., raising funds explicitly for change programs, hiring multicultural change specialists, bringing previously uninvolved students or community members into the change effort). With particular respect to the task of multicultural organizational change, there are different kinds of important resources. For instance, personal or individual resources include people or groups of people who are about these issues, who have information about racism and multiculturalism, skills in teaching and administering in new ways and the passion or will to take action. Organizational resources include funds (for an audit or for training programs), rewards for people prepared to act (teach or administer) in new ways, and other forms of power and persuasion resting in the hands of organizational leaders. And as noted, external resources in the form of community groups, funds and legitimacy can help to rally public resources and pressures in support of the multicultural change effort.

A key resource that all change movements (and countermovements) seek, and that cuts across these categories, is control of the language or the conceptual frame within which a challenge is described (Benford and Snow 2000; McAdam, McCarthy, and Zald 1996). In the sociocultural context of the United States, supported by a belief system that explains powerless groups' problems as caused by themselves (e.g., genetic inadequacy, personal laziness, cultural deficits) and powerful groups' successes as the result of individual merit (e.g., superior talent, hard work), frames that resist and delegitimize the multicultural agenda have not been hard to come by. They can be expressed facilely in such language as "multiculturalism is balkanization," "affirmative action is reverse discrimination," "black/Latino/Latina students and faculty are not competent," or "special curricular programs are destroying the canon of Western civilization." On the other hand, frames challenging racism and other forms of discrimination and promoting multiculturalism may be expressed in language such as "discrimination must end," "diversity is essential for democracy," "fair pay is fair play," "the talents of people of color and women have been underused," or "affirmative action is necessary until negative action ceases."

The Role of External and Internal Constituencies— Opportunities and Constraints

The external social environment both creates pressure for change and constrains the kinds of changes that universities can successfully undertake. For instance, the culture of racism that is so deeply embedded in U.S. society significantly restricts and generates resistance to the possibilities for antiracist and multicultural change. At the same time, the need for educated workers, combined with changing racial demographics and movements for racial justice, drive such change efforts. State and federal courts, national educational spokespersons and policymakers, state legislatures that fund public higher education, major foundations, and the relative health of investment portfolios and alumni giving all affect the opportunities and resources available for multicultural change programs.

Many external publics are concerned with the state of higher education and in particular with its role in sustaining or reshaping racial relations. Often these forces are well organized and exert powerful influence on institutions' racial policies, for better or for worse. The examples include the coalitions of business and military leaders who submitted briefs in the University of Michigan's admissions' court cases: as described by Schmidt (2000): "Several Fortune 500 companies have filed briefs telling the court of the intricate, and mutually beneficial, relationships that they have been forging with Michigan and other public universities to promote diversity both in higher education and the workplace" (A21). Some have prompted multicultural reform by indicating publicly that they wish to hire graduates who can work well in diverse teams. On the other hand, there are the activities of Ward Connery's minions in seeking a ballot initiative to prohibit considerations of race in collegiate admissions.

Designs for significant changes in the educational organization must also be responsive to internal dynamics, especially to the history of the specific organization and unit with regard to multiculturalism and diversity-related issues. However, since what happens (or does not happen) in one unit often affects others, an organization-wide approach to analysis (see figures 3.1 and 3.2), planning, and action can identify strengths, anticipate reverberations, and improve the change process.

Administrative promises to make change, particularly regarding issues as controversial as racism, sexism, and multiculturalism, are sometimes more rhetorical than resolute. This is especially likely when vague commitments are made without specific plans that contain deadlines and responsibilities for action assigned to individuals and units. Image management often is a prime concern of organizational leaders. For instance, as Rowley et al. (2002) point out, "Organizations often articulate formal dispositions and organizational structures, which may only operate as myths, in order to maintain legitimacy within the broader social context" (5–6). Moreover, when overt and blatant incidents of racism or sexism surface on campuses, many local educational leaders focus primarily on protecting the image and reputation of the institution or acceding to powerful political interests fearful of apparent "rebellion."

Chang (2000) suggests that "institutional success at improving racial dynamics might well be a loose coupling of two competing forms—formal, organized, centralized efforts (perhaps originating from senior management) and informal organic patterns that are shaped by institutional culture and open communication (emanating from and occurring within multiple constituencies)" (170). Another way of saying this is that top-down (administratively led) and rationally planned strategies and bottom-up (energized by students, faculty, or community) and emergent strategies may both be employed. Comprehensive changes altering racism and sexism in any organization require top leadership to make explicit and courageous decisions that commit the organization to major innovations. But even the power of senior leaders has limits, and, as University of Maryland president William Kirwan (1998) states, "The role of the president 'can be overstated—true commitment must be a shared responsibility'" (2.9).

As multiple groups join in the change effort, leaders may arise from various organizational locations. Certainly there are examples of significant leadership from the senior administrative ranks: James Duderstadt of the University of Michigan, Donna Shalala of the University of Wisconsin, James Slaughter of Occidental College, Ruth Simmons of Brown University, and other university presidents have articulated major plans or mandates for multicultural change. But other organizational members also may exert leadership. Faculty members, individually or as a group, often have initiated efforts to change the curriculum, pass new race and ethnicity graduation requirements, champion affirmative action, and invent new courses. And at many colleges and universities, students, especially students of color, who have been the victims of overt or covert harassment and discrimination, have precipitated change efforts. Without the efforts of students of color and occasionally their white allies, and without their strong and public protests, significantly fewer leaders would come forth from the senior administration and faculty to provide key resources or support change initiatives. Finally, it is important to draw attention to the process of implementing and sustaining changes. There is many a slip between verbal commitments to change, or even the development of new programs, and their eventual operation and maintenance (Rowley et al. 2002).

In addition, universities are notoriously decentralized institutions, with transient constituencies, multiple centers of power, varying norms of administrative authority and control, and increasingly short periods of appointment for presidents, provosts, and deans. The lack of a clear bottom line, or even ready agreement among internal and external constituencies about the aims and ends of higher education, make for loosely coupled connections among the inputs (student bodies/minds and funds), throughputs (delivery of knowledge and pedagogy), and outputs (student learning, research production, community service) of these organizations (Richardson and Skinner 1990; Weick 1976). Colleges and universities are loosely coupled in another sense; while administrators, faculty, staff, and students are united for a common general purpose, they often operate as quite separate entities, with different reporting lines and different versions of their common tasks (Holton and Phillips 1995). When we add to this mix the frequently heated and highly conflictual issues involved in multicultural change, all organizational members and constituencies face multiple pressures and difficult strategic choices.

In the face of these multiple forces and pressures, successful planning efforts and decisions must include faculty, staff, students, and administrators as well as powerful external stakeholders; students and faculty of color as well as whites; women as well as men; gay and lesbian people as well as heterosexuals; and so on. Disagreements and tensions undoubtedly will arise as a result of such widespread participation, but in addition to legitimacy, plural involvement provides ideas and skills that are more responsive to the needs of multiple groups throughout the organization—especially to those groups most aggrieved.

Appealing to the (White and Male and Senior) Power Structure and Its Supporters (Including Some Persons of Color and Women)

We have suggested throughout the importance of leaders and members, people of different races, ethnicities, and other social categories, working together to create change in an organization's race and gender characteristics. But what are the possible motivations for dominant groups' involving themselves in programs when that participation could well reduce their privileges and their control of organizational resources? On occasion, efforts to reduce sexism and racism in organizations are motivated primarily by the desire of administrators and faculty members to advance social justice and improve educational outcomes for everyone. Clarity about how multicultural change can serve to advance the general welfare of the organization, not just to the advancement of a single group, can promote commitment to multiculturalism by almost everyone, including white and male senior administrators and faculty members and lower-power constituencies who also are committed to the survival and growth of the college or university. Other positive motivations may spring from such self-interest-based factors as (1) the costs of institutional racism and sexism to the organization and its members, both to people of color and women and to white people and men; and (2) new internal rewards for members or units that undertake positive efforts to reduce racism and sexism, or newly instituted sanctions for resistance to change. In addition, some change efforts may be undertaken as an attempt to ameliorate public protests, bad press, and potential litigation or out of a sense of personal guilt or value incongruence.

People and organizations that operate in racist and sexist ways sometimes are not aware of their intentions, behaviors, or programs and their effects. At other times, they act in these ways because someone or some group perceives benefits from such activities, or at least does not accurately perceive the costs of current procedures. Whether that benefit or self-interest is financial, positional (status), or emotional (feeling good about oneself) may not matter as much as the benefit process itself. If college and university leaders clearly see their self-interests linked to the rewards of change and the costs of continued exclusion and discrimination, they may be more likely to support multicultural change. This principle of organizational change, based on self-interest, is articulated clearly by Monaghan (1989) as a way of influencing the behavior of individual faculty members: "Colleges and universities should offer incentives and rewards to faculty members who show a commitment to cultural pluralism, and should hold administrators more accountable for advancing institutional goals to improve opportunities for minority scholars" (A18).

Another set of incentives involves the self-interest of senior white men themselves to reduce the level of overload, stress, and criticism associated with their privileged positions. This incentive speaks to the often invisible costs associated with such positions, including anxiety about performance, guilt about unmerited privilege, and fear of attack. For many overloaded administrators, the concentration of resources in white male hands, with its concomitant burden of responsibility to manage and administer, means that they work hard and long hours, often with minimal colleagueship, and often to their own physical detriment. Whether or not changes wrought via such self-interest also result in changes in the work and life opportunities for others in the organization is key to gaining strong support from others.

Working across Differences with Intergroup Coalitions

In the midst of differences and/or disagreements among people students, from different roles or positions in the organization, or different racial and ethnic groups, the promotion of intergroup coalitions stands as a unique model for bringing them together to support a change effort. Groups with different values, resources, and interests can be expected to pursue their self-interests and compete with other groups seeking or controlling those interests and resources. At the same time, groups that exist together within a single organization or unit have some common interests, most notably a desire to maintain the health of their common unit. Thus, cross-cutting solidarities and interests within an organization can help integrate people across the boundaries of race, gender, class, age, and organizational status or role. The identification and articulation of these common interests, as well as respect for disparate or competing interests, are the conditions for coalition creation. While intergroup coalitions represent an important way to combat racism and sexism, they are likely to be new formations in higher education organizations and not necessarily easy to establish and maintain. Attention must be paid to potential diversity and disagreement within each coalition partner, as well as between partners.

DEALING WITH RESISTANCE TO
MULTICULTURAL CHANGE

Various spokespersons, books, organizations, and conferences have attacked the multicultural challenge to racism in higher education and have suggested reasons and tactics to resist this agenda (Bernstein 1994; D'Souza 1991; Kimball 1990; Steele 1990; Wood 2002; see also the National Association of Scholars' website at www.nas.org). Resistance to multicultural change efforts is normal and should be expected to continue. Efforts that fail to anticipate such resistance fall prey to naïve assumptions about the universal appeal of multiculturalism, the existence of a consensus about social justice and the way to achieve it, the moral rightness of this agenda, and the general goodwill of U.S. educators, students, and the general public.

We neither overemphasize nor demean such resistance; rather, we try to understand its claims and tactics and to distinguish between the rhetoric of resistance, or the shape of public debate, and its underlying sources. Many people have reasonable questions and disagreements about the meaning and value of multiculturalism. Others worry that their own self-interest and comfort, their current privileges and powers, will be diminished by multicultural advances. The purpose of this analysis is not to eliminate dissent from the multicultural struggle, but to try to understand and appreciate it. But understanding resistance does not imply tolerating or accommodating it; understanding resistance means learning how to overcome it as effectively as possible.

The nature and type of resistance to multicultural change in organizations of higher education depend substantially on the origin and power of the challenge and the response of organizational leaders—the dominant cadre. The way in which this leadership group responds to the content of multicultural challenges and change efforts foretells subsequent tactics and events—including further resistance. For instance, consider first the situation in which the leadership cadre itself initiates the multicultural change process (perhaps in the form of a mandate or a design for change). Or if organizational leaders do not initiate the challenge, consider the situation in which they respond positively and proactively to pressure for change from internal groups of protesting students (see chapter 11), faculty advocates, union leaders, or external parties such as government, judicial, or community groups. In these situations, when they initiate the change process or agree with the challenging group's agenda and actively support it, organizational leaders become allies of change advocates. The leaders' concrete role in subsequent action then probably depends on the extent of their agreement with the multicultural change agenda, the resources (material and symbolic) they have at their disposal, and their knowledge of effective change tactics.

Naturally enough, when the leadership cadre of the college or university itself champions the change process, other internal parties may resist implementation of new programs and policies. Moreover, where the multicultural agenda also is being instituted or championed by senior administrators, midlevel administrators and faculty may feel squeezed from above and below—from deans and chairs and from student groups. Since university divisions (constituent colleges and departments) typically have considerable autonomy, they may be slow to act on an agenda championed by the upper administration. In addition, powerful white and male staff, faculty, and students may resist any senior administrative agenda on the basis of not having been consulted. They may feel threatened by the real or imaginary advances of women and people of color and the perceived threat to their status and interests. Then the analysis of resistance, and of plans to overcome it, must be led by the senior administrator champions within the organization.

Second, consider the situation in which the leadership cadre is opposed to the multicultural change agenda. Even in the face of challenges from within or without, or perhaps because of them, organizational leaders may resist major elements of the change effort. Local college leaders may be joined in such a response by faculty and staff colleagues, by some student groups, and by external allies such as associations of educators, political sympathizers, and the media. Then the analysis of resistance, and of tactics to overcome it, must target the leadership cadre itself and its overt or covert allies.

The work of Leeds (1969) and O'Day (1974) classifies types of resistance to change. They include attempts to (1) *nullify* the multicultural agenda through obfuscation, denial, or outright rejection of its claims and requests/demands; (2) *incorporate* or *absorb* the multicultural agenda through efforts to delay action for change, assert institutional acceptance where little exists in reality, engage leaders of the change efforts in other tasks, and even reward challengers by moving them into positions of higher authority that at the same time diminish their ability to maintain their roles as challengers; (3) *sabotage* the multicultural agenda by failing to implement good faith agreements for change or by carrying out agreements in bad faith; and (4) *counterattack* the multicultural agenda by intimidating or harassing its leaders and members, by dividing and fostering competition among challengers, or by mobilizing and supporting other resistant constituencies.

In chapter 6, we drew attention to Theodore's (1986) study of academic women who complained about and took action to fight against employment discrimination based on gender inequity and sexual harassment issues. Her informants reported that senior campus administrators often responded to their complaints and formal grievances with a number of the resistance tactics discussed above: instances of complaints being ignored (nullification), of token responses being made (incorporation), of postponement of hearings (absorption), of promises not kept (sabotage), of the women being blamed for creating the problem in the first place (nullification), and of punitive and retaliatory action (counterattack). When one of these academic women was dissatisfied with local administrators' responses and took her concerns to external EEOC offices, the protestor was not only seen as "displaying aggressive behavior considered inappropriate to both the scholarly and female roles, but she was especially to be resisted if she had shown an additional defiance and disobedience to authority by taking her case off campus" (251). Indeed, Theodore argues that "all women encounter resistance when they challenge the discrimination and ask for equitable treatment; the difference in resistance is only a matter of degree" (254).

In dealing with resistance to multicultural change it is important to keep in mind that the objective of making change is not the same as coming to agreement or even doing away with conflict. In some circumstances, uncovering and escalating underlying conflict may be vital to draw people's attention to problems of discrimination and injustice, to mobilize them to come to the aid of the effort, and to stimulate everyone to learn about multiculturalism.

Education and information can help clarify a multicultural vision, retrieve data about demographic shifts, articulate the value of diversity, and specify the steps involved in achieving change (see, e.g., the materials in chapters 3 and 9). These efforts are most likely to succeed when the sources of resistance include ignorance, lack of vision, difficulties in conceptualizing and planning change, and lack of specific multicultural teaching and administering skills. Educational efforts are unlikely to be effective when large portions of the faculty or administration continue to assert their superior knowledge or the total illegitimacy of multiculturalism.

Cooperative problem solving involves people working together on specific projects or objectives despite potential disagreement on broad goals or interests and values. Thus, it requires a problem that the various parties identify as important to solve and relevant to them all, such as the failure of the current curriculum to excite students of any background, perception by a wide range of the faculty that tenure and mentoring processes are unfair, or the college's inability to recruit and retain good students or faculty generally. Cooperative problem-solving is most likely to be effective where large numbers of people agree that discrimination exists and change must happen, where there is a strong possibility of finding common ground, and where resistance is based on difficulty planning change, procedural disagreement, and time and energy constraints.

Persuasion, as discussed earlier in the section on change strategies, assumes some mutuality of interest and openness on the part of resistors to hear such arguments or appeals, or at least to be influenced by changed incentives and the power on the part of advocates to produce such incentives. It is most likely to be effective when the sources of resistance include substantive disagreement, concern about loss of power and privilege, and monoculturalism or discrimination that is organizationally based.

Providing adequate resources for the effort may help some parties overcome their fear that changes will seriously interfere with their own time, energy, and potential for personal gain. When members already feel that they or their units are disadvantaged or mistreated, these fears may be heightened by the introduction of major organizational change efforts that appear to raise the status of other people, groups, or units (Katz 1992). Efforts to transform the curricula and teaching, to devise new grading and assignment systems, to advise more comprehensively, to deal openly with controversial issues, and to innovate in the classroom all generally require substantial personal investments and additional material resources. All too often multicultural advocates are asked to undertake these challenges on their own time and without extra help—a prescription for burnout, alienation, and resistance.

Coercion and pressure, of varying types, involves developing and exerting sufficient power to force the resistant party to alter its behavior. As noted earlier, examples of pressure range from typical organizational sanctions on faculty and staff (such as merit reviews, wage and salary adjustments, promotions/demotions) to litigation and court actions, to political mobilization efforts by students and occasionally by staff or faculty in the form of protests, demonstrations, boycotts, and strikes. This strategy is likely to be effective only when advocates have access to such power and its use, and is most likely to be necessary in the face of entrenched resistance prompted by strong substantive disagreement, concern with loss of power and privilege, and firmly established and operational institutionalized monoculturalism and discrimination.

This list of ways to deal with resistance and promote change is not complete, and other strategies, or modifications and mixes of these strategies, may be most effective. As suggested earlier with regard to generic change tactics, one might start with a persuasion-based strategy using education and dialogue, and proceed to pressure and coercion only when it becomes clear that mutual listening and regard are absent. Similarly, one might start with requests for cooperative problem-solving and stay with that approach as long as good-faith efforts are evident. In contrast, one might start with threats and displays of power, moving to cooperative problem-solving or education when it appears that willing collaborators are present and committed to work on change.

TRAPS TO AVOID IN MAKING MULTICULTURAL CHANGE

One way to summarize this discussion is to consider some of the common traps in undertaking multicultural change; this may help change planners and advocates develop more successful strategies and avoid failure.

Focusing on crisis management. Crises draw everyone's attention to an issue and often trigger immediate attempts to reduce the crisis and restore normal working operations. At the same time, they are often symptoms of deeper issues (see figures 3.1 and 3.2). Resolving a temporary crisis, however effectively, does not necessarily address the underlying conditions of inequality and/or discrimination. In this context we repeat earlier cautions about the limited utility of a "lecture on diversity" or "diversity training," which have become all too common responses to racial incidents (Katz and Miller 1988). Any serious change effort requires a long-term vision of future possibilities, where the specific current effort is headed, and a plan (or at least the outline of initial steps) for effective ongoing implementation. It also requires written goals, concrete actions, time lines for their accomplishment, and specification of lines of accountability.

Planning and developing multiculturalism as a temporary project. Articulating and designing a short-term innovation—perhaps "a diversity year"—may ease current pressures for change and support some initiatives, but will fail because it does not appreciate the centrality of multiculturalism to the core purposes of higher education. It also fails to appreciate the long-standing history and consequent depth of discrimination and monoculturalism in the contemporary society, including colleges and universities, and thus the likely of retrenchment as soon as the current thrust for change wanes.

Sporadic or nonintegrated planning and implementation. Multicultural change efforts that are not built into the organization's established ways of teaching, learning, and administering can easily be marginalized. Then they may exist as isolated pockets of innovation or are seen as the responsibility of the Human Relations Department, the Affirmative Action Officer, or the Center for African American or Women's Studies, and not as the responsibility of every dean and department chair and every organizational member. If such change efforts are seen as a standard part of faculty and staff roles, both the individuals and their units can be monitored and held accountable for progress on making and institutionalizing change.

Exclusive reliance on integrated planning and implementation. As essential as it is to integrate planning and implementation of changes to achieve multiculturalism into established and official collegiate processes, this is not sufficient (see the discussion of Chang 2000, earlier in this chapter). Given the difficulty of change in the face of resistance of various kinds, change advocates must maintain flexibility and adapt to changing circumstances. This requires a constantly developing network of visionaries, innovators, advocates, and day-to-day supporters who can monitor change and hold officials accountable for meeting specified goals.

Reinventing the wheel. A considerable body of history and literature is now available to shed light on the experience of challenging discrimination on campus (Adams, Bell, and Griffin 1997; Association of American Colleges and Universities 1995; Bowser, Auletta, and Jones 1993; Cheatham and Associates 1991; Dialogues for Diversity 1994; Hurtado et al. 1999; Smith et al. 2002; Valverde and Castenell 1998; and see examples of specific programs and resources in chapter 12). No individual college or university has to develop its agenda or plan entirely on its own. The experience of others can suggest workable alternatives, options that can be carefully considered and then adapted to the local campus situation, vision, and resources.

Relying overmuch on particular activists or elites. Grassroots activists, usually in the form of student protestors and protest organizations, can stimulate the change process. Progressive organizational elites, in the form of a few powerful faculty members, deans, or executive officers, can legitimize, fund, and spearhead the effort. Even their token or rhetorical efforts may be useful. However, it is unwise to let the success of the effort hinge on any single person or small group. Moreover, sustained and effective change typically requires representative activists from both the top and the bottom of the organization, as well as many middle-dwellers, and from persons and groups representing varying racial, ethnic, gender, age, and organizational status.

Limiting tactics to debate and persuasion. As essential as rational debate and verbal persuasion are to the traditional notion of intellectual engagement in the academy, they are not the total answer. Surfacing and escalating conflict and deeply felt emotions are often essential to bring attention to long-ignored problems and to require implementation of needed changes. Moreover, people often are moved by pressure (in terms of financial and other rewards or overt coercion and sanctions), and plans must be made to respond to organizational members who resist or try to sabotage the multicultural change effort.

Limiting tactics to confrontation and pressure. As critical as mobilization for pressure and protest may be, it also is important to be able to sit down, listen, converse, and negotiate with apparent opponents. At appropriate times and places, persuasion, cooperative problem-solving and consensus building are as important as conflict escalation; in the long run they may be the essential steps in long-term institutionalization of change.

Proceeding with inadequate resources. Many change efforts are subtly sabotaged by a shortage of personnel and funds or insufficient attention and support from senior and powerful leaders. Adequate resources, support from leadership cadres, and diversification of responsibilities will be necessary. People who are already working at 100 percent of capacity cannot lead significant change efforts (Katz and Miller 1988). Planners must safeguard against burnout and overload. Volunteer efforts must be accompanied by time off from regular duties, rearrangement of normal obligations, or other forms of release time. Retreats and support networks for those involved in the change effort may be helpful. And all of these efforts will have to be supported with funds.

Exaggerating resistance and overlooking potential allies. Just as it is important not to overlook or deny the existence of resistance, it is important not to overstate it and to categorize all nonsupport as resistance. An entire institution does not have to be transformed, nor convinced of the need for change, for substantial groups of university members to begin to reeducate themselves and their peers, to improve the quality of instruction for and interaction with students and colleagues—especially members of traditionally oppressed groups—and to initiate a more equitable and supportive climate of learning and living. Change leaders must look for, solicit, and trust the participation of actual and potential allies, members of advantaged as well as oppressed groups, even when they are initially invisible.

Failing to monitor and evaluate multicultural changes. Many institutions have developed and implemented innovative programs but have failed to guarantee their maintenance over time. Others, without a plan for assessment or evaluation, have little idea of the long-term impact (positive or negative) of such innovations. Regardless of the organizational dimension or unit(s) in which multicultural innovations are developed (e.g., administrative restructuring or staff retraining, faculty development, curriculum reform, or student programming), efforts to institutionalize such programs and build them into the ongoing structures and cultures of the organization require constant monitoring and occasional assessment of their impact on target groups.

Failing to celebrate success. The effort to challenge racism (and other forms of oppression and privilege) and promote multiculturalism is hard work. It is important to draw attention to the successes of these efforts, perhaps to plan events that reward and honor change advocates and the organizational leaders and members who adopt new ways of working, teaching, and learning. Such rewards also can be institutionalized in the traditional merit system for pay and advancement.

None of the theories or strategies for change making discussed here can be applied automatically to particular colleges and universities and their unique situations and goals. However, all the principles in this chapter, including the analysis of resistance and suggestions for dealing with it and avoiding traps, are relevant to every higher education organization seeking to challenge racism and promote multiculturalism. Change can come by thinking seriously about the options presented here and in the following chapters, fitting them to the local organization, and daring to act vigorously and sensibly.

Chapter Nine

Planning Multicultural Audits*

Colleges and universities can learn many general lessons from the accumulated research on student, faculty, and administrator experience with discrimination on campuses. Some of this literature, along with firsthand reports from students and faculty members, appear in chapters 4–7. However, local change efforts require familiarity with the specific conditions of discrimination in each distinct organizational setting. That level of familiarity requires local data and a process of gathering information to guide change initiatives. Smith (1989) suggests that organizational audits are a critical initial strategy in efforts to reduce discrimination and achieve more multicultural environments. Such audits can help identify problem areas, illuminate the potential for program and institutional changes (see the discussion in chapter 8), and set baselines for evaluating change efforts.

A local assessment or multicultural audit of intergroup issues on campus, institution-wide or for a specific subunit, is in many ways like any other institutional research or data-gathering effort; it requires systematic planning, specific expertise, careful data collection and analysis, thoughtful interpretations, and clear reports and recommendations. And it requires a committed and competent multicultural team that can carry through all these steps. In this chapter we discuss the principles and procedures involved in multicultural audits and provide examples of questions used and data reported in a variety of collegiate efforts. In addition to the examples provided here, a number of other print and web sources provide guidelines for conducting multicultural audits and examples of useful items and instruments (California Post-Secondary Education Commission Report 92-24 1992; Chung 1997; Garcia et al. 2001; Levitan and Wolf 1994; Smith et al. 2002; Tierney 1990; also see the websites

---

*Much of the material in this chapter was published previously in Chesler, 1998, Planning multicultural audits in higher education. *To improve the Academy*, *17*, 171–201. Used with permission of the POD Network.

www.aahe.org/assessment/ and www.usc.edu/dept/education/CUE/projects/
ds/diversityscorecard.html).

BACKGROUND TO AUDITS AND
THE DEVELOPMENT OF CHANGE PLANS

A multicultural audit is not simply an effort to gather and analyze data—it is an intervention into the college's life. The desire to create an audit usually springs from some concern about the current state of affairs and a parallel desire to improve organizational functioning with regard to issues of racial and gender diversity and discrimination. Just acknowledging such a need or objective, coupled with an effort to gather data, necessarily draws attention to these issues and their impacts. Given the level of controversy surrounding these issues, and the potential resistance to gathering or publicizing information that may challenge the college's or a unit's public image and threaten certain groups' privileges and advantages, we can expect the audit to be a focal point for struggle. If the audit succeeds in increasing information and raising consciousness of existing problems, it will probably surface organizational conflicts. The clearly political (and probably conflictual) nature of a multicultural audit must be acknowledged and attended to throughout the stages of design and implementation. Then it can be effectively integrated into a coherent change strategy that is consistent with elements of a persuasion-based or coercion-based approach, or with parts of each (see figure 8.3).

Some higher education organizations have undertaken such audits as a way of appeasing, delaying, or cooling off protesting groups and then have allowed the audits to sit on the shelf. Others, with the best of apparent intentions, have conducted audits without consideration of the broader change process that must result and have thus wasted considerable time between data collection and the introduction of coherent change planning. And some organizations have constructed the audit team as an audit-and-change team from the outset, facilitating a relatively seamless and rapid transition from information to change planning.

Recurrent assessments that are undertaken in good faith serve multiple purposes. They raise the organization's awareness of problems; they may lift the burden of consciousness development from the shoulders of aggrieved constituencies and place it in the center of the organization's or unit's planning efforts; and they can help inform and direct the goals and tactics of a change effort. They can also identify positive and exemplary programs in select subunits or departments of the larger organization. A well-done and respected audit can create a benchmark that when repeated can chart the progress of change efforts and assess their effectiveness over time. By using an organizational lens and providing systemic data in a rigorous fashion, an audit can educate members about their entire organization beyond their personal day-to-day experiences and their individual relationships, departments, or units. For some individuals and groups it can help them learn that things they experienced personally also have been or are being experienced by others. Since members of dominant groups may not comprehend much of the discrimination that exists in colleges and universities or may overlook it entirely, the audit can also serve the function of making covert processes overt. It may educate everyone regarding the continuing existence of problems — matters that can have an impact on or even dramatically contradict the organization's public mission and ideals.

It is important to build the audit into a larger plan for making changes that promote diversity and multiculturalism (see chapter 8 and figure 8.2). The elements of a visionary or progressive plan can be developed using the organizational framework presented there and in chapter 3. Unless a broad perspective is employed and adapted to the local context, an audit may miss its mark. Without links to a concern for change (if not a coherent plan), and a change-planning team with an implementation strategy, a completed audit may end up wasting time and energy and simply sit and gather dust. Or it may become the flashpoint for controversy that detracts from the core struggle over discrimination and over initiatives that might reduce discrimination. Once organizational members provide information via an audit process, they will expect to hear about the results and to witness change; if nothing happens, these frustrated expectations can dramatically raise the level of distrust and tension and subsequent hopelessness and apathy.

The development of clear goals and leadership commitments for the multicultural audit and for appropriate changes are prerequisite to the change process. In some cases such leadership may not initially be forthcoming, and support from organizational leaders may need to be built up over time. In addition, design and data collection efforts should include members of all affected groups: If an audit's concern is a single unit or department, representatives of all membership groups in that department (faculty, students, and staff) should be involved. If the concern is broader, including the entire college or university, multiple actors from a wide variety of units or departments should be involved in the planning and implementation. If the audit is to provide a complete picture of the higher education organization, it should assess all elements of the organization depicted in figures 3.1 and 3.2. Of course, not all audits will reach that broadly; some may focus just on climate, on representation or retention, or on any one or a selected set of the organizational dimensions illustrated in chapter 3. Finally, an audit should be planned in ways that deliberately lead into the creation of recommendations and an action plan for change. Thus, part of the job of the audit is to educate and prepare key personnel, including the group doing the audit, for the change process that it is part of and that will follow.

The working unit for most audits varies. It may include a senior central planning group and/or a specially created and trained team drawn from varied constituencies throughout the organization that makes this work its key focus. An alternative is to contract with an external consultant group to do this work. While hiring external experts has certain advantages, to the extent that key internal constituencies and stakeholders are involved in the design and control of the assessment process, they are more likely to enrich it with experiential knowledge (about the institution's history of struggle with these issues), to own the results, and use them in the change-making process. The goal must be to create a credible audit that is technically sound and substantively meaningful but that does not require endless time and energy that could dissipate resources potentially devoted to achieving organizational change.

Providing data that can guide a change effort is not the same as commissioning an academic research venture. But even if customary research traditions of reliability and validity are not of primary concern, they remain relevant and should be reflected in work that has high credibility and relevance for the issues at hand. This approach is consistent with the tradition of action-research or participatory-action-research, in which a priority on organizational improvement and empowering organizational members has at least equal priority with advances in knowledge (Brown and Tandon 1983; Gaventa 1993; Reason and Bradbury 2001). Thus, the audit should be done in a way that (1) receives support from key organization and/or subunit leaders; (2) involves high participation from members across the unit in data collection and creates substantial trust from these members in the process and findings; (3) develops insights and ideas about the feasibility of alternative goals and strategies to bring about change; (4) involves multiple groups and constituencies in designing and implementing changes based on the data; and (5) builds continuing capacity for assessment (and reassessment) into the school's operations.

PRELIMINARY STEPS

1. *Creating a cultural audit or assessment team.* Great care must be taken in the selection and preparation of the team or unit conducting the audit. The people working together on this task must be able to work as a multicultural team, and the team development process starts with recruiting people who are truly interested in this work and who represent diverse social identity groups, constituencies, and functional units (departments and work sites). A group that is diverse and representative will mirror the larger organization. But though broad representation is useful, it is not a substitute for selecting a group of people who have the commitment and skill to collaborate in doing this difficult job well and reflecting openly and honestly on the unit's current state and its needs for improvements.

Since an audit requires considerable time and energy of team members, supervisors must make sufficient release time available for the internal team. For instance, team members must be able to meet for a two-hour period, perhaps once every two weeks, and still have time to do some preparatory reading and thinking and working between sessions; they may require occasional longer retreat sessions early on and especially during design and report preparation. Since a well-done audit may take a year or more, that commitment may require substantial changes in team members' job assignments—they cannot be expected to undertake such tasks on an overload basis or without support from their supervisors.

Part of the process of developing a multicultural audit team involves creating a working environment and interpersonal relationships that are consistent with a multicultural activity. In chapter 10, we discuss a number of issues involved in creating a multicultural team, including attention to norms, membership, leadership, concepts of team play, and a forthright focus on issues of discrimination at both institutional and interpersonal levels. Unless these issues are attended to, the team will struggle endlessly with its own internalized processes of racism and sexism, with dysfunctional interpersonal and group dynamics, and with the organization's preexisting discriminatory structures and cultures. Numerous examples exist of well-intentioned and competent audit teams foundering on exactly these reefs.

Creating an effective multicultural audit team will take time and energy, and special meetings or retreats probably will be necessary to achieve this goal. Team development issues and racist/sexist/classist baggage are likely to arise throughout the life of the audit, and these internal concerns must be addressed regularly. If the audit is contracted out to an external agency, that agency, too, must be selected and monitored as to its multicultural construction and operation and the liaison between the internal and external teams monitored closely.

In addition to team creation, the multicultural audit team should prepare itself for the audit by

- investigating the nature and history of discrimination, diversity, and multiculturalism in the U.S. society and in higher education in general, and in the particular type of college or university in question (e.g., secular or religious, four-year or two-year, public or private, research oriented or liberal arts, graduate or undergraduate);
- exploring and sharing members' own ideologies, perceptions, and experiences regarding life at the college, especially with regard to intergroup encounters and issues; and
- getting acquainted with the procedures and substance of comparable audits

These preparatory steps emphasize the importance of enlisting social scientists who are experts in organizational matters, scholars of race and diversity issues, faculty development personnel, technical research specialists, multicultural advocates, and staff and student colleagues who could be part of a larger team or group of advisors to the audit and the eventual change effort.

Because the design and conduct of a multicultural audit necessarily involves broader organizational politics (and accompanying power plays), team members will need to be buffered and protected from efforts at co-optation, formal or informal dissatisfaction, resistance, or even retaliation—from peers or from organizational authorities displeased with the findings or the process employed. Thus, lines of reporting and oversight authority need to be clear and maintained. These cautions are especially important since the effort to create a more multicultural organization requires reducing race and gender privilege, and data that surface about such privilege and its discriminatory effects may generate resistance (see the discussion in chapter 8). Thus, the college's or university's leadership cadre must continually mobilize the support and resources (financial, political, emotional) necessary to maintain and follow up the audit and instigate, advocate, and support recommended changes.

2. *Preparing the organization or unit for assessment and discussion of issues and problems.* The issues and problems that occupy most audits include equity-inequity, discrimination, cultural diversity, and multiculturalism throughout any or all of the key dimensions of higher education organizations. Preparation is part of a broader educational and political process that the college's leadership cadre must undertake and it should include

- public clarification of the school's diversity mission and vision, their relationship to other missions and goals, and the role of the audit in this context;
- orientation to the audit of key constituencies and powerful figures in the school; and
- evidence of support and commitment by the president/chancellor, provost, deans, directors, senior faculty, and other formal and informal leaders

Faculty must be centrally involved in this process, both in their roles as teachers and organizational citizens. As experts in understanding and working with the needs and skills of faculty and staff, human resource specialists can serve as aides to the audit team. Other key constituencies include students and staff/administrators. Above all, senior leadership support and commitment are crucial, because the audit team must be able to trust that organizational leaders (or whoever is sponsoring the audit) are sincerely interested in the information, in accurate information no matter how positive or negative, and that they will continue to legitimate the audit as a desirable and accepted activity of the college or particular unit being assessed. Multicultural audit team members must be able to trust that organizational leaders are committed to full reporting of the audit's results and to using them to advance multiculturalism and combat the discrimination that they discover. In the event of lukewarm leadership support, audit advocates will need to generate additional support by demonstrating how their work can make a positive contribution to the organization. Of course, at the outset no one can say whether professed support is real and what actions senior leaders or anyone else may take or commission on the basis of audit results, but if the team does not believe leadership is committed to using the data for multicultural improvement, its members will lose energy and commitment for what may appear to be a waste of time. The commitment of senior leaders will have to be tested and publicly demonstrated—in word and deed.

At times, the initiative for an audit may be generated from low power groups—by students, unionized staff members, part-time lecturers or faculty adjuncts, or other aggrieved stakeholders inside or outside the organization. This situation may occur when groups that raised concerns were ignored, or told that their concerns were insubstantial or unrepresentative or that their complaints were only anecdotal. Their interest in conducting an audit may be to document and make public the nature and extent of their negative experiences in the organization. Under these circumstances, support and commitment from senior leadership may not be vigorous, at least not initially. With luck, it can be garnered and strengthened later in the process. If not, the conduct of the audit itself, regardless of the data, may become part of a public political struggle, and it may need to be conducted more informally (perhaps with less rigor), without official permission, and with clear linkages to mobilized interest groups that can provide some legitimacy and some political cover.

The organizational stage for an officially sponsored audit can be set by establishing good communication and working links with various constituencies and committees of the school (staff advisory committee, executive committee, faculty senate, faculty or staff unions, trustees, student governments), to inform them of the audit, to prepare them to participate in it, and to gain their assistance and legitimation for the effort. It also is vital to gain the cooperation of varied identity and interest groups, including groups of students and faculty of color and women's caucuses. This step is important in promoting and ensuring a high response rate in information gathering, and a high response rate is itself an important aspect of the audit's eventual credibility and utility. However, groups that feel disadvantaged or oppressed by the organization are not likely to trust the audit process any more than they trust the organization in general; they may be unwilling to respond to this effort unless reassured of their safety and confidentiality, the audit's utility and relevance for their lives, and access to the results. Likewise, people and groups (or units) opposed to the multicultural agenda itself may be unwilling to respond to a multicultural audit unless they, too, are reassured that their voices will be heard and their concerns addressed. Establishing clear guidelines for maintaining confidentiality, for protecting the vulnerability of key informants, and distinguishing and separating an audit from evaluations of individuals' performances are important aspects of organizational preparation.

THE DESIGN OF THE AUDIT

3. *Designing the audit itself.* The design phase involves several substeps: (1) deciding which issues to explore; (2) deciding from whom or where (or from what

constituencies or identity groups or interest groups) to seek information; and (3) deciding what information-gathering strategies to use.

The first substep can be facilitated by creating a list of key problems or concerns—the current negatives—and effective policies and practices—the positives. The ensuing list will differ according to the type of school involved and the issues that are locally present and potent. Such a list can start with exploration of specific incidents or grievances that have surfaced. More generally, however, a systematic audit can address many of the organizational dimensions identified in chapter 3. Examples of issues or focuses of the information quest include (italicized terms key these foci to the organizational dimensions of figures 3.1 and 3.2):

- stated *mission* of the college;
- *culture(s)* of the school and its constituent units;
- demographic composition of the *power structure* and decision makers;
- management, leadership, and decision-making practices (*power structure*);
- representation of diverse *membership* in various roles and levels;
- instructional content and processes (*technology*);
- character of research being conducted (*technology*);
- *climate* of social relationships, both formal and informal (among and between students, faculty, and staff);
- *resources* actually or potentially available for the change effort;
- quality of relations and services provided to and received from external communities (*boundaries*);
- positive or negative changes in any of the above organizational dimensions over time
- incidents or public examples of racism, sexism, homophobia, and so forth;
- policies and programs relevant to cultural differences or multicultural issues;
- history of past discrimination and prior or current antidiscrimination efforts;
- interest in or feasibility of particular changes regarding diversity and multiculturalism;
- nature and location of resistance to change.

The second substep involves deciding from whom or what to seek information. Sources of data can include

- individuals and groups (or subgroups) of students, faculty, administrators or higher-level executives, board members, staff members, parents, community members or representatives of the public at large, alumni;
- records (such as personnel files, incident reports, grievance files);
- documents reflecting policies and programs;
- minutes of meetings or events;

- notes and materials from workshops on teaching or conducting research;
- curricula offerings and syllabi.

If the audit focus is narrow—perhaps on the improvement of teaching—omitting some of these sources makes sense. But whether the focus is narrow or broad, it is important to include people of color (and women and members of other obviously or potentially disadvantaged and aggrieved groups) as data sources, for their experience often is highly informative about the covert nature of organizational discrimination. It is important to gather data from white people as well as people of color (and men as well as women), because the contrasts or similarities between various groups' perceptions of the environment will help to clarify the way even apparently fair and just organizations may create different working and learning conditions for people of different backgrounds, social locations, and organizational status and function.

The third substep involves deciding what information-gathering strategies to use. For instance, multiple information-gathering strategies may include

- questionnaires;
- personal interviews;
- small-group interviews (focus groups);
- observations at key organizational sites and of key processes;
- written materials and documents;
- observations and evaluations of classroom teaching;
- reports from special events—hearings or town meetings;
- meetings discussing preliminary reports of the audit; and
- brief ethnographies of student, faculty, and staff life.

Useful, brief, and nontechnical discussions of the comparative advantages and disadvantages of some of these data-gathering methods can be found in almost any research methods textbook in the social sciences. The choice of instruments will depend on the audit's focus and purpose (e.g., interviews will do better at uncovering covert discrimination than will questionnaires) as well as local logistics and resources (e.g., self-report paper-and-pencil questionnaires are much more cost-effective than face-to-face interviews).

Figure 9.1 presents one way to visualize the complex integration of issues, data sources, and data-gathering strategies. The choices of what to look at can be listed under "Issues," and decisions about sources and information-gathering strategies inserted in the boxes going across.

Questionnaires and surveys have been used by many colleges and universities. Among the many, Michigan State University (Social Science Research Bureau 1991) assessed faculty and academic staff members' views of diversity issues; Pennsylvania State University assessed faculty and staff knowledge of

Issues	Individual Surveys				Individual Interviews				Group Inter-views	Organizational Data	
	Student	Faculty	Staff	Alumni	Student	Faculty	Staff	Alumni		Obser-vation	Records

Figure 9.1. Inquiry Issues, Modes, and Sources

disability-related issues (Project Opportunity and Access, Special Education and Rehabilitation Services Program, n.d.) and faculty and student views on lesbian and gay issues (Committee on Lesbian and Gay Concerns 1992); the University of Georgia (Campus Climate Research Group 2002) surveyed lesbian, gay, bisexual, transsexual, and queer students regarding their experiences on campus; Massachusetts Institute of Technology assessed minority students' and alumni's views of the quality of campus life (McBay 1986); Virginia Tech (n.d.-b) surveyed classified staff members' views of diversity issues; the University of Pennsylvania (2001) surveyed faculty members' views of their quality of life; and the School of Dentistry at the University of Michigan assessed student, staff, faculty, and patient views of the School's cultural climate (Multicultural Initiatives Committee 1995). Examples of items used in some of these surveys are provided here. By including these examples, we do not endorse any single item or set of questions, but illustrate a range of topics and question wording. People interested in pursuing these surveys further should examine several entire instruments, as well as websites and relevant scholarly publications, to select focuses and items that best fit their own campus issues and concerns.

The first set of questions that follows is a sample of items from the 1991 Michigan State University report and focuses on the faculty's general acceptance of and support for diversity (Social Science Research Bureau 1991, appendix: 2). It uses a five-point Likert scale for response: 5 = strongly agree, 4 = agree, 3 = neither agree nor disagree, 2 = disagree, and 1 = strongly disagree.

- The dean of my college is strongly committed to increasing the gender diversity of the faculty.
- The chair of my department/school appreciates time I spend fostering multicultural understanding and cooperation.
- Issues of diversity and pluralism are often topics of discussion in my department/unit meetings.

The next set of questions comes from the student portion of a survey conducted at Pennsylvania State University (Committee on Lesbian and Gay Concerns 1992). It uses a five-point Likert scale and asks informants, "How likely are you to respond in the following ways?" The choices: 5 = very unlikely, 4 = unlikely, 3 = not sure, 2 = likely, or 1 = very likely.

- Tell a derogatory gay, lesbian or bisexual joke.
- Tell someone I disapprove of anti-gay, anti-lesbian, or anti-bisexual remarks.
- Avoid taking a particular class because I heard the instructor was a gay man.

The following item is selected from the student portion of a survey that was part of the report from the University of Michigan School of Dentistry (Multicultural Initiatives Committee 1995, appendix B2: 2). That survey used a five-point Likert scale as follows: 5 = always, 4 = often, 3 = sometimes, 2 = rarely, 1 = never, and asks, "How often have you experienced unequal treatment from students?"

- of another gender
- of another ethnic/racial group
- with a physical disability
- with a different sexual orientation
- from a different age group
- from a different religious background

The same question was repeated asking dentistry students how often they experienced unequal treatment from faculty and from staff, and a similar set of questions also was posed to dental school faculty and staff members.

Focus group interviews have been used at the University of California, Berkeley (Duster 1991), the School of Public Health at the University of Michigan (Task Force on Racial and Cultural Concerns 1990), and George Mason University (The Conflict Clinic 1991) to gather the experiences and outlooks of students of color and white students. In the self-study conducted by the University of Michigan's School of Public Health (1990), the following five questions were used to focus group discussions (Task Force on Racial and Cultural Concerns 1990: 5):

- In thinking about your experiences here in the School of Public Health, list the two or three major barriers, problems or concerns that have made you upset or angry, or that have had a negative effect on you.
- As you think of your interactions with faculty, what are things that professors do that are upsetting to you or make you uncomfortable or angry in the classroom or in more private interactions?
- In thinking about your experiences as a graduate student, please describe any interactions with other students in the school, that made you upset or angry.
- Thinking about the content of your courses, how is racism as it affects public health problems dealt with in your classes?
- Thinking about the issues we've talked about, list suggestions or recommendations that you would make to improve the school.

Individual interviews were used by the University of California system (with faculty and students—Justus, Freitag, and Parker 1987), Pennsylvania State University (with lesbian and gay students—Committee on Lesbian and Gay Concerns 1992), San Diego State University (with students and staff and faculty—Social Science Research Laboratory 1999), and LeMoyne College (with department heads—1991), among others. Many of the items used in surveys and group interviews have also been used in individual interview studies.

Observations of group interactions, public meetings, or the behavior of people at key campus locations (dormitory lunchrooms, campus rallies, athletic events, academic forums, etc.) can shed light on the campus climate as well as the success or failure to implement diversity-related policies and practices. To be truly useful, observations and observers should record the situation as fully as possible, leaving the winnowing of important from unimportant details until later analysis. In a somewhat different approach to public meetings, both MIT and Wellesley gathered information by observing open forums or public meetings where issues were discussed or audit data reported (McBay 1986; Task Force on Racism 1989), and the State University of New York (Office of Student Affairs and Academic Programs 1989) investigated and reported in detail a series of "bias-related" activities. Additional examples of items and strategies for use in conducting campus audits focused on diversity are reviewed briefly in Levitan and Wolf (1994); other sources include various research studies on multiculturalism, the experiences of faculty and students with diversity, and so forth.

A number of audits have included questions that can be addressed via the *examination of written organizational policies, procedures, and programs*. For instance, requests may be made for each college or unit to share its plans for increasing minority enrollment and hiring. The response will provide evidence of whether such planning has been done and whether it has been done systematically. Further requests or data collected over time may clarify whether such planning led to the unit's own desired outcomes or to outcomes that met a broader organizational standard. Various units also may be asked to identify the key personnel responsible for dealing, proactively and reactively, with issues related to diversity and multiculturalism. The existence of such named individuals may be taken as important evidence of organizational priorities, and these individuals also may be key informants for other questions. Furthermore, unit policies and programs can be examined to determine if they provide mechanisms to deal with complaints or grievances concerning discrimination, diversity, and multiculturalism. If such mechanisms (ombudspersons, sexual and racial harassment policies, dispute settlement systems, informal or formal grievance procedures) do exist, are they widely publicized and known throughout the unit? With particular respect to the teaching–learning mission of the college or university, the formal and informal curricula of various colleges or departments may be examined (with experts from those units participating) to determine the degree to which courses are inclusive in content and procedures. Green (1989) provides a series of checklists that can be used to investigate and record institutional policies and programs, such as those focused on hiring procedures, admissions practices, campus life activities, and resource allocations.

The examination of *organizational records* also can produce information about diversity in campus membership, and the history of hiring, promotion, and retention of members of different racial and gender categories. For instance, Indiana University (1992), the University of Wisconsin, Madison (Steering Committee on Minority Affairs 1987), and many other institutions report statistical profiles reflecting the existence and representation of students, faculty, and staff of color. The University of Colorado report (Office of Diversity and Equity 2000), in particular, provides a wide range of such profiles, within and across various schools, departments, and units.

Decisions about what to inquire into, where or from whom to gather data, and how to gather them are not independent of one another—choices about what information to seek will influence the choice of strategies used to gather the data and the sources to collect them from. The creation of a time line for completing various survey activities will be useful (although such time lines are notoriously underestimated), as will appropriate division of labor among audit team members, with possible formation of subcommittees. Key questions that a team must address in the creation of an integrative audit design include (Chesler 1998):

- What do we want to achieve—what information do we want (focuses)? Assess attitudes, gather stories about experiences, assess behaviors, assess barriers to change, assess policies and their impact.
- How do we want to achieve our goal—how do we get this information?
  - Committee discussions, questionnaires to people in the school, focus group conversations/interviews, analysis of the curriculum, analysis of statistical data on school membership.
- From whom (where) do we want to get this information?
  - Students, staff, faculty, alumni, patients, school records.
- When do we want each of these pieces delivered?
- Who will do which tasks? (182–82)

Most formal audits' plans for data collection and analysis will have to be approved by an institutional human subjects review board, where issues of accountability and confidentiality are of prime concern. However, such boards, which generally review proposals to conduct research in external environments, may be unaccustomed to dealing with research within their own organization. They may be particularly discomforted by questions probing delicate issues concerning race, gender, and sexual orientation, or by the possibility of "negative" information surfacing. This eventuality suggests one more of the unique properties (and sometimes difficulties) that distinguish a multicultural audit from most other institutional review procedures and research efforts. Careful planning, internal education, and the support of senior leadership should help smooth the path.

CONDUCTING THE AUDIT

4. *Gathering information.* Based on decisions made in designing the audit, the team can now gather the data. Unless the audit team is large, other people and organizational resources will have to participate at this stage. Research departments

or classes, other faculty and staff members, graduate student assistants and interns, and computer experts and other technically skilled personnel may be called upon. Considerable debate currently rages as to whether respondents are more honest and the data more valid when the data gatherers are of the same social background as those they gather it from (e.g., when people of color interview students and faculty of color, women staff members interview women staff, etc.). The verdict is still out, and powerful arguments resound on both sides; audit teams need to be aware of this issue and consider it carefully. They also must assure informants of the confidentiality of their responses. Specific steps involved in gathering the data include

• selecting a sample of people and places to gather information from,
• monitoring the information-gathering process as it occurs, and
• altering the design as required by early responses.

Some collegiate self-reports have used large samples, while others have used relatively small data bases. For example, in the Michigan State University report (Social Science Research Bureau 1991), 775 faculty and academic staff members returned questionnaires; at the University of Pennsylvania (Gender Equity Committee 2001), 483 faculty members returned questionnaires; and at Virginia Tech (n.d.-b) 1,636 classified staff members filled out questionnaires. On the other hand, at LeMoyne College (1991: 44) 64 people "intimately involved with and concerned about diversity" were interviewed; at George Mason University (The Conflict Clinic 1991), 150 people participated in 47 personal interviews and 17 group interviews; at the University of Georgia (Campus Climate Research Group 2002), 82 members of the lesbian, gay, bisexual, transgender, and queer community returned questionnaires; while at the University of California, Berkeley (Duster 1991), 230 students participated in 55 focus groups, some of which were racially and ethnically heterogeneous and others, racially and ethnically homogeneous.

Decisions about sample size may be influenced as much by the availability of resources as by particular inquiry goals or concerns about representativeness or inclusiveness. Obviously, a large questionnaire survey or series of interviews involving many respondents requires more resources and staff assistance than does a smaller project. If extensive individual or group interviews are planned, care must be taken to train interviewers in how to collect the data. Beyond gathering data, specially trained personnel and technical resources will be required to perform the analyses.

As the audit progresses, it may become clear that some questions or focuses of inquiry are not relevant or useful to pursue, while other important focuses may arise from early conversations and responses. Early responses to questionnaires may demonstrate the need for follow-up interviews, and early interview responses may indicate the need for a more representative questionnaire survey. Alterations in the overall plan should be made in order to get the best possible data on emerging matters as they become apparent. While this approach may present some compromise with the traditional research priority on replicability and reliability, in the long run it should pay off with greater validity and relevance.

5. *Preparing the information for analysis.* This stage involves taking the raw data gathered and organizing them in ways that permit systematic analysis. Quantitative data gathered in surveys or from statistical records generally must be coded (reduced to numerical constants) and entered into a computerized system for machine analysis. Qualitative data gathered from individual or group interviews, or from meeting minutes or observations, generally must be transcribed (if recorded on audiotape) and prepared for either manual analysis or electronic analysis via software designed to identify key themes. Technical assistance in both forms of analysis generally is available on most campuses, and audit committees should be encouraged to make use of these resources.

6. *Analyzing the data.* The choice of analytic format depends on the type of data gathered and the degree of analytic sophistication desired. With quantitative data, for instance, in some cases univariate analyses or marginal tabulations of gross data will be adequate, while at other times multivariate and/or regression analyses will be most useful and convincing to audiences. With qualitative data, the analytic format may include tabulation of the number of times various themes or issues arise in interviews, or the presentation of direct excerpted quotes of people's experiences and comments ("narratives" or "stories"). Sometimes personal quotes (presented anonymously) will be more convincing than a vast array of numbers, and sometimes the reverse will be true, depending upon the nature of the data, the audience, and the overall purposes of the audit. Several examples of data gathered in focus groups and analyzed via qualitative methods are included here.

Earlier we presented some of the questions used in the group interviews conducted by the University of Michigan's School of Public Health (Task Force on Racial and Cultural Concerns 1990). The school's report indicates that the data were collected and analyzed by a faculty–student team specially trained in techniques of qualitative interviewing and data analysis. Their inductive coding system generated the following:

The nine most prominent themes that emerged from the interviews are:

1. There are demands on blacks to educate whites to issues of race and racism.
2. Low socioeconomic status is equated with minority status.
3. Issues of race and racism are ignored in course content.
4. Faculty devalue students' experiences and options.
5. Faculty are uninterested and not helpful in advising and counseling students.

6. The grading system is subjective and standards are ambiguous.
7. There is a lack of tolerance for different political and racial perspectives.
8. The lack of ongoing formal or informal dialogue between minority and non-minority students limits cross-racial understanding.
9. Experiences of social exclusion and isolation occur between minority and majority students. (5–6)

When student focus groups were analyzed in the report from the University of California, Berkeley (Duster 1991), a wide range of concerns and issues related to issues of ethnic identity and prejudice or racism emerged. The first excerpt is from a Chicano/Latino student and the second from a white student.

They [African American students] talk about racism and then a Chicano/Latino will go, "Oh yeah, I know what you mean," and they'll just look at you or you know or if you're not dark enough they don't think you've experienced it and I've come out and say, "Well, Chicanos/Latinos face racism, too." But, also I always have to remind them: maybe you have a color barrier, but a lot of Chicanos/Latinos have a language barrier. . . . A lot of times, Chicanos/Latinos, they have a language barrier and it's always there. (35)

Many whites don't feel like they have an ethnic identity at all and I pretty much feel that way too. It's not something that bothers me tremendously but I think that maybe I could be missing something that other people have, that I am not experiencing. (37)

Other student responses to such questions, and their elaborations of these and similar themes, are strikingly similar to the material presented in chapters 4 and 5.

It often is useful to analyze and present data in a comparative format, comparing and contrasting the views or experiences of one group of people with those of another or others (students compared to faculty, white students compared to African American and Latino/a students, men to women, faculty to staff, etc.). These comparisons document and may help explain how people see and experience the school environment differently, as well as highlight important commonalities. For instance, the Michigan State study (Social Science Research Bureau 1991) reports in textual form some of the results of its survey questions (one of which was displayed earlier).

When presented with the statement: "my department has not made a good faith effort to recruit qualified minority faculty," 68.9% of the respondents disagreed. Similarly, when asked this same question relative to women, 69.6% disagreed. While the majority clearly believe that a good faith effort had been made to recruit minority and women to faculty and academic staff positions, nevertheless 15.3% believed their department had *not* made such efforts to recruit minorities and 13.3% believed their department had *not* made such efforts to recruit women. As one might expect, more minority respondents believe that there has not been a good faith effort to recruit qualified minority faculty, however, 4.8% of non-minority men and 21% of non-minority women believe their department has *not* made a good faith effort to recruit qualified minority faculty. By race we find that 62.8% of the African American respondents and 47.1% of the Hispanic respondents believe that there has been a lack of good faith effort to recruit qualified minority faculty while only 33.9% of Asian/Pacific Islanders and 25.8% of the Caucasian respondents agreed with this assessment. (14)

The University of Pennsylvania report (Gender Equity Committee 2001: 7) compared the responses of male and female faculty members to a series of items as illustrated in table 9.1. This report also (quite favorably) compared the University faculty members' responses to reports on gender comparisons from the 1999 National Survey of Post-secondary Faculty. There are many examples of reports of students' attitudes or experiences, most often with comparisons among people of different racial/ethnic groups. Comparisons also can be made among responses from individuals in different schools/colleges, departments, or units. However, if the number of women or persons of color in a particular unit is small, presentations of data that are broken down by race or gender may identify individuals and thus compromise guarantees of confidentiality. Similarly, if a given unit is itself quite small, it, too, might be identifiable in the presentation of data comparing units. While in the latter instance it may be desirable to name and identify units, extra care should be taken to avoid public identification of individuals, even by reporting some breakdowns in the data only in very general terms.

The presentation of faculty, student, or staff profiles is a fairly straightforward matter, using data from records that indicate numbers or percents of people in different units, at different status levels (professor versus associate professor versus assistant professor versus lecturer, or faculty versus staff member), or at different time periods, by race and gender characteristics. The University of California system report (Justus, Freitag, and Parker 1987) compares similar membership data on faculty and administrative representation at California campuses with data from several peer institutions throughout the nation.

Table 9.1.   University of Pennsylvania Faculty Survey

	Men	Women
Satisfied with job overall (%)	86.4*	78.6
Satisfied with salary (%)	70.8*	60.3
Satisfied with benefits (%)	86.7	89.0
Think female faculty are treated unfairly (%)	10.8*	30.2
Think minority faculty are treated unfairly (%)	11.9*	24.1
Average hours worked per week	59.5	58.9

*Indicates that gender gap is statistically significant: $p < .05$.
Source: Adapted with permission from "The Gender Equity Report", *Almanac*, University of Pennsylvania, v48 (14), December 4, 2001.

	Gathered/Organized/Analyzed		
	By Unit	By Social Identity Group	By Status Level or Job Category
1. Paper-and-Pencil Questionnaires			
2. Face-to-Face • Formal-Standardized • Informal-Conversational			
3. Group Interviews • Formal • Informal • Brainstorming			
4. Observations • Nonparticipant • Participant			
5. Records Retrieval			

Figure 9.2.   Comparisons of Data and Responses with Different Data-Gathering Methods

Another comparative frame for analyzing and reporting data examines the similarities and differences in data and findings that develop from the use of different inquiry methods. Figure 9.2 presents a format for comparing information gained from different data gathering methods with responses from varied sources (people or documents in different units or departments, people of different social backgrounds or identity groupings, and people at different status levels in the organization). In the social science literature such methodological integration is called "triangulation," indicating the ways in which multiple perspectives can be brought to bear on a single set of concerns or findings.

REPORTING RESULTS AND
PREPARING THE WAY FOR CHANGE

7. *Preparing a preliminary report.* Once the data are analyzed and a preliminary or draft report written, the audit team can test their interpretation of the data, and

recommendations flowing from it, with others—members of key constituencies (institutional leaders, informal leaders, representatives of traditionally oppressed groups, etc.). Sharing this preliminary material serves several purposes: (1) to test interpretations with people who may have special expertise and who have not been heavily involved in the audit process; (2) to gain new ideas and perspectives the audit team may have overlooked; (3) to test the appropriateness and relevance (or feasibility) of varied recommendations; and (4) to engage others in the broader change process. This step should precede full public disclosure and can help solicit support and advocacy for public feedback sessions later. To the extent these arrangements can be negotiated ahead of time, fewer surprises will present themselves at later stages.

Open discussions of issues of discrimination and multiculturalism often draw heated exchange, and sharing the preliminary report may explore previously hidden conflicts and resistance. For instance, one university's audit team that presented its report to the unit's senior leadership was told flatly that the report was unacceptable. Despite initial assurances that the report would be made public, the leadership group felt that too much of the text was critical of the organization and felt attacked and defensive. The audit team members felt they had acted and reported in good faith and were extremely distressed. They perceived that they were faced with difficult choices: to "gentle" their report in ways that contradicted their findings; to rework the report in ways that contextualized the data and provided some positive findings as well as negative ones; or to quit the process. They chose the second alternative, presented a revised report to their leadership team that stayed true to their findings, negotiated a series of meetings where the leadership team met with them (and an external consultant) to discuss the findings in depth, and then were joined by the leadership group in conducting a public workshop on the report for all organizational members. A number of other audit teams have first presented their findings to leadership groups and then together with these groups have crafted more-public documents. Other teams have operated independently of organizational leaders and moved directly to public or semipublic presentations by publishing a newsletter, posting findings on bulletin boards, or calling public meetings. Under some circumstances the involvement of external groups has helped ensure that audit results are shared widely and that recommendations for change are seriously considered.

8. *Preparing a public report with recommendations and action plans (the beginning of a new phase).* In this final phase, the audit team provides the entire school with feedback or public access to its report, making sure that informants who participated in the data collection process receive this information. Depending on the team's original charge and mission, this phase should also include recommendations for change based on the findings. It is useful to detail the connection between findings and any specific recommendations, indicating clearly the database(s) from which any particular recommendation flows. Such

self-reports also commonly inform readers of sampling procedures that were (or were not) representative of their entire institution, other important limitations or concerns that would affect interpretations of the data, and how the results may be useful in planning and implementing recommendations for change. Examples of these reports, some quite formal and others not, have been cited throughout this chapter.

This final step also may lead to the transformation of the audit team into a change team, or the creation of a new team that will undertake the planning of changes that are based (more or less directly) on the results of the audit and its recommendations. An effective change team might include some members of the audit team, the better to facilitate the transition from data gathering to response, as well as members of the school's leadership cadre and representatives from varied stakeholder groups. Considerations at this stage return to the discussion of the place of the audit in the organization's overall change effort and its plans for multicultural organizational change along the lines of strategies and tactics delineated in chapter 8 (see figures 8.2 and 8.3).

Chapter Ten

Administrative and Faculty Roles in Advancing Multiculturalism

Researchers and practitioners in higher education agree that proactive leadership is crucial for achieving the organization-wide changes needed to combat racism and achieve multiculturalism. In a 1987 report prepared for the University of California system, Justus, Freitag, and Parker (1987) argue that this level of participation is pivotal, regardless of the leadership style of the president:

> Available research on faculty affirmative action . . . does stress the importance of leadership at all levels within the university—from chief executives to deans to department chairs. . . . Significantly, at the most successful institutions we were told that CEOs, whether called Chancellors or Presidents, do make a difference; that the commitment of an institution can be measured by the relative weight the chief executive places on affirmative action success, and his/her ability to translate commitment into action. (50)

Other research and excerpts from the writing and speeches of college presidents (see chapter 7) underscore this point.

With regard to board members or trustees Joan Finney (1991), director of policy studies at the Education Commission of the States, articulated their potential role in transforming monocultural colleges and universities into multicultural campuses:

> What is needed is the political will and leadership from governing boards to support change. . . . How do institutions make such changes? How do campus and board leaders support and provide incentives for change? Simply put: Leaders make it a high priority and then shift resources, rewards and incentives. (17)

Finney is specific in suggesting that boards must determine institutional goals for minority enrollment and graduation rates and regularly monitor progress toward these goals. The board can then hold the senior administration accountable for such goals and include that criterion in performance reviews. However, it is unclear whether and how boards that remain composed predominantly of white men will provide more than rhetorical leadership and support on these issues. Lacking knowledge of the discrimination typically experienced by people of color, monocultural boards are unlikely to recognize and plan to challenge institutionalized racism or to advocate greater social justice.

If senior administrative and board leaders are unable to provide leadership on these issues it is unlikely that departmental chairs and individual faculty members will work together effectively to improve their own and students' quality of life. Indeed, as Massey, Wilger, and Colbeck (1994: 11) note, faculty roles in teaching often are marked by "hollowed collegiality," a state in which "fragmented communication patterns isolate individual faculty members and prevent them from interacting around issues of undergraduate education." Improvement in faculty orientations and skills, and of the support systems undergirding faculty work, can address some of the issues that students of color report concerning their relationships with collegiate faculty, as well as some of the problems both students of color and white students identify relating to issues of diversity and multiculturalism. More effective multicultural designs and formal and informal rewards for proactive faculty behavior can also help them respond to some of the challenges—personal, pedagogical, curricular, and organizational—reported by faculty members in chapter 6.

This chapter focuses on some of the major actions that college and university leaders can pursue to reverse higher education's long-standing exclusion and subordination of people of color. It taps into issues of the power structure, the technology of higher education (represented in the curriculum and pedagogy), and the climate of social relations on campuses, as illustrated in chapters 4–7. It also reflects some of the typical change strategies used by high power groups, as noted in figure 8.1.

ALTERING LEADERSHIP MIRED IN MONOCULTURALISM

While there have always been courageous educational leaders who champion multicultural initiatives, affirmative action and other means of increasing diversity and approaching racial justice in organizational policies and practices were not initiated primarily by higher education institutions themselves. They resulted from the civil rights movement and the consequent external pressures applied by the federal government, the courts, and community advocates, with occasional reinforcement from collegiate actors. Moreover, in some colleges and universities, the lessening of governmental and societal pressure since the mid-1990s has substantially slowed progress toward greater racial diversity. Even more recently, backward movement was evident in the retreat from affirmative action mandated by several federal court rulings (e.g., in the matter of the University of Texas), statewide ballot initiatives (e.g., in California and Washington), and initiatives by state government leaders (e.g., in Florida). This retreat has come partly from the threats of lawsuits by advocates of a "color-blind" view of U.S. history, from people who feel the "racial playing field is now level," from others seeking to protect their positions of relative advantage, and from some who explicitly support notions of white cultural superiority.

The recent Supreme Court decisions in the University of Michigan cases that upheld the use of some forms of affirmative action in higher education may provide other colleges and universities an opening to reconsider their own policies and practices. At this writing it is unclear the degree to which educational leaders will make use of these decisions to improve racial diversity on campuses or to retreat from this goal or the extent to which opposing forces will permit them to do so. Indeed, in a recent article, one of the legal architects of the campaign against affirmative action lays out a future political and legal strategy (Clegg, 2005). He argues that Republican control of both the executive and legislative branches of governments, as well as legal action against some colleges, and public initiatives such as those led by Ward Connerly will help roll back efforts to forthrightly address the systematic exclusion of people of color from higher education (or, in his terms, counter the use of racial preferences to inappropriately promote their inclusion).

Moreover, the likelihood of committed and skillful institutional leadership on this agenda is quite mixed. For instance, in chapter 7 we present the enlightened views of several leading college and university presidents (see also Bowen and Bok 1998). On the other hand, a recent book from widely recognized authorities gives evidence of a general weakness in thinking about antiracism and multiculturalism in higher education. In the *Field Guide to Academic Leadership: A Publication of the National Academy for Academic Leadership* (NAAL) (Diamond 2002), only one of twenty-six chapters ("Diversity Issues") deals explicitly with the pervasive issues of racism and sexism in higher education. This chapter does argue that "diversity can be achieved only when it is pursued in the context of the mission and core values of an institution. Whether you are a board member, president, vice president, dean or department chair, your leadership is needed to help the campus community understand the positive outcome of being truly diverse" (Silver 2002: 358). However, Silver never uses the terms *racism, sexism, white privilege, male privilege,* or *multiculturalism,* nor does the chapter discuss the racial history of U.S. colleges and universities nor offer any data on the racial makeup of organizations of higher education. The remainder of the volume makes only a few references to issues of multiculturalism in campus climate, curriculum, and teaching strategies. As a work that represents in some ways the perspective of a major policy group (NAAL), this book indicates that higher education leadership has a long way to go in understanding the problems of discrimination and the necessity of promoting multiculturalism.

To make progress, Vaughan (1996) recommends that governing boards recruit presidents outside normal pathways and pipelines and create an institutional climate that is more supportive of minority presidents. Search committees and governing boards must be prepared to challenge existing practices and develop explicit search rules that include provisions for compliance with new policies and regular reports on progress (as well as on lack of progress and violations). The preparation for a presidential search also can utilize a diverse campus task force to prepare a statement of the organization's leadership needs, as well as a description of those current local strengths and challenges that highlight the multicultural agenda. A campus-wide assessment, such as described in chapter 9, can aid in establishing up-to-date knowledge of these conditions.

If board members explicitly include in presidential job descriptions the responsibilities for implementing multiculturalism and antiracist and antisexist policies/practices, these particulars will be an asset in advertising for and recruiting well-chosen candidates and in helping to ensure specific attention to these issues in the process of screening, interviewing, and selecting leaders. Boards can strengthen their commitments to this agenda by selecting a search firm that includes within its priorities, competencies, and record of performance the ability to find women and people of color who fit clients' needs, and to locate new leadership attuned to emerging societal conditions and population demographics.

Moreover, if the president's job description emphasizes diversity and multiculturalism, the president can more easily include these matters in her or his day-to-day work. Based on the survey reported in *The American College President* (Corrigan 2002), the issues occupying the most time of presidents in private colleges and universities are fund-raising (77.0 percent), planning (64.4 percent), budget (50.7 percent), board relations (38.5 percent), personnel (37.7 percent), and academic issues (37.1 percent) (respondents were asked to select the four areas that occupy most of their time; therefore, percentages total more than 100). The comparable data for presidents of public universities shows the following pattern of emphasis: planning (54.6 percent), community relations (49.8 percent), budget (49.4 percent), personnel (45.9 percent), fund-raising (44.2 percent), board relations (33.2 percent). The identification of presidents' most important responsibilities shows why their work is so important in achieving diversity and multiculturalism. Planning and budgeting in relation to these priorities has an immense impact on their inclusion in the allocation of resources. A president's time and energy devoted to board relations make her or him the critical channel for communicating with and influencing board members about diversity and multiculturalism. Such leadership can then more fully commit the institution to these important matters, devote time and attention to challenging racism/sexism and promoting multiculturalism in key decisions, and represent this agenda to the organization, the general public, and important stakeholder groups. Because the president plays such a pivotal role in fund-raising, she or he also can educate potential donors about the importance of multiculturalism and its contributions to educational quality, leadership for rapidly changing communities, research innovation, and service that advances the common good.

Each of the other major issues occupying university presidents' time has the potential for contributing to an organization's action against discrimination, its achievement of greater diversity, and a deeper and broader multiculturalism. Effective community relations allow the president and her or his advisers to engage with individuals and groups about the college's commitments to diversity and the issue's relevance to the community and region. In the course of such activities, a president can identify community resources that can help the college achieve its mission—donors, exemplars of multicultural commitment, potential students and adjunct faculty members, a support group of community leaders, and community-based opportunities for research, service, and teaching. The critical challenge for the president, senior administrators, and board members is to model such leadership and vigorously integrate the college's actions and ideas for advancing diversity and antiracism into all its task priorities and missions.

In the effort to increase diversity and multiculturalism, college and university leaders struggle to balance this concern with many other major external and internal pressures. The list of issues occupying presidents' time is daunting (Peterson 1997) and includes constrained resources, the telematics revolution, academic and institutional quality reform, economic productivity improvements, postsecondary relearning, globalization, reverse growing economic and social inequity, conserve and restore the natural environment, resolve conflicts nonviolently, and reduce ever-growing patterns of consumption (Board on Sustainable Development 1999; Milbrath 1989; Rowley, Lujan, and Dolence 1997; Tibbs 1999). The result is great pressure to manage what is often a very large and complex institution, do more with less funding, and still promote innovation. Moreover, the rapidly transformed postsecondary knowledge industry now includes many organizations that are not colleges or universities, such as corporate and government groups that offer training and education, telecommunications companies, producers of computer software and hardware, and entertainment and media organizations (Dill and Sporn 1995; Peterson 1997). Consequently, many colleges and universities (especially those with a significant research or public service orientation) have created joint public-private ventures and are now part of a common industry where organizations compete to produce and market knowledge-based services. The challenge of increasing diversity and reducing discrimination, in the face of society's changing racial and economic demographics, is inseparable from the other major challenges listed earlier.

How these and other challenges are prioritized and responded to depends not only on trustees' and administrators' personal views and commitments regarding

multicultural changes, but on the kind or model of organization that characterizes a particular institution (see the models discussed in chapter 7) and the
change strategy (or strategies, as discussed in chapter 8, and see figure 8.3) pre-
ferred by leaders and supported by local norms. For instance, leaders of bureaucratically organized colleges and universities can generate mandates or policies
that they expect subordinates in the administrative or faculty sectors to adopt and
follow. Leaders of collegially organized systems cannot effectively proceed in
this way; they will need to engage the participation of other staff and senior faculty (at least) peers in order to create more or less consensually agreed-upon
policies and programs. Higher education institutions that operate on the basis of
an openly political model require yet other leadership approaches; here leaders
can anticipate significant conflict and engagement in decisional and implementation processes by more or less organized interest groups, and seeking agreement among diverse groups of faculty, students, staff, and others will involve
substantial negotiation and coalition building. Likewise, efforts to come to
agreement on policies and programs, and more importantly, to adopt, implement,
and sustain the spirit as well as the letter of multicultural change efforts, may
proceed on the basis of either or both persuasion-based or coercion-based tactics
of change. In order to be most effective, presidents and senior staff members or
faculty leaders will need the vision and skills to employ both sets of tactics, and
to know when and where certain tactics will be more effective than others.

In chapter 7, we noted that while people of color and women have made
some inroads into the leadership structures of non–Research I four-year institutions and two-year colleges, far fewer of them have held top administrative
posts in doctoral-level research universities (especially private ones). We emphasized the important message this pattern of white and male domination or
ownership sends to organizational members and to the society about the future
leadership roles of women and people of color—in higher educational institutions and elsewhere.

The retention of administrators of color has proven as challenging as their hiring. In chapter 7, we quote several presidents from underrepresented groups who
called attention to the spurious and unfavorable judgments that disparage them
and support the chilly climate of racism and sexism in colleges and universities.
Colleges and universities need policies and practices that explicitly support ap-
pointees of color when they experience disrespect and discrimination (overt or
subtle) and that help them obtain the resources that they need in order to become
fully effective (information, funding, cooperation, and mentoring).

Most white academics have not experienced a person of color as their immediate supervisor or senior organizational leader, nor have most male academics
experienced a woman as a senior administrator. When they do, traditional prejudices and stereotypes often lead to conscious or unconscious doubts, questions,
or outright challenges to the competency and qualifications of the new senior

staff member. Training programs that include practical examples of multicultural alternatives, case studies, and role playing or skill development can provide organizational members with alternative ways of leading and of responding to leadership in such unfamiliar circumstances. Changing organizational norms and policies to include, support, and reward persons of color and women as legitimate and effective members and leaders of colleges and universities will require new job descriptions, antidiscrimination policies, and appropriate rewards and sanctions that support desired norms.

What are the possibilities for change in the hearts and minds—and skills—of educational leaders? Every person in our society has a specific history and set of personal experiences involving prejudice and stereotyping, racial and gender-based domination or subordination, and conscious or unconscious feelings of intergroup fear and hope, trust and distrust. Educational leaders—board members, administrators, staff and faculty members—who seek to create multicultural organizations and classrooms must learn more about their own racial and gender identities, overcome internalized (and often unconscious) racism, sexism, and homophobia, and gain the skills necessary to act and lead others to act in antiracist and antisexist ways. The focus of this journey is to discover or expand knowledge of one's authentic self in the face of practices of domination and subordination in organizational and societal relationships. Beyond personal knowledge, leaders must acquire the skills needed to become more effective in providing organizational leadership to achieve diversity and multiculturalism. This process of self-development and related professional development is never complete. Members of dominant cultural groups (heterosexuals, whites, men, the upper class) often have more to learn than other groups because their dominance may not have required them to become self-reflective about their cultural assumptions and behaviors.

In a similar vein, many senior and middle-level managers in the staff sectors and faculty in the academic sectors of the organization will need (re)training focused on developing their personal and organizational knowledge and skills in leading and supporting multicultural change. Many of these actors come to managerial or leadership positions without a background or skills in organizational leadership, let alone in planning and leading multicultural change efforts. Preparation for these roles can take the form of supervisor training or faculty development programs operated by in-house human resource or pedagogical experts or can include the externally operated workshops reported by McCauley, Wright, and Harris (2000; see *Dialogues for Diversity* 1994, for examples of essays, role-play situations, and exercises that could be used in such training programs and workshops), or they may take the extended form of multicultural organizational development projects advocated by Jackson and his colleagues (Jackson and Hardiman 1994; Jackson and Holvino 1988) and Katz (1988).

Multicultural Teams

An element often overlooked in administrative change processes, and in the examination of leadership roles, is the use of plural leadership teams. Complex decisions in complex organizations require teamwork and input from multiple actors with divergent perspectives and skills. Musil et al. (1999) argue that the creation of diverse senior administrative teams not only helps bring plural perspectives to bear on key decisions, it also stands as a model for the organization and sends a signal that issues of diversity and multiculturalism are being taken seriously.

Bensimon and Neumann (1993: 123) emphasize the importance of distinguishing between teams that are real and those that are illusory. Illusory leadership teams merely look plural and powerful, but "real teams go beyond the traditional bureaucratic hierarchy led by the president and involve collaborative management styles, ones that truly respect the input of all team members and that engage in mutual decision-making." In their study of leadership teams at fifteen higher education institutions, they make a strong case for diverse teams, providing examples of situations in which the differing social identities of team members permitted presidents and the team to understand and take account of the views of different campus groups. The authors also illustrate the ways in which white male leaders overtly or covertly (often unconsciously) disparaged or demeaned the presence and contributions of female colleagues and colleagues of color. Several of these latter examples mirror issues reported by students, faculty, and administrators of color as noted in chapters 5, 6, and 7—questioning the competence of a female vice president, patronizingly offering to help a female instructor improve her way of presenting herself and her work, and stereotyping "women and minority members by expecting them to assume the role of definer (of issues and concerns) only or always when the team is dealing with gender or minority-related issues" (Bensimon and Neumann 1993: 124). Reflecting on these incidents, the authors warn of the problems of collaboration among people used to dominating others and not accustomed to working together across status and identity lines, especially alerting white male leaders to their role in dealing with their race and gender privilege.

The development of leadership teams in support of multiculturalism generally requires the successful initiation and operation of teams that are themselves diverse. Diverse and multicultural teams are an essential building block in planning and implementing multicultural change, and they increase the likelihood of positive outcomes emerging from the planning and implementation process. However, because most higher education organizations have little experience with multicultural teams, such groups also add a level of difficulty. To be effective, these teams require diversity in membership and leadership, collaboration, creativity, and shared power. New leadership behaviors and plural interpersonal and organizational processes are required both to cope with the differences that accompany their diverse membership and to utilize these differences to enhance creativity, solve problems, and perform tasks.

The establishment of effective multicultural leadership teams begins with member selection. While members of such teams obviously should be diverse by organizational status or location, race, gender, sexual orientation, and other characteristics, it also is important to ensure that potential members are committed to multicultural change and possess key leadership skills; this is not the time or place to try to effect conversion, but rather to select people who are already committed and prepare them to work well together. Once members are selected, they will usually need training and preparation for the process of working together across the lines of separation and distance, privilege and discrimination, and fear and pain that typify intergroup relations in U.S. society. Miller (1988) emphasizes the need for team members to address their own racism and sexism, and Ely (1995) especially stresses the need for members of traditionally dominant groups to examine the ways in which their history has conditioned their attitudes and behaviors toward others. Moreover, team leaders must be attentive to personal or culturally typical differences in ways of handling conflict, approaches to problem solving, communication styles, and understandings of time (Gardenswartz and Rowe 1994). Organizational power and status differences between groups represented on the team also must be addressed, lest struggles for legitimacy and influence within the team take the place of problem solving (Cox 1993).

Once multicultural teams are organized and prepared, they can expect to encounter issues of developing team norms for appropriate behavior (which may be rooted in members' different cultural backgrounds). They will also need to develop ways of encouraging the expression of a wide range of views on organizational problems (views often affected by their own and their group's experience in the organization), shared leadership patterns (since many members of traditionally dominant and subordinate groups may not be accustomed to treating one another as equally important and powerful), and the ability to negotiate differences and come to agreement—or respectful and articulate disagreement—on programs of action. All these issues exemplify the ways diversity may impact team processes, just as they affect classrooms. They can be resolved effectively only if multicultural teams self-consciously attend to their own internal processes.

In addition to dealing with these internal issues, multicultural teams also face external pressures, emanating from the nature of their task as well as from members of their own racial or gender groups, or organizational role/status groups, that expect them to operate as their representatives. Unless such teams are supported by other members of the organization's leadership cadre (including the president), they will function as window dressing rather than as a true organizational resource.

Responding to Crises

Whether or not universities deal with issues of diversity or multiculturalism in proactive and planful ways, they inevitably will face occasional crises and disruptions related to issues of race, gender, class, religious difference, and sexual orientation. Some of these crises may stem from spontaneous reactions to incidents, while others may take the form of carefully orchestrated mobilizations by committed interest groups (see chapter 8). Many university leaders have struggled for ways to respond to complaints and demands from students, faculty, or community members who belong to underrepresented groups. Some of their reactions or proposed solutions may in turn create their own sets of problems. For instance, one common response to such challenges has been the creation of a high-level position to deal explicitly with issues of diversity and multiculturalism. However, this often is instituted as a bureaucratic solution to a highly politicized problem, one with alert and demanding constituencies. As a result, "some universities have found that it is often easier to create such positions than to define them, and, say some observers, easier to hire such administrators than to work with them" (Leatherman 1990: A17).

Davis's (2002) study of affirmative action officers in higher education illustrates the importance to this role of support from the president and other senior leaders. Davis compares thirty institutions that were more successful in recruiting/admitting African American and Latino/a faculty and students with thirty institutions that were less successful in these efforts and concludes that "people with the power to make a difference play a central role in racial diversity initiatives at the successful schools, especially the president, human resource office and faculty" (142). The central roles that these leadership cadres play include providing clear mandates for affirmative action officers, ensuring that their position provides them with the power to pursue this mandate, and generating support from large numbers of administrators and faculty leaders for the affirmative action effort.

Without widespread support and preparation, however, establishing an affirmative action position or similar office may create a ready target for escalated conflict. At Cleveland State University (CSU), for example, the vice president for minority affairs and human relations left after only ten months on the job when the administration allowed his contract to expire. Turmoil followed, with minority students' occupying the administration building; local, state, and national politicians accusing the university leadership of racism; and involvement by Cleveland's Roman Catholic Church leaders. Widely different perspectives emerged concerning the appropriateness of collaborative tactics versus conflict tactics. As the recently departed occupant described it, this position was poorly defined and little more than window dressing. In his eyes, the role was one of "loyal opposition," necessitating confrontation and being inherently "intrusive"

(Leatherman 1990: A20). The president of CSU expressed a somewhat divergent sense of this vice president's role and the turmoil that followed his nonretention:

> Our job as a university is to do the best we can to put the mechanisms in place to obliterate prejudicial and racist attitudes. But you don't do that by decree. You do it by influencing people and working with them to obtain cooperation. . . . You can't in doing this [pressuring for change] destroy the way an academic department works. You can sometimes nudge, sometimes coerce a bit, you can sometimes try to convince. But you can't bludgeon. (Leatherman 1990: A 20)

It is unclear whether this president quoted above recognized the many ways in which pressure is an ongoing tactic in most university administrations, that combating racism and furthering multiculturalism may involve changing the way that academic departments work, that this often cannot be done without tension and occasional conflict, and that pressure may not destroy but help departments improve the ways they operate (see the discussion of both persuasion- and coercion-based change strategies in chapter 8). In situations like the one at CSU, difficulties are commonly blamed on the person appointed to such a position, rather than on the prevailing culture or ongoing organizational resistance. Ironically, the person whose contract was not renewed at CSU was so well regarded that his prior university employer offered to reemploy him with a raise in title and status, as well as university-wide recognition for a new position.

Other observers of affirmative action and "minority affairs" positions note that they are not typically part of the administrative hierarchy, are staff rather than line positions. They also point out that these new roles carry inherent conflicts that involve differing perceptions of the goals, the means that should be used in achieving the goals, and how rapidly changes should be sought. Experienced administrators who have held such positions stress the importance of clear role definition; preparing the faculty, staff, and students to understand the role; and strong support from a president for the role and its occupant. Charles D. Moody, vice provost for minority affairs at the University of Michigan in the 1980s, stated that for minority affairs administrators to succeed, their jobs "must be woven into the fabric and fiber of institutions" (Leatherman 1990: A20). He acknowledged that these roles are so new that such role integration is difficult and consequently may puzzle many people on campus. Moody noted that he had to make clear that his job was "not to defend the university, but to help make changes at the university" (Leatherman 1990: A20). Other occupants of similar positions have addressed the common experience of being caught in the middle, of trying to meet the sometimes-competing demands of underrepresented campus groups seeking change, and of senior administrators (or male and majority faculty) seeking peace and order—or a calm face to show the public. It is often a lonely and thankless job.

Key to the effectiveness of establishing a high-level administrative role focused specifically on minority affairs, antiracism/sexism and/or multiculturalism is the surrounding context of organizational support and action related to those issues. In other words, the location of a specific college on the various continua between monocultural and multicultural (as described in chapter 3) must be identified. Such information would allow the school to fit this role and its occupant to the immediate opportunities and constraints of the organization. For instance, it is unlikely that an organization committed to a monocultural orientation would hire a senior staff member for such a position; at best, or for window-dressing purposes, they might recruit someone into a low-level role to oversee minority concerns. Even if a person was hired under these monocultural circumstances, we would expect major organizational resistance to their efforts. On the other hand, such hires and roles are typical in a transitional stage organization. The key question, then, would be the extent to which the remaining members and climate of the organization are as advanced in the transition effort as are the leaders who initiated the hiring and (hopefully) are supportive of changes accompanying the new position. In addition, it is reasonable to question whether organizational leaders will continue to support the activities associated with this role if such activities begin to challenge the commitments or actions of senior leaders.

Moreover, if this type of role is initiated in the midst of a crisis, within a context of administrative or faculty or student distrust, mobilization, or resistance, its challenges will be greatly different than if it comes about as a desired result of organization-wide, participatory strategic planning. In the former scenario, enlisting the support of administrative and faculty leadership and educating them must receive high priority. These leaders must participate in helping to solve the urgent unmet needs of people of color and other underrepresented groups on the campus. In the latter scenario, significant administrative and faculty understanding and commitment to diversity and multiculturalism may already exist; consequently, supporting and further developing existing initiatives can receive high priority. As Musil et al. (1999) argue, these appointments are likely to be most successful when the role occupant and the senior leadership team make it clear that "the daily responsibility for attending to diversity also belongs to the campus as a whole" (34).

IMPROVING MULTICULTURAL TEACHING
IN RESEARCH-ORIENTED UNIVERSITIES

While transforming the technology of higher education—specifically the curriculum and pedagogical practices—from monocultural or transitional to multicultural is an arena where most universities have made some progress, there are many entrenched forces which prevent further change and innovation. The shape and power of these forces to affect teaching, organizational priorities regarding teaching, and changes in teaching content and pedagogy are not consistent across the full variety of higher education systems (Wright et al. 2004). For instance, it is clear that faculty members and organizational norms at liberal arts colleges and many community colleges value teaching more highly than at Research I universities. Despite these important differences, however, some of the characteristics and norms of these most prestigious research universities still define much of the reality within which all higher education systems operate ("Why Is Research the Rule?" 2000).

Large research-oriented universities, and their stellar departments, gain their reputations and enhance their status (and resources) primarily via the activities of research scholars. These scholars, especially the senior research faculty, enrich the intellectual environment of the university and often are critical stimulants and mentors for interested and committed students. But not all these senior scholars are interested in undergraduate education or are effective undergraduate teachers. Some "buy out" of teaching responsibilities via research grants or scholarly fellowships, and relatively few teach introductory undergraduate classes. A large percentage of undergraduate classes, especially at the introductory level, are taught by lowest status instructors, including junior faculty and increasingly part-time faculty and graduate students. Despite debates about the comparative priorities of research and teaching in the higher education reward structure, and despite some recent evidence of change, the traditional emphasis on research productivity is still the primary basis for scholarly evaluation, promotion and tenure, and merit increases (Boyer Commission on Educating Undergraduates in Research Universities 1998).

Educators' concerns, as well as the growth of publicity, about the lack of attention to undergraduate teaching, has led to a number of meaningful and exciting innovations in undergraduate education (e.g., living-learning communities, undergraduate research internships, first-year seminars, residential colleges, honors studies, community service learning programs, joint efforts linking Academic Affairs to Student Affairs, etc.). However, such innovations have not significantly altered the culture of most departments and divisions nor the infrastructure of rewards and incentives. Nor have they altered those institutional priorities that create substantial reliance on lecture classes of hundreds of students, packed into rows of seats, listening in fifty-minute or longer segments to an expert deliver material impersonally and from a distance.

The typical organizational focus on faculty scholarly productivity within individual disciplinary venues often means that the broader problems and concerns of the undergraduate community (e.g., safety, access to popular courses, campus racial climate, sexual harassment, alcohol abuse, postcollegiate careers, social rules) seldom capture faculty attention. And students' expressed needs or desires (as opposed to the faculty's goals for students' academic learning) are seldom considered as the basis for curriculum design or redesign. Separating the academic curriculum from the daily lives of students also distances the faculty from concerns with those collegiate environments that are oppressive to women, students of color, and other minorities. The student culture and the developmental needs of young people from diverse backgrounds are generally seen as the purview of associate deans and offices of student affairs—student activity specialists, housing departments, counseling centers, and perhaps campus security forces. In particular, racism, sexism, and intergroup relations' problems on campus may be seen by faculty as a nuisance or moral blot, but generally not as a matter deserving academic or classroom attention.

An additional challenge to improving undergraduate education in general is that most faculty have never been taught about teaching as a skill or an art; they typically learned how to teach as apprentices to senior scholars or as a condition of economic survival while graduate students. The academic culture often assumes a level of teaching competence on the basis of outstanding substantive (disciplinary) knowledge, and when problems occur within a culture that does not expect them, and within a structure of faculty power, students generally are seen as the primary culprits (as in victim blaming that asserts incompetent, lazy, or disinterested students). Under these circumstances it is difficult for any faculty member—junior or senior—to ask for help: the admission of problems represents considerable deviance and may be tantamount to announcing substantive intellectual gaps, professional inadequacy, or personal failure. The result often is a culture of silence about teaching and a lack of comfort in talking about what is done (and not done) in the classroom. Tierney and Bensimon (1996) suggest that as a result of some of these trends, "the social fabric of the academic community has been torn asunder" (10). So has the promise of a democratic and humane education for students. Fortunately, several notable exceptions to this tradition do exist and increasingly are described in disciplinary journals devoted to teaching, in faculty development programs, and in training programs and courses for new teaching assistants.

In the face of these organizational tendencies, the background and prior pedagogical training (or lack thereof) of most faculty, especially the older and predominantly white and male faculty, often leave them ill prepared to deal with the unique demands and opportunities present in diverse classrooms. Although McCauley, Wright, and Harris (2000) report the growing popularity of diversity workshops on college campuses, general purpose diversity workshops do not necessarily focus on issues related to instruction. Moreover, faculty of different race, gender, and status, and from varied academic disciplines often have very different experiences in the classroom and thus very different needs for new information and skills. Certainly most faculty members try to be effective teachers and are distressed when they get the message (academic failure, student disrespect, low class enrollment, poor student evaluations) that they are not being effective with or respected or liked by students. When such messages are accompanied or stimulated by students' allegations of racism or sexism, the distress is compounded. This hurt may be covered in a variety of ways: denying concern, retreating from the undergraduate classroom, blaming students for a lack of interest or skill or appreciation of faculty efforts, and so forth. Somewhat less often faculty respond by asking colleagues for help, seeking the advice of faculty development experts, or investing in renewal and relearning of their craft.

BRINGING MULTICULTURALISM INTO THE CLASSROOM

Teaching in a monocultural institution or classroom, about monocultural content, or in monocultural ways, is partial teaching; it is teaching within, about and with a small portion of the range of social variability of knowledge, experience, and practice. However much the larger organization adopts or resists movements toward multiculturalism, the classroom remains a central arena for change. Here teachers and students can reach beyond the familiar to search for more inclusive ways of learning and knowing.

Components of Classroom Change

Despite these structural and cultural pressures, many faculty members try to be excellent instructors who are successful in the task of educating students in a diverse community. Many are also committed to learning how to improve their efforts and to create more multicultural classroom environments. At an organizational level, the effort to improve the quality of instruction, especially instruction in a diverse classroom and with multicultural aims in mind, has been the focus of many faculty development programs. Useful and successful faculty development related to diversity and multiculturalism must include the following elements:

Knowledge of the subject matter, especially with regard to multicultural traditions in the discipline or relevant disciplinary history and major figures involved in race and gender issues
Knowledge of oneself as a person with race, gender, and other social characteristics, and of the conscious and unconscious ways in which we all impact others
Knowledge of the students, and of the relevance of their backgrounds, social identities, and personal learning styles, for classroom learning and interaction
Knowledge of a range of pedagogical and classroom management approaches to teaching in a diverse environment, and of the ways in which one can (re)organize classroom dynamics to reduce negative intergroup dynamics and take

advantage of opportunities for growth in students' racial/ethnic, class, and gender consciousness

Knowledge of the organizational and social (including historical) context, such that one can safely negotiate the cultural norms of the contemporary educational environment

The interaction among these factors emphasizes the complex web of issues involved in classroom instruction. Approaching multicultural administrative leadership or teaching competency involves mastery of all these features (or at least continual growth). We discuss each in more depth in the following sections.

Changing the Subject Matter

Curriculum reform is the most common focus of multiculturally oriented change efforts in higher education and has received extensive coverage in many publications and conferences. While the content of courses is important, it is all too easy to diversify the syllabi without diversifying either the faculty or the students affected by them, without pluralizing or transforming the instructional skills and styles used, and without changing the organizational context in which instruction and learning take place. As a result, multicultural curriculum reform efforts can be a part of or stimulate wider organizational change or it can take the place of more substantial change (e.g., by adding scholars of color to the syllabus without adding any to the faculty or student body or without altering the syllabus itself). Garcia and Smith (1996) emphasize the transformative rather than the ameliorative potential of curricular reform (see the discussion in chapter 8) as follows: "The process of transformation, particularly as we think about educating the new majority, goes beyond adding books to course syllabi and beyond making broad generalizations about new students and their distinctive learning styles. The process goes to the heart of the educational enterprise in terms of what is to be taught, who is to teach it, and how it is to be taught" (265). It is especially important, in this vein, to situate curriculum reform within the larger organizational frame of changes in instructional strategies and assessment techniques, in authority structures, reward systems, and the college climate or culture.

Early curricular reform efforts attempted to incorporate women and people of color into the curriculum via a variety of tactics or "stages" (Schuster and Van Dyne 1985). These stages ranged from the back-to-basics focus on "standards of excellence" in which women and racial minorities were for the most part absent, to a transformed or balanced curriculum more inclusive of the range of human experience to fundamentally rethinking the curriculum as it currently exists.

Another approach to curricular reform has been to infuse individual courses with multicultural content and teaching styles. These efforts have aimed not only to bring long-excluded histories and texts into college classrooms but also to serve all students more effectively by recognizing and accommodating a wider range of learning styles. These efforts have engaged faculty in dealing with important issues of how to teach students to value difference and diversity and think and act critically in the world in which they live. Two especially good anthologies that engage these issues in a variety of courses in the social sciences, natural or physical sciences, mathematics, humanities, education, and nursing are Schoem et al. (1993) and Morey and Kitano (1997). In addition, many academic disciplinary organizations have developed materials aimed at accomplishing these objectives in their particular subject matter areas. Such efforts also require faculty to be alert to organizational and social incidents and struggles involving racism and multiculturalism, so they can be used as subject matter with relevance to students' learning processes.

Distinct from the goals of reforming individual classes are attempts to diversify the curriculum of an entire department or college. For instance, some institutions have designed courses focused on racism, sexism, homophobism, or other forms of discrimination, and others have created a single multiculturally oriented course that every student must take to graduate (Adams, Niss, and Suarez 1991; Humphreys 1997; Musil et al. 1995; Schmitz 1992). This approach has the obvious drawback of leaving the rest of the curriculum intact and thereby implicitly suggesting that while students might need some exposure to multiculturalism, the majority of courses are fine as they are. Other colleges and universities have adopted a "menu" approach to diversifying the curriculum, identifying a number of existing courses as satisfying a multicultural graduation requirement and allowing students to select any course from this list (Adams et al. 1991). This approach provides institutional validation of innovative efforts and is broader than the single-course option. However, it has been criticized because it often does not create clear guidelines about what makes a particular class "multicultural." Finally, some colleges (e.g., the College of Education at San Diego State University and Hunter College) have pursued the broader reform of infusing the entire curriculum with a commitment to prepare students for citizenship and service roles in a diverse democracy (Adams et al. 1991; Morey and Kitano 1997).

Another multicultural reform strategy is the creation of new programs or program areas, especially ones focusing on ethnic or women's studies (Butler and Walter 1991) but also including cross-cutting or inclusive programs such as the Program on Social Justice in Education at the University of Massachusetts, Amherst. Such programs have had great success in opening up opportunities for new courses and for creating positions for faculty of color and women in the academy. At the same time, the programs stand the risk of becoming "ghettoized"—seen as the remote locations where ethnic studies or multiculturalism is supposed to happen, thus leaving the remainder of the curriculum unchanged.

Increasing Knowledge of Oneself and of Students

Faculty who can identify and articulate their own social identities are also likely to be more aware of some of the negative assumptions they may hold about the competencies or credentials (or promise) of students of color. Explicitly with regard to white faculty, self-knowledge increases understanding of, and thus the power to control, some of the fears and concerns reported in chapter 6 (see also Bell et al. 1997; Weinstein and O'Bear 1992) and prevent the expression of the kinds of biased faculty behaviors students identified in prior chapters. Ferren and Geller (1993) argue that it is especially important for faculty to examine their own comfort levels, lack of knowledge, and fears with regard to sexual orientation and other often-overlooked or ignored aspect of diversity in the classroom (e.g., economic class, religion). Moreover, they suggest that faculty should be prepared for opposition: "In seeking full recognition of diversity and support for genuine inclusiveness (especially with regard to sexual orientation) we may well be confronted with resistance, backlash, harassment, moral judgment and negative stereotyping" (101).

Knowledge of the students with whom they are working requires more than the faculty's (often-overlooked) acquaintance with their names. It involves understanding the social identities of students in class and the kinds of attitudes about and experiences with diversity that students bring with them (see chapters 4 and 5, and Adams et al. 1997). This information must be particularized for every teaching–learning situation. Tatum (1992) and Osajima (1995) argue that without generating such knowledge, and sharing it publicly in the classroom, discussions of race, social inequality, or multiculturalism will occur at an abstract level and often encounter vigorous student resistance. Tatum (1992) and Hardiman and Jackson (1992) also explicitly suggest that instructors assess (or help students assess) the stage of students' racial identity development (see also Chesler, Peet, and Sevig 2003).

Several scholars also emphasize the importance of understanding the different learning styles or preferences students may bring with them to the classroom, and the impact that may have on their ability to respond to faculty styles or the ways in which the faculty may want to present and test classroom material. Anderson and colleagues (1988a; Anderson and Adams 1992) present one of the most useful and easily understood distinctions in student learning styles, examining the differences between primarily analytical and primarily relational learners. Analytical learners are comfortable with abstract and impersonal material, well able to focus on detail and to persevere with temporarily unstimulating tasks. Relational learners, on the other hand, tend to "place an emphasis on affective and reality-based learning, a broad and personal approach to the processing of information, a search for relevance and personal meaning in what is taught, and a need for qualitative feedback" (Anderson and Adams 1992: 22).

Clearly the former style is more likely to be represented in traditional higher education classrooms and approaches, especially by faculty who themselves were educated in and are more comfortable in this tradition. Faculty members' attention to theory and research on young adult learning styles can bring to the fore questions about the ways learning styles may differ—primarily by individuals' cognitive and emotional characteristics, but perhaps as well by their gender and class and ethnicity (Anderson and Adams 1992; Auster and MacRone 1994; Kolb 1984; Montgomery and Groat 1998).

Some of the work in this area that ties learning styles to students' race, gender, and class characteristics is dangerously stereotypical and needs to be examined and its recommendations implemented carefully. However, the evidence suggests that people from different cultures and cultural groupings (racial, ethnic, class, gender) may be accustomed to and prefer different learning styles and thus might learn or perform most effectively via different instructional modes (e.g., oral vs. written performance, active vs. passive instruction, individual vs. group projects, and timed vs. power tests). Thoughtful consideration of the best of this work could reduce the occurrence of monocultural and exclusionary assumptions about appropriate student learning styles, motivations, and talent. It also might point the way to a more plural set of approaches to classroom activities and faculty teaching techniques and help draw our attention to the fit between the styles of different groups of students and the dominant cultures of the academy or the particular approach of a given instructor.

Highlighting the similarities and differences between faculty styles and those of students, especially when they have different gender, class, and racial backgrounds and identities, may also increase the faculty's awareness and sensitivity to their differential impact on students. As Montgomery and Groat argue (1998), "the problem is not that faculty/student mismatches sometimes occur, but rather it is the failure to acknowledge and work out the potential conflicts and misunderstandings that undermine student learning" (6–7). Once acknowledged (by teachers and by students), both teaching styles and learning styles can be modified via particular faculty approaches or by students' willing participation in class activities and assignments that extend their range of options.

Expanding Knowledge of Instructional Strategies

With explicit relevance to the classroom, knowledge and use of a wide range of teaching approaches can expand the typical "active lecturer–passive listener" style of classroom organization. Approaches that are better suited to an active and engaged student role include small-group discussions, teamwork, collaborative learning, and independent projects. Above all, faculty must develop classroom approaches that acknowledge and utilize students' diverse orientations and skills in ways that lead to the positive educational and social outcomes identified in prior research. A diverse student body offers this opportunity but only skillful and innovative faculty pedagogies that deliberately engage race and other differences can help realize it.

Focusing on teaching approaches that are suitable for the diverse classroom, Osajima (1995) reports his efforts to invite "students to talk explicitly about the kind of classroom environment that would be most conducive to breaking the silence that often accompanies discussions about race" (137). Canon (1990) engaged students in reacting to a posed set of "multicultural guidelines" for classroom operations. As modified by others, these guidelines typically emphasize the almost universal existence of prejudice and discrimination and thus the need for students and faculty to (1) be alert to (overt or covert) expression of these attitudes; (2) be compassionate with one another's misinformation and sensitivities; (3) be committed to learning together in ways that combat myths and stereotypes; and (4) be invested in creating a safe and productive atmosphere for learning.

A positive and inclusive classroom climate, or a psychologically safe environment for learning, is especially important when students from diverse social groups engage one another. Whether the diversity in a classroom is itself the focus of learning, or incidental to learning about other topics, students who must learn with people from other backgrounds whom they do not know enter uncharted (and often seemingly dangerous) territory. For instance, Auster and MacRone (1994) argue that there is a masculine bias in a classroom style based on argument and challenge. Because of women's socialized and socially constructed communications styles, they often are not as comfortable in such exchanges as men, and their participation and performance in class and their learning may suffer. Under such conditions, attending to the pedagogical process and the nature of relationships among students in the classroom and between instructor and students is essential.

Thus, the classroom is not a neutral or culture-free zone. A creature of the larger educational organization and of the surrounding political environment and economy, it "reflects the cultural norms and traditions established by its predominantly Western white male originators" (Marchesani and Adams 1992: 12). These authors see that tradition reflected in norms of individual performance, reasoned argument, personal objectivity, and sportslike competition. Obviously nothing is wrong or objectionable per se in these traditions, but if they are the only forces in play, they are problematic for those students who are accustomed to or more comfortable with other traditions and fail to broaden the perspectives of students who are comfortable within that tradition.

Conceptualizing and treating the classroom as a social group, as more than an aggregate of individuals, draws attention to the operation of peer influences and group norms. Such norms not only support or constrain active learning postures and student commitment to classroom work; they also influence student seating patterns (racially and gender separate or not), and the development (or not) of integrated study groups or social connections. Students' prior educational experiences, and the influence of institutionalized discrimination, mean that power differentials typically exist in the classroom between students of color and white students, between male and female students, between students of working class and middle- or upper-class backgrounds, between heterosexual students and homosexual students, between able-bodied students and students with disabilities, between Christian students and Jewish or Muslim or Hindu students. Students generally act out their socially learned positions in the social and educational hierarchy, resulting in major differences in feelings of empowerment, competence, willingness to take risks in academic inquiry, relations with classmates, approaches to the instructor, and access to other academic resources. Fair play, as well as a concern to provide positive educational experiences for all students requires faculty members to pay deliberate and proactive attention to these dynamics and to initiate structures, processes, and norms to equalize all students' access to and exercise of classroom power and resources.

Collaborative learning designs, or the organization of students into teams or study groups that work and learn together, is especially appropriate for the diverse classroom. Based in part on studies of cooperative learning in desegregated public elementary and secondary schools, Aronson and Patnos (1978), Cohen (1994), and Johnson and Johnson (1987) have generated a number of principles relevant for higher education as well. The creation of teams of students of varying academic abilities and styles and of differing social identity characteristics may be the starting point for such interactive learning or "jigsaw learning" designs. Several faculty members comment on whether and how to create such teams in chapter 6. As they note, and as we emphasize, simply creating diversity, in class or in smaller workgroups, does not ensure cooperation and mutual learning. Instruction in and attention to group process, building in individual and well as collective accountability for group products, eliminating in-group competition, and designing group tasks and allocating resources and roles in ways that do not permit higher-status students to dominate are important supplements. For most students (of whatever race and gender), the development of the skills and values of working together in teams is an important preparatory step.

These and other principles of an effective multicultural pedagogy are relevant for all classrooms, regardless of subject matter. In addition, and to the extent consistent with disciplinary and course objectives, personal and group reflection and discussion of the influence of racial/ethnic, gender, and other social identities on classroom processes, and on the subject matter itself, can help make covert classroom dynamics visible and amenable to challenge and alteration.

No matter how well a faculty member prepares herself or himself and the classroom for open and trusting forms of discussion and interaction, no matter how much power equalization occurs, no matter how much discussion takes place about guidelines and ways of working together, on occasion things will be said or done (by faculty or students) that give offense and generate passionate and often angry emotions. Our national history of racial discrimination and ignorance, as well as politicized intergroup relations, make such events inevitable. Such events may be "teachable moments," but only if the emotional level created thereby is manageable and translatable into common learning endeavor. Under such charged circumstances, faculty members often fear losing classroom control, and many students dive for cover. The Derek Bok Center for Teaching and Learning at Harvard University (1992) has developed a series of suggestions for what instructors may do when these "hot moments" occur. They suggest asking students to step back and talk about what they have seen and can learn from such an event or exchange, making a journal assignment that invites students to reflect on the situation and its meaning for them (perhaps for discussion at the next class meeting), discussing differences in students' personal or culturally based comfort with such passion or argument, and using the situation to reflect on patterns of involvement or airtime and role taking in the class. Above all, they emphasize that hot moments may not be disastrous; they may also be the openings to the engagement of previously unengaged students and deeply honest reflection, exchange, and learning — when handled effectively and courageously by faculty and students alike.

But it is not just students who experience hot moments, and it is not just their emotional reactions that must be dealt with. Faculty also have their hot buttons or emotional triggers set off by classroom events. They then must deal with their own internal states (anger, fear, joy) in order to be able to turn such events into teachable moments for themselves and the class. Chesler and Zuniga (1991) describe one on-the-spot intervention into a classroom moment that centered on homosexuality and heterosexism. Faced with a heated argument between two students, which threatened to explode when other students started scapegoating one of the participants, the instructors vigorously intervened to stop the conversation and asked the two primary combatants to come into the middle of the room, sit facing one another, and then engage in a tightly facilitated dialogue. The straightforward engagement with a combustible situation not only produced rich conversation and exchange on the matter at hand, it also provided students with new models for reacting to intense disagreements. Other examples of faculty responses to difficult classroom situations are reported in part 7 of Schoem at al. (1993). They often require new skills and practices and willingness to deal with mistakes and conflict, as well as the exhilaration of new insights and relationships.

Knowledge of the Organizational and Social Context

It is not sufficient to rely upon the personal motivations of individual administrators or faculty as the gateway to personal/functional development programs. Such efforts are more likely to be successful when tied to the institution's mission, supported by reward systems, promoted at the highest levels of the college or university, and encouraged by local departments and peers. Then, change in faculty members' approaches to instruction will be supported and given meaning by the organization's cultures and structures. In their case study analysis of a faculty development effort at Emory University, Frost and Teodorescu (2001) report), "In most conversations participants called for new structures to support teaching . . . (a) promoting interdisciplinary teaching, (b) implementing change at multiple levels, and (c) improving the physical infrastructure" (410–11). Despite the potential that organizational change offers, Terenzio (2002) reports that most faculty development programs still focus on individual faculty members and their individual teaching skills and fail to address the academy's broader culture and structure. Such efforts must address the feeling of isolation and alienation experienced by many faculty of color and white women faculty. Cooperative and team-teaching designs and enhanced interpersonal support and sharing of classroom innovation can help advance multicultural teaching. These more ambitious faculty development programs will have to focus on and be supported by institutional leaders who espouse transformational goals; they will need more adequate resources (in terms of time, space, and funds); and they must provide clear rewards to staff and participants (Bland and Bergquist 1997).

As individual faculty members alter their classroom styles, especially if they share their innovative efforts with colleagues, the organization's approach to instruction and perhaps its cultural openness to differences can begin to shift. As students experience faculty members trying to instruct them in different ways, they too may begin to change and to see new options for their own ways of learning and of working with others. As concrete teaching approaches and the organizational culture of instruction change, the individuals living and learning within these institutions may follow suit. Organizations and individuals change together, and one set of changes often leads to another (Antonio 2003).

Table 10.1 outlines different course components and levels of change in the effort to move from a monocultural to a multicultural curriculum and classroom, or in Kitano's language, from "exclusive" to "transformed" (Kitano 1997). Changes in these classrooms may mirror the changes in organizational stages of monoculturalism to multiculturalism portrayed in figure 3.2. Revising a course involves developing new content—reading lists, textbooks, lectures; approaching a multicultural curriculum often involves the use of new paradigms, ones that reconsider and (re)present material from the point of view of nondominant groups. It also requires the use of alternative pedagogies, instructional strategies, and activities that involve students more directly in creating knowledge based on or tested against their own experience. Alternative methods to assess student knowledge will move beyond standardized tests, or perhaps beyond tests of any sort, to student-designed projects and self-assessments. Finally, the management of classroom dynamics in multicultural settings attends deliberately and proactively to patterns of interaction among diverse groups of students, ensuring equity in student participation by challenging appearances of masculine bias, racial/ethnic privilege, or dominance of interaction by any group.

The process of changing from a monocultural to a multicultural classroom environment does not have to happen in all these components at the same time; in-

Table 10.1.   A Model for Multicultural Course Change: Examining Course Components

Component	Stage of Course Development		
	Exclusive (Monocultural)	Inclusive (Transitional)	Transformed (Multicultural)
Content	Gives traditional mainstream experiences and perspectives; adds authors from different backgrounds who confirm traditional perspectives or support stereotypes.	Adds alternative perspectives through materials, readings, speakers; analyzes historical exclusion of alternative perspectives.	Reconceptualizes the content through a shift in paradigm or approach; presents content through nondominant perspective.
Instructional strategies and activities	Mainly lecture and other didactic methods; question-and-answer discussions; instructor as purveyor of knowledge.	Instructor as purveyor of knowledge but uses a variety of methods to relate new knowledge to previous experience, engage students in constructing knowledge, build critical thinking skills, and encourage peer learning.	Change in power structure so students and instructor learn from each other; methods center on student experience and knowledge such as analyzing concepts against personal experience.
Assessment of student knowledge	Primarily examinations and papers.	Multiple methods and alternatives to standard exams and papers, perhaps with student choice.	Alternatives that focus on student growth: action-oriented projects, self-assessment, reflection on the course.
Classroom dynamics	Focus exclusively on content; avoidance of social issues in classroom; minimal student participation.	Acknowledgement and processing of social issues in classroom; promoting equity in student participation.	Challenging of biased views and sharing of diverse perspectives; ensuring equity in student participation.

Source: Adapted from A. I. Morey and M. K. Kitano (Eds.) *Multicultural Course Transformation in Higher Education: A Broader Truth.* Published by Allyn and Bacon, Boston, MA. Copyright © 1997 by Pearson Education. Reprinted by permission of the publisher.

deed, change in any of these components is likely to influence change in the others. Moreover, progress is not likely to be linear—from monocultural to transitional to multicultural—and there typically will be starts and stops, progress and regress, along the way. Finally, planning and implementing such changes may best be done by many committed colleagues working together, even within the context of a disinterested or resistant department or unit.

Many colleges and universities have established special units that focus on these issues in the improvement of faculty skills and techniques related to antiracism/ antisexism and multiculturalism. Called "faculty development centers," "centers for the improvement of instruction," "teaching excellence centers," and so on, these units are focal arenas for the generation and delivery of faculty development programs. Describing one such center at the University of Hawaii, Wunsch and Chattergy (1991) describe a broad agenda for faculty development programs focused on multiculturalism. Their agenda includes new faculty orientation, teaching assistant training, department chair leadership development, instructional development programs, incentive and reward programs, and classroom/campus research. Some centers also publish occasional papers detailing innovative instructional strategies, sponsor theater troupes that conduct dramatic portrayals of classroom issues, and sponsor departmental retreats for faculty.

In other such programs, faculty have discussed their own experiences with discrimination or inappropriate treatment by students or have attempted to solve common classroom problems in intergroup relations. Fox (2001: chaps. 8 and 9) provides a compendium of materials, activities, scenarios, discussion topics, and guidelines for intergroup interaction that can be used in faculty workshops or in faculty discussions with students. Brief descriptions of a wide range of workshops, seminars, and other faculty development activities (of varying duration and disciplinary focus) supported by foundation grants and the American Association of Colleges and Universities are provided in Musil et al. (1995). Other relevant materials are available on the websites of various instructional centers, most particularly those of Arizona State University (Intergroup Relations Center 2003), the University of Minnesota (Center for Teaching and Learning Services 2003), and the University of Washington (Center for Instructional Development and Research 2002). Descriptions of many of these efforts have been collected and published by other university centers and agencies (see, e.g., *Dialogues for Diversity* 1994; Silverman and Welty 1993). The activities' educational power is multiplied when they depict situations similar to those faculty actually have experienced (or can readily imagine occurring), when they capture the faculty's own expertise as well as concern, and when colleagues can engage each other with their different responses—and the reasons underlying these differences—in an atmosphere of trusting and open exploration.

Faculty development units have also implemented programs aimed at the faculty of the future—current graduate students who are assisting in the instructional process. Some of these efforts combine instruction for faculty and graduate assistants together, and others conduct these sessions separately. Faculty developers at the University of Massachusetts's Center for Teaching offered a series of self-contained workshops, a luncheon seminar series, and a variety of resource materials (Ouellett and Sorcinelli 1995). In a special pilot project, they brought together nine graduate teaching assistant and faculty teams. Each team participated in a two-day intensive workshop and a monthly informal dinner seminar and designed a discipline-based project for its home department. As Ouellett and Sorcinelli note, over and above the typical issues and resistance encountered in multicultural development programs, complex issues arose in the attempt to work simultaneously with faculty and graduate students (differential status, airtime, and views about the possibilities for change). However, careful facilitation enabled participants to overcome these problems and create "a core of faculty and TA partners interested in issues of teaching, learning and social diversity" (216).

PERSONAL DEVELOPMENT
AND ORGANIZATIONAL CHANGE

The effort to develop more inclusive leadership styles, generate new courses and programs, and broaden the faculty's teaching approaches will require altered institutional structures. Senior, mostly male and white, administrators and faculty may need special training to acquire the necessary new skill sets and perspectives, but their colleagues and students who are women and people of color may need grounding and preparation as well. Chism (1998) and Patrick and Fletcher (1998) address these issues directly in advising faculty and staff members who design and implement personal development programs to focus on the necessity of institutional transformation.

Mentoring as a Process of Personal Development

Initiatives to improve administrators' performance and faculty instruction may take the form of both formal and informal mentoring activities that include a wide range of institutional, instructional, and career-related concerns (Ragins and Cotton 1999). Young professionals often prefer mentors and role models like themselves (probably because they perceive that these role models will have experienced difficulties and challenges similar to their own), but this often is not feasible for people of color and women in many academic fields and roles (Rowe 1993). Indeed, in chapter 6, several faculty who did actively mentor younger colleagues discuss how their commitments to these roles added up to a substantial burden of extra work. As a result of these skewed membership patterns, cross-race and cross-gender mentoring is the norm, and this reality sets the stage for relationships in which gender and race and status/rank/power may interact to reproduce many of the difficulties present in a racist and sexist society and organization. For instance, Thomas (1989) notes that "whites and blacks can enact the history of race relations, with all its difficulty and promise, in their everyday interaction, in the micro-dynamics of supervision and mentoring, and in career planning" (280) (the same, of course, is true for cross-gender mentoring). Thus, careful preparation for new patterns of intergroup relationships is crucial to the success of intergroup mentoring.

Peer mentoring represents another strategy that simultaneously builds a sense of community and deemphasizes organizational norms of expertise rooted in seniority and hierarchy. Friendship circles and study and writing groups may help young faculty learn material and support one another while avoiding constant competition, negative interactions, or concerns about senior colleagues' reactions. As Rowe (1993) suggests, peer "Networks provide skills, training and contacts for their members, they enhance mentoring, help to identify complaints and concerns, and help teach the institution what it needs to know to change its structures appropriately. Networks also provide comfort and support" (39).

Tierney and Bensimon (1996) argue that collective mentoring, where senior colleagues take responsibility for creating mentoring teams, is a formal and collective organizational task, part of the organization's responsibility to orient and socialize its new members. As such, "Mentoring need not take place only in a senior faculty member's office or an orientation session at the beginning of the school year. The mail room, the faculty lounge, and any number of other institutional locations have potential for socializing individuals to the culture of the department and organization" (56).

For the potential benefits of personal development programs to be realized, the organization's reward system, culture, norms, and definitions of tasks and functions must value and encourage these activities as central to organizational goals. In colleges and universities throughout the nation, creative and courageous faculty and administrators are trying new ways of teaching, managing, and leading. The critical step is for them and their institutions to move beyond individual pockets of innovation to systemic change. Without ongoing support in terms of new organizational designs and peer/supervisor responses, individuals are unlikely to sustain new approaches to the classroom or to administrative tasks, or to challenge entrenched patterns of personal and institutional discrimination. Speaking specifically about the fields of science and engineering, Ginorio (1995) argues that women and people of color, especially, need to find a meaningful community, one that "would not include . . . outdated ideas of what a successful culture of science is: competitive, all engrossing, demanding to the exclusion of any other interest, and open only to the handful of individuals who can pass all the tests of misunderstood manhood that are demanded today" (32). Above all else, as both Chesler and Chesler (2002) and Frost and Teodorescu

(2001) suggest, the building of a supportive community, one that encourages and assists colleagues in trying new behaviors related to multicultural classroom and unit objectives, is essential to support both personal and organizational change. The lack of such trusting and supportive communities escalates the sense of alienation and marginalization reported by so many women faculty and faculty of color, echoes of the hollowed collegiality so prominent in the culture of teaching in major research universities. Such organizational communities cannot only reduce discrimination and support multiculturalism, they can improve the quality of life for all members of the higher educational system.

Chapter Eleven

Student Programs and Initiatives Promoting Multiculturalism

Young people attending higher education institutions are a select group. Institutional admissions practices as well as student self-selection processes mark college and university students as different from their noncollegiate age-mates in a variety of ways. Institutions of higher education also vary significantly in their degree of selectivity and in the criteria they use to select which students may attend. They differ in the amount of attention they pay to preparing students for future roles as responsible and active citizens in a pluralistic and multicultural democracy. And they differ in the extent to which academic offices and personnel and student affairs offices and personnel collaborate with one another in attending to students' social development and citizenship preparation. What is common, however, is students' desire to learn information, intellectual skills, and ways of relating to others that will stand them in good stead in their postcollegiate careers and prepare them for rewarding futures in a more democratic and multicultural society.

In this chapter, we begin by examining a variety of cocurricular programs that deliberately and proactively involve students in efforts to learn about people and cultures: about both themselves and those different from themselves, about the ways the larger society provides opportunities and limits to their lives, and about the knowledge and skills they need to participate in a diverse democracy. We then consider patterns of student activism and the ways in which students at many colleges and universities have mobilized to advance multiculturalism and social justice in the face of both new opportunities and local efforts at retrenchment. Rather than focus on academic courses, we highlight programs that depart from traditional academic offerings and that attempt to bridge the divide between academic and student life and/or to improve the quality of student intergroup experiences on campus. We explore both administratively directed, or at least facilitated, change processes as well as those involving challenges by traditionally low power groups (e.g., students and people of color). (See the discussion of change strategies in chapter 8.) The agenda in many of these efforts, sometimes stated and sometimes not, is to go beyond narrow academic objectives to stimulate young people to think and behave in ways that transform the injustices in their world.

The advent of structural diversity—the increased number of students of color on campus—provides myriad opportunities for students to learn together and to create new and positive forms of intergroup relations. But structural or representational diversity does not guarantee positive outcomes. As noted in chapters 4 and 5, unplanned diversity can also sustain isolation and separation and reproduce prior messages of minority inadequacy, majority arrogance and ignorance, and the generally negative state of intergroup relations in the society at large. Thus the need exists for thoughtful and proactive programming in order to reach multicultural objectives.

STUDENT AFFAIRS/STUDENT LIFE INITIATIVES

To increase the potential for positive lessons and growth, students and institutions must transcend casual intergroup contact and enter into sustained interaction. For instance, Pascarella (Pascarella et al. 1996; Pascarella and Terenzini 1991) suggests that more than one casual or extended intergroup experience or event is necessary to affect students' openness to diversity and challenge; an accumulation of interrelated experiences over time, interactions that call for a serious level of engagement, are crucial. These accumulated experiences can occur in classrooms, in student resident halls, in student organizations and activities, and, in the best of situations, in all arenas of student life.

In the past several decades, college and university staffs have generated a wide variety of programs designed to provide opportunities for students to learn about and improve racial and intergroup relations on campus, as well as to consider their own future roles in a diverse democracy. Many of these programs, initially undertaken in response to crises and flareups of racial tension and protest, aimed at easing the pain and sense of discrimination experienced by students of color. More recently, however, attention has focused on activities that might educate all students to multicultural issues at a deeper level. These ongoing activities try to proactively counter the racial attitudes and behaviors with which many students enter college and that might otherwise escalate into tensions that lead to destructive conflict. Most of these programs have been undertaken by student affairs professionals—nonfaculty staff members directly concerned with the quality of student life on campus. In some instances, key faculty members have been instrumental in initiating, sustaining, and/or sponsoring such efforts. And in the best scenarios, long-term collaboration has linked student affairs and academic affairs offices in these programs.

Powell (1998) discusses a variety of multiculturally oriented informal (or cocurricular) instructional programs that student affairs departments have undertaken, including student leadership development programs, debate and discussion clubs, celebrations of multiethnic traditions, mentoring, psychological counseling services, residential life and education programs, training of students in conflict resolution skills, and precollege orientation sessions—to name just a few. One focus is to help groups of students form identity-specific groups; another is to help prepare students to explore differences (even disagreements) and commonalities in guided interactions across identity groups. Fostering both intragroup and intergroup associations is not contradictory: it is important for members of majority groups (e.g., white students, Christians, heterosexuals) and minority groups (students of color, Jewish students, gays/lesbians) to feel secure in their own identity and relationships in order to reach out and relate successfully with members of other groups.

Services Oriented to Students of Particular Identity Groups

Many colleges and universities also have units dedicated to providing supportive services to identified student groups. For instance, student services offices often have staffs and programs oriented to serving groups of students of color, sometimes a single staff for all groups of students of color but more typically separate staffs for African American students, Hispanic or Latino/a student groups, Native American students, Asian American students, and foreign students. Many institutions also have an office serving gay, lesbian, bisexual, and transgender (LGBT) students, although the level of funding and institutionalization of such operations varies considerably. Similarly, offices providing special services for women students and for students with different abilities and physical or mental disabilities are common throughout higher education.

Collectively, these units provide services such as academic counseling and advice, academic tutoring assistance, advocacy for special needs (e.g., translators for deaf students or special materials for blind students), social identity-based programs and support groups, educational events and materials directed at the broader collegiate audience, links to local community supporters, referrals to peer groups on campus, social events, advice in dealing with discriminatory behavior, career preparation and referrals, and psychological support and counseling. Specifically with regard to psychological counseling services, a considerable literature attempts to address the different developmental needs of students with different racial/ethnic or sexual orientation identities, their experiences in largely white and heterosexual campuses, and therefore the different services and counseling styles or approaches that may be most appropriate for furthering their growth and development.

These offices also often serve as informal political gathering spaces or organizing venues for student groups seeking influence or planning protest or change campaigns. Such activities may place the student affairs professionals staffing these offices in the political conflict of potentially serving two masters—change-oriented students and order-oriented administrators (or change-oriented administrators committed to different programs or a different timeline than students), and how they play out their roles can have enormous influence on the level of trust students have in the institution's capacity to respond to their needs and concerns.

Diversity Workshops

Many colleges and universities have invested in racial awareness workshops and sensitivity workshops for all members of the college community, especially for students. McCauley, Wright, and Harris (2000) review results from a survey of 281 higher education institutions, noting that 73 percent use "diversity workshops" of one sort or another. Of course, these announcements tell us little about the impact of the programs, merely that they exist as a popular option. Evidence from a review of corporate diversity programs suggests that when implemented in conjunction with affirmative action plans, they can have a significant effect on organizational outcomes (Kalev, Dobbin, and Kelly 2004). To the extent that such efforts help disentangle or unload the "knapsack of white privilege" (MacIntosh 1989), they can promote greater awareness on the part of white students and greater assumption of responsibility for their interracial intentions and behaviors; this evolution may in turn help all students learn about the outlooks and experiences of their peers of different races and ethnicities. Hurtado et al. (1999: 36) cite research that confirms "the importance of workshops to promote white students' willingness to learn about and have contact with others from a different racial/ethnic background." Such workshops may serve as meaningful antidotes to prevalent patterns of racial isolation and separation, particularly on campuses where the fraternity and sorority system is marked by racial division (Appel et al. 1995). Perhaps even more important, Astin (1993) reports that "participating in a racial or cultural awareness workshop had a significant positive effect on end-of-first-year openness to diversity and challenge" (189). Many examples of case studies, dilemmas, provocative essays, and quotes from students that have been used as stimuli and aids in such workshops and ongoing discussion groups have been collected in *Dialogues for Diversity: Community and Ethnicity on Campus* (1994). The message from many of these efforts is that they work best when they go beyond surface exchanges to serious explorations of the realities of different people's lives in a racist and sexist society and organization.

While brief or short-term workshops may represent structured opportunities for students to come into contact with and learn about others, and to learn and practice new forms of intergroup behavior, growth toward a multicultural perspective and a multicultural campus is likely only if students are able to develop relationships that are sustained over time, if the diversity they represent becomes a topic for exploration and conversation, and if the members of these diverse groups engage in focused interactions that require task collaboration (joint schoolwork, social events, or problem-solving activities).

Multicultural Programming in Residence Halls

Students who live in collegiate and university residence halls (quite common for underclass students) participate in an arena of the most sustained and intimate peer interactions and exchanges. Here, in this "critical mass" (Lomotey 1990; Smith et al. 1997), often in students' most vulnerable and impressionable years, peer associations are most likely to develop and influence students' social and academic behavior and pursuits (see, e.g., Rimling 1999; Schroeder, Mable, and Associates, 1994). More than twenty years ago, Rimling and Miltenberger (1981) argued:

> The primary purpose of residence halls must be educational, not managerial. The residence hall staff must choose whether they are going to be monitors of student behavior, or facilitators of student growth, because it is much simpler for residence halls to function as hotels than it is for them to be an extension of the educational experience of the college. (22)

But what does this pursuit mean in the context of higher education's efforts to create diverse and multicultural environments?

Most discussions of residence hall programming are limited to an identification of the cultural differences between people of different racial/ethnic, gender, ability, and sexual orientation groupings, and a general notion that such differences should be presented to and perhaps discussed among students (e.g., see the chapter headings and content in Rimling 1999). But this scope is simply not sufficient. As students of different backgrounds encounter one another, the potential exists for formal and informal learning about one's own and others' social identities and histories, boundary crossing, and positive intergroup relationships. At the same time, these environs may be the staging ground for the solidification of lines of division and the forestalling of positive encounters and growth. Despite optimism and positive programming, residence halls are also often the prime sites of critical racist and sexist incidents, such as rape and sexual harassment, gay bashing, racist graffiti, and more subtle forms of separatism and exclusion. Indeed, with particular regard to issues of sexual orientation, residence hall staff often deal with the subtle kinds of "harassment and abuse [that] may provide warnings to other bisexuals, lesbians and gays to 'stay in the closet'" (O'Bear 1991: 47; see also Bourassa and Shipton 1991; Robinson 1998).

The growth of living–learning communities or residential colleges within large universities represents another organizational-level effort to gain maximum educational advantage from students' experiences of living and learning in close association and collaboration with one another. If a deliberate focus of such communities is intergroup or multicultural issues, then intensive intellectual and experiential programming can become the core of students' collegiate agenda.

Students as Mediators of Campus Intergroup Conflict

The engagement of diverse groups of students as campus mediators or conflict intervenors offers another example of the kind of problem-solving activities and tasks that can make a difference in intergroup relations. Programs to train students these roles are under way at Arizona State University, the University of California at Los Angeles, Carnegie Mellon University, and George Mason University. As Hurtado et al. (1999: 82) report, such programs provide students (and sometimes faculty and staff as well) with "practical strategies and skills they can use when dealing with tension and conflict between groups."

Brown and Mazza (1991) also describe a program that involves students in reducing prejudice and welcoming diversity on campus, based on principles developed by the National Coalition-Building Institute. Teams of students, faculty, and staff are trained in various matters including: the formation of stereotypes, inter- and intragroup oppression, skills in change making, and the ability to handle intergroup conflict. Once trained, these teams are available to educate various groups on campus, to respond to campus incidents, and to provide training for the construction of additional teams. They also provide a model and example of the possibilities of cross-identity group and cross-status collaboration in such efforts.

These programs go beyond raising students' awareness, and beyond encouraging or facilitating border-crossing relationships. Their power and potential rest on the development of skills and on the active roles participants are expected to play in working together to improve the quality of intergroup life on campus. As they engage in these activities, students work with one another in common tasks of problem solving and conflict intervention or resolution; in addition, their work educates other students about interpersonal and intergroup issues, potentially reducing intergroup tension and improving the campus climate.

COMMUNITY SERVICE LEARNING

Students who do more than learn together—who work or undertake action projects together—are more likely to develop new forms of awareness and collaboration. Many colleges and universities have developed community service learning programs in which students perform service in local communities while participating in reflective seminars for academic credit. O'Grady (2000) notes the development of student involvement in community service, ranging from the Roosevelt administration's creation of the Civilian Conservation Corps, through the formation of the Peace Corps and VISTA (Volunteers in Service to America) in the 1960s, to the National Service Act of 1993. These programs have gained substantial attention in the academic and popular press and are a key component of higher education's commitment to create a sense of civic responsibility among students (Hollander and Saltmarsh 2000). A recent study of more than 63,000 students at 276 colleges indicates that over 60 percent of college students expect to participate in such programs or otherwise volunteer in a local community agency (National Survey of Student Engagement 2000). What distinguishes community service learning programs from other volunteer or service work is their emphasis on academic learning and their structural support for such linkages between action and reflection for applying academic knowledge to real life situations (Hollander and Saltmarsh 2000; Kraft 1998).

A number of scholars have argued that several different but potentially overlapping goals characterize community service learning (Morton 1995). Kahne and Westheimer (1996) and Checkoway (2000) distinguish between programs focused on charity and those focused on social change. Programs focused on charity work to provide services to oppressed and disadvantaged populations, primarily in the form of governmental or private support. Social change programs attempt to weaken or disestablish community structures of racism, sexism, and social inequality and/or to alter the allocation of resources to oppressed populations. While the service focused on social change is less common, it clearly holds substantial potential for student and community transformation.

The multicultural frame of community service learning (O'Grady 2000) is especially potent when diverse groups of college students are involved, and when their work—in seminars and at field sites—focuses on their interactions with one another as well as with underserved or oppressed community members and agencies. Once again, it is not simply participation in such programs that makes a difference; the quality of interaction and reflection that students undertake together is the crucial factor. Through their work at community sites, many students step beyond the boundaries of the classroom and university and come into sustained contact with communities much more diverse in race and class than those in which they grew up.

The chances for reflection and academic inquiry built into such efforts ask students to examine not only the communities in which they are placed, and the social forces that create and maintain differential privilege and advantage, but also their own social backgrounds and collective enmeshment in these patterns. Without sustained and guided reflection and intellectual attention to such issues, many students will fail to learn new race, class, and gender lessons from community participation; they are just as likely to reinforce their prior and often simplistic (mis)understandings of these social structures and dynamics (e.g., "most people on welfare do not wish to work," "only lower-class men batter women"). As Hondagneu-Sotelo and Raskoff (1994) report, students in service learning classes may often "reach unwarranted, often racist conclusions, based on selective perceptions . . . through the lens of prejudice and individualism" (250). (See Rabow, Chin, and Fahimian 1999 for a closer examination of these tensions and ways to resolve them productively.)

Such service learning experiences may take a different shape in those colleges and universities where the differences between campus and community, and between the dominant racial/class compositions of the student and civic communities, are less dramatic. For example, at many community colleges and urban universities students may undertake community service learning activities in the very communities in which they grew up and live. Under these circumstances, service programs are likely to be sustained beyond a one or two semester timeline, become more permanent partnerships for students and agencies alike, and may lead to ongoing efforts to create agency or community change.

Some community service learning programs are organized as extracurricular activities, while others are embedded deeply in the academic program, linked to other courses, and treated as an integral (in some cases mandatory) aspect of students' higher education (Rice and Pollack 2000). Some are integrated into residential living arrangements joining efforts to create diverse communities of students as well as students working in diverse communities—the "living learning communities" (Galura et al. 2004). The American Association of Higher Education has produced a series of eighteen monographs aimed at promoting the disciplinary integration of service learning (for examples from social science courses, see Bohmer and Briggs 1991; Calderon and Farrell 1996; Ostrow, Hesser, and Enos 1999). However, such integrated efforts are still relatively rare; the National Survey of Student Engagement (NSSE) suggests that less that 15 percent of students will engage in community service as part of a "regular course" (NSSE 2000).

Although outcomes are mixed, some studies indicate that as students of different racial groups collaborate in community service learning enterprises, they may achieve a deeper understanding of one another and their diverse cultures (Aberle-Grasse 2002; Astin and Sax 1998; Kezar and Rhoads 2001), new appreciations for diversity, an ability to place themselves in others' shoes (Eyler, Giles, and Braxton 1997) decreases in traditional and modern racism and racial prejudice (Greene and Diehm 1995; Myers-Lipton 1996), and the ability to work with diverse others (Osborne, Hammerick, and Hensley 1998). Some studies also indicate increases in students' understanding of the structural realities of U.S. society, of their own racial privileges, and of the enduring power of racism and classism in communities and community institutions (Aberle-Grasse 2002). In a similar vein are the reports that students engaged in these programs develop more positive "civic attitudes," to learn about social change (Kellogg 1999), and to gain greater sense of their ability to have positive impact on the world (Miller 1997).

INTERGROUP DIALOGUE

A relatively new and popular approach to multicultural programming is the intergroup dialogue. Several colleges report adopting one or another form of intergroup dialogue; Arizona State University, the University of Illinois, the University of Maryland, the University of Massachusetts, the University of Michigan, Mount Holyoke College, and the University of Washington are among the pioneers. Intergroup dialogue brings together students (and occasionally faculty and staff) from different social backgrounds and identity groups to increase their awareness and understanding of one another. As Schoem et al. (2001) explain, "Intergroup dialogue is a form of democratic practice, engagement, problem-solving, and education involving face-to-face, focused, facilitated, and confidential discussions occurring over time between two or more groups of people defined by their different social identities" (6; see also Du Bois and Hutson 1997). Thus, a dialogue is more than mere talk and exchange of information; it involves the creation of a communicative relationship. Without a relationship among the parties, there is little hope for mutual understanding or for the joining of different perspectives in the creation of new levels of perception, meaning—and action.

Intergroup dialogue has its origins in a long tradition of research and intervention around racial (and other) relations in schools and communities (Kramer and Weiner 1994). A critical assumption is that under certain conditions (equal status relations, sustained interaction, self-disclosure, empathic connection, engagement in a common and important task), groups of people who are markedly different from and even in conflict with one another can improve their mutual understanding and relationships. Intergroup dialogue as a form of learning that can lead to collective social action also has roots in the tradition of community education/empowerment and action research, popularized in the 1970s by organizational and community change advocates like Freire (1970), Tandon (1981), and others. Through dialogue, previously separated groups can begin to understand one another, understand their own and others' social locations and their origins, and build the trusting connections that enable them to undertake collective action. Moreover, when distinctive social groups, some of whom may have been in conflict with one another, undertake dialogue and collective action, they may form more or less formal alliances or coalitions (Anner 1996).

Many students of various social groupings do wish to talk with, learn about, learn from, learn with, and work for individual and social change with others. But students who have little prior experience with one another may engage in dialogue

programs for varied reasons and may encounter difficulty in talking openly with
one another. For instance, several reports suggest that white students often come
to an intergroup dialogue (or to almost any interracial encounter) in order to learn
things about others and to make new friends; students of color often come to an
intergroup dialogue in order to teach things to others and to change the conditions
of their own organizational and societal lives (Duster 1991). This core asymmetry
may make it difficult for people of different backgrounds to share common dialogue objectives, let alone develop a common language or trust in the possibility
of a mutually satisfying enterprise.

Although different intergroup dialogues take various shapes, most use a
small-group format, with ten to eighteen students, equally representing the recognized social identity groups, participating in a given dialogue. These small
groups of students typically meet for two hours a week for seven to fourteen
weeks (a half or full semester). One noteworthy exception is reported by Rabow
(2002), who undertook dialogic encounters as a regular feature of a large class
in race relations. One dialogue model brings students together from two contrasting groups, perhaps ones that have a history of conflict (e.g., whites and
blacks, or blacks and Latinos/as, or men and women, or men of color and
women of color, or gays and straights). In another model, students from various
groups meet, and the focus of work may include exploration of multiple identities simultaneously. The deliberate intention of both approaches is to comple-
ment academic material (usually readings) with intense and intimate challenges
and exchanges among students from different racial and ethnic backgrounds.

To be sure, every participant has multiple social identities operating simultaneously, and this intricacy enriches explorations of the primary identity being
explored in the group that brings students to a particular encounter. Explorations
of these identities are further enhanced when (as is the case for most students)
they include one or more "target" (oppressed or discriminated against) identities
and one or more "agent" (privileged or advantaged) identities.

Over the years, Zuniga and her colleagues (Zuniga and Nagda 1993; Zuniga,
Nagda, and Sevig 2002; Zuniga et al. 1996) developed and refined a conceptual
framework for a twelve-session intergroup dialogue. The sessions are grouped into
four stages, which build on one another in a potent intellectual and emotional dynamic. Stage 1, "Group Beginnings," introduces participants to one another and to
the nature of the dialogue. This stage is the time and place for discussion of ground
rules such as confidentiality, openness, and refraining from verbal abuse or trash-
ing of others. In stage 2, which generally involves three or four sessions, participants engage in "Exploring Differences and Commonalities." Each person's multiple identities are explored in progressively deeper and more intimate conversations,
much like peeling the layers of an onion. Particular attention is paid to the way individual social identities have their roots in group phenomena—the history of one's
own and others' groups in social systems of advantage and disadvantage, privilege

and oppression. Stage 3, "Exploring and Dialoguing about Hot Topics," involves several sessions that focus on specific issues that often divide groups. At this point students are grounded in potentially heated discussion of specific current matters, and the commitment to stay in dialogue (as opposed to moving to a different form of encounter) is severely tested. In addition to group discussions, most dialogue programs at this stage use interactive exercises, readings, journals, and a final reflection paper to help students explore deeply embedded attitudes, personal blind spots or cultural ignorance, and the impact of covert or unintended actions. Stage 4, "Action Planning and Alliance Building," lasts one to three sessions and asks, "Where do we go from here?" This stage poses the possibility of students working together within and across social identity groups to take action to alter societal, community, or organizational forms of discrimination and privilege.

As Nagda and Zuniga (2003) suggest, mature forms of intergroup dialogue go beyond interpersonal understanding, to "examine ways in which group differences are situated in systems of oppression and privilege, and to explore ways to challenge the effects of such systems" (5). This important form of education (and potentially of action) stretches from the micro to the macro, from an expanded understanding of oneself and one's relationships with others to the nature of socially organized power and privilege. The ability to create more just organizations and institutions depends on the ability to talk and work together across racial, class, gender, and other boundaries. Social justice also requires widespread social and economic change, but effective dialogue is a necessary component of such large-scale change efforts as well as an outcome of such collaborative work. Vasques-Scalera (1999) argues that it is the combination of personal intellectual, emotional, and experiential activities, engaged in a supportive intergroup context, that is the key dynamic in this educational effort to help students gain the skills and knowledge (of self and others) for life in a multicultural society.

Research evaluating the effects of this innovation is still in its infancy, but Gurin (1999) notes that the integration of content and peer interaction occurring in intergroup dialogue often leads to growth in students' active thinking, civic engagement, acceptance of difference as compatible with societal unity, mutuality in orientation to their own groups and others, and understanding of conflict as a normal and healthy aspect of social life. Hurtado (2001) also argues that dialogue programs have a positive impact on white students' racial learning, and Zuniga et al. (1995) report the programs' role in reducing racial prejudice.

PROBLEMS AND CHALLENGES IN PROGRAMS ORIENTED TOWARD STUDENTS

One critical challenge in all these student-oriented programs involves *maintaining a balance between emphasizing separate social identities and building a transgroup consciousness or community*. Part of the intergroup dialogue process focuses on individuals' separate social identities, the better to help students understand themselves and their own group. Another part focuses on helping students understand others' identities, cultures, social experiences, and outlooks. While student service and service learning programs may not emphasize these issues as directly as do intergroup dialogues, they often generate similar insights. It is also important for all students to understand and appreciate both differences and commonalities and to bond as a community, cutting across separate identity groups' interests, ideologies, and social locations. But it is important to do this in a real, impassioned, committed way, not in a way that masks important differences and ignores inevitable conflicts.

A second critical challenge involves *determining the extent to which undergraduate students who participate in these programs also can be involved as facilitators, guides, or educators of their peers*. At some universities, students are trained specifically for leadership roles as resident hall advisors, peer counselors, and facilitators of community service and multicultural educational efforts (Beale, Thompson, and Chesler 2001; Chesler, Fritz, and Knife-Gould 2002; Hatcher 1995; Zuniga et al. 1996). With faculty guidance and oversight, but leading and instructing their peers directly, students can add a more democratic educational practice to these programs. Vasques-Scalera (1999), in research with peer facilitators of intergroup dialogues, reports some of the key benefits in personal esteem and confidence, multicultural awareness, leadership skills, and intergroup behavior that may accrue to students who play leadership roles in these and other programs. Such peer-led efforts are rare but nevertheless noteworthy, especially since students have often been a significant force in the initiation of these programs and in the advocacy of multicultural change on campuses throughout the nation.

A third challenge involves *establishing how the faculty or staff instructors in these programs play out their own identities, roles, and personae*—with one another (as a team) and with students. After all, if these are student-focused or student-generated initiatives, the natural assertion of older faculty or staff direction and control potentially robs them of their unique student nature. The authority that faculty or staff instructors usually carry in such situations is magnified by age differences, by these instructors' location in the status system, and by the credit-granting hierarchy of the academy. If faculty or staff and students work as a team in such programs they must figure out how to work together well, both to provide effective training and to operate as a model for others. If the instructors/trainers/supervisors come from different sectors of the university, they may have to struggle with the attributions of greater expertise, authority, and aloofness often attributed to university faculty (and the corollary lesser status accorded to student affairs personnel).

A final challenge involves *negotiating the very life and structure/culture of such programs within the larger academic structure of the university and creating/ sustaining collaboration between offices of student affairs (vice presidents or deans of students, residence hall directors, etc.) and offices of academic affairs (provosts, deans, and departments).* Collaboration between these entities often is difficult. Few faculty adopt active roles in these ventures, and many of those that do are academically marginal themselves or operate with an attitude of superior knowledge embedded in their faculty roles. Sometimes student affairs personnel, who feel primarily responsible for programs focused on students' social and moral development, are also loath to cooperate fully with potential academic colleagues. Moreover, gaining and sustaining course-credit legitimacy for student-oriented, nontraditional multicultural learning, as well as academic credibility for intellectual work accomplished through innovative (especially if peer-led) programs, requires constant boundary management. The good news is that several of the initiatives discussed in this chapter have gained academic credit in a number of different universities, and have established effective interunit collaborations.

In addition, interunit and town–gown relations are often complicated and may be threatened when university students—outsiders to surrounding communities and to faculty-led departments—attempt to study and change race, class, and gender relations in local systems. Residence advisor education, student mediation activities, collegiate dialogues, and service learning efforts are clearly defensible as educationally valuable. But as soon as these programs become involved in change efforts, especially efforts deliberately planned by groups of people—inside the academy or in the local environment—colleagues and community members may raise concerns about objectivity, political correctness, and the forceful impositions of values.

The contemporary collegiate landscape is full of many varieties of these student-oriented and often student-initiated efforts. Some focus merely on acknowledging and celebrating differences and learning about "the other." The more important efforts, from our point of view, focus on the nature of organized privilege, and the location of affluent white students as more or less conscious purveyors of privilege—and of privilege's other side of disadvantage and oppression. Regardless of their focus, these activities often help students see the contradictions between the type of education their college or university normally provides and the promise of intense explorations of intergroup issues, and of the gap between work on racial justice and curricular avoidance of these issues. These gaps cannot be closed, nor these activities sustained, without parallel changes in the operations and curricula of departments and the larger collegiate or university environment. Efforts to achieve multiculturalism in these student life arenas of higher education also must be linked to similar efforts involving faculty and administrative staffs.

STUDENT MOBILIZATION AND ACTIVISM

Distinct from but related to the programmatic efforts to educate students to function as multicultural citizens are the many efforts on the part of students as activists themselves to change universities and the larger world in which they are embedded. Contrary to their typical role as "receivers" of knowledge, students have historically offered quite cogent critiques of and challenges to systems of inequality. However, students have never commanded much influence in the traditional power structures of U.S. higher education. Student government organizations, even when representative, seldom have a meaningful role in collegiate decision making. Graduate students—wiser, older, often with longer tenure and in the role of apprentice faculty—have more status but still only negligible influence in determining their curriculum and pedagogical processes and in shaping larger university matters.

Of course, important exceptions do exist. In some other societies students play more powerful roles in university governance, often through "legitimate" and official channels but also via periodic mobilization efforts and consequent activism. At the margins of mainstream U.S. higher education a democratic tradition has long seen students as collaborators and sought to integrate their voices. Noteworthy experiments with powerful student roles have occurred at Antioch College, Black Mountain College, and a variety of other work-focused and small residential colleges. Despite these departures, the dominant tradition has placed students on the lowest rung in official organizational decision making and power. The tradition of "adultism/ageism" in higher education—combining a fear or distrust of youth with assumptions of adult expertise and strong pressures to control student behavior—has relegated students to a dependent organizational status. U.S. institutions of higher education also have avoided legitimate student influence by excluding or assimilating members of those groups who might most wish to alter traditional educational patterns—students of color, women, and members of economically disadvantaged groups. Students from more privileged backgrounds have more opportunity and therefore less need to exert influence in social organizations that already advance their personal and collective interests.

In classrooms students also are often cast in the role of passive recipients of knowledge presented by distant faculty experts. Naturally, then, when students have pressed their views and interests on collegiate curricular or pedagogical matters, or on political or cultural matters affecting the collegiate environment, they often have done so in ways that depart from normal organizational procedures and have mobilized outside normal channels of participation, influence, and authority. In particular, student mobilizations (in the form of petitions, demonstrations, protests, boycotts, and occasional violence) have been key elements, perhaps *the* key element, in the historic struggle to challenge racism and other forms of discrimination and promote multiculturalism in higher education.

They often are examples of the pressure-oriented strategies pursued by low-power groups discussed in chapter 8.

We do not attempt here a detailed history of student mobilization around public issues, nor do we offer a comprehensive chronicle of examples; several other volumes do this task well (Altbach and Lomotey 1991; Astin et al. 1975; Levine 1998; Light and Spiegel 1977; Rhoads 1998b; Yamane 2001). But we do draw attention to some of the issues and campaigns of the past several decades that have helped shape student efforts around racial and ethnic issues and multiculturalism. Some of these mobilizations were focused on issues related directly to students' educational experience, while others focused on issues of social and political justice arising primarily outside the academy.

The Tradition of Student Mobilization

Students' challenges to collegiate policies and programs are as old as schools themselves. But the 1960s in the United States stands as a landmark, a time when contemporary student activism took organized shape in ways that still define it. In the latter half of the twentieth century, the post–world war experience brought to the fore of American society an older college population, the growth of international outlooks, a burgeoning movement for civil rights, a series of increasingly unpopular wars or "police actions" around the world, and a movement to resist these wars (culminating in opposition to the draft and protests against the Vietnam War and the tragedy at Kent State). Public apathy and confusion about civil rights at home and wars abroad helped fuel student involvement. As students at one school organized for collective action on such issues, their actions spread to other campuses, generating new cadres of activists.

The growth of student mobilization efforts was also located in students' struggle against the *in locus parentis* rules of university administrations. The concept of the university as substitute parent meant that university officials took responsibility for the socialization and social control of young people while they were on campus. Vice presidents and deans of student affairs often oversaw all aspects of students' nonacademic lives, from residence halls to social events to personal decisions about lifestyles and intimate partners (Rhoads 1998b). Closely related in time, the collegiate movement for "free speech" and a renewed sense of student political mobilization around civil rights took its lead from organizing by black students (and their white allies) in the southern states (Hayden 1988, especially chap. 2; McAdam 1988) and at institutions like the University of California at Berkeley (Heirich 1977). Related to other movements, and through the efforts of organizations like Students for a Democratic Society (born at Michigan but presaged by events and mobilizations elsewhere), primarily white student political organizations and actions also spread throughout the nation (Gitlin 1987; Hayden 1988; Miller 1987; Sales 1973). Thus, while campus actions in the latter third of the twentieth century sometimes focused on local educational policy, they most often intersected with broad societal issues and constituencies.

The Necessity for Racial Struggle

The civil rights revolution significantly influenced students' consciousness and activity around racism and related issues of social discrimination experienced in the United States in the 1960s. As black students in the South used their colleges (and high schools and churches) as organizing arenas for wholesale challenges to the segregation of public facilities, their efforts galvanized substantial portions of the young adult society (McAdam 1988; Morris 1984). Many white students from the North went south to join the student-generated or energized organizations of the civil rights movement (especially the Student Nonviolent Coordinating Committee, the Southern Christian Leadership Conference, and the Congress on Racial Equality). When they returned to their northern schools and communities, many brought back a commitment to continue the fight for racial equality, along with new skills and tactics in social organizing and protest (Rhoads 1998b). In the late 1960s and 1970s, sustained northern protests around campus-related racial issues occurred at Columbia University, Cornell University, and the University of Michigan, to name but a few sites. In the 1980s, students on many campuses campaigned to convince their colleges and the government to get rid of investments in companies doing business with the South African apartheid regime.

Once out of the bottle, the genie of student mobilization and protest was hard to put back. Successive generations of students learned that they could express their views about race, gender, and class issues on their campuses and in their communities, and that protest tactics could influence educational and social policies. In fact, as Yamane (2001) notes, student mobilization has been key to multicultural change (see also Astin et al. 1975): "the likelihood of a campus having a department or program in ethnic studies, urban studies, or women's studies increases with the presence of groups willing to apply pressure" (17–18). White students often joined with their African American, Chicano/a or Latino/a, and Asian American colleagues to press for the adoption of curricular reforms and specialized programs and centers that responded to their groups' histories and learning agendas (Munoz 1989). In a particular case, Bauder (1998) documents the role of LGBT students' petitions, legislative lobbying, and protests in the Indiana University decision to create a special campus office to serve their needs.

Activist students learned that they could organize other students, both on their own campus and beyond, to explore their needs and views on local, regional, and national issues. One example of the historic consistency and cross-generational influence of student mobilization efforts is reflected in the University of Michigan student demands of the 1970s–1990s. In 1970 and again in 1987, groups of students of color, joined by small numbers of whites, responded to racial incidents on campus by presenting the university administration with proposals and demands (Black Action Movement 1970; United Coalition against Racism 1987). In each case, their demands focused on the organizational roots of the racial discrimination practiced by white students, faculty, and administrators, including concerns about admissions, financial aid, and the creation of safe environments for students of color. While the university consistently responded with efforts at change, the limited response to the organized student movement in the 1970s and 1980s did not fundamentally alter the institutional basis of racism. Persisting conditions of disadvantage and discrimination led to overt incidents and sporadic protest about these same concerns in the 1990s. As the university's affirmative action admissions cases arose, student mobilization resurfaced in 2002–2003, this time joining current students with some of their forebears. Although the University of Michigan's experience in this regard is especially public and dramatic, the underlying themes are by no means unique.

Over the years, student activists on many campuses discovered adult organizations (such as unions, political parties, and identity-based movements) and issue-oriented organizations with whom they could make common cause or create cross-generational coalitions. The issue-oriented alliances included African American and Latino/a groups, pro-Israel and pro-Palestinian groups, right-to-life and prochoice groups, antisweatshop campaigners, and environmental protection activists.

Many student mobilizations and campaigns have erupted more or less spontaneously, spurred by racist campus incidents or intergroup tensions. In some cases, administrative responses to initial protest—or the conspicuous absence of a rapid and effective response—escalated tension and fueled movement development. As Gordon (1991) points out with regard to the experience of Arizona State University, "A precipitating conflict incident will not, in and of itself, generate a general collective reaction unless a socially combustible situation has developed over time" (235). Thus, organized and sustained protest activity is most likely to be linked with student activists' sense that administrative officials responsible for campus policies are either untrustworthy on their face or nonresponsive to claims of discrimination or injustice (Altbach 1989). The combination of long-standing grievances, protest activity, and administrative responses that seek immediate (and often punitive) reestablishment of order, or that deny or ignore activism, often provide the "combustible situation."

Contemporary Student Mobilizations

Contemporary student mobilizations vary broadly in their nature and depth. Many formed in response to specific incidents of discrimination the limits of campus programming or to the limits of existing efforts to bring multiculturalism to campus. We present a few examples:

- In the fall of 1999, several students of color at Pennsylvania State University reported receiving racist e-mail. The Black Caucus and Student Minority

Advisement Team helped organize a rally against racial intolerance, which led to student demands that the university expand the teaching of African American issues and the history of racism. Later demands included hiring more minority faculty, developing an Africana Studies Research Institute, and adding more scholarships for students of color. Dissatisfied with the speed and nature of the administration's response, students met with members of the State Legislative Black Caucus, demonstrated at a varsity football spring practice game, and occupied a campus center (www.collegian.psu .edu/archive).

- In 2001, protests developed at Duke University over an ad that ran in the *Chronicle*, the independent daily student newspaper, opposing reparations for slavery. Protests and sit-ins took place at the *Chronicle*'s office, and the Duke Student Movement raised objections to the paucity of black faculty and senior administrators, voiced the need for a new Multicultural Center and Center for Black Culture, and demanded a yearly report on the treatment of minority students (www.chronicle.duke.edu/story).
- In the fall of 2001, members of a fraternity at Louisville University wore blackface and dressed as criminals and pimps at a house party. Students and their faculty allies called for suspension of the fraternity and, dismayed by the delays and inadequacy of administrative response, demanded the resignation of administrators in the Office of Student Life (www.louisville.cardinal).
- In the fall and winter of 1997–1998, students at Iowa State University mobilized to increase diversity on campus. The September 29th Movement, allied with the Black Student Alliance, the Lesbian-Gay-Bisexual-Transsexual and Allies Alliance, the Vietnamese Student Association, and the Asian-Pacific-American Awareness Coalition, sponsored rallies, a teach-in, and a "wait-in" in the office of the university president (www.daily.iastate.edu).
- In the fall of 2000, the Students of Color Coalition at the University of Michigan occupied the offices of a secret undergraduate society located in official university space. The society had displayed Native American artifacts and invented American Indian names for its members (www.pub.umich.edu/daily).
- At numerous colleges and universities, campaigns have focused on the elimination of athletic mascots and cheers that use Native American symbols and tribal names. And every year, at countless campuses across the nation, the celebration of Martin Luther King Day is an occasion for speeches and reflections on the state of local efforts at multiculturalism. Similarly, the Supreme Court's consideration of affirmative action issues in the University of Michigan case was a stimulus for student mobilization and campaigns (both for and against these policies) at Michigan and elsewhere.

Other recent examples are reported and analyzed in extensive case studies by Rhoads (1998b) and Yamane (2001). Rhoads's analyses focus on (1) celebrations of National Coming Out Day at Pennsylvania State University, students' requests to add a sexual orientation clause to the university's statement of nondiscrimination, and their demands for the expansion of domestic partner benefits and equal treatment for gay/lesbian/bisexual students in the ROTC program; (2) a student movement to create a Chicano Studies Program at the University of California at Los Angeles; (3) student mobilization to resist attempts by the Michigan governor to eliminate tuition waivers for state-born Native Americans; (4) the mobilization of a strike and boycott of classes by students at Mills College to resist and eventually overturn a presidential and board decision to make the college coeducational—and a later student campaign calling for greater racial diversity among the faculty; and (5) African American students' leadership of multiple groups' demonstrations and protests of the Rutgers University president's suggestion that African American students might not "have that genetic, hereditary background to have a higher average [SAT score]" (193). Yamane's studies focus on (1) black student activists' response to a fraternity party's depiction of "a black native complete with a bone through the nose in front of the house to welcome partygoers" (30) leading to protests and the development of a multicultural education requirement at the University of Wisconsin at Madison; and (2) student mobilization, with faculty assistance, leading to the creation of a required undergraduate course in American cultures and an American Cultures Center to oversee implementation of the requirement at the University of California–Berkeley.

Other recent student mobilizations have focused on the ways in which racial or class difference, privilege and justice are embedded in the culture and operating structures of their colleges and in the national and regional politics.

- At Harvard, students staged a three-week occupation of the president's office in order to call attention to the low wages paid to university custodial and food-service workers—the "living wage" campaign (Brown 2002). And at a number of other universities, graduate student instructors have organized (and some have unionized) to press for increased pay and better working conditions and benefits—in some cases striking or creating a work stoppage to press their demands.
- At several universities, students targeted corporations' links to overseas factories that were alleged to have poor working conditions and antiunion policies. On nearly one hundred campuses, students joined United Students Against Sweatshops (USAS) and pressed their administrations to join the Worker Rights Consortium and challenge sweatshop conditions in the production of wearing apparel (Featherstone and USAS 2002). At the University of Wisconsin thousands of students signed pledges not to work for companies that have accumulated poor records of environmental stewardship (Brown 2002).
- Mallory (1998) discusses a variety of political roles and agendas pursued by LGBT student organizations. They include advocacy and protests related to

efforts to attain equal partner benefits for students and staff members, nondiscrimination clauses specific to heterosexism, LGBT-oriented academic programs and centers, and student services offices dedicated to helping meet their social, educational, and medical needs.
• At colleges and universities throughout the country, students have joined campus-level political parties and campaigned actively to elect local, state, and national representatives of their choice. Other students have become involved in local and national mobilizations and actions focused on the environment, especially when a link could be made to race and class injustice (e.g., The Clamshell Alliance, Student Environmental Action Coalition; also see Bryant 2002). Others have organized to push for need-blind admissions policies that do not turn away qualified applicants because of financial need.

None of the changes that appeared to flow from these student-initiated protests occurred without struggle, and many promised changes have been implemented in only modified or weakened fashion over the intervening years. The same transient status that has helped to exclude students from major official roles in university decision making weakens their ability to monitor change over time and to sustain the political pressure that brought about change in the first place. As the president of the University of Maryland Lesbian, Gay, Bisexual Alliance noted:

> It is true that the University of Maryland, College Park, has taken some steps in acknowledging diversity when it comes to lesbian, gay, and bisexual issues. . . . These efforts were brought about with some student media pressure on the administration . . . but the students were shut out of the critical decision-making process once the administration was deciding what to do. (Kalathas 1988: 5/4)

It appears that student mobilization efforts are most likely to be successful when they occur with the assistance of, or in coalition with, key faculty members and administrators, or with external social movements and organizations. Involvement of organizations such as the National Association for the Advancement of Colored People (NAACP), Public Interest Research Groups, and the Republican or Democratic Party on campus matters greatly strengthens students' power and presence.

Identity Politics and Issue Politics: Coalitions

Some of these and other student mobilizations and protests represent *identity politics* (organizing on the basis of issues affecting one's social identity group), while others involve *issue politics* (organizing on the basis of commitment to particular issues that may crosscut identities). The particular underlying principle often affects who becomes involved and the nature of racial, ethnic, and class interaction among participants. For instance, mobilizations focusing on racist or sexist incidents may more quickly engage students of color, women students, or gay and lesbian students whose safety and security are directly affected by these events. Antisweatshop and environmental protest movements are likely to draw activists whose identities do not make them obvious targets of campus discrimination; thus these movements are often dominated by white and affluent students, although recent environmental justice initiatives have drawn a mix of students of color and white students. However, as Featherstone and USAS note (2002), "Some student activists of color sense that white student activists work on third world issues (e.g., sweatshops, environmental pollution, and disease in less affluent nations) because domestic issues in the United States, almost by definition, involve race, which white student activists don't want to talk about" (65). Race and gender distrust, or just differing agendas, affect the possibilities of intergroup coalitions for change on campus just as elsewhere in the society.

However, it would be an error to see the kind of identity politics and campaigns on college campuses as always problematic or necessarily isolationist and divisive. To the contrary, where students organize around racial and ethnic issues, identity politics have usually energized and empowered broadly based constituencies and interracial coalitions. Most notably, student actions supporting the retention of affirmative action policies in collegiate admissions have generally been interracial, with both white students and students of color playing significant roles. These alliances, borne in struggle, often teach important lessons about the nature of race relations, organizational and societal racism, and the possibilities of interracial coalitions for change. While the student actions have probably not affected recent court decisions (certainly not as much as amicus briefs from military and corporate leaders in the recent University of Michigan cases), they have had significant impact on the nature of campus discussions and policies regarding multiculturalism.

Organizing trends come and go, and the issues that grab the attention of students may change over time. But concerns with race and racism remain a central focus of student activism. And student efforts are often *the prime motivator and influence* on changes in policies and programs of higher education. The increased diversity of campus populations itself helps to sustain efforts on behalf of multicultural issues. As Astin (1993) argues, "emphasizing diversity on campus seems to enhance the likelihood that students will engage in some kind of protest activity during their undergraduate years" (153). Diversity brings with it contact with people who are different. When collegiate programs take advantage of this diversity by promoting sustained "informal interactional diversity" (Gurin 1999), students learn about one another, about their different traditions, about the impact of institutionalized racism and other forms of discrimination on everyone, and about the necessities of life in a diverse democracy. The productive tension accompanying such learning can stimulate social activism, itself a forum for learning.

LINKING STUDENT INITIATIVES
TO ORGANIZATIONAL CHANGE

The personal and interpersonal gains from student-oriented initiatives and mobilization efforts can translate into organizational change efforts in several ways. They reflect a variety of the influence strategies delineated in figure 8.3. For instance, individual student actions may take a variety of forms, beyond increased awareness or respect, including (1) decisions to participate in additional educational events, whether through formal classes or in informal community settings; (2) efforts to (re)educate peers, as in challenges to jokes that disparage particular groups on the basis of race, ethnicity, gender, religion, class, or sexual orientation; (3) direct challenges to institutional or community policies and practices (on admissions, racial profiling, sexual harassment, curricular content, etc.) that discriminate against or negatively affect students of color, women, or LGBT students or that privilege heterosexual white men (or various combinations of the above).

Beyond individual actions, and more powerful in their potential impact on organizational and community structures, are the collective actions or mobilization efforts undertaken by groups of students (and sometimes students and faculty and staff) working together. Isaacs (1996) argues that dialogue programs have the potential to "produce coordinated action among collectives, and to bring about genuine social change" (20). Some dialogue programs conducted within institutions of higher education have aimed beyond learning as the only outcome and have attempted to help students engage in intergroup actions for change.

With particular regard to community service learning, Rhoads (1998a) notes, "For students to see themselves as agents of social change, often it is necessary to have contact with diverse individuals and groups whose struggles might in some way connect to the lives of the students" (40). In the community service learning program Rhoads set up in Washington, D.C., students engage in work with homelessness in ways that help them "learn about the many ways that they might [help] alter the circumstances of homeless citizens beyond the obvious path of providing a hot meal or a warm place to sleep" (42). Participants in this effort work to alter these circumstances directly or to lessen the impact of homelessness on people's lives.

It is also likely that some dialogue or community service learning programs may effect organizational change as they enlighten faculty and administrators, expand those members' awareness of teaching options, and even involve them directly in curricular or institutional reform. Thus, student-oriented programs that involve those university members may lead to administrator and staff retraining and faculty development (particularly in the context of Burbules's (1993) work on pedagogical innovations), as well as different forms of faculty–staff–student encounters.

If any of these student-oriented efforts are to have significant impact on the surrounding collegiate environment and operations, they will have to reach beyond students and student affairs professionals themselves. As argued in chapter 8, such organizational change requires cooperation and proactive leadership from senior administrators and faculty, education of faculty and staff and students regarding all forms of overt and covert discrimination, hiring of minority staff and faculty, honest naming of and rapid responses to incidents of overt harassment or discrimination, and regular programming that meets the particular needs of traditionally disadvantaged groups.

Chapter Twelve

Examples of Collegiate/University Multicultural Change Recommendations

Policy and program innovations and changes that seek to address discrimination and approach multiculturalism are planned or underway in colleges and universities across the nation. They encompass many of the dimensions of organizational life outlined in figures 3.1 and 3.2 and some of the change strategies depicted in figures 8.2 and 8.3. Various compendia describe a broad range of these innovations (Musil et al. 1995; Musil et al. 1999; "Diversity" website, www.inform .umd.edu/diversityweb) and many other plans have been reported in local assessments or research studies, collegiate commission and committee reports, campus publications, and local websites.[1]

The plans and programs reviewed here constitute important innovations and changes, despite in many cases incorporating problematic assumptions and offering limited means to address fundamental problems. Some campus plans are full of rhetoric about change but unclear about strategies of implementation. Some reports are long on assessment or documentation of problems but short on specific solutions and concrete programs. Others provide exemplary detail on innovative practices that appear to have been implemented and even institutionalized. Working from the recommendations in these reports, we unfortunately often do not know which programs have been implemented or their impact; there has been very little systematic evaluation of most of these efforts. Where possible, we comment on the recommended plans in terms of their likelihood of adoption and their potential contribution to a more fully multicultural university.

We first suggest a series of questions or analytical frames of reference to consider when assessing the probable effectiveness of such efforts. We then organize these innovations by the dimension of higher education organizations to which they seem most pertinent (see figures 3.1, 3.2, and 12.1). In presenting these specific programs and innovations, we critically view the extent to which they appear to conform to our criteria for challenging discrimination and promoting multiculturalism.

266

CRITICAL ANALYSIS OF INNOVATIVE
AND TRANSFORMATIVE EFFORTS

In order to maintain an analytic perspective, it is important to examine the assumptions these plans appear to make about collegiate organizations, their likelihood of being implemented and maintained, and their probable efficacy at dealing with organizational racism and social injustice. Several essential questions can be posed to frame an analysis:

1. What vision of multiculturalism (or diversity) and what understanding of the problems of racism and discrimination are evident in organizational statements?
2. Which programs most sensibly address problems of racism and other forms of discrimination and approach the goals of multiculturalism in higher education? Which most explicitly and effectively begin to alter core cultural assumptions and structures or processes that reproduce inequality/discrimination/ disadvantage for some and privilege/advantage for others? And which programs are most likely to interrupt the continued exercise of white and male privilege and to approach social justice?
3. Which organizational dimensions do varied programs focus on? To what extent do they address multiple dimensions of organizational discrimination? Do they focus on central or peripheral functions, and to what extent are administrative/faculty/staff leaders and students and other staff members involved in their planning and execution?
4. To what extent are plans based on data about the local organization or unit(s) and their members? Are these data publicly available and shared?
5. Which programs are most responsive to the hopes, pains, and pressures that students, faculty, and staff members of socially disadvantaged and oppressed groups feel? Which programs address white (and white male) members' concerns and reach out to involve them in multicultural change efforts?
6. Which programs are most likely to achieve substantial change, rather than minor reforms or simple add-ons, in organizational life? To what extent is multiculturalism treated as close to the heart of the institution (in climate, pedagogy, power structures, etc.) rather than as a series of add-ons?
7. Which programs are most likely to be implemented and sustained—perhaps in the face of resistance? Is rhetoric likely to be transformed into action and policy into program? Is ongoing support likely for new programs or for changes?

The typical recommendations and innovations that appear in a number of campus reports are summarized in figure 12.1.

Figure 12.1.   Examples of Diversity/Multicultural Programs/Activities Fit to the Organizational Model

---

Mission
   Forthright policy statements
   Explicit attention to multiple groups' needs/interests
   Links to other missions (excellence, community leadership, globalization, etc.)
   Organization-wide planning and evaluation procedures
Culture (overt/covert, formal/informal, dominant/subordinate)
   Revised codes of conduct/speech
   Training in race/gender awareness for administrators/faculty/staff/students
   New criteria for norms and rewards (e.g., merit pay)
   Opportunities for different cultures to gain/give support and flourish
   Explicit valuing of different identity groups in the organization
   Revised organizational symbols and icons
   Revised organizational narratives to include history of discrimination and of
      challengers
Power and governance (formal/informal leadership, decision making)
   Administrative proaction on issues, strong response to incidents
   Leadership that represents diverse groups and statuses
   New offices to address diversity in administration, academic units, and student
      services
   Mentoring and access for underrepresented groups
   Challenge to existing order seen as opportunity for change
   Support for middle managers
   Unit responsibility/accountability for multicultural progress in every depart-
      ment and unit
   Acceptance of and support for student initiatives in challenging discrimination
   Explicit collaboration among board, administration, faculty, and alumni in ad-
      vocating multicultural change
   Use of diverse leadership teams and advisory committees
Membership
   Plans to recruit/admit diverse student body
   Plans for soliciting/recruiting faculty, staff, and administrators from underrep-
      resented groups
   Plans for postrecruitment retention and advancement of students, faculty, staff,
      and administrators
Social relations and social climate (communication, interaction)
   Antidiscrimination training for staff, faculty, administration, and students
   Support for plural forms of dress, emotional expression, and communication
   Support for white men desiring to change
   Training managers/supervisors in multicultural competencies and teamwork
   Use of multicultural teams and teamwork
   Encouragement of informal social events for work groups
   Support groups and caucuses
   Mentoring members of underrepresented groups

Assessment and feedback regarding member satisfaction
Explicit procedures for assessing progress on multicultural agenda
Recognition and redress of previously ignored forms of harassment
Interpersonal, interdisciplinary and interunit communication and collaboration
Technology (curriculum, pedagogy)
New courses and majors
Introduction of diverse and multicultural material into existing courses
Support for use of alternative research epistemologies, methods, audiences
Retraining and support programs for faculty (faculty development)
Targeted rewards for outstanding multicultural teaching
Use of broader range of instructional methods
Resources (funds, persons)
Resources targeted for innovative recruitment, enrollment/hiring, retention/advancement
Special funds for innovative multicultural programs and innovators
Special funds for incorporating multicultural topics/methods into research
Fairness in salary and other forms of resource distribution
Mentoring and retention/advancement of people from underrepresented groups
Boundary management (external relations, suppliers/markets/constituencies)
Outreach to local secondary schools
Placement of graduates and arrangements with recruiters
Service to communities, especially underrepresented communities
Proactive challenges to community discrimination
Support for minority contractors, suppliers
Changes in accreditation standards and procedures

Source: Chesler and Crowfoot, 1990, Racism on Campus. In W. Mays (Ed.), *Ethics and higher education* (pp. 195–230). New York: Macmillan. Copyright © 1990 by American Council on Education and Macmillan Publishing Company, a Division of Macmillan, Inc. Reproduced with permission of Greenwood Publishing Group, Inc., Westport, CT.

PROGRAMS FOR MULTICULTURAL CHANGE

Mission

The U.S. Office of Education (2004) reports that 74 percent of colleges and universities "acknowledge a commitment to diversity of some sort in their mission statement" (1). Most of these institutions' statements explicitly address racial and ethnic diversity, but other categories of difference often are included. Even more importantly, Musil and her colleagues (Musil et al. 1999) argue that many colleges and universities have gone beyond the effort to diversify their student membership to include concern about the benefits of diversity for students of all races/ethnicities, about its implications for the canon and for research methods/topics, about the future of a multicultural and democratic society, and about preparing students for success in an interdependent global society.

Several large universities have articulated in their mission statements an explicit commitment to various forms of diversity. For instance, Virginia Tech's vision of the future states (Virginia Tech, n.d.-a):

> Virginia Tech must guide its future so that it will become a university that not only accommodates, but also embraces and reflects, the diversity of opinions, races and cultures that will most certainly be our future. . . . The university community must embrace diversity in a manner that will cause Virginia Tech's students to embrace it as well, thus strengthening their academic and personal skills and competencies so they can serve effectively. (2)

And the University of Wisconsin System has developed a comprehensive plan that "especially targets institutional racism as a pernicious phenomenon and seeks to eradicate the impact it has on all students, faculty, and staff members" (Lyall 1994: appendix A).

Some smaller institutions, liberal arts colleges, and religiously oriented colleges have expressed similar core values in their mission statements or restatements. For instance, LeMoyne College (1991) articulates several possible rationales for their commitment to a focus on diversity in community life, as follows:

> Because diversity is part of the universe, has God's sanction, and ought to be affirmed. . . . Because the college's commitment to social justice dictates that it work affirmatively to educate persons from groups that have been or are victims of prejudice and discrimination. . . . Because the European American majority stands to gain a great deal from learning more about the rich history and cultural achievements of African Americans, Hispanics, Native Americans, and non-American and non-Western cultures. . . . And because the Western or European tradition has a great deal of value to offer to African Americans, Hispanics, Native Americans, and persons from non-American and non-Western cultures. (33)

As a Catholic institution, LeMoyne's sense of its multicultural mission obviously is integrated into its view of its religious educational mission.

Various mission statements differ in the rationales they offer for organizational action, and these differences then influence what a college or university works on and achieves. Some statements still use the language of diversity to address the need to acknowledge and "celebrate" different cultures. Although most present the diversity or multicultural agenda as a matter of substantial concern, only a few explicitly address the core issues of institutionalized privilege and discrimination that lie at the root of racism and sexism and classism in higher education and most thereby fail to espouse a critical form of multiculturalism. Very few mission statements "own" their institution's involvement in a history of societal discrimination. A few explicitly suggest that all collegiate members, including the majority of white people, gain from advances in racial diversity; the argument that such action is good for the entire university differs fundamentally from the argument that it is done to benefit particular groups. A multicultural approach to challenging racism requires going beyond transitional notions of tolerance, celebration of difference, and promotion of equal opportunity to include conceptions of social justice and commitments to reducing multiple forms of group oppression and privilege.

Mission statements alone do not carry the power for change. Putting such rhetoric on display in public view is not the same as mobilizing organizational resources to change policy and practice. We should cherish but not necessarily rely on enlightened mission statements unless they are developed in broadly participatory ways, periodically updated, and translated into sustained action for change on the following organizational dimensions.

Culture

Several institutions recognized the necessity of changing their institutional culture and of creating a priority for multiple forms of cultural identification, exchange, and transformation. Some institutions developed programs to infuse the campus with images of cultural difference and efforts to increase intercultural contact, primarily among students. For instance, the report of a survey conducted at Indiana State University included a recommendation to, "Explore ways of dedicating attractive living spaces to multicultural themes to promote intergroup contact: Given that ISU is the first introduction to other cultures for four out of ten white American students, a more visible display of themes may help students realize there is a world beyond their immediate environment" (Office of Institutional Research and Testing, n.d.: 7). Other campuses have engaged academic departments and community agencies in portraying the music and arts of different groups and nations to demonstrate alternatives to the dominant Eurocentric culture.

Consensus-based cultural exchange of this sort, while useful, is not the same as cultural change, however, and the latter requires a sustained, long-term systemic approach and, perhaps, conflict and struggle. In this context, administrators at George Mason University stressed one key element in the change process: the necessity of challenging offensive acts. They planned to "Develop new incident response/conflict resolution procedures for cross-cultural incidents; . . . and [to] recognize that such incidents are the responsibility of the whole campus community" (Conflict Clinic 1991: 12). For its part, Skidmore College recognized the need for an institution-wide focus on cultural change efforts: "the task of making diversity an integral part of its institutional culture must be a campus-wide enterprise involving every office and department" (Office of Diversity and Affirmative Action 2002: 9).

Cultural change can take many forms, but if institutional racism is partly a cultural phenomenon—a socially constructed process of devaluing people based on assumptions about the meaning and value of their life and work—then its opponents must challenge and alter the culture supporting such racism. Thus, it may be appropriate and useful to establish separate support groups for students, colleagues, and staff of color, to create culturally specific programs and events, and to design culturally separate student housing or social units. In a parallel vein, it is equally important to provide opportunities for a community that crosses these boundaries, for intergroup support systems and living arrangements (see Gurin 1999, and chapters 4 and 5 about the importance of informal social contacts). But while these efforts may provide culturally distinct groups with safe havens within an alien environment, or with opportunities for productive intergroup contact and exchange, that alien and often hostile environment itself must eventually change. Focusing on modifying individuals' attitudes or behaviors, or celebrating diverse traditions, may be useful and important, but they do not generally translate into systemic cultural change. For this to occur, progressive forces must emphasize culture-changing designs that focus attention on altering the overwhelming power of the white male Eurocentric tradition.

Some programs that focus on organizational climate assert the need for a culture of civility in the face of differences and for conflict intervention or mediation programs to deal with hostile incidents or confrontations among groups (see the discussion in chapter 11). Indeed, the call for trained intervenors (often specially prepared students) in student intergroup disputes is popular in public elementary and secondary school systems as well as in colleges. George Mason University, Syracuse University, and UCLA (each with support from the William and Flora Hewlett Foundation's Program in Conflict Resolution Theory and Practice) have led the way in this effort. Similarly, many colleges have adopted plans to alter campus cultures or to promote civility with codes of conduct and sanctions for acts of racial and sexual harassment. Antagonistic court cases and media have challenged and sometimes ridiculed such plans as examples of unconstitutional limitations on freedom of speech and of an institutional dogma of political correctness. However, as Rhoads (1997) argues, creating a truly inclusive campus environment specifically for lesbian, gay, and bisexual people requires not only "College and university leaders . . . to demonstratively and publicly express their condemnation of hate speech and other forms of verbal and physical intimidation," but to follow such rhetoric with procedures and penalties (198). But once again, such efforts do not necessarily address problems in the basic culture of the organization: only comprehensive efforts that address core aspects of the dominant culture can successfully move the organization from episodic and reactive mediation or educational intervention to proactive challenges to prejudice and discrimination.

Power Structure and Decision Making

If colleges and universities are to advance toward multiculturalism, the power structure of the organization must be mobilized behind this effort. Locating the responsibility and commitment for such progress at the highest levels of the organization, the Brown University (2000) Diversity Report recommends that "the President and Provost assume full responsibility as the final authorities accountable for Brown's affirmative action plan and vision of diversity, pluralism and community" (4). Identifying the responsibility for action and pushing it farther down into the organization, the Kent State University (2001) plan recommends that the provost hold "deans, chairs and directors accountable for creating and maintaining a climate inclusive of diversity within each Regional campus, as well as colleges/offices" (13).

The dominance of older white males entrenched in patterns of decentralized authority and faculty autonomy help maintain traditional forms of power in most of our highly competitive undergraduate colleges and large research-oriented universities. As a result, the common call for the recruitment, training, and advancement of members of traditionally underrepresented and oppressed groups into higher-level faculty and administrative positions is a partial response to the existing monocultural structures of power in most higher education organizations. As one example, the Michigan State University report recommended that "the University [administration] . . . identify women and minority faculty with exceptional ability and promise who may wish to consider senior administrative leadership positions" (Social Science Research Bureau 1991: 15).

But replacing one set of people with another is not necessarily a long-term solution. New power holders from previously underrepresented groups often hold positions that lack authority. In fact, the most common example is the movement of members of underrepresented groups into high-level staff rather than line positions, or into powerful roles in less prestigious arenas of organizational life. Thus, persons of color and women may occupy roles as vice presidents or deans of student affairs, community affairs, and minority affairs, rather than as academic provosts or vice presidents for financial affairs; and as deans of schools of social work, education, and public health, rather than as deans of schools of liberal arts, law, business, engineering, or medicine. Moreover, once they are placed in positions of traditional and mainstream authority prevailing elites may hold them accountable for keeping their particular constituencies in check, thereby easing the life of senior white and male power holders. They may also find that older traditions and personal representatives of prevailing elites severely limit their new roles. A central question, then, is to what extent new and more diverse members of the elite can or will operate differently from their white male predecessors?

Efforts to alter the structure of higher education institutions in order to deal better with problems of racism and to promote multiculturalism often entail creating special commissions or new offices dedicated to these concerns. For instance, Marshall University is one of a variety of institutions that established a special office whose mission is to "promote equitable and fair treatment in every aspect of campus life," including preventing discrimination, resolving disputes and complaints about discrimination, and organizing educational activities to prevent or eliminate discrimination (Office of Equity Programs 2002: 1–2). More specifically, Pennsylvania State University established a Commission on Lesbian, Gay, Bisexual and Transgender Equity, "to improve the climate for diversity within Penn State and specifically to address issues affecting the welfare of lesbian, gay, bisexual and transgender (LGBT) members of the University Community" and to advise the university president (Committee on Lesbian and Gay Concerns 1992: 1). However, clearly locating responsibility for action on this agenda in a single office may have the effect of relieving other offices, administrators, and faculty members of their responsibility for action. Moreover, unless they wield real power in the organization, such offices often constitute window-dressing. It is vital that such new structures and offices not be insular or isolated, and that they be linked to the nexus of power in the organization. It is important to avoid creating these offices as ghettos or barrios for administrators of color who continue to be excluded from other more powerful deanships or provostships. Such racialized patterns are common in the private sector (Collins 1997), and they are a clear sign of structural intransigence. Multicultural change requires not only adding to structures that already exist but fundamentally opening up these structures to members of underrepresented groups, altering exclusionary models of staffing and operation, assigning them major resources, and providing them with the power and leadership support to impact others in the organization.

Absent effective antiracist and multicultural leadership, neither new positions nor new people in old positions are likely to make a difference. Plans for transforming systems of racial, gender, and class privilege, rather than merely preserving them with minor adaptations, must be linked to greater democratization in general, and not based on a narrowly designed system of elite rule. Certainly expanded systems of governance should include representatives of the governed, especially those traditionally excluded from governance processes, in the design and implementation of multicultural policies and programs. Indeed, Davis (2002) argues that the involvement of persons of color in the design of local affirmative action efforts was a key ingredient in colleges' success in achieving diversity. In addition, traditional authoritarian modes of power wielding need to be replaced with alternative models of collaborative or transformative power sharing. But with the exception of the University of Massachusetts report (Hurst 1987)—a study commissioned after major racial conflict on campus and conducted by an external group—the reports reviewed here do not provide detailed examples of democratized institutional decisional systems with meaningful faculty and student representation and participation.

Membership

Current debates, litigation, and protests for and against affirmative action admissions' programs highlight the contentious nature of membership issues in the academy. Many colleges and universities throughout the nation have expressed a commitment to advancing student and faculty diversity but are struggling to make sense of the shifting legal and political grounds beneath them. Following the Supreme Court's 2003 decisions in the University of Michigan cases, the Bush administration has advocated "race-neutral" admissions procedures (U.S. Office of Education 2004), making a distinction between "developmental" and "admissions" approaches to diversity. Developmental approaches emphasize expansion of the applicant pool through outreach to and partnerships that offer special courses in disadvantaged secondary schools, recruitment centers in underserved areas and community colleges, and more financial aid to students in low-income areas. Race-neutral admissions approaches emphasize more comprehensive reviews of applicants, the use of class rank (such as in Florida, California, and Texas), admissions lotteries, and special attention to students from poor and working-class backgrounds. Examples of developmental plans in action include the University of Wisconsin System's (Lyall 1994: 9) recommendation that "the most comprehensive campus recruitment strategies include long-range plans that integrate extensive pre-college programming with systematic efforts to increase future enrollment," and the University of Vermont's "adoption" of a high school in New York City in order to build a pool of African American and Latino/a applicants (Steinberg 2001). In addition, several colleges and universities have used alternative admissions' approaches by discontinuing or reducing their reliance on SAT scores (or at the graduate level, GRE scores), partly in recognition of these tests' failure to accurately predict academic performance for minority students (Harris and Nettles 1996).

A reliance on "race-neutral" procedures in a racialized and race conscious society is literally impossible; like "color blindness," race neutrality is always affected by structural and cultural influences. In ignoring these factors, race neutral admissions procedures divert attention from the historic and contemporary forms of institutionalized racism that are part of our society. Developmental plans, while essential in the long run for helping to reform an unequal and oppressive system of public education, can do little to alter current college attendance patterns. They also require major reinvestments and changes in segregated and failing elementary and secondary school systems and in the economically and politically oppressed communities they serve. Even if they were successful in producing future generations of qualified students, such efforts would take years to bear fruition in the form of guaranteeing equal access of poor people and people of color to higher education. The admissions plans suggested in the U.S. Department of Education document substitute concerns about class and/or a reliance on luck (lotteries) as ways of dealing with fundamental racial inequality and oppression. By refusing to deliberately attend to and remediate racial inequality in admissions, and the complex relationships between race and class, these race-neutral programs fail to address current inequalities in higher education.

A number of higher education institutions have recognized that diversification of the student body requires efforts beyond recruitment and admission: these efforts typically include heightened attention to campus climate concerns and curricular or pedagogical innovations. Based on a series of case studies of ten public universities, Richardson and Skinner (1996) argue that interventions to improve the retention of students of color require the provision of greater financial aid, assistance with transitions to college (through summer programs), mentoring, workshops to improve study skills, and psychosocial support for life in a culturally alien environment.

Beyond concerns with student membership issues, the report of the Committee on the Status of Women Faculty at Caltech (2001) directly addressed the issue of faculty membership: "Caltech needs to hire more women faculty, be more proactive in nurturing gifted junior faculty, and make itself friendlier to the working family" (2). A subsequent comment, however, indicated agreement with the president's view that "we must be willing to modify our traditional assumptions to create a more welcoming environment. We will do this while keeping in mind our fundamental goal of academic excellence, recognizing that intellectual achievement is Caltech's premier contribution to the world" (2). This language implies that modifying traditional assumptions (and hiring operations) may challenge the goal of excellence; other colleges and universities have expressed their intention to increase the representation of people of color and women on their faculties without such implications of diminished excellence or with the positive argument that academic excellence requires diversity.

Some institutions have dealt emphatically with the implications in chapters 7 and 10 of the necessity to increase the representation of women and people of color within administrative ranks/positions. For instance, in commenting on the goal of developing a diverse management team, the Pennsylvania State University (n.d.) report states:

> Progress in placing African Americans into important leadership positions has been fairly impressive. However, in recent years several African American employees have assumed executive-level positions at other institutions following unsuccessful efforts to advance at Penn State. While some progress has also been made in the representation of women in managerial positions, it still lags behind the overall representation of women in the workforce. In addition, other historically underrepresented groups are virtually absent from the managerial ranks at all levels of the organization. (1)

In the effort to retain and advance people of color and women in their faculty and staff, specialized support and mentoring programs, family-friendly policies, and other programs suited to the particular needs of these populations must be in place. In all of these institutions sustained, long-term commitment, allocation of resources, and periodic evaluations are essential.

Climate and Social Relations

Many campus reports and recommendations include efforts to deal directly with the quality of intergroup social, academic, and working relationships. For instance, the University of California, Berkeley report (Duster 1991) pays considerable attention to students' views of their informal relationships—in and out of class—with students of other races and ethnicities. Indeed, this report identifies and decries the trend toward racial/ethnic separatism in student communities, both as a preferred-group lifestyle and as a response to perceptions of exclusionary treatment and harassment. Clearly any effort to address these issues must be proactive rather than reactive, and must acknowledge both the pre-college experiences with separation and prejudice that many students enter with and the campus conditions that sustain these patterns.

Many colleges and universities have attempted to create a more inclusive campus climate by instituting programs that respond to discriminatory graffiti, hate speech, and incidents of discrimination. For instance:

- Students organized a "This is our home" campaign in response to hateful graffiti (Bentley College n.d.).
- Administrators at Indiana State University made sanctions for posting hateful graffiti clear to students and staff (Office of Institutional Research and Testing 1995).
- Administrators at the University of Colorado at Boulder developed a Bias Motivated Incident Response Team as part of an effort to create a welcoming and enriching environment for all members of the university (Office of Diversity and Equity 2000).

Others have designed proactive programs to either anticipate or prevent such events.

- Advisers at the University of Nebraska–Lincoln suggested conducting workshops and establishing ombuds services and support services to foster a campus climate where tolerance and respect occur (1999).
- At Duke University students organized a one-day campaign for campus members to wear shirts saying "Gay, fine by me" (Rooney 2003; Zernicke 2004). This activity was replicated at several other institutions (e.g., Notre Dame; Fosmoe 2004).

Sometimes student initiative is responsible for the initiation of new programs (e.g., the Bentley and Duke examples). For instance, as part of a response to white supremacist leafleting and a shooting rampage targeting Asian students, an Indiana University program, Conversations About Race, developed in campus residence halls, spread to the larger campus community, and eventually was adapted into a two-day seminar for academic credit (www.studycircles.org). In chapter 11, we reviewed other special curricular or extracurricular programs using intergroup dialogue and conflict mediation skills that are underway at a number of institutions. While programs of this sort are useful, they could be even more effective if integrated into a curriculum that focuses on such issues. Efforts to introduce notions of civility, democratic behavior, or good intergroup relations into universities' curricular programs place issues of cultural transformation at the heart of the moral enterprise of education rather than at the individual and special-program periphery.

Campus climate diagnoses or interventions that key on the student climate often overlook the degree to which the actions of the faculty, administration, and board of trustees determine much of the culture that students enter into and participate in. Defining this as a student problem, or solely as a problem in interpersonal relationships, often means that departments or offices of student affairs, rather than the faculty or the institution as a whole, are presumed to have sole responsibility for dealing with it. Indeed, the age- and experience-based domination and distance that often bedevil faculty–student interactions may have as great an impact on student alienation and conflict as do race or gender dynamics. These generationally determined systems of status and power often constitute the bedrock social structure of the institution and may make any change in a more egalitarian direction difficult unless it, too, is challenged and remediated.

In addition, the transitory nature of the student body means that change efforts must be organized in ways that are repeated every year; thus, to be effective, they must be institutionalized, and such institutionalization requires significant collaboration and participation from longer-term members of the university community. Focusing on students may also ignore ways in which racism and other forms of discrimination are institutionalized in the structure and culture of the higher education organization itself—and among the faculty, staff, and administrative offices. Challenging discrimination in the campus climate must be seen as an academic priority as well as a student management priority, and it must be integrated into curricular planning, pedagogical selections, coursework, research projects, and administrative agendae. It also is important for climate improvement efforts to focus on the reeducation of white people—students and faculty and staff—about race and other forms of discrimination, and to challenge the ways in which white hegemony influences everything else that occurs on campus.

Many of the interventions normally directed at students' relationships and interactions—racial awareness and education activities, sensitivity sessions, intergroup social events, intragroup social and support activities, residence hall and fraternity/sorority living unit innovations and educational programs, service learning options, conflict resolution and mediation training, and so on—should also be planned for staff, administrators, and faculty members, or at least should be implemented for students in ways that involve these other constituencies. For example, in order to overcome the isolation and exclusion from informal social and working relations that faculty of color often experience, Indiana University (1992) suggests that the university "develop plans to include campus climate issues in evaluating faculty and staff performance" (41). Indeed, the Indiana report explicitly advocates that, as part of this inquiry, interviews be conducted with "minority faculty members who elect to stay at Indiana University in order to appraise the comfort level each minority faculty member perceives" (44).

Technology—Curriculum and Pedagogy

In the midst of great national debate about whether a canon of core knowledge does or should exist in various disciplines—and if so, what elements it should contain—many universities have advocated new course requirements designed to increase students' experience with and academic understanding of issues of difference and domination in intergroup relationships. Surveys reported in Musil and various coauthors (Musil et al. 1995, 1999), as well as several other Association of American Colleges and Universities' reports (Humphreys 1997; Association of American Colleges and Universities 1995; see also Schmitz 1992), identify numerous innovative curricular efforts to prepare students for life in a diverse democracy (see chapter 10). Despite the fears of some opponents, advancing multiculturalism does not require destruction and replacement of the traditional curriculum. But it does require coherent analysis of the curriculum, including discussions of why certain views and definitions of what should be taught and learned prevail and others do not.

Innovative pedagogy that responds to a more diverse campus and classroom environment is much less often addressed in these reports, but chapter 10 provides a number of relevant suggestions and examples. Among the faculty improvement workshops described in Musil et al. (1999) and Musil et al. (1995) are off-site and on-site efforts, independent study, group sessions, one-shot workshops, several-week seminars, and exchanges between institutions. Some programs also include stipends for participating faculty. The Association of American Colleges and Universities sponsors summer institutes on these issues and has collaborated with the University of Maryland to make such resources available on the Internet (www.inform.umd.edu/diversityweb).

One useful innovation is the implementation of more faculty development efforts (and the released time that would support such efforts) that focus on collaborative teaching conducted by both faculty colleagues and students. To the extent that wisdom and skill in intergroup relations are not solely the property of faculty and staff members, pedagogical innovations may place skilled students in the lead of peer-directed learning environments and activities. The Berkeley report (Duster 1991), for instance, advises that "American Culture courses could lend themselves particularly well to a new pedagogical format. Given that these lectures are being newly formed and developed around the idea of comparative ethnic-racial perspectives, instructors need to be open to the idea that both they and their students are simultaneously engaged in a learning process that aims at being explicitly comparative" (61). Other examples of student peer-led educational programs focusing on multiculturalism are illustrated in chapter 11.

One priority of the U.S. system of higher education, especially in research-oriented universities, is the pursuit of truth and the generation of scientific knowledge. In this regard, some scholars have argued that different cultures may prefer or be more attuned to different epistemological styles, and a fund of scientific (social and natural) knowledge and artistic (visual and literary) experience that is not reflected in or represented best in a Western, rationalist, and semipositivist epistemological framework. Without falling into essentialist arguments, pursuing this claim seems important, as does consideration of its relevance for the pluralistic pursuit of knowledge. Collegiate representatives of oppressed social communities who wish to conduct research that directly serves these communities may benefit from alternative research visions and methods, such as participatory action research and community based research. These issues are seldom addressed in campus self-reports and plans.

Resources

Few programs and recommendations can be implemented and sustained without a continued infusion or reallocation of resources and many colleges and universities have recognized this reality. For instance, the Ohio State University (2000) "authorized $500,000 in new funding for scholarship programs, including funds for transfer students, designed to increase diversity" (2). These efforts to provide additional scholarship funds for students from underrepresented groups represent a meaningful response to research indicating that "minority students report more financial need than their nonminority counterparts" (Harris and Nettles 1996: 339).

In addition to supporting students, resources also can be deployed to aid the recruitment of women faculty and faculty of color as well as research on multiculturally relevant issues. The University of Michigan report (Office of Affirmative Action and Office of Minority Affairs 1992: 12) suggests that the university "Provide full funding for minority hiring (of faculty) from central rather than unit funds." This approach mirrors many other institutions' establishment of "targets of opportunity," an incentive-based arrangement wherein departments that hire faculty of color (or in some cases women faculty) do not have to spend departmental funds to do so; thus, they gain an extra position and an extra colleague. Resources also can be used to enhance the infrastructure of support for diversity and multicultural efforts. For instance, the University of Maryland has developed a Faculty Support Award to "encourage faculty to engage in diversity-related research by providing funds for extra and/or specialized research time and/or a course 'buy-out'" (Office of Human Relations Programs 2003: 1). Many grant or award programs are in place at various colleges to support faculty in reorganizing existing courses or preparing new curricula, to support student groups in designing cultural and intercultural events, and to support staff members in organizing educational sessions. The search for additional resources to meet these needs could tap previously overlooked sources of private (alumnus/a and community) donations that explicitly share the college's multicultural agenda.

Resources may be human as well as financial. Thus, the George Mason University report (Conflict Clinic 1991) further suggests the need to "tap the resources of existing culturally diverse organizations (e.g., student clubs) in developing responses to cross-cultural friction on campus" (12). This example begins to cross the boundary between staff and faculty planning initiatives and the involvement of students as codevelopers and implementers of such programs. It does not cross the boundary between the university and its surrounding communities, however, nor does it reach out to diverse community resources (people, history, ideas, or sites for internships).

Altering the incentive and reward system, which embodies the normative frame for allocating many resources, is another appropriate change goal. Linking resources to the underlying reward system of the unit begins to tie such efforts to the core mission and culture of the institution. The organization speaks and acts through the control and allocation of resources. Funds, however, are neither the only nor in every case the most important resource and many institutions have found it easier to fund multicultural innovations than to expend the necessary time and energy to alter the organization's culture and structure in ways that bring these innovations into the mainstream of organizational life and sustain them over time.

Boundary Systems

Every organization must interact with its external environment and must find ways to survive and prosper in the context of societal and community events and relationships. For universities and colleges, managing these boundaries and relationships affects student and faculty recruitment, housing opportunities for university personnel, action on a service mission, fund-raising, and many other things. A higher education organization committed to multiculturalism must take

a proactive stance regarding antiracism and antisexism in the geographic and political community where it is located. This in turn will require the institution to
develop collaborative relationships with local and state legislators, local political and economic elites, and organizations and groups of people not traditionally
represented in community power structures. The institutions will also have to relate to communities on more egalitarian and collaborative grounds than has historically been the case.

Aside from concerns about student recruitment, addressed earlier in this chapter, efforts to attend to other aspects of the diversity agenda beyond the campus
boundaries may engage colleges and universities in joint academic-community
programming. The report for Mount St. Mary's College (Haldeman, n.d.) en-
dorses an effort "to build bridges with the community and to become part of the
revitalization of Los Angeles through civic work and involvement" and the development of internships with local educational and youth-serving agencies (1).

Some reports provide examples of boundary-spanning activities that focus on
universities' relationships with suppliers of goods and materials and with local
businesses. For instance, Washington University established an Office of Supplier Diversity to help create and sustain viable minority businesses in St. Louis
and to increase minority representation in the workplace (Washington University in St. Louis 2002–2003). Not only does the University of Maryland direct
work to minority businesses, but its Minority Business Enterprise works with
"the governor's office of minority affairs, placing notices in trade publications
that reach minority businesses, attending special events and fairs, and establishing 'strategic partnerships' with groups such as the Maryland Minority Contractors Association and Hispanic Contractors Association, all in order to identify
and retain more minority vendors" (University of Maryland, College Park, and
Association of American Colleges and Universities 1998: 6.17).

The multicultural agenda poses a number of dilemmas for managing the boundary systems of contemporary higher education organizations. First, in the absence
of a substantial and equitable number of students, faculty, staff, and administrators
representing varied identity groups inside the organization, the institution must
breach traditional boundaries and develop new approaches to recruitment, admissions, or hiring and retention. The Smith College report (1989) suggests that alumnae be more fully involved in campus change efforts; this is another example of
boundary reformation, since alumnae's involvement in these roles requires their
being more fully exposed to, oriented to, and trained in the multicultural change
process. Such effort may also stimulate additional alumnus/a financial support for
these initiatives.

New organizational members may seek to build and retain ties with their old
communities and traditions of origin in ways that differ from previous linkages
generated by white male members. That, too, may breach historic boundaries
and create the need for more socially just policies, such as greater ties with and

services provided to K–12 educational systems, curricula that offer students opportunities for community service learning, research that directly serves the political and economic interests of local communities, intellectual and cultural events that address community needs and traditions, organizational decision making that involves the participation of community leaders, and so on.

In some cases, collaborative relationships with state and municipal higher education agencies can help support campus multicultural initiatives. For instance, Hurtado et al. (1999) argue that "state higher education policies can provide the necessary infrastructure through funding, introduction of new programs, and reforms that require changes in public systems of higher education" (58). State political leaders and legislatures also may provide critical financial resources to public colleges and universities (including community colleges), and in so doing support greater diversity and the hope for multicultural change on campus. Or they can act in ways that limit public colleges' multicultural change efforts. These political actors and other community organizations also may become members of external coalitions that can generate broadly based public support for or opposition to affirmative action programs and other multicultural initiatives.

An overriding boundary issue is the effect of current trends in the U.S. society toward social and political retrenchment on issues of racial, economic, and social justice in higher education. Major campaigns have been waged recently against progressive racial policies and programs initiated during the civil rights movement, against advancement of equal rights and protection of gay and lesbian people, and in favor of economic policies that ignore the needs of economically deprived groups and increase the gaps between wealthy and nonwealthy citizens. All these trends impact local communities and through them the populations of young families and students seeking higher education. Many colleges and universities have been passive in the face of the boundary-penetrating developments, "passing on" societal changes in the form of more restrictive curricula, diminished financial aid packages, and the abandonment of racial diversity as part of their admissions and hiring policies. Others have tried to buffer their student, faculty, and staff members from these trends, refusing to alter or eliminate policies and programs that attempt to address the needs of diverse collegiate populations. A few others, however, have elected to actively counter these trends, continuing to develop and implement curricular changes that address the needs of varied racial, ethnic, and gender groups, modifying admissions and hiring policies in ways that conform to current court standards while still guaranteeing a diverse collegiate membership, and instituting financial aid packages that address the needs of families and students who face shrinking economic resources. Many of the attempts to implement the innovative policies and programs reviewed in this chapter, as well as others discussed throughout this volume, will have to negotiate pressures originating outside the boundaries of higher education institutions.

CONCLUSIONS

Examining reports of plans and programs is a poor substitute for actual obser-
vation of programs in practice, but it does clarify some of the critical questions
raised earlier in this chapter. The vision of multiculturalism that these plans and
programs seek to address, and their diagnostic knowledge of local racism and
discrimination, vary considerably. Some efforts focus on diversity as a path to
greater representation of people of different social origins on campus—as students, as faculty, as staff, and as senior administrators. Others identify the existence of prejudice and discrimination, usually at the level of individuals, and
seek to mitigate or eradicate these. Few directly mention or discuss racism, sexism, heterosexism, and other forms of institutionalized discrimination or of sustained white male privilege and advantage, as we approach them. And fewer still
seriously attempt to challenge and transform such institutional discrimination
and domination. A broad multicultural vision of the sort we propose in figure 3.2
is missing in most of these reports.

Many of the proposed programs reviewed here exist only on paper, as suggestions made by special committees or as the dreams of a leadership cadre or of an
alienated group. We do not have information on their disposition, and whether or
which recommendations have been implemented. Moreover, many of those that
appear to have been implemented and remain operational appear to lack coherent
assessments or evaluations. If universities themselves lack information about the
results of new programs and change attempts they cannot successfully determine
their progress toward multiculturalism or correct for unanticipated results. Under
such circumstances, neither they nor we know the efficacy of these efforts in addressing root problems of organizational and societal discrimination. One can
only wonder why so few evaluative studies of multicultural change efforts are
broadly available: perhaps they are available locally, perhaps no one wants to take
the risk of knowing what actually works and does not work.

Some plans and programs address only one or two of the organizational dimensions illustrated in figures 3.2 and 12.1. The most common foci of single-
focus plans are membership, climate, and curriculum. Much less often addressed
are pedagogy, power structures, and boundary systems. Other reports address
multiple dimensions, and some even link the dimensions into something approaching an integrated strategic plan for innovation and change. For instance,
rather than merely suggesting a workshop for faculty interested in curriculum
change, they may identify and plan ways for senior leaders to sponsor such
workshops, to ensure rewards for participating faculty who use the results in innovative classroom designs, and to demonstrate their own commitment to
change by attending such events.

Few of these reports and plans specify the change strategies that would be
used to implement any of the recommendations, an essential step illustrated in

figure 8.2. Indeed, under what circumstances might such efforts actually be implemented and succeed or fail? Certainly, little progress will occur and be sustained unless there is clear agreement among organizational leaders, and between leaders and other major constituencies, as to the nature of the problem(s) at hand and potential changes and their role in planning and implementation. If efforts to undertake change are not integrated or coordinated in a systematic plan the multicultural effort relies on temporary and ad hoc innovators and innovations instead of the ongoing power of organizational energy, skill, and structure. Davis (2002) emphasizes the importance of a strong mandate for action from senior leaders and their follow-through with allocations of key resources such as funds, time, and energy. And Richardson and Skinner (1996) stress the importance of accountability and senior leaders' expectations that action will be taken. If these are some of the key ingredients for success, it is not hard to imagine why and how many change efforts fail to be implemented, to overcome resistance, or even to start.

In the absence of strong and supportive leadership from traditional power figures, and continuity of commitment in the face of leadership turnover, multicultural change advocates will have to organize and innovate independently and from the grassroots. In most institutions individuals can find space to try out new programs on their own initiative—in classrooms, faculty meetings, residence halls, student clubs and associations, staff units, and the like. Such agency and commitment is the lifeblood of many faculty and staff members. As these efforts take place, are publicized, and are networked with similar ventures, and as advocates or innovators link to one another, they can become a significant force for change across a broad spectrum of the college or university. Thus, while leadership from above is important, justice-minded challengers to organizational discrimination need not (and should not) wait for, be beholden to, or be limited by a lack of such leadership. Indeed, efforts to transform pockets of innovation into systemic change often are at the core of pressure-based tactics of change in the face of hesitant or recalcitrant educational leadership.

It is clear that few of the innovations reported here, and few of the campus plans and reports cited, seriously approach the vision of a multicultural organization articulated in figure 3.2. Even in their current state, however, the suggestions outlined here constitute useful starting points for many institutions. For colleges that have yet to begin, the change plans cited and those available in locally published or Internet access form provide concrete examples of the kinds of steps necessary for multicultural change, and to move from a monocultural to a transitional stage. For those institutions where planning is underway and change is in motion, these plans may highlight areas left unexamined. While none provides a complete map, taken together the reports cited and the suggestions listed in figure 12.1 offer markers for what it means to begin to take antiracism and multiculturalism seriously within higher educational organizations.

NOTE

1. Most plans or reports that are listed in this chapter as accessed on university websites were accessed during 2002 and 2003. Although the exact date of authorship of some of these postings is unclear (thus the designation "n.d."), we assume their presence on universities' official websites means that the institution considered them to be up-to-date and relevant as of 2002 or 2003. Some of these website reports, as well as others, were also available in printed form and were distributed by colleges and universities with or without a publication date indicated.

Part Four

THE FUTURE?

In this final section, we look to the future of challenges to racism and other forms of discrimination and efforts to promote multiculturalism and justice in higher education organizations. We examine the current and probably future landscape of struggles for equality and justice and consider its implications for higher education. Then we review and summarize the major issues discussed throughout this volume, those involving the key conceptual frames, the reports of experiences of major actors in colleges and universities, and the central strategies and tactics of organizational change.

Chapter Thirteen

Looking toward the Future

There are multiple visions of what multiculturalism means and what a multicultural system of higher education might look like. While we have provided definitions and concrete images of more just educational institutions, and how to move in that direction, we know many questions remain unanswered. Hopefully colleges and universities will move away from monocultural and discriminatory traditions of the past, and beyond an assimilationist orientation in which institutions are controlled by affluent and older white males and their supporters. As they approach multiculturalism and social justice, we undoubtedly will discover additional ways to organize more egalitarian and effective systems of higher education.

The effort to challenge racism, sexism, and other forms of social discrimination and to promote multiculturalism in higher education presents many difficulties. Creating a more multicultural organization with a more inclusive sense of community, while simultaneously supporting identity group commitments and ties, is a major intellectual and programmatic challenge. As colleges and universities undertake this challenging new task, we know that forces within them will resist change, especially change in a multicultural direction. Disciplinary commitments to traditional academic content and processes, and efforts to justify them as markers of quality and excellence, help maintain life as it is in these organizations. Whether the root of resistance lies in entrenched loyalty to tradition, in an unwillingness to let go of assumptions about the importance of "merit" as traditionally defined, in bureaucratic ossification, or in the defense of privilege, the resistance persists. Perhaps more important, we know that all attempts to bring greater justice to higher education must engage all the institutionalized forms of social discrimination that exist in the larger society—in the culture of racial and economic privilege, in the unbalanced distribution of wealth and other material resources, in unequal access to clean water and air, in neighborhood and elementary school segregation, in the lack of ability to determine one's own life opportunities and future. Often only innovation or pressure from the margins of the institution, from internal outliers and external community agencies and social movements, will make the difference.

But it is worthwhile for colleges and universities to take on the tasks of challenging racism and other forms of discrimination and promoting multicultural change. These institutions play a vital role in maintaining the best elements of our current society and in creating a more just social order. They are the socializers and gatekeepers of opportunities for young people who are the society's most important resource. The great minds collected in universities at their best generate alternative visions of the ways people and organizations can live and work together. They also invent and design theories and strategies of change that can propel groups and organizations in a multicultural direction. The students who move through these institutions are often thirsty for knowledge and are concerned with the quality of life in their own communities and impending careers. To the extent that these young people can learn the nature of societal discrimination and oppression, the roots of intergroup problems, and how to live and work productively across traditional group boundaries, hope endures. To the extent that higher education organizations can teach change skills and can model new social relations based on common interests, power sharing, and collaboration, that hope may be realized. Despite the current failings and limits of our higher education institutions, the potential for change, and the importance of such change, remain. We must engage in these struggles of multicultural transformation. Failing to do so makes us complicit in sustaining racism and other forms of social inequality. Failing to do so betrays critical elements of the unique American dream.

THE CURRENT POLITICAL MOMENT

These are clearly dangerous times, and the new century is one of rapid and unprecedented change. Among its changing conditions are globalization of the economy and culture; rapid population growth, particularly among people of color living in poverty; powerful technologies such as biological weapons, artificial intelligence, genetic engineering, and ever faster and more complicated information processing. Increasing affluence occurs for a numerical minority of humans amidst great economic and social inequities between and within countries and global regions. Starvation and disease affect the less wealthy nations of the world, weapons of mass destruction proliferate, and an unstable international order prevails. The arrival of the "end of nature" signifies that humans are increasingly a major influence on environmental changes (e.g., land use, atmospheric greenhouse gas levels and climate change, oceanic dead zones, and depletion of nonrenewable sources of energy). A growing world population creates increased pressure on food supplies, land and water resources, and economic and educational opportunities. The combination of these factors results in patterns of environmental injustice, as the effects of economic and environmental stratification are visited most powerfully on communities of poor people and people of color around the globe. Long-standing patterns of social domination and subordination are facilitated and exacerbated by the increased reliance on military and violent means of control, parallel technologies of cultural hegemony, and economic pressure creating marginalization and exclusion. As these patterns are challenged the specters of international wars of terrorism, internal civil strife, and state repression increase. Whether international institutions and democratic states can survive as such in the face of these developments is unclear. As noted by Ruth Simmons (2002), president of Brown University, "Whatever the implications of globalism, we know that all of our lives are being irrevocably affected by the startling changes that are now shaping the world" (16).

In the United States, rising domestic inequality in wealth and income levels looms large across racial and class lines, and mass incarceration of people of color leaves many college age young people outside the opportunity structure. In addition, opposition to efforts to counter discrimination against people of color and LGBTQ people has gained momentum and reached our courts and legislatures.

These demographic and economic transformations, and their related cultural challenges, promote innovation but also generate renewed resistance. The underlying conflicts of a world divided by race and gender and class become more visible in struggles over cherished traditions and contemporary resources. In a time of major challenges, those with courage and vision are compelled to act. In a place of confused alternatives, those with clear vision will command the stage. People committed to challenging racism and other forms of discrimination must be able to articulate the vision and mobilize the skills required to act on the multicultural agenda as a key element of future societal stability.

TWENTY-FIRST-CENTURY LEADERSHIP FOR MULTICULTURALISM IN HIGHER EDUCATION

As U.S. colleges and universities uncritically embrace technology development and joint ventures with economic elites they privilege service to the private corporate sector and the public governmental sector in ways that often threaten independent inquiry and service to more varied publics. Financial starvation of the public sector has led to budget cuts throughout higher education, and we can anticipate that innovative efforts to challenge discrimination will continue to be among the first sets of programs to be threatened. Moreover, in the face of narrow victories in the Supreme Court and continuing litigation and political campaigning (see, e.g., Clegg 2005), it will take bold administrative and faculty action to maintain successful affirmative admissions designs and related financial aid programs necessary to enroll and retain students from less wealthy backgrounds. Even when substantial numbers of students, faculty, and staff from underrepresented groups are present on campus, continued resistance to their presence, to their more than symbolic participation, and to their advancement, will make their path perilous. The foremost question facing higher education leaders will be how to prepare diverse groups of students for these challenges. Answering this question will require choosing between preparing students for the old social order rooted in colonialism and postcolonialism or for an emerging order based on interdependence and collaboration among people who differ from one another in many ways. We will either maintain long-standing systems of white privilege and racial discrimination or provide leadership for a more just future.

Amid these difficult challenges, windows of opportunity for multicultural change will open. Demographic changes and market demands make it inevitable that more people of color will enter the ranks of our colleges and universities. The increased entry of members of these groups leads unavoidably, albeit slowly, to challenges to and changes in the culture of social relationships on campus. Their sense of agency, even in the face of marginalization and stigma, is a critical resource for change and a call for enlightened white support. The resultant accommodations in organizational structures and processes require all members to learn new ways of administering, teaching, and learning. Alice Chandler (1991), president of the State University of New York at New Paltz, echoes several other university leaders quoted earlier:

> American society faces an important choice whether to adopt and reconcile its differing peoples and cultural traditions or to splinter into cultural and social apartheid. . . . The history of the United States is a mixed picture of welcome and intolerance for immigrant groups. Today the fragmentation and polarization of American society is more complex. The tensions, resentments and polarizations bred by an underlying social structure find reflection on our campuses today. Racial minorities and white students all too often meet as strangers who have inherited fears of each other. One-quarter of all college presidents and two-thirds of all presidents of research and doctorate institutions say racial tensions and hostilities are a moderate to major problem on their campuses, reports Ernest Boyer. Social cleavages along racial and ethnic lines are widely visible. (4–5)

Educational leaders and their multiple constituencies will face even harder choices between democratic traditions supportive of multiculturalism and long-established patterns characterized by white male privilege and the stratification of higher education institutions.

DRAWING LESSONS FROM THIS BOOK

The major lessons we have learned in creating this work, and that we emphasize in concluding our effort, can be summarized in three areas: first, the conceptual frameworks presented in chapters 1–3; second, insights into the experiences of key actors dealing with racial and other forms of discrimination in higher education organizations presented in chapters 4–7; third, a set of strategic considerations that can guide the development of new programs and related efforts to promote multiculturalism and approach justice presented in chapters 8–12.

Conceptual Frameworks

We have argued that certain conceptual frames—ways of understanding the world—are central in the effort to challenge discrimination and promote multiculturalism.

- Racism, sexism, and other forms of discrimination are institutionalized in our society. Such institutionalized discrimination goes hand in hand with privilege and advantage for most white people, most men, most people of upper- and upper-middle-class backgrounds, heterosexuals, and Christians.
- Such institutionalized discrimination and privilege can be maintained even if those who gain from it are not acting intentionally to harm others and those who suffer from it are not doing anything to merit such treatment.
- Such institutionalized discrimination undergirds the operations of higher education organizations and has resulted in a long history of systematic exclusion and maltreatment of underrepresented and subordinated groups in U.S. colleges and universities.
- The institutionalization of discrimination toward some and corollary privileges for others are present in the organizational structure and processes of colleges, and the managerial and instructional behavior of boards, administrations, faculty, staff, and students. They occur in every dimension of the educational organization and help maintain the status quo.
- Except in response to crises, higher education places a lower priority on reducing discrimination and advancing multiculturalism than on other priorities such as fund-raising, academic excellence, departmental rankings and prestige, and intercollegiate sports programs.
- Domestic and global transformations, along with growing consciousness of the privileges of race and gender and wealth, represent major pressures on higher education organizations to change in the direction of greater justice.

Experiences of Key Actors

In addition, we have argued that these societal and organizational factors affect the experience and behavior of all members of higher education organizations. Several chapters report some of the ways in which students, faculty, and administrative officers experience their lives in colleges and universities.

- Many white students report ignorance about their own and others' racial memberships and history, and ignorance of the advantages and disadvantages associated with their own and others' racial status. They report feeling racially awkward in the presence of students of color, at best unsure how to behave toward and react to them (and at worst having misconceptions about their presence and resistance to it).
- Students of color in predominantly white colleges and universities often report being stereotyped and stigmatized in interracial peer relationships, and that life in these institutions is especially burdensome.
- Students of color in predominantly white colleges and universities often report being stereotyped and overlooked by white faculty, being called upon to represent their race/ethnicity, and finding their heritage and concerns missing from the curriculum.
- Many students of color and white students also report positive intergroup encounters and significant changes in their identities, knowledge, and outlooks as a function of collaborative learning in diverse educational communities.
- Faculty of color and women faculty, underrepresented in the academy, consistently report their scholarly credentials and status being questioned and their authority challenged, sometimes in implicit terms and sometimes explicitly, by students and by colleagues.
- White and male faculty often report an inability or unwillingness to proactively deal with subtle and covert racial/ethnic issues and incidents in the classroom and confusion about how to react to such issues when they arise overtly.
- Few faculty, regardless of race/ethnicity, gender, status, or discipline, report familiarity with and use of a wide range of pedagogical options for dealing with diverse classrooms and intergroup issues.
- Faculty committed to working on issues of discrimination and oppression report struggles with formations of racial and gender power—among students and often between themselves and students.
- Some faculty of color and white faculty report the intellectual excitement and sense of satisfaction that they experience when teaching diverse groups of students and especially in raising with them issues of intergroup discrimination, privilege, and patterns of engagement.
- Administrators of color and women administrators are underrepresented in the academy (and on its governing boards), especially in elite research-oriented institutions.
- Administrators of color and women administrators report many of the same tensions and experiences as do faculty and students of color and women.
- Those colleagues who do challenge discrimination or proactively engage the multicultural agenda often report minimal skill in change making and a lack of support or even resistance from peers and organizational leaders.

- In the midst of these tendencies, courageous white people and people of color constantly emerge to take leadership roles in challenging racism and other forms of discrimination and promoting multiculturalism (with or without institutional support).

Strategic Considerations for Change

These conceptual frames and reports from studies with members of colleges and universities lead to a focus on the strategies and tactics of organizational change that might challenge racism and other forms of discrimination and promote multiculturalism. In most organizations, under most circumstances, the choice of change strategies and tactics involves complex, often contradictory, considerations.

- Forthright leadership from the college or university president, senior administrators, and senior faculty is important to legitimate and drive a multicultural change effort.
- Campus-wide and specific-unit cultural audits or assessments can provide data about the existence of discrimination, the needs of various campus groups, and the tactical opportunities for change.
- Curricular and pedagogical innovations are necessary to take advantage of the opportunity diversity provides and to help students develop multicultural competencies.
- Faculty development efforts are an important ingredient in meeting the faculty's need to expand their curricular and pedagogical options and to be more effective teachers in diverse classrooms. Parallel programs for administrators and staff members can advance the quality of campus life, the effectiveness of multicultural leadership teams, student services, and cocurricular activities.
- Intergroup collaboration, within and across groups of students, faculty, and staff, is an important ingredient of a multicultural change process. A key organizational learning agenda is the development of the new skills and attitudes required to create and sustain effective intergroup coalitions or teams.
- Change agents must figure out how to make substantial change in their institution while surviving and even thriving as members (with acknowledgment of some of membership's own privileges). Despite the often oppressive nature of life in these institutions, and of resistance to change, some members continue to exert their sense of agency and promote more just environments.
- Change advocates must learn how to operate from both the margin and the center of higher education organizations, from positions of power and from positions far removed from traditional centers of operational power, with internal allies and external coalition partners.
- Coercive or pressure-oriented change tactics and persuasion or cooperation-oriented tactics must both be considered, as appropriate in given situations, with knowledge about each's specific resources and opportunities (as well as risks).

- Since race- and gender-based advantages are sustained by the power structure, the membership, culture, and operational power of organizations and classrooms must be altered for multicultural change to occur.
- Students—especially but not exclusively students from underrepresented groups—have been a prime stimulus for challenges to campus discrimination and often are an untapped political and human resource in the multicultural change process.
- Substantial alterations in the allocation of resources to higher education organizations, and in the internal distribution of such resources, must accompany social justice-oriented change efforts.
- Organizations are vulnerable to petitions and pressure from external constituencies; therefore, alumni, parents, business leaders, local community members, accreditation agencies, state educational and legislative officials, and other local and national executives and judiciaries have crucial roles to play in the multicultural change effort. Collegiate leaders must plan how to mobilize these parties to assist in challenging discrimination and promoting multiculturalism.
- College leaders, faculty, and students can improve the climate of intergroup relations among students on campus in general by selecting from among the innovative programs under way in many colleges and universities.

We have provided a quick view (and some guidelines for analysis and assessment) of some of the many efforts to move from monocultural to transitional stages of development, and even to promote multiculturalism, that are under way in colleges and universities across the nation. These efforts should be analyzed carefully to see whether plans have progressed to the implementation stage, if key actors have walked the talk of their publications and reports, and if programs have been evaluated or monitored in ways that teach us about their relative success and ways of making further progress.

AND NOW TO WORK . . .

It is now up to university boards, presidents, administrators, staff, faculty, students, and concerned citizens (whether from underrepresented or well-represented groups) to take the next steps. The actions they take, that we all take, will determine not only the shape of our colleges and universities in the years to come, but the shape and welfare of our nation and emerging global institutions.

References

Aberle-Grasse, M. 2002. The Washington study-service year of Eastern Mennonite University. *American Behavioral Scientist*, *43*(5), 848–57.

Academe. 2003, May–June. Notabene. Pp. 7–8.

Achieving diversity: Race-neutral alternatives in American education. 2004. Washington, D.C.: United States Department of Education, Office of Civil Rights.

Adams, D. 1995. *Education for extinction: American Indians and the boarding school experience: 1875–1928*. Lawrence: University of Kansas Press.

Adams, J., Niss, J., and Suarez, C. 1991. *Multicultural education: A rationale for development and implementation*. Macomb. Western Illinois University Foundation.

Adams, M., Bell, L., and Griffin, P. (Eds.). 1997. *Teaching for diversity and social justice: A sourcebook*. New York: Routledge.

Adams, M., Jones, J., and Tatum, B. 1997. Knowing our students. In M. Adams, L. Bell, and P. Griffin (Eds.), *Teaching for diversity and social justice: A sourcebook* (pp. 311–26). New York: Routledge.

Aguirre, A. 1995. A Chicano farmworker in academe. In R. Padilla and R. Chavez (Eds.), *The leaning ivory tower: Latino professors in American universities* (pp. 17–28). Albany: State University of New York Press.

Allen, W. 1986. *Gender and campus race differences in black student academic performance, racial attitudes and college satisfaction*. Atlanta: Southern Educational Foundation.

———. 1988. The education of Black students on white campuses: What quality the experience. In M. Nettles (Ed.), *Toward black undergraduate student equality in American higher education* (pp. 57–86). Westport, Conn.: Greenwood.

———. 1992. The color of success: African-American college student outcomes at predominantly White and historically Black public universities. *Harvard Educational Review*, *62*(1), 26–44.

Allen, W., Epps, E., Guillory, E., Suh, S., and Stassen, M. 2002. Outsiders within: Race, gender and faculty status in U.S. higher education. In W. Smith, P. Altbach, and K. Lomotey (Eds.), *The racial crisis in American higher education: Continuing challenges for the twenty-first century* (pp. 189–220). Albany: State University of New York Press.

Allen, W., Epps, E., and Haniff, N. 1991. *College in black and white: African-American Students in predominantly white and in historically black public universities.* Albany: State University of New York Press.

Allen, W., and Jewell, J. 2002. A backward glance forward: Past, present and future perspectives on historically Black colleges and universities. *Review of Higher Education,* *25*(3), 241–61.

Allen-Brown, V. 1998. African-American women faculty and administrators. In L. Valverde and L. Castenell (Eds.), *The multicultural campus: Strategies for transforming higher education* (pp. 169–87). Walnut Creek, Calif.: Alta Mira.

Almaguer, T. 1994. *Racial fault lines: The historical origins of white supremacy in California.* Berkeley: University of California Press.

Altbach, P. 1989. Perspectives on student political activism. *Comparative Education,* *25*(1), 97–110.

Altbach, P., and Lomotey, K. (Eds.). 1991. *The racial crisis in American higher education.* Albany: State University of New York Press.

Alvarez, R., and Lutterman, K. (Eds.). 1979. *Discrimination in organizations.* San Francisco: Jossey-Bass.

American Council on Education. 1999. *Making the case for affirmative action in higher education.* Washington, D.C.: Author.

———. 2002a, December 9. ACE report shows rate of increase in number of women and minority presidents slowing. *Higher Education and National Affairs, 51*(22), 1–2. Accessed at www.acenet.edu/hena/issues, August 2003.

———. 2002b. Executive summary and selected tables. In *The American college president.* Accessed at www.acenet.edu/programs/policy/president-study/index.cfm, August 2003.

American Society of Engineering Education. 2001. *Profiles of engineering and engineering technology colleges.* Washington, D.C.: Author.

Anderson, J. 1988a. Cognitive styles and multicultural populations. *Journal of Teacher Education, 38,* 1–8.

———. 1988b. *The education of blacks in the South: 1860–1955.* Chapel Hill: University of North Carolina Press.

Anderson, J., and Adams, M. 1992. Acknowledging the learning styles of diverse student populations: Implications for instructional design. *New Directions for Teaching and Learning, 49,* 19–33.

Anner, J. 1996. *Beyond identity politics.* Boston: South End.

Antonio, A. 2001. Diversity and the influence of friendship groups in college. *Review of Higher Education, 25*(1), 63–89.

———. 2003. Diverse student bodies, diverse faculties. *Academe, 89*(6), 14–17.

Appel M., Cartwright, D., Smith, D., and Wolf, L. 1995. *Studying the impact of diversity initiatives on students.* Washington, D.C.: Association of American Colleges and Universities.

Aronson, E., and Patnos, S. 1978. *The jigsaw classroom: Building cooperation in the classroom.* Beverly Hills, Calif.: Sage.

Association of American Colleges and Universities. 1995. *American pluralism and the college curriculum: Higher education in a diverse democracy.* Washington, D.C.

Astin, A. 1993. *What matters in college: Four critical years revisited.* San Francisco: Jossey-Bass.

Astin, A., Astin, H., Bayer, A., and Bisconti, A. 1975. *The power of protest: A national study of student and faculty disruptions with implications for the future.* San Francisco: Jossey-Bass.

Astin, A., and Sax, J. 1998. How undergraduates are affected by service participation. *Journal of College Student Development, 39*(3), 251–63.

Astin, H., Antonio, A., Cress, C., and Astin, A. 1997. *Race and ethnicity in the American professoriate, 1995–1996.* Los Angeles: University of California Press.

Astin, H., Astin, A., Bisconti, A., and Frankel, H. 1972. *Higher education and the disadvantaged student.* Washington, D.C.: Human Service Press.

Auster, C., and MacRone, M. 1994. The classroom as a negotiated setting: An empirical study of the effects of faculty members' behavior on students' participation. *Teaching Sociology, 22*, 289–99.

Austin, A. 1990. Faculty cultures, faculty values. In W. Tierney (Ed.), *Assessing academic climates and cultures* (pp. 61–74). San Francisco: Jossey-Bass.

Badwound, E., and Tierney, W. 1996. Leadership and American Indian values: The tribal college dilemma. In C. Turner, M. Garcia, A. Nora, and L. Rendon (Eds.), *Racial and ethnic diversity in higher education* (pp. 441–45). Needham, Mass.: Simon & Schuster.

Baldridge, V. 1971. *Power and conflict in the university.* New York: Wiley.

Baldridge, V., Curtis, D., Ecker, G., and Riley, G. 1977. Alternative models of governance in higher education. In G. Riley and V. Baldridge (Eds.), *Governing academic organizations: New problems, new perspectives* (pp. 2–41). Berkeley, Calif.: McCutchan.

Banks, J. 1995. Multicultural education: Its effects on students' racial and gender role attitudes. In J. Banks and C. Banks (Eds.), *Handbook of research on multicultural education* (pp. 617–27). New York: Macmillan.

Bauder, D. 1998. Establishing a visible presence on campus. In R. Sanlo (Ed.), *Working with lesbian, gay, bisexual and transgender college students* (pp. 95–103). Westport, Conn.: Greenwood.

Bayh, B. 1989, April 17. Let's tear off their hoods. *Newsweek.*

Beale, R., Thompson, M., and Chesler, M. 2001. Training peer facilitators for intergroup dialogue leadership. In D. Schoem and S. Hurtado (Eds.), *Intergroup dialogue: Deliberative democracy in school, college, community and workplace* (pp. 227–46). Ann Arbor: University of Michigan Press.

Becker, R., and McSherry, M. 2002, June 10. Higher degree of debt for new grads. *Chicago Tribune,* 1, 14*ff.*

Bell, D. 2004. *Silent covenants:* Brown v. Board of Ed *and the unfulfilled hopes for racial reform.* New York: Oxford University Press.

Bell, L., Washington, S., Weinstein, G., and Love, B. 1997. Knowing ourselves as instructors. In M. Adams, L. Bell, and P. Griffin (Eds.), *Teaching for diversity and social justice* (pp. 299–310). New York: Routledge.

Benford, R., and Snow, D. 2000. Framing processes and social movements: An overview and assessment. *Annual Review of Sociology*, *26*, 611–39.

Bennett, C. 1995. Research on racial issues in American higher education. In J. Banks and C. Banks (Eds.), *Handbook of research on multicultural education* (pp. 663–81). New York: Macmillan.

Bensimon, E. 1989. The meaning of "good presidential leadership": A frame analysis. *Review of Higher Education*, *12*(2), 107–23.

Bensimon, E., and Neumann, A. 1993. *Redesigning collegiate leadership*. Baltimore: Johns Hopkins University Press.

Bensimon, E., Neumann, A., and Birnbaum, R. 1989. *Making sense of administrative leadership: The "L" word in higher education*. ASHE-ERIC Higher Education Report, No. 1. Washington, D.C.: School of Education and Human Development, George Washington University.

Bentley College. n.d. Diversity update. Accessed at http://ecampus.bentley.edu/dept/hr /diversity/update.html, May 2002.

Berg, L. 1993. Racialization in academic discourse. *Urban Geography*, *14*(2), 194–200.

Bernstein, R. 1994. *Dictatorship of virtue: Multiculturalism and the battle for America's future*. New York: Knopf.

Black, L. 1995. Stupid rich bastards. In B. Dews and C. Law (Eds.), *This fine place so far from home* (pp. 13–25). Philadelphia: Temple University Press.

Black Action Movement. 1970. *List of demands III*. Ann Arbor, Mich.: Author.

Blackshire-Belay, C. 1998, July–August. The status of minority faculty members in the academy. *Academe*, 30–36.

Blalock, T. 1967. *Toward a theory of minority-group relations*. New York: Wiley.

Bland, C., and Berquist, W. 1997. *The vitality of senior faculty members: Snow on the roof—Fire in the furnace*. ASHE-ERIC Higher Education Report, Vol. 25, No. 7. Washington, D.C.: ERIC Clearinghouse on Higher Education.

Blauner, R. 1972. *Racial oppression in America*. New York: Harper & Row.

Bloom, A. 1987. *The closing of the American mind*. New York: Simon & Schuster.

Blumer, H. 1958. Race prejudice as a sense of group position. *Pacific Sociological Review*, *1*, 3–7.

Board on Sustainable Development, Policy Division, National Research Council, 1999. *Our common journey: A transition toward sustainability*. Washington, D.C.: National Academy Press.

Bobo, L. 1999. Prejudice as group position: Microfoundations of a sociological approach to racism and race relations. *Journal of Social Issues*, *55*(3), 445–72.

Bobo, L., J. Kluegel, and R. Smith. 1997. Laissez-faire racism: The crystallization of a kinder, gentler, antiblack ideology. In S. Tuch and J. Martin (Eds.), *Racial attitudes in the 1990s: Continuity and change* (pp. 14–42). Westport, Conn.: Praeger.

Bohmer, S., and Briggs, J. 1991. Teaching privileged students about gender, race and class oppression. *Teaching Sociology*, *19*, 154–63.

Bolman, L., and Deal, T. 1984. *Modern approaches to understanding and managing organizations*. San Francisco: Jossey-Bass.

Bonacich, E. 1989. Racism in the deep structure of U.S. higher education: When affirmative action is not enough. In A. Yogev and S. Tomlinson (Eds.), *International perspectives on education and society* (pp. 3–15). Greenwich, Conn.: JAI.

Bonilla-Silva, E. 2001. *White supremacy and racism in the post–civil rights era.* Boulder, Colo.: Rienner.

Bonilla-Silva, E., and Forman, T. 2000. "I'm not a racist but . . .": Mapping white college students' racial ideology in the USA. *Discourse and Society, 11,* 50–85.

Bonilla-Silva, E., and Lewis, A. 1999. "The new racism": Toward an analysis of the U.S. racial structure, 1960s–1990s. In P. Wong (Ed.), *Race, nation and citizenship* (pp. 55–101). Boulder, Colo.: Westview.

Bourassa, D. 1991. How white students and students of color organize and interact on campus. *New Directions for Student Services, 56,* 13–24.

Bourassa, D., and Shipton, B. 1991. Addressing lesbian and gay issues in residence hall environments. In N. Evans and V. Wall (Eds.), *Beyond tolerance: Gays, lesbians and bisexuals on campus* (pp. 77–96). Alexandria, Va.: American College Personnel Association.

Bowen, W., and Bok, D. 1998. *The shape of the river: The long-term consequences of considering race in college and university admissions.* Princeton, N.J.: Princeton University Press.

Bowman, P., and Smith, W. 2002. Racial ideology in the campus community: Engaging cross-ethnic differences and challenges. In W. Smith, P. Altbach, and K. Lomotey (Eds.), *The racial crisis in American higher education: Continuing challenges for the twenty-first century* (pp. 103–20). Albany: State University of New York Press.

Bowser, B., Auletta, G., and Jones, T. 1993. *Confronting diversity issues on campus: Survival skills for scholars.* Newbury Park, Calif.: Sage.

Boyer Commission on Educating Undergraduates in the Research University. 1998. *Reinventing undergraduate education: A blueprint for America's research universities.* Stony Brook: State University of New York Press.

Bransford, J., Brown, A., and Cocking, R. (Eds.). 2000. *How people learn: Brain, mind, experience and school.* Washington, D.C.: National Academy Press.

Brief for amicus curiae 63: Leading American businesses in support of respondents. 2003. Accessed at www.umich.edu/urel/admissions/legal/gra-amicus-ussc/um.html, June 2003.

Brief of the American Educational Research Association, the Association of American Colleges and Universities, and the American Association for Higher Education as amici curiae in support for the respondents. 2003. Accessed at www.umich.edu/urel/admissions/legal/gra-amicus-ussc/um.html, June 2003.

Brief of the Amicus Curiae of the American Psychological Association in Support for the Respondents. 2003. Accessed at www.umich.edu/urel/admissions/legal/gra-amicus-ussc/um.html, June 2003.

Brint, S., and Karabel, J. 1989. *The diversity dream: Community colleges and the promise of educational opportunity in America 1900–1985.* New York: Oxford University Press.

Brown, C., and Mazza, G. 1991. Peer training strategies for welcoming diversity. *New Directions for Student Services, 56,* 39–51.

Brown, D. 1983. *Managing conflict at organizational interfaces.* Cambridge, Mass.: Addison-Wesley.

Brown, D., and Tandon, R. 1983. Ideology and political economy in inquiry: Action research and participatory action research. *Journal of Applied Behavioral Science, 19*(3), 277–94.

Brown, J. 2002. Giving it the old college outcry. *Utne Reader*, *109*, 20.

Brown, M., Carnoy, E., Currie, E., Duster, T., Oppenheimer, D., Schultz, M., and Wellman, D. 2003. *Whitewashing race: The myth of a color-blind society*. Berkeley: University of California Press.

Brown University. 2002, May 5. Executive summary, diversity report. *George Street Journal*. Accessed at www.brown.edu/Administration/George_Street_Journal/diversity.html, May 2002.

Brubacher, J., and Rudy, W. 1997. *Higher education in transition: A history of American colleges and universities* (4th ed.). New Brunswick, N.J.: Transaction.

Bryant, B. 2002. *Environmental advocacy: Working for economic and environmental justice*. Ann Arbor, Mich.: Bunyan Bryant.

Burbules, N. 1993. *Dialogue in teaching: Theory and practice*. New York: Teachers College Press.

Burke, W. 2002. *Organizational change: Theory and practice*. Thousand Oaks, Calif.: Sage.

Butler, J., and Walter, J. 1991. Praxis and the prospect of curriculum transformation. In J. Butler and J. Walter (Eds.), *Transforming the curriculum: Ethnic and women's studies* (pp. 325–30). Albany: State University of New York Press.

Calderon, J., and Farrell, B. 1996. Doing sociology: Connecting the classroom experience with a multi-ethnic school district. *Teaching Sociology*, *24*, 46–63.

California Post-Secondary Education Commission. 1992. *Resource guide for assessing campus climates*. Report 92-24. Sacramento: Author.

Calhoun, C. 1999. The changing character of college: Institutional transformation in American higher education. In B. Pescosolido and R. Aminzade (Eds.), *The social worlds of higher education* (pp. 487–95). Thousand Oaks, Calif.: Pine Forge.

Campus Climate Advisory Committee. n.d. *Report and recommendations of the Campus Climate Advisory Committee*. San Jose, Calif.: San Jose State University. Accessed at www.sjsu.edu/campus_climate/committee/report/recommendations.html, May 2002.

Campus Climate Research Group. 2002. *In the shadow of the arch: Safety and acceptance of lesbian, gay, bisexual, transgender and queer students at the University of Georgia*. Athens: University of Georgia Press.

Canon, L. 1990. Fostering positive race, class and gender dynamics in the classroom. *Women's Studies Quarterly*, *1 and 2*, 126–33.

Carby, H. 1992. The multicultural wars. In G. Dent (Ed.), *Black popular culture* (pp. 187–99). Seattle: Seattle Day Press.

Carmichael, S., and Hamilton, C. 1976. *Black power*. New York: Vintage.

Carnevale, A. 2003. Seize the moment. In D. Leon (Ed.), *Latinos in higher education* (pp. 9–36). Amsterdam: JAI.

Carter, D. 1991. Fostering a multicultural curriculum: Principles for presidents. In D. Carter and A. Chandler (Eds.), *AASCU issues*. Washington, D.C.: American Association of State Colleges and Universities.

CAWMSET. 2000. *Land of plenty: Diversity is America's competitive edge in science, engineering and technology*. Arlington, Va.: Congressional Commission on the Advancement of Women and Minorities in Science, Engineering and Technology.

Center for Instructional Development and Research. 2002. *Working with diverse groups of students*. Seattle: University of Washington. Accessed at http://depts.washington.edu/cidrweb/DiversityTools.htnp, June 2003.

Center for Teaching and Learning Services. 2003. *Diversity toolkit*. Minneapolis: University of Minnesota. Accessed at www.umn.edu/ohr/teachlearn/diversity.html, June 2003.

Chan, K., and Hune, S. 1995. Racialization and panethnicity: From Asians in America to Asian Americans. In W. Hawley and A. Jackson (Eds.), *Toward a common destiny* (pp. 205–33). San Francisco: Jossey-Bass.

Chan, S. 1991. *Asian Americans: An interpretive history*. Boston: Twayne.

Chandler, A. 1991. Fostering a multicultural curriculum: Principles for presidents. In D. Carter and A. Chandler (Eds.), *AASCU Issues* (pp. 3–8). Washington, D.C.: American Association of State Colleges and Universities.

Chang, M. 2000. Improving campus racial dynamics: A balancing act among competing interests. *Review of Higher Education*, *23*(2), 153–75.

———. 2002. Preservation or transformation: Where's the real educational discourse on diversity? *Review of Higher Education*, *25*(2), 125–40.

Chang, M., and Kiang, P. 2002. New challenges of representing Asian American students in US higher education. In W. Smith, P. Altbach, and K. Lomotey (Eds.), *The racial crisis in American higher education: Continuing challenges for the 21st century* (pp. 137–58). Albany: State University of New York Press.

Cheatham, H., and Associates (Eds.). 1991. *Cultural pluralism on campus*. Lanham, Md.: American College Personnel Association and University Press of America.

Checkoway, B. 2000, July–August. Public service—our new mission. *Academe*, 24–28.

Chesler, M. 1996. Protecting the investment: Understanding and responding to resistance. *Diversity Factor*, *4*(3), 2–10.

———. 1998. Planning multicultural audits in higher education. *To Improve the Academy*, *17*, 171–201.

Chesler, M., and Crowfoot, J. 1990. Racism on campus. In W. Mays (Ed.), *Ethics and higher education* (pp. 195–230). New York: Macmillan.

Chesler, M., Fritz, J., and Knife-Gould, A. 2002. Training peer facilitators for community service learning leadership. *Michigan Journal of Community Service Learning*, *9*(2), 58–76.

Chesler, M., and Peet, M. 2002. White students' views of affirmative action on campus. *Diversity Factor*, *10*(2), 21–27.

Chesler, M., Peet, M., and Sevig, T. 2003. Blinded by whiteness: The development of white college students' racial awareness. In A. Doane and E. Bonilla-Silva (Eds.), *Whiteout: The continuing significance of race* (pp. 215–30). New York: Routledge.

Chesler, M., Wilson, M., and Malani, A. 1993. Perceptions of faculty behavior by students of color. *Michigan Journal of Political Science*, *16*, 54–79.

Chesler, M., and Zuniga, X. 1991. Dealing with prejudice and conflict in the classroom: The Pink Triangle Exercise. *Teaching Sociology*, *19*(2), 173–81.

Chesler, N., and Chesler, M. 2002. Gender-informed mentoring strategies for women engineering scholars: On establishing a "caring community." *Journal of Engineering Education*, *91*(1), 49–55.

Chin, R., and Benne, K. 1969. General strategies for affecting change in human systems. In W. Bennis, K. Benne, and R. Chin (Eds.), *The planning of change* (pp. 22–45). New York: Holt, Rinehart & Winston.

Chism, N. 1998. The role of faculty developers in institutional change: From the basement to the front office. *To Improve the Academy*, *17*, 141–54.

Chung, W. 1997. Auditing the organizational culture for diversity: A conceptual framework. In C. Brown, C. Snedeker, and B. Sykes (Eds.), *Conflict and diversity* (pp. 63–83). Cresskill, N.J.: Hampton.

CIRP: Cooperative Institutional Research Program. 2000. Entering student survey. Los Angeles: Higher Education Research Institute, University of California at Los Angeles.

Clark, B. 1970. *The distinctive college: Antioch, Reed and Swarthmore.* New York: Aldine.

———. 1983. *The higher education system.* Berkeley: University of California Press.

Clark, S., and Corcoran, M. 1986. Perspectives on the professional socialization of women faculty: A case of accumulative disadvantage. *Journal of Higher Education, 57,* 20–43.

Clegg, R. 2005, January 14. Time has not favored racial preferences. *Chronicle of Higher Education,* B10–B11.

Clotfelter, C. 2004. *After* Brown: *The rise and retreat of school desegregation.* Princeton, N.J.: Princeton University Press.

Cloud, R. 1952. *Education in California: Leaders, organizers and accomplishments of the first hundred years.* Stanford, Calif.: Stanford University Press.

Cohen, E. 1994. *Designing groupwork: Strategies for the heterogeneous classroom* (2nd ed.). New York: Teachers College Press.

Collins, S. 1997. *Black corporate executives: The making and breaking of a black middle class.* Philadelphia: Temple University Press.

Committee on Lesbian and Gay Concerns. 1992. *College level planning program: Faculty and academic staff diversity survey.* State College: Pennsylvania State University.

Committee on the Status of Women Faculty at Caltech. 2001. *Final report.* Pasadena: California Institute of Technology.

Conflict Clinic. 1991. *Cross-cultural conflict and consensus building opportunities in the George Mason community.* Alexandria, Va.: George Mason University.

Consolidated brief of Lt. Gen. Julius Becton et al. as amici curiae in support of respondents. 2003. Accessed at www.umich.edu/urel/admissions/legal/gra-amici-ussc/um-html, June 2003.

Cornell, S. 1988. *Return of the native.* New York: Oxford University Press.

Corrigan, M. 2002. *American college president: 2002 edition.* Washington, D.C.: American Council on Education. Accessed at www.acenet.edu/program/policy/president-study/index.cfm, June 2003.

Cose, E. 1993. *The rage of a privileged class.* New York: HarperCollins.

Cox, T. 1991. The multicultural organization. *The Executive, 5*(2), 34–47.

———. 1993. *Cultural diversity in organizations.* San Francisco: Berrett-Koehler.

Crenshaw, K. 1989. Foreword: Toward a race-conscious pedagogy in legal education. *National Black Law Journal, 11*(1), 1–14.

———. 1997. Color-blind dreams and racial nightmares. In T. Morrison and C. Lacour (Eds.), *Birth of a nationhood* (pp. 97–168). New York: Pantheon.

Crichlow, W., Goodwin, S., Shakes, G., and Swartz, E. 1990. Multicultural ways of knowing: Implications for practice. *Journal of Education, 172,* 101–17.

Croteau, J., and Lark, J. 1995. On being lesbian, gay or bisexual in student affairs: A national survey of experiences on the job. *NASPA Journal, 32*(3), 189–97.

Croteau, J., and von Destinon, M. 1994. A national survey of job search experiences of lesbian, gay and bisexual student affairs professionals. *Journal of College Student Development*, *35*, 40–45.

Crowfoot, J., and Chesler, M. 1974. Contemporary perspectives on planned social change. *Journal of Applied Behavioral Science*, *10*, 287–303.

D'Souza, D. 1991. *Illiberal education: The politics of race and sex on campus*. New York: Free Press.

Davis, L. 2002. Racial diversity in higher education: Ingredients for success and failure. *Journal of Applied Behavioral Science*, *38*(2), 137–55.

Derek Bok Center for Teaching and Learning. 1992. *Tips for teachers: Encouraging students in a racially diverse classroom*. Cambridge, Mass.: Harvard University. Accessed at http://bokcenter.harvard.edu/docs/TFTrace.html, May 2002.

Dews, B., and Law, C. (Eds.). 1995. *This fine place so far from home*. Philadelphia: Temple University Press.

Dey, E. 1994. Dimensions of stress: A recent survey. *Review of Higher Education*, *17*(3), 305–22.

Dialogues for diversity: Community and ethnicity on campus. 1994. Phoenix, Ariz.: Accrediting Commission for Senior Colleges and Universities of the Western Association of Schools and Colleges and Oryx Press.

Diamond, R. (Ed.). 2002. *Field guide to academic leadership: A publication of the National Academy for Academic Leadership*. San Francisco: Jossey-Bass.

Dill, D. 1982. The management of academic culture: Notes on the management of meaning and social integration. *Higher Education*, *11*, 303–20.

Dill, D., and Sporn, B. 1995. The implications of a postindustrial environment for the university: An introduction. In D. Dill and B. Sporn (Eds.), *Emerging patterns of social demand and university reform* (pp. 1–19). Tarrytown, N.Y.: Elsevier Science and Pergamon (with International Association of Universities).

Doane, A. 1997. White identity and race relations in the 1990s. In G. Carter (Ed.), *Perspectives on current social problems* (pp. 151–59). Boston: Allyn & Bacon.

Doane, A. 2003. Rethinking whiteness studies. In A. Doane and E. Bonilla-Silva (Eds.), *White out: The continuing significance of racism* (pp. 3–20). New York: Routledge.

Dovidio, J., and Gaertner, S. 1986. Prejudice, discrimination and racism: Historical trends and contemporary approaches. In J. Dovidio and S. Gaertner (Eds.), *Prejudice, discrimination and racism* (pp. 1–34). Orlando, Fla.: Academic Press.

Dovidio, J., Mann, J., and Gaertner, S. 1989. Resistance to affirmative action: The implications of aversive racism. In F. Blanchard and F. Crosby (Eds.), *Affirmative action in perspective* (pp. 83–102). New York: Springer.

Drake, S., and Cayton, H. 1993 [1945]. *Black metropolis*. Chicago: University of Chicago Press.

Du Bois, P., and Hutson, J. 1997. *Bridging the racial divide: Interracial dialogue in America*. Brattleboro, Vt.: Center for Living Democracy.

DuBois, W. 1968. *Dusk of dawn*. New York: Schocken.

———. 1996 [1899]. *The Philadelphia Negro*. Philadelphia: University of Pennsylvania Press.

Duster, T. 1991. *The diversity project*. Berkeley: Institute for the Study of Social Change, University of California at Berkeley.

Elfin, M., and Burke, S. 1993, April 19. Race on campus: Segregation is growing. *U.S. News & World Report*, pp. 52–56.

Ely, R. 1995. The role of dominant identity and experience in organizational work on diversity. In S. Jackson and M. Ruderman (Eds.), *Diversity in work teams* (pp. 161–86). Washington, D.C.: American Psychological Association.

Essed, P. 1991. *Understanding everyday racism: An interdisciplinary theory*. Newbury Park, Calif.: Sage.

———. 1997. Racial intimidation: Sociopolitical implications of the use of racial slurs. In S. Higgins (Ed.), *The language and politics of exclusion: Others in discourse* (pp. 131–52). Thousand Oaks, Calif.: Sage.

Etkowitz, H., Kemelgor, C., and Uzzi, B. 2000. *Athena unbound: The advancement of women in science and technology*. New York: Cambridge University Press.

Eyler, J., Giles, D., and Braxton, J. 1997. The impact of service learning on college students. *Michigan Journal of Community Service Learning*, *4*, 5–15.

Falbo, T., Contreras, H., and Avalos, M. 2003. Transition points from high school to college. In D. Leon (Ed.), *Latinos in higher education* (pp. 59–72). Amsterdam: JAI.

Fanon, F. (1967). *Black skins white masks*. New York: Grove.

Farley, R. 1995. *State of the union: America in the 1990s*. New York: Russell Sage Foundation.

Feagin, J. 2000. *Racist America: Roots, current realities and future reparations*. New York: Routledge.

———. (Ed.). 2002. *The continuing significance of racism: U.S. colleges and universities*. Washington, D.C.: American Council on Education.

Feagin, J., and Feagin, C. 1986. *Discrimination American style: Institutional racism and sexism*. Englewood Cliffs, N.J.: Prentice Hall.

———. 1999. *Racial and ethnic relations* (6th ed.). Upper Saddle River, N.J.: Prentice Hall.

Feagin, J., and Sikes, W. 1994. *Living with racism*. Boston: Beacon.

Feagin, J., and Vera, H. 1995. *White racism*. New York: Routledge.

Feagin, J., Vera, H., and Imani, N. 1996. *The agony of education: Black students at white colleges and universities*. New York: Routledge.

Featherstone, L., and University Students Against Sweatshops 2002. *Students Against Sweatshops*. New York: Verso.

Ferren, A., and Geller, W. 1993. Faculty development's role in promoting an inclusive community: Addressing sexual orientation. *To Improve the Academy*, *12*, 97–108.

Fields, C. 1988. The Hispanic pipeline: Leaking and needing repair. *Change*, *20*(3), 20–27.

Fine, M., Powell, L., Weiss, L., and Wong, L. (Eds.). 1997. *Off white: Readings on race, power and society*. New York: Routledge.

Fine, M., and Weiss, L. 1998. *The unknown city: The lives of poor and working class young adults*. Boston: Beacon.

Finney, J. 1991, May–June. Opening the minority pipeline. *AGB Reports*, 16–19.

Fish, S. 1993, November. Reverse racism, or pow the pot got to call the kettle black. *Atlantic Monthly*, *272*, 128–36.

Fiske, E. 1988. The undergraduate Hispanic experience: A case of juggling two cultures. *Change*, *20*(3), 28–33.

Flagg, B. 1993. "Was blind but now I see": White race consciousness and the requirement of discriminatory intent. *Michigan Law Review*, *91*, 953–56.

Fleming, J. 1984. *Blacks in college: A comparative study of students' success in black and white institutions*. San Francisco: Jossey-Bass.

Floyd, C. 1995. Governing boards and trustees. *Review of Higher Education*, *19*(2), 93–110.

Fogg, P. 2003, December 19. So many committees, so little time. *Chronicle of Higher Education*, *50*(17), A14–A15, A17.

Forman, T. 2001. Social determinates of white youth's racial attitudes: Evidence from a national survey. *Sociological Studies of Children and Youth*, *8*, 173–207.

Fosmoe, M. 2004, March 19. ND students don T-shirts to support gays, lesbians: The University of Notre Dame turns down request for gay-straight alliance. *South Bend Tribune*, D1.

Fox, H. 2001. *When race breaks out*. New York: Lang.

Frankenberg, E., and Lee, C. 2002. Race in American public schools: Rapidly resegregating school districts. Cambridge, Mass.: Civil Rights Project, Harvard University. Accessed at www.researchmatters.harvard.edu.

Frankenberg, R. 1993. Growing up white: Racism and the social geography of childhood. *Feminist Review*, *45*, 51–84.

Frankenberg, R. 1994. *White women, race matters: The social construction of whiteness*. Minneapolis: University of Minnesota Press.

Franklin, J., and Moss, A. 1988. *From slavery to freedom* (6th ed.). New York: Knopf.

Fraser, S. (Ed.). 1995. *The bell curve wars: Race, intelligence and the future of America*. New York: Basic Books.

Freedman, J. 1991, September–October. Diversity and Dartmouth. *Change*, *23*(5), 15–31.

Friere, P. 1970. *Pedagogy of the oppressed*. New York: Seabury.

Fries-Britt, S., and Turner, B. 2002. Uneven stories: Successful black collegians at a black and a white campus. *Review of Higher Education*, *25*(3), 315–30.

Frost, S., and Teodorescu, D. 2001. Teaching excellence: How faculty guided change at a research university. *Review of Higher Education*, *24*(4), 397–415.

Gallagher, C. 1995. White reconstruction in the university. *Socialist Review*, *24*(1/2), 165–87.

Galura, J., Pasque, P., Schoem, D., and Howard, J. (Eds.). 2004. *Engaging the whole of service learning, diversity and learning communities*. Ann Arbor, Mich.: OCSL Press.

Garcia, M. (Ed.). 2000. *Succeeding in an academic career: A guide for faculty of color*. Westport, Conn.: Greenwood.

Garcia, M., Hudgins, C., Musil, C., Nettles, M., Sedlacek, W., and Smith, D. 2001. *Assessing campus diversity initiatives: A guide for campus practitioners*. Washington, D.C.: Association of American Colleges and Universities.

Garcia, M., and Smith, D. 1996. Reflecting inclusiveness in the college curriculum. In R. Rendon, L. Hope, and Associates (Eds.), *Educating a new majority* (pp. 265–88). San Francisco: Jossey-Bass.

Gardenswartz, L., and Rowe, A. 1994. *Diverse teams at work*. New York: McGraw-Hill.

Garland, J. 2002. Response: What will our students remember? In J. Feagin (Ed.), *The continuing significance of racism: U.S. colleges and universities* (pp. 37–39). Washington, D.C.: American Council on Education.

Garza, H. 1993. Second-class academics: Chicano/Latino faculty in U.S. universities. *New Directions for Teaching and Learning*, *53*, 33–41.

Gaventa, J. 1993. The powerful, the powerless and the experts: Knowledge struggles in an information age. In P. Park, M. Brydon-Miller, S. Hall, and T. Jackson (Eds.), *Voices of change: Participatory research in the United States and Canada* (pp. 21–40). Westport, Conn.: Bergin & Garvey.

Gender Equity Committee. 2001, December 4. The gender equity report (executive summary). *Almanac supplement*. Philadelphia: University of Pennsylvania.

Ginorio, A. 1995. A culture of meaningful community. In *Bridging the gender gap in engineering and science* (pp. 29–32). Pittsburgh: Carnegie Mellon University.

Giroux, H. 1998. The politics of insurgent multiculturalism in the era of the Los Angeles uprising. In H. Shapiro and D. Purpel (Eds.), *Critical social issues in American education: Transformation in a postmodern world* (pp. 181–98). Mahwah, N.J.: Erlbaum.

Gitenstein, B. 2002. Response: Reaping our own sweet fruit. In J. Feagin (Ed.), *The continuing significance of racism: U.S. colleges and universities* (pp. 41–45). Washington, D.C.: American Council on Education.

Gitlin, T. 1987. *The sixties: Years of hope, days of rage*. New York: Bantam.

Glater, J. 2004, June 13. Diversity plan shaped in Texas is under attack. *New York Times*, 1.

Gmelch, W. 1995. Department chairs under siege: Resolving the web of conflict. *New Directions for Higher Education*, *92*, 35–42.

Goodman, D. 2001. *Promoting diversity and social justice: Educating people from privileged groups*. Thousand Oaks, Calif.: Sage.

Gordon, L. 1991. Race relations and attitudes at Arizona State University. In P. Altbach and K. Lomotey (Eds.), *The racial crisis in American higher education* (pp. 233–48). Albany: State University of New York Press.

Gossett, T. 1975. *Race: The history of an idea in America*. Dallas, Tex.: Southern Methodist University Press.

Gould, S. 1999. Race and theory: Culture, poverty and adaptation to discrimination in Wilson and Ogbu. *Sociological Theory*, *17*, 171–200.

Gratz et al. v. Bollinger et al. 2003. 123 S. Ct.: #02-576. *Supreme Court Reporter (Interim Edition)* (pp. 2411–46). Washington, D.C.: West.

Green, M. 1989. *Minorities on campus: A handbook for enhancing diversity*. Washington, D.C.: American Council on Education.

Greenberg, M. 2004, June 18. How the GI bill changed higher education. *Chronicle of Higher Education*, B9–B11.

Greene, D., and Diehm, G. 1995. Educational outcomes of a service integration effort. *Michigan Journal of Community Service Learning*, *2*, 54–62.

Gross, E., and Grambsch, P. 1977. Power structures in universities and colleges. In G. Riley and V. Baldridge (Eds.), *Governing academic organizations* (pp. 27–41). Berkeley, Calif.: McCutchan.

Grutter v. Bollinger et al. 2003. 123 S. Ct.: #02-241. *Supreme Court Reporter (Interim Edition)* (pp. 2325–74). Washington, D.C.: West.

Guglielmo, T. 2003. *White on arrival: Italians and race in Chicago.* New York: Oxford University Press.

Gurin, P. 1999. Selections from *The Compelling Need for Diversity in Higher Education*: Expert reports in defense of the University of Michigan: Expert report of Patricia Gurin. *Equity and Excellence in Education, 32*(2), 37–62.

Gurin, P., Dey, E., Gurin, G., and Hurtado, S. 2004. The educational value of diversity. In P. Gurin, J. Lehman, and E. Lewis (Eds.), *Defending diversity* (pp. 97–188). Ann Arbor: University of Michigan Press.

Gurin, P., Dey, E., Hurtado, S., and Gurin, G. 2002. Diversity and higher education: Theory and impact on educational outcomes. *Harvard Educational Review, 72*(3), 330–67.

Hacker, A. 1992. *Two nations: Black and white, separate, hostile and unequal.* New York: Scribner's.

Haldeman, P. n.d. *Urban engagement and civic responsibility program.* Los Angeles: Mount Saint Mary's College.

Hall, S. 1990. The whites of their eyes: Racist ideologies and the media. In M. Alvarado and J. Thompson (Eds.), *The media reader* (pp. 7–23). London: British Film Institute.

Hamilton, K. 2003, August 28. An overlooked oasis. *Black Issues in Higher Education,* 22–27.

Hardiman, R., and Jackson, B. 1992. Racial identity development: Understanding racial dynamics in college classrooms and on campus. *New Directions in Teaching and Learning, 52,* 21–38.

Haro, R. 1995. Held to a higher standard: Latino executive selection in higher education. In R. Padilla and R. Chavez (Eds.), *The leaning ivory tower* (pp. 189–207). Albany: State University of New York Press.

Harris, C. 1993. Whiteness as property. *Harvard Law Review, 106,* 1710–91.

Harris, S., and Nettles, M. 1996. Ensuring campus climates that embrace diversity. In L. Rendon, R. Hope, and Associates (Eds.), *Educating a new majority: Transforming America's educational system for diversity* (pp. 300–71). San Francisco: Jossey-Bass.

Hassamani. N. 1973. *The thoughts and experiences of six technical college presidents regarding leadership on cultural diver*sity. Unpublished Ph.D. dissertation, University of Minnesota, Minneapolis.

Hatcher, S. (Ed.). 1995. *Peer programs on the college campus.* New York: Teachers College Press.

Hayden, T. 1988. *Reunion.* New York: Random House.

Heirich, M. 1977. *Spiral of conflict: Berkeley 1964.* New York: Columbia University Press.

Heiser, R., and Almquist, A. 1971. *The other Californians: Prejudice and discrimination under Spain, Mexico and the United States to 1920.* Berkeley: University of California Press.

Herrnstein, R., and Murray, C. 1994. *The bell curve: Intelligence and class structure in American life.* New York. Free Press.

Higham, J. 1963. *Strangers in the land.* New York: Atheneum.

Hollander, E., and Saltmarsh, J. 2000, July–August. The engaged university. *Academe*, 29–32.

Holton, S., and Phillips, G. 1995. Can't live with them, can't live without them: Faculty and administrators in conflict. *New Directions for Higher Education*, *92*, 43–50.

Hondagneu-Sotelo, P., and Raskoff, S. 1994. Community service learning: Promises and problems. *Teaching Sociology*, *22*, 248–54.

hooks, b. 1990. *Yearning: Race, gender and cultural politics*. Boston: South End.

Hopwood v. State of Texas. 1996. 116 S.Ct. 2580–81.

Hughes, M. 1997. Symbolic racism, old-fashioned racism, and whites' opposition to affirmative action. In S. Tuch and J. Martin (Eds.), *Racial attitudes in the 1990s: Continuity and change* (pp. 45–75). Westport, Conn.: Praeger.

Hummell, M., and Steele, C. 1996. The learning community: A program to address issues of academic achievement and retention. *Journal of Intergroup Relations*, *23*(2), 28–33.

Humphreys, D. 1997. *General education and American commitments*. Washington, D.C.: Association of American Colleges and Universities.

Humphreys, S. 1995. The role of women graduate students. In *Bridging the gender gap in engineering and science* (pp. 33–40). Pittsburgh: Carnegie Mellon University.

Hunt, J., Bell, L., Wei, W., and Ingle, G. 1992. Monoculturalism to multiculturalism: Lessons from three public universities. *New Directions in Teaching and Learning*, *52*, 101–14.

Hurst, F. 1987. *Report on University of Massachusetts investigation*. Amherst: University of Massachusetts at Amherst.

Hurtado, S. 1994. The institutional climate for talented Latino students. *Research in Higher Education*, *35*(1), 21–41.

——. 2001. Research and Evaluation on Intergroup Dialogues. In D. Schoem and S. Hurtado (Eds.), *Intergroup dialogue: Deliberative democracy in school, college, workplace and community* (pp. 22–36). Ann Arbor: University of Michigan Press.

Hurtado, S., Dey, E., and Trevino, L. 1994. *Exclusion or self-segregation: Interaction across racial/ethnic groups on campus*. Paper presented to meetings of the American Educational Research Association, New Orleans.

Hurtado, S., Engberg, M., Ponjuan, L., and Landresman, L. 2002. Students' precollege preparation for participation in a diverse democracy. *Research in Higher Education*, *43*(2), 163–86.

Hurtado, S., Milem, J., Clayton-Pederson, A., and Allen, W. 1999. *Enacting diverse learning environments: Improving the climate for racial/ethnic diversity in higher education*. ASHE-ERIC Higher Education Report, Vol. 26, No. 8. Washington, D.C.: George Washington University.

Indiana University. 1992. *The Hoosier plan for minority enhancement*. Unpublished manuscript. Bloomington: Author.

Intergroup Relations Center. 2003. *Faculty resources*. Phoenix: Arizona State University. Accessed at www.asu.edu/provost/intergroup/resources/facresources.html, June 2003.

Isaacs, W. 1996, January–February. The process and potential of dialogue in social change. *Educational Technology*, 20–30.

Jackson, B., and Hardiman, R. 1994. Multicultural organizational development. In E. Cross, J. Katz, F. Miller, and E. Seashore (Eds.), *The promise of diversity* (pp. 231–39). New York: Irwin and NTL.

Jackson, B., and Holvino, E. 1988. *Multicultural organizational development*. Working paper #11. Ann Arbor: University of Michigan, Program on Conflict Management Alternatives.

Jacobs, J. 1963. *The death and life of great American cities*. New York. Vintage.

Jacoby, R., and Glauberman, N. (Eds.). 1995. *The bell curve debate: History, documents, opinions*. New York: Times Books.

Johnson, D., and Johnson, R. 1987. *Learning together and alone: Cooperative, competitive and individualistic learning* (2nd ed.). Englewood Cliffs, N.J.: Prentice Hall.

Johnsrud, L. 1993. Women and minority faculty experiences: Defining and responding to diverse realities. *New Directions for Teaching and Learning, 53*, 3–16.

Jones, J. 1970. *Prejudice and racism*. Reading, Mass.: Addison-Wesley.

Justus, S., Freitag, S., and Parker, L. 1987. *The University of California in the twenty-first century*. Los Angeles: University of California.

Kahne, J., and Westheimer, J. 1996, May. In the service of what? The politics of service-learning. *Phi Delta Kappan*, 593–99.

Kailin, J. 2002. *Antiracist education: From theory to practice*. Lanham, Md.: Rowman & Littlefield.

Kalathas, S. 1988. Student leadership. In *Diversity blueprint: A planning manual for colleges and universities* (p. 5.4). Washington, D.C.: University of Maryland, College Park, and Association of American Colleges and Universities.

Kalev, A., Dobbin, F., and Kelly, E. 2004. *Two to tango: Affirmative action, diversity programs and women and African Americans in management*. Paper presented to meetings of ICOS, University of Michigan, Ann Arbor.

Katz, D., and Kahn R. 1978. *The social psychology of organizations*. New York. Wiley.

Katz, J. [Joseph]. 1991. White faculty struggling with the effects of racism. In P. Altbach and K. Lomotey (Eds.), *The racial crisis in American higher education* (pp. 187–96). Albany: State University of New York Press.

Katz, J. [Judith]. 1988. *Facing the challenge of diversity and multiculturalism*. Working Paper #13. Ann Arbor: University of Michigan, Program on Conflict Management Alternatives.

———. 1992. Resistance is part of the change process. *Cultural Diversity at Work, 5*(1), 10–11.

Katz, J., and Miller, F. 1988. Between monoculturalism and multiculturalism: Traps awaiting the organization. *OD Practitioner, 20*(3), 105–11.

Keller, G. 2001. The new demographics of higher education. *Review of Higher Education, 24*(3), 219–35.

Kellogg, W. 1999. Toward more transformative service-learning: Experiences from an urban environmental problem-solving class. *Michigan Journal of Community Service Learning, 6*, 63–73.

Kenny, L. 2000. *Daughters of suburbia: Growing up white, middle class and female*. New Brunswick, N.J.: Rutgers University Press.

Kent State University. 2001. *Diversity implementation plan 2001–2005: A framework to foster diversity at Kent State University's eight-campus system*. Kent, Ohio: Author.

Kezar, A., and Rhoads, R. 2001. The dynamic tension of service-learning: A philosophical perspective. *Journal of Higher Education, 72*(2), 148–71.

Kidwell, C. 1994. Higher education issues in Native-American communities. In M. Justiz, R. Wilson, and L. Bjork (Eds.), *Minorities in higher education* (pp. 239–57). Phoenix, Ariz.: American Council on Education and Oryx Press.

Kimball, R. 1990. *Tenured radicals*. New York: Harper & Row.

Kincheloe, J., and Steinberg, R. (Eds.). 1996. *Measured lies: The bell curve examined.* New York. St. Martin's.

Kinder, D., and Sanders, L. 1996. *Divided by color: Racial politics and democratic ideals*. Chicago: University of Chicago Press.

Kinder, D., and Sears, D. 1981. Prejudice and politics: Symbolic racism versus racial threats to the good life. *Journal of Personality and Social Psychology*, *40*, 414–31.

Kirwan, W. 1998. Leadership statement. In *Diversity blueprint: A planning manual for colleges and universities* (pp. 2.5–2.6). Washington, D.C.: University of Maryland, College Park, and Association of American Colleges and Universities.

Kitano, M. 1997. What a course will look like after multicultural change. In A. Morrey and M. Kitano (Eds.), *Multicultural course transformation in higher education: A broader truth* (pp. 18–34). Needham Heights, Mass.: Allyn & Bacon.

Knowles, M., and Harleston, B. 1997. *Achieving diversity in the professoriate: Challenges and opportunities,* Washington D.C.: American Council on Education.

Kochman, T. 1981. *Black and white: Styles in conflict*. Chicago: University of Chicago Press.

Kolb, D. [David] 1981. Learning styles and disciplinary differences. In A. Chickering and Associates (Eds.), *The modern American college: Responding to the new realities of diverse students and a changing society* (pp. 232–55). San Francisco: Jossey-Bass.

——. 1984. *Experiential learning: Experience as the source of learning and development*. Englewood Cliffs, N.J.: Prentice Hall.

Kolb, D. [Deborah] 1986. Who are organizational third parties and what do they do? *Research on Negotiation in Organizations*, *1*, 207–27.

——. 1992. Women's work: Peacemaking in organizations. In D. Kolb and J. Bartunek (Eds.), *Hidden conflict in organizations* (pp. 63–91). Thousand Oaks, Calif.: Sage.

Kotler, P., and Murphy, P. 1991. Strategic planning for higher education. In M. Peterson (Ed.), *Organization and governance in higher education* (pp. 239–52). Needham, Mass.: Ginn.

Kraft, R. 1998. Service learning: An introduction to its theory, practice and effects. In J. Craig (Ed.), *Advances in educational research, Vol. 3*. Washington, D.C.: National Library of Education.

Kramer, M., and Weiner, S. 1994. *Dialogues for diversity*. Washington, D.C.: American Council on Education and Oryx Press.

Krysan, M., and Lewis, A. (Eds.). 2004. *The changing terrain of race and ethnicity*. New York: Russell Sage Foundation.

Kuh, G., and Whitt, E. 1988. *The invisible tapestry: Culture in American colleges and universities*. ASHE-ERIC Higher Education Report, Vol. 15, No. 1. Washington, D.C.: George Washington University.

Kulis, S., Chong, Y., and Shaw, H. 1999. Discriminatory organizational contexts and black scientists on postsecondary faculties. *Research in Higher Education*, *40*(2), 115–48.

LaFlesche, F. 1963. *The middle five: Indian schoolboys of the Omaha tribe.* Madison: University of Wisconsin Press.

LaPaglia, N. 1995. Working-class women as academics: Seeing in two directions awkwardly. In B. Dews and C. Law (Eds.), *This fine place so far from home* (pp. 177–86). Philadelphia: Temple University Press.

Lawrence, C. 1987. The id, the ego and equal protection: Reckoning with unconscious racism. *Stanford Law Review, 39*, 317–88.

Le, C. 2001a. The first Asian Americans. *Asian-Nation.* Accessed at www.asian-nation.org/history.html, January 2002.

———. 2001b. The new wave of Asian immigration. *Asian-Nation.* Accessed at www.asian-nation.org/history.html, January 2002.

Leatherman, C. 1990, September 12. Turmoil at Cleveland State over black administrator's departure focuses attention on issues facing minority-affairs officials. *Chronicle of Higher Education,* A17, A20.

Leeds, R. 1969. The absorption of protest. In W. Bennis, K. Benne, and R. Chin (Eds.), *The planning of change* (pp. 194–207). New York: Holt, Rinehart & Winston.

Leon, D. 2003. Building a leap for Latinos in higher education. In D. Leon (Ed.), *Latinos in higher education* (pp. 193–205). Amsterdam: JAI.

LeMoyne College. 1991. *Self-study presented to the Commission on Higher Education of The Middle States Association.* Syracuse, N.Y.: Author.

Lempert, R., Chambers D., and Adams, T. 2000. Michigan's minority graduates in practice: The river runs through the law school. *Law and Social Inquiry, 25,* 395–505.

Levine, A. (Ed.). 1998. *Higher learning in America.* Baltimore: Johns Hopkins University Press.

Levitan, T., and Wolf, L. 1994. Assessing diversity on campus: A resource guide. *New Directions for Institutional Research, 81,* 87–100.

Lewis, A. 2001. There is no "race" in the schoolyard: Colorblind ideology in an (almost) all white school. *American Educational Research Journal, 38*(4), 781–812.

———. 2004. What group? Studying whites and whiteness in an era of color-blindness. *Sociological Theory, 22*(4), 622–45.

Lewis, A., Chesler, M., and Forman, T. 2000. The impact of "colorblind" ideologies on students of color: Intergroup relations at a predominantly white university. *Journal of Negro Education, 69*(1/2), 74–91.

Light, D., and J. Spiegel (Eds.). 1977. *The dynamics of university protest.* Chicago: Nelson-Hall.

Lipset, S., and Ladd, E. 1985. The changing social origins of American academics. In M. Finkelstein (Ed.), *ASHE reader on faculty and faculty issues in colleges and universities* (pp. 28–43). Lexington, Mass.: Ginn.

Litwack, L. 1998. *Trouble in mind: Black southerners in the age of Jim Crow.* New York: Vintage.

Lively, K. 2000, September 15. Diversity increases among presidents. *Chronicle of Higher Education, 47*(3), A31–A34.

Lomawaima, T. 1995. Educating Native Americans. In J. Banks and C. Banks (Eds.), *Handbook of research on multicultural education* (pp. 331–47). New York: Macmillan.

Lomotey, K. 1990, April. *Culture and its artifacts in higher education: Their impact on the enrollment and retention of African-American students.* Paper presented at meetings of the AERA, Boston. (ERIC, ED319339.)

Lorde, A. 1984. *Sister outsider.* Freedom, Calif.: Crossing.

Lucas, C. 1994. *American higher education: A history.* New York: St. Martin's.

Lyall, K. 1994. *Design for diversity: Increasing participation and graduation: A midpoint review.* Madison: University of Wisconsin.

MacIntosh, P. 1989, July–August. White privilege: Unpacking the invisible knapsack. *Peace and Freedom,* 10–12.

Maclay, K. 1988. Berkeley faculty considers mandatory minority course. *Black Issues in Higher Education,* 5(20), 15.

Madsen, H. 1997a. *Composition of governing boards of independent colleges and universities, 1997.* AGB Occasional Paper #36. Washington, D.C.: Association of Governing Boards of Universities and Colleges.

——. 1997b. *Composition of governing boards of public colleges and universities, 1997.* AGB Occasional Paper #37. Washington, D.C.: Association of Governing Boards of Universities and Colleges.

Mallory, S. 1998. Lesbian, gay, bisexual and transgender student organizations: An overview. In R. Sanlo (Ed.), *Working with lesbian, gay, bisexual and transgender college students* (pp. 321–28). Westport, Conn.: Greenwood.

Marable, M. 2000. *How capitalism underdeveloped black America.* Boston: South End.

Marchesani, L., and Adams, M. 1992. Dynamics of diversity in the teaching–learning process: A faculty development model for analysis and action. *New Directions in Teaching and Learning,* 52, 9–20.

Margolis, E., and Romero, M. 1998. The department is very male, very white, very old and very conservative: The functioning of the "hidden curriculum" in graduate sociology departments. *Harvard Educational Review,* 68(1), 1–32.

Marsden, G. 1994. *The soul of the American university: From Protestant establishment to established nonbelief.* New York: Oxford University Press.

Martin, I., and Siehl, C. 1983, Autumn. Organizational culture and counterculture: An uneasy symbiosis. *Organizational Dynamics,* 52–64.

Masland, A. 1985. Organizational culture in the study of higher education. *Review of Higher Education,* 8, 157–68.

Mason, M., and Goulden, M. 2002, November 21–27. Do babies matter? The effect of family formation on the lifelong careers of academic men and women. *Academe.*

Massey, D., and Denton, N. 1993. *American apartheid: Segregation and the making of the underclass.* Cambridge, Mass.: Harvard University Press.

Massey, W., Wilger, A., and Colbeck, C. 1994, July–August. Overcoming "'hollowed" collegiality: Departmental cultures and teaching quality. *Change,* 11–20.

Matlock, J., Gurin, G., and Wade-Golden, K. 2002. *The Michigan Student Study: Student expectations and experiences with racial/ethnic diversity.* Ann Arbor: University of Michigan Office of Academic Multicultural Initiatives.

Mazurek, R. 1995. Class composition and reform in departments of English: A personal account. In B. Dews and C. Law, *This fine place so far from home* (pp. 249–63). Philadelphia: Temple University Press.

McAdam, D. 1988. *Freedom summer*. New York: Oxford University Press.

McAdam, D., McCarthy, J., and Zald, M. 1996. Introduction: Opportunities, mobilizing structures and framing processes. In D. McAdam, J. McCarthy, and M. Zald (Eds.), *Comparative perspectives on social movements: Political opportunities, mobilizing structures and cultural framings* (pp. 1–20). Cambridge: Cambridge University Press.

McAdam, D., and Scott, R. 2002. Organizations and movements. In G. Davis, D. McAdam, R. Scott, and M. Zald (Eds.), *Organization theory/social movement theory*. New York: Cambridge University Press.

McBay, S. 1986. *The racial climate on the MIT campus*. Cambridge: Massachusetts Institute of Technology—Minority Issues Study Group.

McCarthy, C. 1995. Multicultural policy: Discourses on racial inequality in American education. In R. Ng, J. Scane, and P. Staton (Eds.), *Anti-racism, feminism and critical approaches to education* (pp. 21–44). Westport, Conn.: Bergin & Garvey.

McCauley, C., Wright, M., and Harris, M. 2000. Diversity workshops on campus: A survey of current practice at US colleges and universities. *College Student Journal*, *34*(1), 100–14.

McClelland, K., and Auster, C. 1990. Public platitudes and hidden treasures: Racial climates at predominantly white liberal arts colleges. *Journal of Higher Education*, *61*(6), 607–42.

McConaghy, J. 1983.Modern racism, ambivalence and the modern racism scale. In J. Dovidio and S. Gaertner (Eds.), *Prejudice, discrimination and racism: Theory and research* (pp. 91–126). New York Academic Press.

McCune, P. 2001, May–June. What do disabilities have to do with diversity? *About Campus*, 5–12.

Merton, R. (1949). Discrimination and the American creed. In R. MacIver (Ed.), *Discrimination and national welfare* (pp. 99–126). New York. Harper & Row.

Messner, M. 2000. White guy habitus in the classroom. *Men and Masculinities*, *2*(4), 457–69.

Meyerson, D. 2001. *Tempered radicals*. Boston: Harvard Business School Press.

Meyerson, D., and Scully, M. 1995. Tempered radicalism and the politics of ambivalence and change. *Organizational Science*, *6*, 585–600.

Milbrath, L. 1989. *Envisioning a sustainable society: Learning our way out*. Albany: State University of New York Press.

Miller, F. 1988. Moving a team to multiculturalism. In B. Reddy and K. Jamieson (Eds.), *Team building: Blueprints for productivity and satisfaction* (pp. 192–97). Alexandria, Va., and San Diego, Calif.: NTL Institute and University Associates.

Miller, J. 1987. *Democracy in the streets*. New York: Simon & Schuster.

———. 1997. The impact of service-learning experience on students' sense of power. *Michigan Journal of Community Service Learning*, *4*, 16–21.

Mingle, J. 1978. Faculty and departmental response to increased black enrollment. *Journal of Higher Education*, *49*(3), 201–17.

Mintz, B., and Rothblum, E. 1997. *Lesbians in academia: Degrees of freedom*. New York: Routledge.

Monaghan, P. 1989. Action, not just policy change, seen needed to improve minority scholars' opportunities. *Chronicle of Higher Education*, *35*(26), A1, 18.

Monette, G. 1998. Leadership statement. In *Diversity blueprint: A planning manual for colleges and universities* (p. 1.3). Washington, D.C.: University of Maryland, College Park, and Association of American Colleges and Universities.

Montejano, D. 1987. *Anglos and Mexicans in the making of Texas: 1836–1986.* Austin: University of Texas Press.

Montgomery, S., and Groat, L. 1998. Student learning styles and their implications for teaching. *CRLT Occasional Papers #10.* Ann Arbor: University of Michigan, Center for Research on Learning and Teaching.

Morey, A., and Kitano, M. (Eds.). 1997. *Multicultural course transformation in higher education: A broader truth.* Needham Heights, Mass.: Allyn & Bacon.

Morris, A. 1984. *The origins of the civil rights movement.* New York: Free Press.

Morton, K. 1995. The irony of service: Charity, project and social change in service-learning. *Michigan Journal of Community Service Learning, 2,* 19–32.

Moses, Y. 1989. *Black women in academe: Issues and strategies.* Washington, D.C.: Association of American Colleges.

Moses, Y. 1994. The role of female chief academic officers in institutionalizing cultural diversity in the academy. In J. Davis (Ed.), *Coloring the halls of ivy* (pp. 45–58). Bolton, Mass.: Anker.

Multicultural Initiatives Committee, University of Michigan School of Dentistry. 1995. *Multicultural audit.* Ann Arbor: University of Michigan School of Dentistry.

Munoz, C. 1989. *Youth, identity, power: The Chicano movement.* New York: Verso.

Musil, C., Garcia, M., Hudgins, C., Nettles, M., Sedlacek, W., and Smith, D. 1999. *To form a more perfect union.* Washington, D.C.: Association of American Colleges and Universities.

Musil, C., Garcia, M., Moses, Y., and Smith, D. 1995. *Diversity in higher education: A work in progress.* Washington D.C.: Association of American Colleges and Universities.

Myers-Lipton, S. 1996. Effects of a comprehensive service-learning program on college students' level of modern racism. *Michigan Journal of Community Service Learning, 3,* 44–54.

Nagda, B., and Zuniga, X. 2003. Fostering meaningful racial engagement through inter-group dialogue. *Group Process and Intergroup Relations, 6*(1), 111–28.

National Center for Educational Statistics. 1998. *Digest of educational statistics, 1998.* Washington, D.C.: U.S. Department of Education.

———. 1999. *1999 Study of Postsecondary Faculty (NSOPF99).* Washington, D.C.: U.S. Department of Education.

———. 2001. *Fall staff, 1999 Integrated Post Secondary Education Data Systems (IPEDS).* Washington, D.C.: U.S. Department of Education. Accessed at nces.ed.gov/programs/digest/d02/Tables, June 2003.

———. 2002. *Digest of educational statistics, 2002.* Washington, D.C.: U.S. Department of Education.

National Survey of Student Engagement: National benchmarks of effective educational practice. 2000. Bloomington: Indiana University Center for Post Secondary Research and Training.

Niemann, Y., and Dovidio, J. 1998. Tenure, race/ethnicity and attitudes toward affirmative action: A matter of self interest? *Sociological Perspectives, 41*(4), 783–96.

O'Bear, K. 1991. Homophobia. In N. Evans and V. Wall (Eds.), *Beyond tolerance: Gays, lesbians and bisexuals on campus* (pp. 39–66). Alexandria, Va.: American College Personnel Association.

O'Day, R. 1974. Intimidation rituals: Reactions to reform. *Journal of Applied Behavioral Science*, *10*(3), 373–86.

Office of Affirmative Action and Office of Minority Affairs. 1992. *Faculty, staff and students of color: A statistical profile for academic years 1981–82 through 1991–92*. Ann Arbor: University of Michigan.

Office of Diversity and Affirmative Action. 2002. *Equal opportunity, affirmative action and diversity policy for the Skidmore College community*. Saratoga Springs, N.Y.: Skidmore College.

Office of Diversity and Equity. 2000. *Diversity and equity: A blueprint for action—First state of the campus diversity report*. Boulder: University of Colorado.

Office of Equity Programs. 2002. *EEO/AA*. Huntington, Va.: Marshall University. Accessed at www.marshall.edu/eeoaa/, May 2003.

Office of Human Relations Programs. 2003. *Faculty support awards*. College Park: University of Maryland, College Park. Accessed at www.inform.umd.edu/ohrp/faculty /fsa.html, May 2003.

Office of Institutional Research and Testing. n.d. *A survey of the national origin climate at Indiana State University: Summary report*. Terre Haute: Indiana State University. Accessed at www.indstate.edu/oirt/clim1/home.html, May 2002.

Office of Student Affairs and Academic Programs. 1989. *Campus climate and bias-related behavior*. Albany: State University of New York.

O'Grady, C. 2000. Integrating service learning and multicultural education: An overview. In C. O'Grady (Ed.), *Integrating service learning and multicultural education in colleges and universities* (pp. 1–19). Mahwah, N.J.: Erlbaum.

Ohio State University. 2000. *A diversity action plan for The Ohio State University*. Columbus, Ohio. Accessed at www.acs.ohio-state.edu/diversityplan/index-1.html, June 2003.

Oliver, B., and Davis, J. 1994. Things they don't teach you about being a dean. In J. Davis (Ed.), *Coloring the halls of ivy* (pp. 59–70). Bolton, Mass.: Anker.

Oliver, M., Rodriguez, C., and Mikelson, R. 1985. Brown and black in white: The social adjustment and academic performance of Chicano and black students in a predominately white university. *Urban Review*, *17*, 3–23.

Oliver, M., and Shapiro, T. 1995. *Black wealth, white wealth*. New York: Routledge.

Olneck, M. 1990. The recurring dream: Symbolism and ideology in intercultural and multicultural education. *American Journal of Education*, *98*(2), 147–74.

Omi, M., and Winant, H. 1994. *Racial formation in the United States: From the 1960s to the 1990s*. New York: Routledge.

Ong, P., and Hee, S. 1993. The growth of the Asian Pacific American population: Twenty million in 2020. In *The state of Asian Pacific American: A public policy report: Policy issues to the year 2020* (pp. 11–23). Los Angeles: LEAP Asian Pacific American Public Policy Institute and UCLA Asian American Studies Center.

Orfield, G., Bachmeier, M., James, D., and Eitle, T. 1997. Deepening segregation in American public schools: A special report from the Harvard project on school desegregation. *Equity and Excellence in Education*, *30*(2), 5–24.

Orfield, G., and Gordon, N. 2001. *Schools more separate: Consequences of a decade of resegregation*. Cambridge, Mass.: Harvard University, The Civil Rights Project.

Osajima, K. 1993. The hidden injuries of race. In L. Revilla, G. Nomura, S. Wong, and S. Hune (Eds.), *Bearing dreams, shaping visions* (pp. 81–91). Pullman: Washington State University Press.

———. 1995. Racial politics and the invisibility of Asian-Americans in higher education. *Educational Foundations*, *9*(1), 35–53.

Osborne, R., Hammerich, S., and Hensley, C. 1998. Student effects of service-learning: Tracking change across a semester. *Michigan Journal of Community Service Learning*, *5*, 5–13.

Ostrow, J. Hesser, G., and Enos, S. (Eds.). 1999. *Cultivating the sociological imagination: Concepts and models for service-learning in sociology*. Washington, D.C.: American Association of Higher Education.

Ouellete, M., and Sorcinelli, M. 1995. Teaching and learning in the diverse classroom: A faculty and TA partnership program. *To Improve the Academy*, *14*, 205–19.

Padilla, R., and Chavez, R. (Eds.). 1995. *The leaning ivory tower: Latino professors in American universities*. Albany: State University of New York Press.

Palmer, P. 1987. Community conflict and ways of knowing. *Change*, *19*(5), 20–25.

Pang, V. 1995. Asian Pacific American students: A diverse and complex population. In J. Banks and C. Banks (Eds.), *Handbook of research on multicultural education* (pp. 412–24). New York: Macmillan.

Pascarella, E., and Terenzini, P. 1991. *How college affects students*. San Francisco: Jossey-Bass.

Pascarella, E., Whitt, E., Nora, A., Edison, L., Hagedorn, L., and Terenzini, P. 1996. What have we learned from the first year of the National Study of Student Engagement. *Journal of College Student Development*, *37*(2), 182–92.

Patrick, S., and Fletcher, J. 1998. Faculty developers as change agents: Transforming colleges and universities into learning organizations. *To Improve the Academy*, *14*, 205–17.

Paulsen, M., and St. John, E. 2002. Social class and college costs: Examining the financial nexus between college choice and persistence. *Journal of Higher Education*, *73*(2), 189–236.

Peckham, I. 1995. Complicity in class codes: The exclusionary function of higher education. In B. Dews and C. Law (Eds.), *This fine place so far from home* (pp. 263–75). Philadelphia: Temple University Press.

Pennsylvania State University. n.d. *A framework to foster diversity at Penn State: 1998–2003 (diversifying university leadership and management)*. University Park: Author. Accessed at www.equity.psu.edu/Framework/leaders.html, May 2003.

Perry, P. 2002. *Shades of white: White kids and racial identities in high school*. Durham, N.C.: Duke University Press.

Peterson, M. 1997. Using contextual planning to transform institutions. In M. Peterson, D. Dill, L. Mets, and Associates (Eds.), *Planning and management for a changing environment: A handbook on redesigning postsecondary institutions* (pp. 127–57). San Francisco: Jossey-Bass.

Peterson, M., Blackburn, R., Gamson, Z., Arce, C., Davenport, R., and Mingle, J. 1978. *Black students on white campuses: The impacts of increased black enrollments.* Ann Arbor: University of Michigan, Institute for Social Research.

Peterson, M., and Spencer, M. 1990. Understanding academic culture and climate. *New Directions for Institutional Research, 68,* 3–18.

Pincus, F. 1996. Discrimination comes in many forms: Individual, institutional, and structural. *American Behavioral Scientist, 40,* 186–94.

———. 2000. Reverse discrimination vs. white privilege: An empirical study of alleged victims of affirmative action. *Race and Society, 3,* 1–22.

Platt, A. 2000. End game: The rise and fall of affirmative action in higher education. In A. Aguirre and D. Baker (Eds.), *Structured inequality in the United States* (pp. 319–29). Upper Saddle River, N.J.: Prentice Hall.

Powell, M. 1998. Campus climate and students of color. In J. Valverde and L. Castenell (Eds.), *The multicultural campus: Strategies for transforming higher education* (pp. 95–118). Walnut Creek, Calif.: Sage and Alta Mira.

President's Council of Economic Advisers. 1998. *Changing America: Indicators of social and economic well being by race and Hispanic origin.* Washington, D.C.: U.S. Government Printing Office.

Project Opportunity and Access, Special Education and Rehabilitation Services Program. n.d. *Faculty and staff survey of disability knowledge.* University Park: Pennsylvania State University. Accessed at www.ed.psu.edu/poa.asp, June 2003.

Rabow, J. 2002. *Voices of pain, voices of hope.* Dubuque, Iowa: Kendall-Hunt.

Rabow, J., Chin, and Fahiminian, N. 1999. *Tutoring matters.* Philadelphia: Temple University Press.

Racial backlash flares at colleges. 2001. Accessed at www.cnn.com/2001/fyi/teachers .ednews/09/21/ec.campus.backlash/.

Ragins, B., and Cotton, J. 1999. Mentor functions and outcomes: A comparison of men and women in formal and informal mentoring relationships. *Journal of Applied Psychology, 84*(4), 529–50.

Reason, P., and Bradbury, H. (Eds.). 2001. *Handbook of action research: Participation, inquiry and practice.* Thousand Oaks, Calif.: Sage.

Regents of the University of California v. Baake. 1978. 438 U.S. 265.

Reyes, M. de la luz, and Halcon, J. 1988. Racism in academia: The old wolf revisited. *Harvard Educational Review, 58*(3), 299–314.

Rezai-Rashti, G. 1995. Multicultural education, anti-racist education, and critical pedagogy: Reflections on everyday practice. In R. Ng, J. Scane, and P. Staton (Eds.), *Anti-racism, feminism and critical approaches to education* (pp. 3–20). Westport, Conn.: Bergin & Garvey.

Rhoads, R. 1997. Toward a more inclusive vision of affirmative action: Improving campus environments for lesbian, gay and bisexual people. In M. Garcia (Ed.), *Affirmative action's testament of hope: Strategies for a new era in higher education* (pp. 181–204). Albany: State University of New York Press.

———. 1998a. Critical multiculturalism and service-learning. *New Directions for Teaching and Learning, 73,* 39–46.

——. 1998b. *Freedom's web: Student activism in an age of cultural diversity.* Baltimore: Johns Hopkins University Press.

Rice, K., and Pollack, S. 2000. Developing a critical pedagogy of service learning: Preparing self-reflective culturally aware, and responsive community participants. In C. O'Grady (Ed.), *Integrating service learning and multicultural education in colleges and universities* (pp. 115–34). Mahwah, N.J.: Erlbaum.

Richards, H. 1994. Reflections of a mother confessor: African American women's roles and power relationships in historically white institutions. In J. Davis (Ed.), *Coloring the halls of ivy* (pp. 37–44). Bolton, Mass.: Anker.

Richardson, R., Simmons, H., and de los Santos, A. 1987. Graduating minority students: Lessons from ten success stories. *Change, 19*(3), 20–26.

Richardson, R., and Skinner, E. 1990. Adapting to diversity: Organizational influences on student achievement. *Journal of Higher Education, 61*(5), 485–511.

——. 1996. Improving access and achievement. In R. Richardson and E. Skinner (Eds.), *Achieving quality and diversity: Universities in a multicultural society* (pp. 227–54). New York: American Council on Education and Oryx Press.

Rimling, G. (Ed.). 1999. *The resident assistant* (5th ed.). Dubuque, Iowa: Kendall-Hunt.

Rimling, G., and Miltenberger, L. 1981. *The resident assistant: Working with college students in residence halls.* Dubuque, Iowa: Kendall-Hunt.

Robinson, M. 1998. The residence hall: A home away from home. In R. Sanlo (Ed.), *Working with lesbian, gay, bisexual and transgender college students* (pp. 53–66). Westport, Conn.: Greenwood.

Roediger, D. 1991. *The wages of whiteness: Race and the making of the American working class.* New York: Verso.

Rooney, M. 2003, June 13. Shirt alert. *Chronicle of Higher Education,* 6.

Rowe, M. 1993, March–April. Fostering diversity: Some major hurdles remain. *Change,* 35–39.

Rowley, L., Hurtado, S., and Ponjuan, L. 2002, April 2. *Organizational rhetoric or reality? The disparities between avowed commitment to diversity and formal programs and initiatives in higher education institutions.* Paper presented at American Educational Research Association, New Orleans.

Rowley, L., Lujan, H., and Dolence, M. 1997. *Strategic change in colleges and universities: Planning to survive and prosper.* San Francisco: Jossey-Bass.

Rudenstine, N. 1996, April 19. Why a diverse student body is important. *Chronicle of Higher Education, 42*(32), B1–B2.

Ryan, W. 1971. *Blaming the victim.* New York: Pantheon.

Sagaria, M. 2002. An exploratory model of filtering in administrative searches. *Journal of Higher Education, 73*(6), 677–710.

Said, E. 1978. *Orientalism.* New York: Vintage.

Sales, K. 1973. *SDS.* New York: Random House.

Savage, S. 1976. *Blacks in the West.* Westport, Conn.: Greenwood.

Sax, J., and Arredondo, M. 1999. Student attitudes toward affirmative action in higher education: Findings from a national study. *Research in Higher Education, 40*(4), 439–59.

Sax, J., Astin, A., Korn, W., and Gilmartin, S. 1999. *The American college teacher: National norms for the 1998–99 HERI Faculty Survey.* Los Angeles: n.p.

Saxton, A. 1990. *The rise and fall of the white republic: Class politics and mass culture in nineteenth-century America.* London: Verso.

Schlesinger, L. 1992. *The disuniting of America.* New York: Norton.

Schmidt, P. 2000, November 24. Legal allies. *Chronicle of Higher Education*, A21.

——. 2004, March 19. Not just for minority students anymore. *Chronicle of Higher Education*, A17–A20.

Schmitz, B. 1992. *Core curriculum and cultural pluralism.* Washington, D.C.: Association of American Colleges and Universities.

Schoem, D., Frankel, L., Zuniga, X., and Lewis, E. (Eds.). 1993. *Multicultural teaching in the university.* Westport, Conn.: Praeger.

Schoem, D., Hurtado, S., Sevig, T., Chesler, M., and Sumida, S. 2001. Intergroup dialogue: Democracy at work in theory and practice. In D. Schoem and S. Hurtado (Eds.), *Intergroup dialogue: Deliberative democracy in school, college, workplace and community* (pp. 1–22). Ann Arbor. University of Michigan Press.

Schroeder, C., Mable, P., and Associates. 1994. *Realizing the educational potential of residence halls.* San Francisco: Jossey-Bass.

Schuman, H., Steeh, C., Bobo, L., and Krysan, M. 1997. *Racial attitudes in America: Trends and interpretations.* Cambridge, Mass.: Harvard University Press.

Schuster, M., and Van Dyne, S. (Eds.). 1985. *Women's place in the academy: Transforming the liberal arts curriculum.* Totowa, N.J.: Rowman & Allanheld.

Sears, J. 2002. The institutional climate for lesbian, gay and bisexual education faculty: What is the pivotal frame of reference? *Journal of Homosexuality*, *43*(1), 11–37.

Silver, J. 2002. Diversity issues. In R. Diamond (Ed.), *Field guide to academic leadership* (pp. 357–72). San Francisco: Jossey-Bass.

Silverman, R., and Welty, W. 1993. *Case studies in diversity for faculty development.* New York: Pace University, Center for Case Studies in Education.

Simmons, R. 2002. Reinventing education: From the elite to the unlimited. *The Presidency*, 5(2), 16–23.

Slaughter, J. 1998. Leadership statement. In *Diversity blueprint: A planning manual for colleges and universities* (p. 8.2). Washington, D.C.: University of Maryland, College Park and Association of American Colleges and Universities.

Sleeter, C., and Grant, C. 1988. An analysis of multicultural education in the United States. In N. Hidalgo, C. McDowell, and E. Siddle (Eds.), *Facing racism in education* (pp. 138–61). Cambridge, Mass.: Harvard University Press.

Smith, D. 1989. *The challenge of diversity: Involvement or alienation in the academy.* ASHE-ERIC Report #5. Washington, D.C.: George Washington University School of Education and Human Development.

Smith, D., Altbach, P., and Lomotey, K. (Eds.). 2003. *The racial crisis in American higher education: Continuing challenges for the twenty-first century.* Albany: State University of New York Press.

Smith, D., Gerbick, G., Figueroa, M., Watkins, G., Levitan, T., Moore, L., Merchant, P., Beliak, H., and Figueroa, B. 1997. *Diversity works: The emerging picture of how students benefit.* Washington, D.C.: n.p.

Smith, D., Parker, S., Clayton-Pederson, A., Osei-Kofi, N., Richards, G., Teraguchi, D., and Figueroa, M. 2002. *Campus diversity initiative evaluation project resources kit.* Claremont, Calif.: Claremont Graduate University School of Educational Studies.

Smith, E., and Witt, S. 1993. A comparative study of occupational stress among African American and White university faculty: A research note. *Research in Higher Education, 34*, 2.

Smith College. 1989. *The Smith design for institutional diversity.* Northampton, Mass.: Author.

Sniderman, P., and Piazza, T. 1993. *The scar of race.* Cambridge, Mass.: Harvard University Press.

Snipp, M. 1995. American Indian studies. In J. Banks and C. Banks (Eds.), *Handbook of research on multicultural education* (pp. 245–58). New York: Macmillan.

Social Science Research Bureau. 1991. *College level planning program: Faculty and academic staff diversity survey.* East Lansing: Michigan State University.

Social Science Research Laboratory. 1999. *Survey of SDSU faculty/staff/students regarding campus climate issues.* San Diego, Calif.: San Diego State University.

Solórzano, D., Ceja, M., and Yosso, T. 2000. Critical race theory, racial microaggressions and campus racial climate. *Journal of Negro Education, 69*(1/2), 60–73.

Sporn, B. 1999. *Adaptive university structures.* Philadelphia: Kingsley.

St. John, E. 1991. The impact of student financial aid: A review of recent research. *Journal of Student Financial Aid, 21*(1), 18–32.

Standing Bear, L. 1975. *My people the Sioux.* Lincoln: University of Nebraska Press.

Starr, P. 1992, Winter. Civil reconstruction: What to do without affirmative action. *American Prospect,* 7–16.

Stassen, M. 1995. White faculty members and racial diversity: A theory and its implications. *The Review of Higher Education, 18*(4), 361–91.

Steele, C. 1997. A threat in the air: How stereotypes shape intellectual identity and performance. *American Psychologist, 52*, 613–29.

Steele, S. 1990. *The content of our character.* New York: St. Martin's.

Steering Committee on Minority Affairs. 1987. *Final report.* Madison: University of Wisconsin.

Steinberg, J. 2001, December 26. The University of Vermont builds a pool of recruits in the Bronx. *New York Times,* A1.

Steinberg, S. 1996. The ignominious origins of ethnic pluralism in America. In C. Turner, M. Garcia, A. Nora, and L. Rendon (Eds.), *Racial and ethnic diversity in higher education* (pp. 59–68). Needham Heights, Mass.: Simon & Schuster.

Stikes, C. 1984. *Black students in higher education.* Edwardsville: Southern Illinois University Press.

Stuck, M. 1997. The lesbian experience: An analysis. In B. Mintz and E. Rothblum (Eds.), *Lesbians in academia: Degrees of freedom* (pp. 210–20). New York: Routledge.

Sugrue, T. 1996. *The origins of the urban crisis.* Princeton, N.J.: Princeton University Press.

Suzuki, B. 1994. Higher education issues in the Asian American community. In M. Justiz, R. Wilson, and L. Bjork (Eds.), *Minorities in higher education* (pp. 258–85). Phoenix, Ariz.: American Council on Higher Education and Oryx Press.

Takaki, R. 1989. An educated and culturally literate person must study America's multicultural reality. *Chronicle of Higher Education*, *35*(26), B1–B2.

——. 1993. *A different mirror: A history of multicultural America*. Boston: Little, Brown.

Tandon, R. 1981. Dialogue as inquiry and intervention. In P. Reason and J. Rowan (Eds.), *Human inquiry* (pp. 293–301). New York: Wiley.

Task Force on Racial and Cultural Concerns. 1990. *A report of student concerns about issues of race and racism in the school of public health*. Ann Arbor: University of Michigan School of Public Health.

Task Force on Racism. 1989. *Report of the Task Force on Racism—Draft*. Wellesley, Mass.: Wellesley College.

Tatum, B. 1992. Teaching about race, learning about racism: The application of racial identity development theory in the classroom. *Harvard Educational Review*, *62*, 1–24.

Tatum, B. 1997. *Why are all the black kids sitting together in the cafeteria? And other conversations about race*. New York: Basic Books.

Terenzio, M. 2002. Professional development across the academic career: An engine for implementing a new faculty-institutional compact. In L. McMillin and J. Berberet (Eds.), *A new academic compact: Revisioning the relationship between faculty and their institutions* (pp. 29–60). Bolton, Mass.: Anker.

Terry, R. 1981. The negative impact on white values. In B. Bowser and J. Hunt (Eds.), *The impact of racism on white Americans* (pp. 119–51). Beverly Hills, Calif.: Sage.

Theodore, A. 1986. *The campus troublemakers: Academic women in protest*. Houston, Tex.: Cap and Gown Press.

Thomas, D. 1989. Mentoring and irrationality: The role of racial taboos. *Human Resource Management*, *28*(2), 279–90.

Thomas, G. 1991. *Black students in higher education: Conditions and experiences in the 1970s*. Westport, Conn.: Greenwood.

Thornton, R. 2001. Trends among American Indians in the United States. In J. Smelser, W. Wilson, and F. Mitchell (Eds.), *America beginning: Racial trends and their consequences* (pp. 135–69). Washington, D.C.: National Academy Press.

Tibbs, H. 1999. Deeper news. *Journal of the Global Business Network* (Special issue on sustainability). 3(1), 1–76.

Tien, C. 1998. Challenges and opportunities for leaders of color. In L. Valverde and L. Castenell Jr. (Eds.), *The multicultural campus: Strategies for transforming higher education* (pp. 33–48). Walnut Creek, Calif.: Alta Mira.

Tierney, W. (Ed.). 1990. *Assessing academic climates and cultures: New direction for institutional research*. San Francisco: Jossey-Bass.

——. 1993. The college experiences of Native Americans: A critical analysis. In L. Weiss and M. Fine (Eds.), *Beyond silenced voices* (pp. 309–34). Albany: State University of New York Press.

——. 1996. Understanding domestic partner benefits. *Diversity Factor*, *15*(1), 27–23.

Tierney, W., and Bensimon, E. 1996. *Promotion and tenure: Community and socialization in academe*. Albany: State University of New York Press.

Tolbert, P., Simons, T., Andrews, A., and Rhee, J. 1995. The effects of gender composition in academic departments on faculty turnover. *Industrial and Labor Relations Review*, *48*(3), 562–79.

Trower, C., and Chait, R. 2002, March–April. Faculty diversity: Too little for too long. *Harvard Magazine*, 33–37.

Trueba, E. 1998. Race and ethnicity in academia. In L. Valverde and L. Castenell Jr. (Eds.), *The multicultural campus: Strategies for transforming higher education.* (pp. 70–93) Walnut Creek, Calif.: Alta Mira.

Trujillo, C. 1986. A comparative examination of classroom interactions between professors and minority and non-minority college students. *American Educational Research Journal, 23*, 629–42.

Tschechtelin, J. 1999. A white president of a predominantly black college speaks out about race. *Community College Journal, 69*(3), 6–10.

Turner, C. 1997. *Welcoming diversity on campus: The need for transformation of university culture.* Minneapolis: Interdisciplinary Program in Public Policy and Minority Communities, University of Minnesota.

Turner, C., and Myers, S. 2000. *Faculty of color in academe: Bittersweet success.* Boston: Allyn & Bacon.

Turner Sotello-Viernes, C., Myers, S., and Creswell, J. 1999. Exploring underrepresentation: The case of faculty of color in the Midwest. *Journal of Higher Education, 70*(1), 27–59.

United Coalition against Racism. 1987. *Selected proposals and demands to counter racism at the University of Michigan.* Ann Arbor: Author.

United States Commission on Civil Rights. 1994. Employment discrimination against Asian Americans. In F. Pincus and H. Erlich (Eds.), *Race and ethnic conflict* (pp. 133–44). Boulder, Colo.: Westview.

United States Office of Education. 2004. *Race-Neutral Alternatives in Postsecondary Education: Innovative Approaches to Diversity.* Washington, DC (Office of Civil Rights).

University Committee on Minority Issues. 1989. *Building a multiracial, multicultural university community.* Palo Alto, Calif.: Stanford University.

University of Maryland College Park and Association of American Colleges and Universities 1998. *Diversity blueprint: A planning manual for colleges and universities.* Washington, D.C.: Author.

University of Nebraska–Lincoln 1999. *Comprehensive diversity plan for the University of Nebraska–Lincoln.* Lincoln: Author. Accessed at www.unl.edu/svcaa/priorities/diversity/diversityplan.html, May 2002.

University of Pennsylvania. 2001. The gender equity report. *Almanac, 48*(14), i–vii.

U.S. Census Bureau. 2002. *Statistical abstract of the United States, 2002.* Washington, D.C.: U.S. Department of Commerce.

Valverde, L., and Castenell, L. (Eds.). 1998. *The multicultural campus: Strategies for transforming higher education.* Walnut Creek, Calif.: Alta Mira.

Vasques-Scalera, C. 1999. *Democracy, diversity, dialogue: Education for critical multicultural citizenship.* Unpublished Ph.D. dissertation, University of Michigan, Ann Arbor.

Vaughan, G. 1996. Paradox and promise: Leadership and the neglected minorities. *New Directions for Community Colleges, 94*, 5–12.

Virginia Tech. n.d.-a. *Diversity strategic plan: Mission and vision.* Blacksburg: Author Accessed at http://dsp.multicultural.vt.edu/mission, June 2003.

———. n.d.-b. *The staff assessment of campus climate*. Blacksburg: Author. Accessed at http://dsp.multicultural.vt.edu/climate/staff.shmtl, June 2003.

Washington, M. 1996. The minority student in college: A historical analysis. In C. Turner, M. Garcia, A. Nora, and L. Rendon (Eds.), *Racial and ethnic diversity in higher education* (pp. 69–82). Needham Heights, Mass.: Simon & Schuster.

Washington University in St. Louis. 2002–2003. *Supplier diversity initiative*. St. Louis, Mo.: Author. Accessed at http://supplierdiversity.wustl.edu/, June 2003.

Weick, K. 1976. Educational organizations as loosely coupled systems. *Administrative Science Quarterly*, *17*(1), 1–19.

———. 1984. Small wins. *American Psychologist*, *39*(1), 40–49.

Weinberg, M. 1977. *A chance to learn: The history of race and education in the United States*. New York: Cambridge University Press.

Weinstein, G., and O'Bear, K. 1992. Bias issues in the classroom: Encounters with the teaching self. *New Directions in Teaching and Learning*, *52*, 39–50.

Wessler, S., and Moss, M. 2001. *Hate crimes on campus*. U.S. Bureau of Justice Assistance Monograph #3. Washington, D.C.: U.S. Department of Justice.

Why is research the rule? 2000. *Change*, *32*, 53.

Willie, C., and McCord, A. 1972. *Black students and white colleges*. New York: Praeger.

Wills, J. 1996. Who needs multicultural education? White students, U.S. history, and the construction of a usable past. *Anthropology and Education Quarterly*, *27*(3), 365–89.

Wilson, R. [Reginald]. 1994a. Foreword. In J. Davis (Ed.), *Coloring the halls of ivy* (pp. xi–xii). Bolton, Mass.: Anker.

———. 1994b. The participation of African Americans in American higher education. In M. Justiz, R. Wilson, and L. Bjork (Eds.), *Minorities in higher education* (pp. 195–209). Phoenix, Ariz.: American Council on Higher Education, Oryx Press.

Wilson, R. [Robin]. 2003, December 5. How babies alter careers for academics. *Chronicle of Higher Education*, *20*(15), A1, A6–A7.

Winant, H. 2001. *The world is a ghetto: Race and democracy since WW II*. New York: Basic Books.

Wolfman, B. 1990, September 12. College leaders must act firmly to end racial resegregation on their campuses. *Chronicle of Higher Education*.

Wood, P. 2002, March–April. Diversity. *American Spectator*, 52–60.

Woodbrooks, C. 1991. *The construction of identity through the presentation of self: Black women candidates interviewing for administrative positions in a research university*. Unpublished Ph.D. dissertation, Ohio State University, Columbus.

Woodson, C. 1997. *The miseducation of the American Negro*. New York: AMS Press.

Wollenberg, C. 1976. *All deliberate speed: Segregation and exclusion in California schools 1855–1975*. Berkeley: University of California Press.

Wright, L. 1994. One drop of blood: Push for multiracial category in the census. *New Yorker*, *70*, 46–50.

Wright, M. Assar, N., Kain, E., Kramer, L., Howery, C., McKinney, K., Glass, B., and Atkinson, M. 2004. Greedy institutions: The importance of institutional context for teaching in higher education. *Teaching Sociology*, *32*, 144–59.

Wunsch, M., and Chattergy, V. 1991. Managing diversity through faculty development. *To Improve the Academy*, *10*, 141–50.

Yamane, D. 2001. *Student movements for multiculturalism.* Baltimore: Johns Hopkins University Press.

Young, I. 1994. Gender as seriality: Thinking about women as a collective. *Signs, 19*(3), 713–38.

Zald, M., and Berger, M. (1978). Social movements in organizations: Coups d'état, bureaucratic insurgency and mass rebellions. *American Journal of Sociology, 83,* 823–61.

Zernicke, K. 2004, January 18. Duke students use T-shirts to say it's OK to be gay. *New York Times (Education Supplement).* Section 4A, 7.

Zhao, Y. 2002, June 19. Students protest plan to change test policy. *New York Times,* A13.

Zorn, J. 1986, July 7. Ethics, values best imparted by example. *University Record,* 8.

Zumeta, W. 2001. Public policy and accountability in higher education: Lessons from the past and present for the new millennium. In D. Heller (Ed.), *The states and public higher education policy* (pp. 155–97). Baltimore: Johns Hopkins University Press.

Zuniga, X., and Nagda, B. 1993. Dialogue groups: An innovative approach to multicultural learning. In D. Schoem, L. Frankel, X. Zuniga, and E. Lewis (Eds.), *Multicultural teaching in the university* (pp. 233–48). Westport, Conn.: Praeger.

Zuniga, X., Nagda, B., and Sevig, T. 2002. Intergroup dialogues: An educational model for cultivating engagement across differences. *Equity and Excellence in Education, 35*(1), 7–17.

Zuniga, X., Nagda, B., Sevig, T., Thompson, M., and Dey, E. 1995. *Speaking the unspeakable: Student learning outcomes in intergroup dialogues on a college campus.* Paper presented at meetings of the American Society for Higher Education, Orlando, Fla.

Zuniga, X., Vasques, C., Sevig, T., and Nagda, B. 1996. *Dismantling the walls: Peer-facilitated inter-race/ethnic dialogue processes and experiences.* Working Paper #49. Ann Arbor: University of Michigan—Program in Conflict Management Alternatives.

Index

administration of university, 58–61, 147,
155–61, 178, 264–65; administrators
of color, 157–60, 220, 276, 294;
affirmative action officers, 60, 224;
diversity and, 152–55; at elite
institutions, 161–64, 294; experience
with race, 155–61; female
administrators, 157–60, 222, 276, 294;
governing board, 58, 152–53; models
of, 148–51, 220; presidents, 62,
161–64, 273; senior administrators,
161–64, 217, 219, 273; support for
multicultural change, 156, 187, 199,
215–19, 262–65
affirmative action: and campus climate,
91; focus on black admissions, 110; in
higher education, 7, 41–44, 60–61; in
hiring, 123, 158, 215; law suits and,
156, 216–17; opposition to, 91–93,
110–11, 183, 217; race neutral
admissions policies, 43, 275;
resentment and, 110–11; statewide
ballot initiatives, 217; support for,
95–96, 123, 184; and white students,
90–96
African American students. *See* students
of color
Asian American: educational achievement,
38, 40; faculty. (*See* faculty of color);

immigrants. (*See* immigrants, Asian);
as model minority, 37, 102, 159;
students. (*See* students of color)
assimilation: historical 31–32; and
organizational stage of change, 69;
orientation of organization, *172*, 289;
pressure to assimilate, 107–10; alumni
involvement, 282

Bakke v. Board of Regents, 42. *See also*
affirmative action
black students. *See* African American
students
Brown v. Board of Education, 33. *See*
also segregation

Chicano. *See* Latino
climate: campus, 50, 276; classroom, 234.
See also organizational dimensions,
social relations; climate
college preparation, 17–18, 36, 38–39, 44
color blindness, 9, 14–15; and race-
neutral policies, 275; and white
students, 83–84, 106
community college, 18, 39, 155; and
administrators of color, 62, 15
community involvement. *See*
organizational dimensions, boundary
management

About the Authors

Mark Chesler is Professor Emeritus of sociology at the University of Michigan and executive director of Community Resources, Ltd., Ann Arbor, Michigan. His work on this volume is the outgrowth of several decades of research and action in the field of intergroup relations, racism, multiple forms of discrimination, and organizational/community change. He has been a central agent in University of Michigan programs in community service learning, intergroup dialogues, and faculty development.

Amanda Lewis is assistant professor of sociology and African-American Studies and a Faculty Fellow at the Institute for Research on Race and Public Policy at the University of Illinois at Chicago. The junior member of this team, she began working on this volume while finishing her Ph.D. in sociology at the University of Michigan. This project builds on much of her previous work, which has focused on ways of studying how race shapes daily life in K–12 education, and on the contours and manifestations of whiteness and racism.

James Crowfoot is Professor Emeritus of Natural Resources and Urban and Regional Planning and Dean Emeritus of the School of Natural Resources and Environment at the University of Michigan. Formerly he was director of the Pew Scholars Program on Conservation and the Environment. He also is the former president of Antioch College, Yellow Springs, Ohio. His contributions to this book continue his long-time work on organizational change in higher education and on advocacy for socioenvironmental change, including preservation of the natural environment and the pursuit of social and economic justice to overcome racism and other forms of oppression.